COLORISM

Investigating a Global Phenomenon with
Implications for Research, Policy, and Practice

EDITED BY
KAMILAH MARIE WOODSON, PHD

FIELDING UNIVERSITY PRESS

KATRINA S. ROGERS
PRESIDENT, FIELDING GRADUATE UNIVERSITY

MONIQUE L. SNOWDEN
PROVOST, FIELDING GRADUATE UNIVERSITY

JEAN-PIERRE ISBOUTS
EDITOR, FIELDING UNIVERSITY PRESS

COLORISM: INVESTIGATING A GLOBAL PHENOMENON

EDITOR:
KAMILAH MARIE WOODSON

CONTRIBUTORS:

JOSEPHINE M. ALMANZAR
JOYELL ARSCOTT
PAULA A. BARBEL
TERRA L. BOWEN-REID
DWAYNE M. BRYANT
JO-ANNE MANSWELL BUTTY
DARLENE G. COLSON
ANTONIO M. COOPER
MAYA CORNEILLE
DANIELLE D. DICKENS
PATRICIA S. DIXON
JANICIA DUGAS
ZOEANN FINZI-ADAMS
MARISA FRANCO
O'SHAN D. GADSDEN
KRISTEN GAYLE
NANA K.O. GYESIE
JAMAL H. N. HAILEY
K. MELCHOR QUICK HALL
P. QUICK HALL

Naomi M. Hall-Byers
Ashley Hill
Courtney C. Hives-Gunn
Charnel Hollier
Leah P. Hollis
Ronald E. Hopson
Marilyn M. Irving
Martinque K. Jones
Steve Kniffley
Velma LaPoint
Anna K. Lee
Stacey McDonald Lowe
Afia Mbilishaka
Kathryn Aimee McFarland
Jannis F. Moody
J. Rajasekaran
Petra A. Robinson
Taasogle Daryl M. Rowe
Shannon N. Smith
Sarah J. Stewart
Walter Stamp
Kevin Washington
Brittany M. Williams
David Blake Willis
Kalima Young
Sinead N. Younge

COLORISM

Library of Congress Cataloging-in-Publication data
Colorism: Investigating a Global Phenomenon, by Kamilah M. Woodson (Ed.)
1. Social Sciences-Topics in Diversity

TABLE OF CONTENTS

Section III. Colorism in the Workplace

Section IV. Global Colorism

Section V. Colorism Redefined

Section VI. Colorism, Social Justice, and Liberation

Foreword

Taasogle Daryl M. Rowe
Professor Emeritus, Pepperdine University

Today we still have a major problem with how we think and write about the impact of the horrific period when Western Europeans trafficked millions of Africans into bondage; evidenced by the idea that most historical reflections of that era, and it's byproducts, are dominated by the very group of privileged men that organized and implemented the terror campaign. One of the most heinous and deceitful inventions out of the West was this thing called "slave", reference to its creation as "slavery", and construction of a racial classification system for ranking humans. Race and its correlate – racism – have been primary constructs used to describe, catalogue, examine and teach about human differences, repeatedly in pernicious ways. As Markus (2008) argues, the intent of race, as a cultural construct, is to reinforce the real and implicit power of one group's authority over another, across time. Put simply, whenever we use the construct of race, we reinforce the real and implicit power differentials of Whites and the other, especially Black/African people. Race is simply a construct and has become a worldview used as a strategy for justifying the dehumanization of persons of African ancestry (Smedley, 1999).

This malevolent classification system led to a level of depopulation, forced relocation and exercise of terror of such scope and ferocity that we can only speculate about its full consequences on the life trajectories of Black/African people over space and time. Nonetheless, one of its enduring effects was to seek to fully dehumanize more than thirty percent of the entire human population while holding harmless the perpetrators of this horrific crime against humanity.

Whether in anthropology, the arts, criminology, economics, education, geography, history, law, linguistics, literature, philosophy, political science, sociology, or psychology, the negation of African human agency and the elevation of European ideas, practices, products and institutions (Markus & Hamedani, 2007) as the baselines, norms or standards against which all others are evaluated have been embedded in the underlying principles of most academic disciplines (Smedley, 1999) and social norms and values. These European or Eurocentric principles undermine the humanity of the overwhelming majority of humans by failing to study, explore and examine how the majority of humans understand themselves, others and the world. Conceptually, these Eurocentric principles, or lies, of which race has been one of the most persistent, have been grounded in arbitrary meanings about both the status and worth of humans that were imposed on the facts of phenotypic variations in humans (Grills, Aird, & Rowe, 2016; Smedley & Smedley, 2005).

These lies, codified through the written word, passed down through an integrated cultural meaning system, and reified through a pseudo-scientific methodology have sought to eradicate African experience from the progression of human history; eliminate the spiritness of African agency; and undermine the authenticity and authority of African human expressiveness. The next result is that for almost 500 years, the world has been fed toxic lies about people of African ancestry and those lies continue to exact a heavy toll on Black/African people in almost every conceivable way. It is past time that we stop letting others teach those lies as truth; and that we stop repeating them to each other, and ourselves. Invalidating these lies require our collective genius, fearless pursuit and cooperative engagement. We must seed the development of a wide-range of strategies emerging out of the various disciplines of the Academy that are centered in the restoration of African human agency – whether in the humanities, social sciences, natural sciences, formal sciences, or professions. And since the method of most disciplines ground new knowledge on prior knowledge – those Eurocentric lies still provide the foundation for how the academic disciplines are framed, taught, researched and practiced (Grills, Aird & Rowe, 2016).

Dr. Kamilah Woodson's work reflects such a challenge to the colonizing application of western social sciences' ideas, practices and products; although it is difficult for many of us to think about African human agency unencumbered by the limiting perspectives of the west. This work, *Colorism: Investigating A Global Phenomenon with Implications for Policy, Research, and Practice,* fearlessly seeks to throw off the shackles of conceptual incarceration (Nobles, 1986) that reinforces a reliance on western ideas, practices and products, particularly related to skin color variation, and its byproducts, among persons of African ancestry.

Colorism, as an area of academic exploration, is another iteration of one of the toxic lies fed to persons of African ancestry, which advances that our individual and collective value is primarily determined based on the closeness of our skin pigmentation or color to persons of European ancestry. Simply stated, colorism is the practice of discrimination by which those with lighter skin are treated more favorably than those with darker skin, or as Burke (2008, p. 17) stated, "the allocation of privilege and disadvantage according to the lightness or darkness of one's skin". "Colorism is a persistent problem for people of color in the USA. Colorism, or skin color stratification, is a process that privileges light-skinned people of color over dark in areas such as income, education, housing, and the marriage market. Colorism is directly related to the larger system of racism in the USA and around the world. The color complex is also exported around the globe, in part through US media images, and helps to sustain the multibillion-dollar skin bleaching and cosmetic surgery industries" (Hunter, 2007, p.237). And yet, it is grounded in a series of interconnected lies that undermine African/Black human agency.

As Nobles (2015) has argued, what today is framed as colorism, grew out of "a pathological belief that the African was less than human and as such could rightly be the subject of death and destruction in the service of human exploitation and domination. For the African American, the very fabric of American society was and is woven with savagery, hostility, segregation, defamation, physical brutality, political domination, character assassination, economic exploitation, cultural denigration, and psychic terrorism (n.d.)". These inhuman assaults occurred during the horrific era of forced bondage, wherein European landowners forcibly raped African women, with impunity. The offspring of those ruthless violations often were then offered slight advantages, relative to their peers, resulting in a perverse valuing of lighter skin coloration, almost as if the vicious assaults were minimized or normalized. This is where the lie of privileging lighter skin tones originated, out of the denigration of African human agency, value and worth.

During forced bondage, African women had no authority over their bodies, and European landowners routinely terrorized Africans using rape as an enforcement strategy, resulting in more and more offspring of lighter skin tones. However, since the aim was to build an economically exploitative system that required the destruction of African human agency, laws were passed to ensure that even lighter skin-toned offspring of African women held in bondage, would remain in bondage (Jackson-Lowman, 2013). This is the historical legacy of the phenomenon we refer to as colorism, the institutionalization and internalization of a valuing system that denigrates darker-skin tones (and their correlating phenotypic features – hair texture/length, body image/ physique, and perceived attractiveness/facial features) and venerates lighter-skin tones (and their correlating features), while implicitly overlooking and/or rejecting the vicious system that produced it.

In various ways, Dr. Woodson's career has led her to interrogating the interrelated factors and features of colorism and its damaging effects on persons of African ancestry.

Kamilah's engagement with the field of psychology was influenced by her pressing need to make the field more accessible to her community, broadly defined. Early in her career she travelled to Ghana, West Africa, where she worked to gain a clearer understanding of the continuing importance of oppression among and between African people. Her desire to understand the worldwide impact forced bondage and historic human trafficking has had on various populations of African ancestry led her to travel for research conferences or study to countries including Egypt, South Africa, the Caribbean, Cuba, Mexico, France, Amsterdam, Prague and Hong Kong . All of which, have equipped her with the tools necessary to better train culturally diverse students in doctoral programs, conduct culturally relevant research, and to work in diverse cultural environments. Similarly, Dr. Woodson was awarded a Fulbright Hays Summer Seminar Award in which she travelled to Brazil, where she explored Brazilian remnants of the triangular human trafficking scheme with both her students and colleagues, as she continued to develop comprehensive approaches to working with populations of African ancestry who struggle with the trans-generational effects of the epoch of human trafficking. This has been admirable, and further underscores her commitment to life-long learning, professional development, and to doing work that promotes the advancement of African human agency throughout the Diaspora.

In particular, much of her work focuses on the psychological impacts of colorism and its myriad effects on women of color, especially women of African ancestry. Her scholarly achievements demonstrate her already established leadership skill gaining her national and international recognition. Dr. Woodson has a blend of energy and critical discourse that has stimulated colleagues while challenging them to explore the limits of psychology for effecting change for marginalized populations, especially members of Black/African communities. Dr. Woodson has the theoretical flexibility and multi-contextualist frameworks that allow her to translate a variety of content domains into cogent modules that others can easily digest; she creates a space that is simultaneously engaging and challenging and has assembled a team of scholars to examine colorism from a variety of perspectives.

Colorism: Investigating A Global Phenomenon with Implications for Policy, Research, and Practice, is a powerful contribution that looks behind the curtain of color-consciousness, many of its considerable byproducts, and its damaging effects within the extended African community. It provides penetrating insights into the historical, cultural, relational, and personal challenges that these internalized lies about African human agency wreaks within and between persons of African ancestry. These lies are at the root of the fear, disrespect, hostility, and discrimination too often directed at people of African ancestry. I encourage you to read this volume with excitement and energy, seeking to uncover new ways of thinking about old patterns that have limited persons of African ancestry from reclaiming our agency. I leave you with the words of Ayi Kwei Armah (2002, pp. 136-137),

"…Our teachers in the European academy made it clear that to pass their roadblocks into the future we would have to leave everything African, and transit through the footbaths of Europe first. Singly…It was not so much that we went out to embrace the deadly lie. We looked at its sheer power, and in the despair drilled into us as obedient novices, acquiesced in it… In the fields of triumphant power we left our minds for dead. And yet under the chaos of the slaughterhouse of souls, sometimes a mind here, another there, refused to die…"

Dr. Woodson and her colleagues' minds have refused to die, let yours awaken, as well.

References

Armah, A. K. (2002). *KMT: In the house of life, an epistemic novel.* Popenguine, Senegal: Per Ankh.

Burke, M. (2008). Colorism. In W. Darity Jr. (Eds.), *International encyclopedia of the social sciences, 2,* 17-18. Detroit, MI: Thomson Gale.

Grills, C. N., Aird, E. G., & Rowe, D. M. (2016). Breathe, Baby, Breathe: Clearing the Way for the Emotional Emancipation of Black People. *Cultural Studies ↔ Critical Methodologies,* 1-11. Permissions.nav DOI: 10.1177/1532708616634839 csc.sagepub.com.

Hunter, M. (2007). The Persistent Problem of Colorism: Skin Tone, Status, and Inequality. *Sociology Compass, 1*(1), 237-254.

Jackson-Lowman, H. (2013). An analysis of the impact of Eurocentric concepts of beauty on the lives of African American women. In H. Jackson-Lowman (Ed.) *African American women: Living at the crossroads of race, gender, class, and culture.* Cognella Academic Publishing, 155-172.

Markus, H. R. (2008). Pride, prejudice, and ambivalence: Toward a unified theory of race and ethnicity. *American Psychologist, 63,* 651-671.

Markus, H. R., & Hamedani, M. G. (2007). Sociocultural psychology: The dynamic interdependence among self systems and social systems. In S. Kitayama & D. Cohen (Eds.), *Handbook of cultural psychology* (pp. 3-46). New York: Guilford Press.

Nobles, W.W. (1986). *African psychology: Towards its Reclamation, Reascension and Revitalization.* Oakland, California: Institute for the Advanced Study of Black Family Life and Culture.

Nobles, W. W., Rowe, D. M. (2015). Why the Lies Were Propagated and Why and How the Lies Persist. Presented at Valuing Black Lives: The Annual Global Emotional Emancipation Summit in conjunction with The Honorable Karen Bass, (D.CA), Ranking Member, Africa Subcommittee, U.S. House of Representatives, Washington, DC.

Smedley, A. (1999). *Race in North America: Origin and evolution of a worldview* (2nd ed.). Boulder, CO: Westview Press.

Smedley, A., & Smedley, B. D. (2005). Race as biology is fiction, racism as a social problem is real: Anthropological and historical perspectives on the social construction of race. *American Psychologist, 60*, 16--26. doi:10.1037/0003-066X.60.1.16.

Preface

Kamilah Marie Woodson
Howard University

The challenges with formal and informal discussions of colorism and all of its historic and contemporary attributes, are that the perceptions of clinicians, theorists, educators, psychology trainers, and researchers impact their interpretations of what the phenomena is, as well as its relative power. Worldview, culture, and lived experiences seemingly influence what is studied about colorism and how communities and families have based relational and economic decisions on colorist ideologies. What's fascinating to me is that from a social constructionist perspective, it may be argued that colorist ideologies permeate all aspects of society in various contexts. As such, the main objective of this volume is to provide a one stop solution for interested readers—ranging from clinicians, to theorists, to educators and psychology trainers, and researchers—on the history, scope, current trends and implications of colorism. In brief, colorism commonly has been defined as a prejudice or discrimination in which human beings receive differing social treatment based on the complexion of their skin (Burton, Bonilla-Silva, Ray, Buckelew, & Freeman, 2010).

Colorism differs from racism, however, it is observed both within one's own ethnic group and between groups. It asserts the beliefs that people who have more Eurocentric phenotypic features receive preferential or prejudicial treatment, both within and between races. Also apparent but less mentioned and not included in the aforementioned definition, is the reverse, where those with Eurocentric phenotypic features are discriminated against as well, suggesting that colorist ideologies are contextual and nuanced. The presence of colorism prevails among communities of African descent, having been engrained into society and internalized by individuals of the African Diaspora. Specifically, the effect of this internalized colorism has been seen in preferences of skin color/ hair texture and has been noted in the research (Woodson, 2002) as having both a historic and present (multigenerational) connection to the self-concept and self-esteem of African Americans. Research suggests that Colorism, like the experience of any other trauma, may result in self-destructive behaviors, acting out, and or negative coping mechanisms (Burton, et al. 2010). Unresolved colorist ideologies can even give rise to more diagnostic concerns like narcissism, depression, anxiety, PTDS, disordered eating, and facial/ body dysmorphia.

The above notwithstanding, scholars are just now beginning to recognize that the scope and impact of colorism is much broader than originally conceptualized. This is true both in terms of how it has been defined in the literature (i.e., as primarily a skin color issue), and in terms of the many different ways in which it manifests among individuals and groups, across the global spectrum—particularly within the African Diaspora. Although originating within the context of skin color among Africans in America, in my experience and purview of the literature, it has become increasingly clear that colorism is about more than just skin color. In fact, while skin color indeed may be a most salient feature, the contributions of other aspects of the European aesthetic, such as hair texture/length, body image/physique, and perceived attractiveness/facial features, may be of equal importance, and must not be ignored. They function as individual and or intersecting identities. This book will explore this notion and provide the basis for a reconceptualization of colorism that I believe will be more inclusive and useful for researchers and clinicians.

It also has become clear that colorism is a much more pervasive and global phenomenon than originally thought. In fact, it seems that wherever European domination exists (or has existed), so to exists a preference for the European aesthetic. As such, a tenacious worldview of "good and bad" skin color, for example, has been internalized by generations of White people and people of color (Hall, 2003; Tummala-Narra, 2007). Yet, the global impact of colorism among other cultures across the globe has not been well articulated or even acknowledged in extant literature. As such, this book aims to highlight and describe colorism from a global perspective, with chapter contributions from scholars with diverse geographic and cultural lenses—charged to speak about the nature, scope and impact of colorism from their corner of the globe (for example, West African, Indian, Middle Eastern, Hispanic American, etc.).

This volume also offers a more expansive discussion of the influence of internalized colorism (e.g., in terms of skin color, hair texture, body image, etc.), with particular emphasis on issues of psychosocial and physical health—including health disparities—among persons of color. In addition, I intend to explore the connection between colorism and other, less well studied social arenas (e.g., family functions, the media, academic and workplace environments, romantic relationships, etc.).

In sum, the concept of colorism has evolved such that it requires a "reconceptualization;" one that includes: (a) a redefining of colorism that acknowledges the contributions of other aspects of the European aesthetic, such as skin color, hair texture/length, body image, and perceived attractiveness, (b) a recognition that colorism not only impacts Africans in American, but also has a global footprint that manifests in almost every corner of the world, (c) provides an understanding of colorism as a developmental phenomenon; one that takes root in family dynamics and spreads through almost every aspect of society (e.g., academic environments, the workplace/ employment, healthcare (health disparities), the media, social policy, etc., and (d) explains the scope and implications of colorism as a multigenerational phenomenon. It is my hope that the *Ancestors* are proud of this effort!

References

Burton, L., Bonilla-Silva, E., Ray, V., Buckelew, R. & Freeman, E.H. (2010). Duke University critical race theories: Colorism, and the decade's research on families of color. *Journal of Marriage and Family*: 440 - 459. DOI:10.1111/j.1741-3737.2010.00712.x

Hall, R. E. (2003). Skin color as post-colonial hierarchy: A global strategy for conflict resolution. *Journal of Black Psychology*, 137, 41-53.

Tummala-Narra, P. (2007). Skin color and the therapeutic relationship. *Psychoanalytic Psychology,* 24(2), 255--270

Woodson, K.M. (2002). The impact of hair texture and skin color among African American men and women during mate selection on the expression of risky sexual behaviors. Unpublished Dissertation, California School of Professional Psychology, LA

Introduction:
Color, Caste, and Kinsmen

Jannis F. Moody
Texas Southern University

The Center for Race and Gender (2005) assert that "colorism is in effect when one's complexion becomes the basis for awarding, restricting or denying access to power and resources in various arenas of society, producing a skin tone hierarchy" (http://crg.berkeley.edu.programs/programs). The phenomenon of colorism, an intraracial discrimination based primarily on skin color or complexion, privileges lighter-skinned Blacks and penalizes darker-skinned Blacks (Allen, Telles, & Hunter, 2000; Hunter, 2007, 2008; Russell, Wilson, & Hall, 1992). The racially discriminatory nature of colorism is easily identifiable as an outgrowth of racial discrimination. Russell et. al. (1993) argue that "racial supremacy, mostly White supremacy, informs the principle of colorism", with colorism being rooted and cultivated during slavery.

White slaveholders established and maintained a hierarchy among slaves based on complexion (Gasman & Tudico, 2009). Russell et al. (1993) traced the inception of colorism within the African American community to the miscegenation between White men and Black female slaves, and occasionally between White men and Black male slaves or freedmen, resulting in the birth of biracial and mulatto children. These biracial and mulatto children, who were considered slaves despite parentage, were often granted special treatment (Du Bois, 1903; Frazier, 1957; Keith and Herring, 1991). Whiteness was associated with civility, virtue and beauty, while Blackness was associated with being untamed, sinful, and revolting (Hill, 2002). The closer to White one was phenotypically, the better, which resulted in preferential treatment for lighter-skinned slaves, in comparison to the harsher treatment of darker-skinned slaves (Johnson, 2001).

It was believed that darker-skinned slaves were considered "healthier", more suited for physical labor, better able to withstand the climate, and that darker skin represented labor and intellectual degradation; whereas lighter-skinned slaves were believed to be better suited for more intellectual and skilled tasks (Kerr, 2005; Johnson, 2001; Neal & Wilson, 1989; Toplin, 1979). Mulatto slaves were considered delicate, thereby worthy of serving in the house because of their European-like physical appearances

(Johnson, 1996; Kerr, 2005). Lighter-skinned slaves were more likely to live in the slave master's house and be assigned to more desirable tasks like housework, caring for the master's children, and the position of field foreman, which was a position of authority, allowing for the assertion of power over darker-skinned slaves working in the fields. Conversely, darker-skinned slaves were more likely to be forced into physical labor, sometimes at the orders of lighter-skinned slaves, being assigned more physically laborious tasks such as picking cotton, harvesting the fields, building structures and smelting iron (Frazier, 1957; Keith & Herring, 1991). The power differential created by assigning lighter-skinned slaves to the authoritarian position of field foreman over the darker-skinned slaves in the field only served to further the divide created by the establishment of the complexion hierarchy. The betrayal of and lack of sympathy for the darker-skinned slaves by some of the lighter-skinned slaves seeded and cultivated the notion that their kin was not always their brother (Taylor, 2009).

Lighter-skinned and mulatto slaves maintained higher value at the slave market, particularly lighter-skinned female slaves (Taylor, 2009). Black female slaves with light skin, long hair, and White European physical features were an indication of high social status for White slaveholders, as these women were sold at a much higher prices than darker-skinned female slaves (Hughes & Hertel, 1990; Johnson, 2001). Slave-owners' records depict lighter-skinned Black women as smarter, kinder, gentler, more attractive, and most frequently, described as more delicate than darker-skinned Black women (Johnson, 2001). These lighter-skinned slave women were actively sought after by White men, especially for participation in such affairs as the New Orleans' Quadroon Balls. The quadroon balls were social affairs that allowed White men the opportunity to meet and potentially match with fairer-skinned upper-class Creole girls who had been educated and groomed specifically for careers as mistresses (Bontemps, 1945).

According to the literature, not only were lighter-skinned slaves more likely to reap such benefits as living in the slave master's house and the assignment of more desirable tasks, but it is reported that many also benefited from manumission at the hands of their White slave-owning fathers (African American Lives, 2006; Toplin; 1979). According to Toplin (1979), lighter-skinned slaves were more likely to receive an education and their freedom papers, reporting at least one instance wherein a freed mulatto was given his own slaves and a plantation. Toplin (1979) also reported that some lighter-skinned slaves were able to completely evade slavery by "passing" as White (Toplin, 1979). Bennett, (2001) noted that many fairer-skinned mulattoes, quadroons (a person with one-quarter Black or African heritage and three-fourths White or European heritage), and octaroons (a person with seven-eighth White and one-eighth Black heritage) took advantage the opportunity afforded by their fairer skin to access freedom and the possibility of upward mobility by choosing to live their lives as a White person.

Many lighter-skinned slaves were taught to read, granted access to education, provided with apprenticeships, and exposed to wealthy White traditions (Frazier, 1957; Keith & Herring, 1991; Kephart, 1948). Despite it being illegal for slaves to read or be educated, as the White majority considered it a "threat to their ability to control and manipulate enslaved Africans" (Williams, 2004, p. 8), a number of slaveholders deemed it economically advantageous to educate their slaves, subsequently doing so. Many lighter-skinned slaves used their education and adopted White values to assimilate into White America, differentiating themselves from their darker-skinned brethren (Frazier, 1957; Gatewood, 2000; Kephart, 1948; Russell, Wilson, and Hall, 1993), and further dissociating themselves by socializing exclusively with other mulattoes or other fairer-skinned Blacks.

Though this complexion hierarchy was established by White slaveholders during slavery, its true reign of terror on Black communities began when this manufactured hierarchy was adopted and internalized by Black communities (Harvey et al., 2005). This melanin based caste system fostered the proliferation of internal racism, and eventually classism in the Black community (Golden, 2004; Frazier, 1957; Kerr, 2005), creating a fatal dichotomy of division amongst Blacks that fostered opposition to one another, as opposed to unifying them to confront slave masters or hate mongering Whites (Toplin, 1979). As classism took root in the Black community, many lighter-skinned Blacks and mulattoes accessed the benefits of privilege afforded by the combination of skin color, informal education acquired while living in plantation houses, and adoption of White values, to assimilate into White culture (Jones, 2000), subsequently increasing their access to social mobility, and further differentiating themselves from the "submerged masses" (Taylor, 2009). More specifically, color privilege better positioned fairer-skinned Blacks for formal educational opportunities (Gasman & Abiola, 2016), with historically Black colleges and universities (HBCU's) contributing to the creation of the Black bourgeoisie (Taylor, 2009), and furthering the stratification of the Black community by social class.

Any discourse around the dynamics of this intraracial phenomena in the Black community must address the complex relationship between colorism, HBCU's, and social class, with social class often serving as a determinant for access to education and the social mobility associated therewith. Access to educational opportunities were not the same for darker-skinned Blacks as they were for lighter-skinned Blacks. Frazier (1957) and Gatewood (2000) argued that HBCU's in the United States have been a significant determinant of the socioeconomic status of Black men and women, with education having served as the primary social factor for the establishment of the Black bourgeoisie. The social science literature also documents the various ways (i.e., brown paper bag tests, blue vein societies, etc.) in which many Black churches, fraternities, sororities, and social clubs further distanced themselves from darker-skinned Blacks in an effort to preserve elite and color-conscious circles (Giddings, 2007; Hall, 1992; Maddox & Gray, 2002). This stratification by privilege served to further increase the rift among Blacks (Gatewood, 2000) , as a function of the same intraracial discrimination phenomenon that has, according to Gasman & Abiola (2006), "successfully suppressed and fragmented Black communities by manufacturing social division and spurring intragroup friction, hostility and animosity".

The impact of colorism is multidimensional in that it has the potential for psychological, social, and/or emotional implications for all Blacks impacted by it, including those privileged by it. The roots of this brand of internal racism and intragroup discrimination lie in slavery and have had "a critical influence on the psyche of Blacks that, arguably, is still significant today (Norwood, 2014). From informing individual development and socialization processes, to its influence on the systemic dynamics that inform and maintain social norms, standards of beauty, mate selection, and class; to its shaping the demographic constellations of Black communities; and most dangerously, to its contribution to the contentious division that serves as a barrier to the collective liberation of diasporic African people…colorism's reign of terror on the Black community spans across centuries. In this edition, a collection of experts embark upon a comprehensive examination of the roots and far reaching multigenerational implications of this melanin based hierarchy and its system of intraracial discrimination.

References

African American lives [Television series episode]. (2006). In L. A. Gladsjo, G. Judd, J. Sweet, Youngelson (Producers), *African American Lives*. Arlington, VA: Public Broadcasting Services.

Allen, W., Telles, E., & Hunter, M. (2000). Skin color, income and education: A comparison of African Americans and Mexican Americans. *National Journal of Sociology, 12,* 129--180.

Bennett, J. (2001). Toni Morrison and the burden of the passing narrative. *African American Review, 35*(2): 205--17.

Bontemps, A. (1945). *They Seek A City.* Garden City, NY: Double Day. Definition of Colorism by the Center for Race and Gender, (2005). Retrieved October 24, 2005, from http://crg.berkeley.edu/programs/programs.html.

DuBois, W., ed. (2003). *The Negro Problem*. New York: Humanity Books. Original work published in 1903.

Frazier, F. E. (1957). *Black bourgeoisie: The book that brought the shock of self-revelation to the middle-class Blacks in America*. New York: Free Press Paperbacks.

Gasman, M., & Abiola, U. (2015). Colorism Within the Historically Black Colleges and Universities (HBCUs). *Theory Into Practice, 55*(1), 39-45. DOI:10.1080/00405841.2016.1119018

Gasman, M., & Tudico, C. L. (2008). *Historically black colleges and universities triumphs, troubles, and taboos*. New York, NY: Palgrave Macmillan.

Gatewood, W. B. (2000). *Aristocrats of color: The educated Black elite, 1880-1920*. Fayetteville, AR: University of Arkansas Press.

Giddings, P. (2007). *In search of sisterhood: Delta Sigma Theta and the challenge of the Black sorority movement*. New York, NY: Willow Morrow.

Golden, M. (2004). *Don't play in the sun: One woman's journey through the color complex*. New York, NY: Anchor Books.

Hall, R. E. (1992). Bias among African Americans regarding skin color: Implications for work practice. *Research on Social Work Practice, 2,* 479--486.

Harvey, R. D., LaNeach, N., Pridgen, E., & Gocial, T. M., (2005). The intragroup stigmatization of skin tone among Black Americans. *Journal of Black Psychology, 31*(3): 237--53.

Hill, M. (2002). Skin color and the perception of attractiveness among African Americans: Does gender make a difference? *Social Psychology Quarterly,* 65(1): 77--91.

Hughes, M. & Hertel, B. R. (1990). The significance of color remains: A study of life changes, mate and ethnic consciousness among black Americans. *Social Forces, 68,* 1105--1120.

Hunter, M. (2008). The cost of color: What we pay for being black and brown. In R. E. Hall (Ed.) *Racism in the 21st Century* (pp. 63-76). New York, NY: Springer

Hunter, M. (2007). The persistent problem of colorism: Skin tone, status, and inequality. *Sociology Compass, 1,* 237--254.

Johnson, W. (2001). *Soul by soul: Life inside the antebellum slave market*. Cambridge, MA: Harvard University Press.

Johnson, W. B. (1996). *Black Savannah*, 1788-1864. Fayetteville, AR: University of Arkansas Press.

Jones, T. (2000). Shades of brown: The law of skin color. *Duke Law Journal, 49*(6): 1487--557.

Maddox, K. B. & Gray, S. A. (2002). Cognitive representations of Black Americans: Reexploring the role of skin tone. *Personality & Social Psychology Bulletin, 28,* 250--259.

Norwood, K. J. (Ed.) (2014). *Color matters: Skin tone bias and the myth of a post-racial America*. New York, NY: Routledge.

Keith, V., and C., Herring, (1991). Skin tone and stratification in the Black community. *American Journal of Sociology, 97*(3): 760.

Kephart, W., (2005). Is the American Negro becoming lighter? An analysis of the sociological and biological trends. *American Sociological Review, 13*(4): 437--443.

Kerr, A. E. (2005). The paper bag principle: The law of skin color. *Duke Law Journal, 49,* 1487-1557.

Neal, A. M., & Wilson, M. L. (1989). The role of skin color and features in the Black community: Implications for Black women and therapy. *Clinical Psychology Review, 9,* 323-333.

Russell, K., Wilson, M., & Hall, R. (1992). *The color complex: The politics of skin color among African Americans*. New York, NY: Harcourt Brace Jovanovich Publishers.

Taylor, B. (2009). Color and Class: The promulgation of elitist attitudes at Black colleges. In M. Gasman & C. Tudico (Eds.) *Historically black colleges and universities triumphs, troubles, and taboos*. (pp.189-206). New York, NY: Palgrave Macmillan.

Toplin, R. (1979). Between Black and White: Attitudes toward Southern mulattoes, 1820-1861. *Journal of Southern History, 45*(2): 185-200.

Williams, J. (2004). *I'll find a way or make one. A tribute to historically Black colleges and universities.* New York, NY: Harper Collins.

CHAPTER 1.

The Colorist Identity Convergence Model:
A Re-Conceptualization of Colorism Among Black women

Kamilah Marie Woodson
Howard University

Introduction

According to Hill (2002), Drake and Cayton (1945) cited the observations of an African American physician in an attempt to provide insight into the source of colorism: "Any Negro who is honest will admit that he is dominated by the standards of the society he is brought up in…..All our early concepts of desirable physical attributes come from the white man…The average Negro may say that he is proud to be Black. This is more or less a defense mechanism" (pp.495-496).

Social Scientists have long been interested in identity development, which has been defined as a phenomenological experience of coming to understand oneself; identity is lived discourse (Thomas, Hacker & Hoxha, 2011). According to Thomas, Hacker & Hoxha (2011), the early research on social identity and identity development processes focused on the role of race/ethnicity, often addressing the question, "What does it mean to be African American?" They further remind us that the infamous Clark doll studies suggest that African American children were internalizing negative stereotypes of their race and suffering from low self-esteem as the children often chose the White dolls as having more positive characteristics (Clark and Clark, 1947; Spencer, 2008; Thomas, Hacker & Hoxha, 2011). This however is not surprising, as the most insidious effect of white supremacy racism has been its impact on how people of color view their physical appearance, which largely contributes to one's core sense of self. Throughout the world, the globalization of Eurocentric standards of beauty has resulted in the development of trillion dollar industries that support it, the marketing of images that reify it, the structuring of policies that reward it, and the enactment of interpersonal and personal behavioral routines that emulate it (Jackson-Lowman, 2013). Recognizing domination over groups of people, through mechanisms such as colonialism and slavery, can help us to readily understand the power that has been associated with Eurocentric standards of beauty, skin color in particular. In postcolonial times, the skin color hierarchy on a societal level continues to dominate attitudes, behavior, and policies on a global scale, and impacts identity development on an individual level.

Currently, the literature suggests the phenomenon of colorism is defined as a prejudice or discrimination in which human beings receive differing social treatment based on the complexion of their skin (Burton, Bonilla-Silva, Ray, Buckelew, & Freeman, 2010). Colorism differs from racism in that it is observed both within one's own ethnic group and between groups. It asserts the beliefs that people who have more Eurocentric phenotypic features receive preferential or prejudicial treatment, both within and between races. The presence of colorism prevails among communities of African descent, having been engrained into society and internalized by individuals of the African Diaspora. Specifically, the effect of this internalized colorism has been seen in preferences of skin color/ hair texture and has been noted in the research (Woodson, 2002; Finzi-Smith, 2015; Haileab, 2018) as having both a historic and present connection to the self-concept and self-esteem of African Americans. Black women have had to negotiate the intersection of race, class, politics, and personal appearance in their daily lives; for many, this often results in psychological challenges and or distress. Colorism, like the experience of any other trauma, may result in self-destructive behaviors, acting out, negative coping mechanisms (Burton, Bonilla-Silva, Ray, Buckelew, & Freeman, 2010), and often has adverse psychological consequences. Although a preponderance of the literature speaks to this phenomenon as it relates to skin color, one could argue that this literature is short sighted and or underdeveloped, and that colorism is multidimensional, leading to the development of various colorist identities.

The various identities associated with colorism are the skin color identity, hair texture/length identity, body image (physique) identity and facial features (perceived attractiveness) identity. For example, relative to African American women, one could have developed an identity as the "darker skinned girl", or even be referred to as the girl with the "good hair" regardless of skin color. Someone else could be known as the "shapely or thick girl", while another could be lauded for their European facial features. Consequently, it is the combination of these factors; however subtle they may be, that create a composite identity, and sense of self. It is at the apex of these various identities that self-concept is developed. Where one of the various identities is perceived by self or others as inadequate or displeasing, compensatory realizations can occur on one or more of these colorist factors, which helps to mitigate the negative impact of having perceivably less favorable characteristics on one or more of the other colorists factors (identities). It is then, that the manifestation of the perception of these factors that informs colorist ideologies. Moreover, colorism exists relative to the intersections of these various identities. Therefore, the phenotypic intersections or the convergence could be a real concern and can be quite remarkable given the variability of the aforementioned factors (See Figure 1.) Although there is an intersection of these factors at the core of identity development, the issue of skin color is often the most salient and the most discussed, in this country and in other cultures around the world. In order to understand the development of colorist identities, that again impact the core sense of self, an established comprehensive identity development model was consulted and adapted, redefining colorism.

Theoretical Framework

The theoretical framework that undergirds the Colorist Identity Development Model is the Model of Multiple Dimensions of Identity (MMDI) (Jones and McEwen, 2000). The Model was utilized to explain the dynamic formulations of the core sense of self (Jones and McEwen, 2000), while addressing the development of socially constructed identities. Although the field has considered differences relative to gender, age, race and other identities, many of the models have not adequately addressed the intersection of these constructs, while including others like education, socioeconomic status and sexual orientation. Jones & McEwen (2000) also suggest that the interaction and intersection of multiple identities under development could best be understood as a conical structure, like a helix, with varying radii and heights (see figure 1.). Overall, the Model of Multiple Dimensions of Identity, through various cross sections, enables the presentation of intersections and interactions among identity development dimensions or between multiple identities not seen in other models. This model was adapted as it further speaks to identity as both defined internally by self and externally by others, which provides a platform for a better understanding of multiple identities and underscores the importance of relative salience, sociocultural context and overlapping identities (Jones McEwen, 2000). The Colorist Identity Development Model attempts to advance the existing model by providing a more robust understanding of identity by fine tuning the multiple dimensions of identity while redefining the core self.

The adapted MMDI depicts the Colorist Identity Convergence Model (CICM) and can be viewed as the ultimate pictorial representation of intersectionality. This model too submits that one's personal identity (core self) and other multiple identities might relate at any one point in time. It further proposes that identity can be understood and experienced differently at different points in time particularly in relation to one's personal identity (Colorist Identity) and in terms of the relative prominence of each dimension. The representation in the model of the relationship of the dots on the intersecting circles to the core identity suggests the evolving nature of identity and the changing salience of the various multiple identities. The model does not represent a developmental process; however, it does underscore the importance of the interaction and the interface among one's multiple identities and hints at factors that contribute to the development of identity (contextual influences).

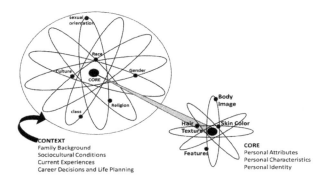

Figure 1. The Colorist Identity Convergence Model (Woodson, 2020) (Adapted from the Model of Multiple Dimensions of Identity -Jones and McEwen, 2000)

The Colorist Identity Convergence Model

Black women lead a very complex existence. They contend with the aforementioned impingers on their Colorist Identities and somehow manage to have a positive overall self-concept. This conceptual model suggests how critical it is to examine and understand the complexities of identity development and provides a developmental snapshot of the most salient dimensions of an individual's identity. It speaks to how the individual experiences those dimensions and provides a blueprint for the individual's future growth and development(Jones & McEwen, 2000).One could argue examining each area individually does not explain the phenomena, but that the understanding of the convergence and or intersections of the various identities (skin, hair, body and attractiveness/features) helps better explicate self-esteem in Black women. Thus, the core identity in this conceptual model can be described as personal identity (Jones & McEwen, 2000). It may be further important to recognize that these women being at the apex of an adequate level of affirmation on one or more of these colorist factors helps to mitigate the negative impact of having a perception of a less favorable characteristic on the other identities. Although much of the literature in the aforementioned colorist identities is directional in favor of Eurocentric Ideals, it is also vital to note that actual phenotypes are less significant, and the more important piece here, is to recognize that the major factor is how African American women are contextually socialized to think and feel about their particular constellations of features. Thus, the point of contention from a psychological perspective, rests in perceived value verses actual phenotypic presentation and or positioning on the colorist identity continuums. Each colorist identity has multifaceted underpinnings and commands intentional attention and description.

Skin Color Identity

Skin Color Identity is based on color consciousness, which is the unnatural assignment of mental or moral traits based upon physical skin color, which can be either positive or negative (Akbar, 1984 Woodson, 2002). According to Akbar, (1984), the African's black skin was considered as evidence for his cursed state to serve as a slave. Despite this notion of "blackness", white masters and overseers, again, routinely engaged in sex with their female captives. Although most Black women participated in these unions against their will, there were some who acquiesced with the hope that the status of their children would be better than their own (Frazier, 1957; Myrdal, 1962; Parrish, 1994; Neal & Wilson, 1989; Woodson, 2002). This was the beginning of the notion of having lighter skin signified higher social status. As a result of the increased race mixing, another "race of people" developed, mulattoes, those with skin color and hair texture closer to that of the slave-master. To maintain their rationale for slavery, they instituted the "one drop rule". That rule stated that if a person had one drop of "black" blood in them, they would have the same social status of Africans. So, on some level, this could have begun to unify the captives. Apparently, once the enslavers saw unity and experienced organized uprisings, they devised a plan to cause division between Blacks, to keep them from unifying, by causing some to feel superior to others based on hair texture and skin color. (Willie Lynch Papers, 1999; Wade, 1996; Okazawa-Rey, Robinson, & Ward, 1986; Boyd-Franklin, 1991; Woodson, 2002). Wyatt (1997) states, "In essence, group solidarity, particularly the historical pattern of drawing on group membership for individual identity ("I am because we are..."), became more precarious" (p.16). Wyatt (1997) further states, "Self-preservation was sometimes maintained at the expense of someone else. And frequently the group was powerless to protect the individual from the master" (p.16).

Although this authenticity of this letter has been challenged in recent years, it provides a theoretical explanation for the phenomenon that is observable among some African Americans today.

Willie Lynch Doctrine of 1712:

"In my bag here, I have a full proof method for controlling your Black slaves. I guarantee every one of you that, if installed correctly, it will control the slaves for at least 300 hundred years. My method is simple. Any member of your family or your overseer can use it. I have outlined a number of differences among the slaves; and I take these differences and make them bigger. I use fear, distrust and envy for control purposes. These methods have worked on my modest plantation in the West Indies and it will work throughout the South. Take this simple little list of differences and think about them. On top of my list is "age," but it's there only because it starts with an "a." The second is "color" or shade. There is intelligence, size, sex, sizes of plantations, status on plantations, attitude of owners, whether the slaves live in the valley, on a hill, East, West, North, South, have fine hair, course hair, or is tall or short. Now that you have a list of differences, I shall give you an outline of action, but before that, I shall assure you that distrust is stronger than trust and envy stronger than adulation, respect or admiration. The Black slaves after receiving this indoctrination shall carry on and will become self-refueling and self-generating for hundreds of years, maybe thousands. Don't forget, you must pitch the old black male vs. the young black male, and the young black male against the old black male. You must use the dark skin slaves vs. the light skin slaves, and the light skin slaves vs. the dark skin slaves. You must use the female vs. the male, and the male vs. the female. You must also have white servants and overseers [who] distrust all Blacks. But it is necessary that your slaves trust and depend on us. They must love, respect and trust only us. Gentlemen, these kits are your keys to control. Use them. Have your wives and children use them, never miss an opportunity. If used intensely for one year, the slaves themselves will remain perpetually distrustful. Thank you, gentlemen." (Lynch, 1999, pp8-9; Parks and Woodson, 2002).

Hughes & Hertel, (1990) cite two main reasons for the higher status enjoyed by lighter skinned captives in the south: First, many white slave owners were related by kinship to their lighter skinned captives and therefore favored them with better positions and better educational opportunities. Second, light skin increased the chances of acculturation because lighter skinned slaves were more likely than those with dark skin to be trained in skilled trades and made into house servants (Hughes & Hertel, 1990). However, according to Gail Wyatt (1997), there were consequences for the privilege of being a house captive. The closer your proximity to the big house, the more likely it was that you were involved in a sexual liaison with a white family member on a routine basis. These unions created children whose skin color, features, and hair texture confirmed that sex/rape was part of the bargain for being a house worker. Wyatt (1997) further states, the fairer skinned population was encouraged by their masters to think of themselves as better than those who toiled in the fields. In reality, their mothers suffered privileged abusive or coerced relationships. The schisms that resulted from alleged class differences based on skin color grew both within and outside of slave quarters (Wyatt, 1997). The results of this were observable beyond enslavement. Russell, Wilson, & Hall (1995), stated, "Before the Civil War, the degree of pigmentation could mean the difference between living free and enslavement." (p.41).

Post-Slavery Color Consciousness
The preferential treatment of mulattoes by Whites had laid the groundwork for a pattern of color classism in Black America (Russell et al., 1995; Hill, 2002; Gullickson, 2005). Post slavery, the "paper bag" and "hair comb" test reinforced negative ideas related to hair texture and skin color, by offering fringe benefits based on these physical characteristics. (Bond & Cash, 1992; Neal & Wilson, 1989; Gullickson, 2005; Kerr, 2005) Since slavery, variations in skin color and features have divided the educated from the ignorant, the well-off from the poor, and the "attractive" from the "plain" (Russell et al., 1995; Gullickson, 2005). "Preferential treatment given by both Black and White cultures to African Americans with light skin and other Caucasoid attributes has conveyed to many Blacks that the more physically conformed to the White majority standard of beauty, the more rewarding their lives would be" (Gatewood, 1988; Bond & Cash, 1992; Landor & Halpern, 2016). According to Rooks (1996), in the early 1900's, there were often advertisements that suggested this would be the case. One advertisement noted by Rooks (1996) read, "Lighter Your Dark Skin": "Race men and women protect your future…be attractive. Throw off the chains that have held you back form prosperity and happiness that rightly belong to you. Apply Black and White Ointment (for white or colored folks) as directed on the package…be the envy of everybody."(p.30) For African Americans, skin color functioned as a marker of a

racial identity, which often was spoken of as simply inferior; therefore, products were marketed to offer African Americans the opportunity to try to lessen the shame of such a marker (Rooks, 1996). Beauty manufacturers in the nineteenth century targeted skin color and hair texture- the two characteristics African Americans had to change if they expected to fit into American society (Rooks, 1996). Consequently, African Americans have considered fair skin, White facial features, and White hair type to be more attractive than dark skin, Black features, and Black hair type (Wade, 1996).

According to Keith and Monroe, (2016), ethnoracial and color discrimination intersect in that, skin complexion is perhaps the primary physical feature that is used to ascribe racial classification and value when interacting with others. Decades ago, Lakoff & Scherr (1984), posited that beauty is power and, many women have gained social success banking on the social marketability of their perceived physical attractiveness (Robinson & Ward, 1995). Hughes & Hertel, (1990) reported that a comparison of the main effects for skin color from 1950to 1980 shows that the effects of skin color have not changed appreciably. In 2020, this is still observable. Although Fair-skinned African Americans still fare better economically, vocationally, and educationally (Wade,1996); practically speaking, the value placed on skin color is contextual and contingent upon the belief and values of the observer and receiver of the messages. For example, the "one" darker-skinned person in the family could be celebrated and treated better than the lighter skinned family members, often as a result of variations in paternity, leading to a very positive self-concept; thus, one could argue that the actual complexion or hue of the skin does not necessarily dictate self-worth, or treatment, but it is how one is made to feel about their complexion-whatever shade they have, is what is most salient and significant. Russell et al., (1995) echo this sentiment as they suggest levels of self-esteem relative to skin color and hair texture would truly depend to the values the subject's family of origin, circle of friends, and the immediate environment (Russell et. al, 1995).

Hair texture and Hair Length Identity

Hair is one element that is a determinant of attractive appearance and is said to be an important factor to all women (Oriowo, 2016). Thus, the "good hair" and "bad hair" distinction is probably the most indelible construction of hair that occupies the psyche of African Americans (Banks, 2000). As feelings and attitudes about hair texture, length, and style have many complex determinants, these sensitivities and concerns may be symbolic of an African American's feelings about other aspects of themselves

(Green, White & Whitten, 2000). It appears as if this is intensified for African American women because the history of American racism, as was discussed earlier, has included a conspicuous devaluation of African physical features and the establishment of beauty standards based on idealized depictions of White women's features (Hall, 1995; Martin, 1964; Neal & Wilson, 1989; Green et al., 2000 Jackson-Lowman, 2013). As physical appearance and attractiveness are more salient social variables for women than for men, and are often seen as the major determinant in calculating a woman's social value or status, women experience greater overt distress and unconscious conflict about their hair and its relationship to their attractiveness (Green et al., 2000).

Historical Significance of Hair

Prior to the institution of slavery, hair had a very different meaning and purpose for Africans. According to Byrd & Tharps (2014) ever since African civilizations bloomed, hairstyles have been used to indicate a person's marital status, geographic location, age, religion, ethnic identity, wealth, and rank within the community. They further state that in some to the cultures a person's surname could be ascertained simply by examining the hair because each clan had its own unique hairstyle (Byrd & Tharps, 2014). Unfortunately, upon their arrival in America, African captives were forced to alter the traditions of hairstyling and grooming once treasured on the continent of Africa. Presumably the enslavers shaved the heads of their new enslaved Africans for what they considered sanitary reasons, but the effect was much more insidious (Byrd & Tharps, 2014). According to Byrd & Tharps, (2014), a shaved head in an African's eyes back then, can be interpreted as taking away someone's identity. "The shaved head was the first step the Europeans took to erase the African's culture and alter the relationship between the African and his or her hair" (Byrd & Tharps, 2014,p.11). Arriving without their signature hairstyles, the Africans entered the New World, just as the Europeans intended, like anonymous chattel (Byrd & Tharps, 2014).

As was mentioned previously, enslavers created distinct differences between enslaved Africans based to their skin color as well as their hair texture. Adjectives used to describe natural African hair are "bad", "nappy", "coarse" and or "wild", thus implying that it needs to be "fixed" or "controlled". These words reflect shame and insecurity, therefore compelling most Africans to try to alter it. Curly and kinky hair was glorified in West African societies; however, it became a symbol of inferiority once enslaved Africans reached the shores of America, and the pride and elegance that once symbolized curly and kinky hair immediately became a badge of racial inferiority (Banks, 2000). Words used to describe Africans who had hair textures similar to textures of the Caucasian slave owners were "good", "curly", "soft", "nice", or a "good grade of hair", thus causing this particular subgroup of enslaved Africans to feel superior to those who did not have this particular hair type or texture based on the preferential treatment they received. The quest for straight hair was often a torturous obsession for the captives. Africans found that they had to use household products to straighten their hair (Byrd & Tharps, 2014). Instead of using the palm oil they were accustomed to, they took to using oil-based products and equipment to achieve certain styles, like bacon grease and butter to condition hair, make it shine, and to prepare it for pressing (Byrd & Tharps, 2014). They also used cornmeal and kerosene as scalp cleaners and used lye mixed with potatoes to at time straighten the hair. Unfortunately, with using the lye, it would often eat the skin right off a person's head (Bryd & Tharps, 2014). This wasn't however, just about conforming to the prevailing fashions of the day. Straight hair translated to economic opportunity and social advantage and continues to current carry this meaning today for many African Americans in certain contexts.

Black women, themselves have internalized the concept of good hair and bad hair and within their own ranks propagated the notion that darker-skinned Blacks with kinkier hair were less attractive, less intelligent, and worth less than their lighter –hued brothers and sisters with straighter hair (Byrd & Tharps, 2014). Anecdotal evidence suggests that distinct groups emerged that were formed based on the texture of a person's hair. In some churches a fine-toothed comb was hung from the front door, and all persons wanting to join the church had to be able to pass the comb smoothly through their hair and if it was too "kinky" membership was denied (Parks & Woodson, 2002; Byrd & Tharps, 2014). This was known as the infamous "Comb test". This type of blatant discrimination not only occurred in churches and social organizations but is also rumored to have occurred in the admissions process in historically black institutions.

According to Byrd & Tharps, (2014) during this time, institutions like Howard (established in 1867), Hampton (1868), and Spelman (1881) were founded to educate the "Black elite", but judging from photographs of the early graduates, it seems as if one of the unspoken requirements for admissions was a skin tone or hair texture that showcased a Caucasian ancestor. Therefore, life after slavery for many Blacks meant a continued obsession with straightening the hair and lightening the skin to feel good about one's self and to be accepted by both Blacks and Whites. Advertisements for skin lighteners and hair straighteners marketed by white companies suggest to Blacks that only through changing physical features will persons of African descent be afforded class mobility within African American communities and social acceptance by the dominant culture (Rooks, 1996). Unfortunately, to gain access to the American dream it was imperative that African Americans attempt to make White people more comfortable with their very presence (Byrd & Tharps, 2014). Woodson (2002), sites an example of the stressful experience of trying to look "presentable" as described by Assata Shakur:

> . . . I had always hated frying my hair—burnt ears, a smokey straightening comb, and the stink of your own hair burning. How many nights I spent trying to sleep on curlers, bound with scarves that cut into my head like a tourniquet. . . Afraid to go to the beach, afraid to walk in the rain, afraid to make passionate love on hot summer nights if I had to go to work in the morning. Afraid my hair would "go back." The permanent was even worse: trying to sit calmly while lye was eati ng its way into my brain…Clumps of hair falling out. . . (Imarogbe, 2001; Shakur, 1987, p.174)

The fact that many women do not have this experience because they have been born with physical characteristics that are compatible with the European aesthetics has set the stage for the inevitable competition between the "haves" and the have nots". Another example of this was a letter written to *Ebony* Magazine:

> "I truly need help with this one. I am a 26 year-old woman and I've been with my 29 year-old boyfriend for three years. I deeply love him and we've been talking about marriage lately. Recently, I let my hair grow very long. Once during love making, my boyfriend said, I love your beautiful long hair. It's just like a white girl's. This comment shattered my heart, not to mention my whole world. I love being Black and I'm proud to be a Black woman. Since this incident, I've noticed how much he talks about his best friend's wife who is white. When I discussed his comment about my hair with him, he said I am overreacting. I don't think I am. I can't help but wonder if he really wants a white woman. I've considered breaking up with him. I just can't seem to get that comment he made out of my mind. Please help. (Ebony, 1996, p.6; Woodson, 2002).

Although these examples are different, they shed light on the experiences of women as it relates to their interactions with their male counterparts who too, have been unable to "…escape the confusing conundrum of experiencing pressure from family, peers, and/or society to have hair textures and partners that result in privileges within the Black community and the dominant culture…" (Green et al., 2000, p.172; Oriowo,

2016). Further, it is important to note that African Americans at either ends of the color or hair texture continuum may experience low self-worth or dissatisfaction with their hair. Every year, Afrikan American women give billions of dollars to a hair care beauty industry, which for the most part, is no longer owned by people of Afrikan ancestry (Jackson-Lowman, 2013). Jackson Lowman (2013) further states that we buy straight, often Indian or Asian hair for the purposes of weaves and extensions, and purchase wigs and hair care products making the owners of these businesses rich, as a result of our obsessions. Oriowo, (2016) underscores this by stating that the Black hair business is said to be half a billion dollar business with the potential to be a trillion dollar business.

Body Image /Physique Identity

Conflicting information has been found regarding differences between Black and White women's perceptions of beauty. The majority of the research with Black women participants indicates that Black women are more accepting than White women of a larger body sizes, define beauty as comprised of personality traits more than physical characteristics, and consider other Black women as allies rather than competitors (Parker et al., 1995;Poran, 2006) Yet other work indicates that Black, White and Latina women all share perceptions of dominant standards of beauty and hold similar definitions of beauty. Much of the body image research on Black women has tended to simply verify the notion that what concerns White women most does not concern Black women (Poran, 2006; Capodilupo and Kim, 2013); however, qualitative work adds a more comprehensive understanding of this nuanced phenomena. Contrary to the theories that present Black women as immune to mainstream cultural preferences for thinness, these women do present the thin ideal as a standard to which they are expected to adhere. The only departure is relative to being both "thin" and "curvy". Capodilupo and Kim (2013) conducted a study and found, that in the face of these opposing pressures, participants reported engaging in some psychological negotiation between meeting the expectations of the dominant White culture versus the Black subculture, which resulted in either internalizing the thin ideal, actively opposing mainstream beauty standards, endorsing and Afrocentric aesthetic, the "Thick Ideal" and/or achieving self-acceptance.

The Poran (2006) study remarkably adds to the literature by dispelling myths about Black women and body image concerns. In the Poran (2006) qualitative study of body image among Black women, it was found that the prevailing standard of beauty was recognized, the pressure of the standard was acknowledged and actively critiqued; suggesting that immunity from White body image ideals is a misnomer, and an active negotiation occurs. This study further states that the perceived preferences of Black men were felt as pressure rather than a safeguard. The participants by in large expressed a goal of being liked by men, and regardless of how smart or successful a woman may be, they believed her primary concern must be to look beautiful for men. Additionally this data set yielded data that posits that physique standards for women vary across race among men, and that other women are not seen as those with whom one could commiserate of find solace, but are viewed as sources of pressure via competition and intimidation. For Black women, one's self image is experienced as delicate and shifting in relation to those who are judging one's body or who are perceived as forcing a comparison that fosters a negative judgment of one's self. Further, the internalization of the images, the projections onto other women and the consequential effects on personal relationships is alarming. Just viewing how other women are judged is enough to trigger a feeling of hatred toward the woman that is receiving a positive assessment of her body. Finally when discussing images of Black women in the media, one of the participants in the aforementioned study stated, "It's funny because um they're giving us these pictures for us to identify with and buy the product, but really it's not really what's happening…We're trying to live up to what they put out there…like subliminal messages" (Poran, 2006).

In sum, Poran (2006), states that Black women are not comfortable with their bodies and did not convey high body image esteem. Rather, they talked about great discomfort, the strong awareness of social pressures for specific body types, and various attempts to either reconcile with or resign oneself to, multiple sources that are telling them that they are not quite good enough. The women did not convey a story of protection from mainstream ideals, but one of conflicting pressures. Black women also receive overt and subliminal messages within the African American Community as well. That message is not only be thin, but to also be curvaceous. An example of this is relative to the lyrics of popular rap and R& B artists. These songs state:

"I'm lookin for a yellow bone long haired star
Thick in the hips come get in my car" - Soulja Boy
"I like them long hair, thick, red bone" - Lil Wayne
"Yellow rims, yellow big booty yellow bones" - Gucci Mane
"Yellow model chic, yellow bottle sippin" - Chris Brown
"Yellow bone passenger, they see us they say oh boy" - Rick Ross

Moreover, Bledman (2011) conducted a study looking at the ideal body shape of Black college women. Seventy-nine Black women enrolled in a diverse college setting completed online survey instruments designed to measure concerns about body shape, body image and shape satisfaction. In particular, the author used the Reese Figure Rating Scale (RFRS) (Patt, Lane, Finney, Yane and Becker, 2002) which is one of the only figure rating scales to be standardized on Black women. Of particular note, the RFRS was developed by increasing the BMI of each image, paying particular attention to thighs, abdomen and breast. Results indicated that Black college women experienced body shape dissatisfaction, suggesting that the participants may have wanted to alter these specific areas in order to be more satisfied with their body shape. Further, data suggests that when Black women seek surgery, they often want procedures related to achieving a curvaceous body shape such as liposuction, fat grafting, and buttock lifts and augmentation (ASPS, 2015; Hollier, 2018). Powell-Hicks (2013), in a sample that mostly consisted of Black female college students, found that Black women college who did not feel close to their cultural standards of beauty were more likely to choose cosmetic survey (Hollier; 2018). However, the issue is that Black women, including Black college women, who desire undergo plastic surgery may not be able to afford the cost of a certified plastic surgeon. They may instead obtain services on the black market which may lead to extreme illness and death for some patients (Rokeshia & Jung, 2017). Rokeshia and Jung (2017) found that Black women in the United States and South Africa were less likely to engage in plastic surgery from a certified plastic surgeon due to socioeconomic status. These statistics and findings suggest that clinicians should consider body shape as component of body image dissatisfaction, especially since Black women, are generally more likely to get plastic surgeries to achieve a curvaceous ideal (Hollier, 2018).

Facial Features and Attractiveness Identity

Research on physical attractiveness has identified clear advantages to individuals viewed as attractive. Compared with persons seen as unattractive, attractive people are perceived as more likeable more desirable as romantic partners, more honest and cooperative, and more competent and intelligent (Collins 1996; Hill 2002) As a result, persons perceived as attractive enjoy numerous social benefits as attractive enjoy numerous social benefits including better job opportunities and higher incomes (Umberson and Hughes, 1987). As one African American child casually remarked during a doll study, "I don't like being Black; I will be rich if I am like a white doll" (Hill, 2002). This suggests that success is sometimes equated with whiteness during childhood among African American girls. Although some research indicates that Black women do not compare themselves against white images of beauty, it is important to note that Black images of beauty are becoming more "White-like", and this may influence women's perceptions of media, themselves, and other women (Poran, 2006); thus, Black women seeking to be perceived by others as feminine and attractive may feel compelled to emulate whiteness (Hill, 2002), or may emulate whiteness inadvertently. Also of note, the majority of beauty products marketed toward women of color are designed to aid them in looking more phenotypically white. Although this is the case, there are only a few Black women who have risen to the status of mainstream sex symbols, for example, Lena Horne, and Halle Berry. Ironically however, in an interview with the *Washington Informer* in 1965 Lena Horne stated,

> "To some Negros light color is far from being a status symbol; in fact, it's quite the opposite. It is evidence that your image has been corrupted by White people... On the one hand, much money was spent on hair straighteners and skin lighteners. On the other hand you were put down for being naturally closer to the prevailing ideal of beauty...I didn't know whether I was supposed to be proud of my color or ashamed of it." (Levine, 2007, p.249)

This paradox exists seemingly as a result of slavery and the within group discrimination that occurs. To justify racial slavery, slave holding interests espoused a white supremacist ideology which held that persons of African descent were innately inferior to whites. Whiteness became identified with all that is civilized, virtuous, and beautiful while is in blackness in opposition, with all that is lowly, sinful and ugly. In this racialized context phenotypic expression came to be the preeminent indicator of social standing and moral character; physical traits such as eye color, nose shape, facial shape, and lip prominence became powerfully loaded symbols of beauty, merit and prestige (Hill, 2002).

Physical attractiveness is considered extremely important to women in current society. In the United States, many women strive for physical perfection, and much attention is focused on the way they look (Sewell, 2013). Evolutionary psychologists propose that physical attractiveness is an indicator of good health and high reproduction in men and women; however, since men are primarily driven by the attractiveness of a potential mate, women have to place a higher emphasis on physical attractiveness as compared to their male counterparts (Ha, Overbeek, & Engels, 2010; Landor & Halpern, 2016). Although all romantic relationships are not heterosexual; it is important to note that what is perceived as attractive tends to be similar across the sexuality continuum. One predictor of physical attractiveness is facial traits and or features (Currie & Little,

2009; Little, 2014). Little (2014) states that human faces vary in different ways and that these facial variations impact whether the person is perceived as attractive or not. Additionally, Little (2014) as well as other researchers suggest that facial attractiveness is closely related to the following constructs: "youth, weight, color, symmetry, masculinity, and femininity, health, good behavior and personality." Further, youthful looking faces are perceived as more desirable and individuals tend rate younger faces as more attractive than older faces (Egan & Cordan, 2009; Little, 2014).

In an analysis of African American women's literature, the subject of Black women's physical beauty occurs with such frequency in the writing of Black women that it indicates that they have been deeply affected (Hill 2002). Moreover, Fears (1998) conducted a study in which they hypothesized through their meta -analysis of popular media periodicals that there would be significantly more representations of Black women as primary newsmakers whose appearance represents the typical Eurotypic (white and or Caucasian facial type than there will be of Black women with an Afrotypic Black and or African American facial type). They found that female models were depicted most often with Eurotypic features. They also noted that there was more frequent usage of the terms or descriptors beautiful, gorgeous, lovely etc., to describe physical attractiveness in texts that accompany photos of Black women whose appearance represents the typical Eurotypic facial type rather that the Afrotypic facial type. This research was conducted decades ago, and in 2020, the same can be observed.

Conclusion

African American women lead an extremely complicated existence. They contend with racism, sexism, and colorism etc., yet they somehow manage to have a resilience, strength and show up performing "Black Girl Magic". This conceptual model suggests how critical it is to examine and understand the complexities of colorist identity, as most, if not all self-esteem measures lack the power and specificity to capture the nuances of this construct. The Colorist Identity Model by and large, provides a framework for an individual's growth and identity development (Jones & McEwen, 2000). Focusing on one area of development does not speak to the dynamic processes or the phenomena but understanding the convergence and or intersections of the various identities (skin, hair, body and attractiveness/features) helps better illuminate the core sense of self in Black women.

Although the preoccupation with phenotypic presentation can be traced back to enslavement, in 2020, the same sort of desire to be accepted, to be acceptable, not only by Whites but also by and among African Americans can be observed. It can be gleaned that the aesthetically beautiful standard set for African American women, is to have long flowing tresses, be a size 6, to have medium to light skin and facial features commiserate with White people in most environments. However, there are times when the status quo is not the most desirable, and characteristics that are commiserate with African features are more desirable, i.e., the "Thick Ideal." An example of this is "White Colorism", which in this context, is defined as the desire of Whites to have the phenotypic expressions typically associated with that of African Americans. Thusly, White colorist ideologies are also an observable phenomenon needing more examination. For example, many of the popular reality TV stars and social media models, who are White, have augmented their bodies to have features typically commiserate with African American women. White women and women from other races are getting cosmetic surgery to have large buttocks, large breasts, thick(full) lips, they darken their skin (though tanning, sprays and makeup) and wear their hair in styles like braids, locks and other hairstyles similar to that of African American women. This is the biggest paradox; such that, many White women emulate Black women, while Black women work to emulate White women. Seemingly both perceive the power of the other and attempt to compensate.

Implications for Research, Policy and Practice

The Colorist Identity Convergence Model, (CICM) was presented as a theoretical framework to document colorism from a developmental theoretical perspective; however, from an empirical perspective, the model should be tested and validated. It is expected that information yielded from the validation of the model would inform and assist in the creation of a colorist identity development scale, perhaps with four subscales (skin color, hair texture/length, body image/physique and attractiveness/facial features). Researchers could also advance the literature on the "redefined definition" of colorism with the goal of generating data that can be used to inform policies on multiple levels in multiple contexts. Interestingly, in 2019, the CROWN Act, an acronym that stands for "Creating a Respectful and Open World for Natural Hair" was passed in California, which was created to ensure protection against discrimination based on hair texture and protective styles. The Crown Act has been passed in other states like Florida; however, more data documenting the importance of this phenomena could aid in providing the foundation for the development of other policies that protect against colorism. The contexts that could benefit from more policies are in legal settings, educational settings, and health care settings, to name a few. The CICM also supposes implications for clinicians.

Clinicians should make sure that they are aware of their own unconscious beliefs, biases and preferences. Clinicians also need to make sure that they feel comfortable discussing colorism (including the aforementioned colorist identities). In terms of the consequence of these various identities, it is key for the clinician to attend to the distress of the African American women who does not have certain features that are known to be most attractive, particularly to their male counter parts. Many African American women have truly bought into the European aesthetic and are participating in a form of self- hatred, while some may not have. Kambon (1992), noted that the act of hair straightening is a form of self -hatred, and even characterizes it as pathological. He stated, "...I am thoroughly convinced that there is a powerful pathological dimension to African's approach to so called hair 'grooming' under the Culturally Misoriented conditions of White supremacy domination" (Kambon, 1992, p.142). He also states, disfiguring our African physical features in order to achieve the 'European/Caucasian-look,' and by implication greater self-acceptance (under a social system of White supremacy domination), has now become so common among Africans in America that this gross form of mental disorder is literally taken for granted throughout the community (Kambon, 1992). Now Dr. Kambon's perspective may appear radical, however, it underscores that a range of perspectives exist among clinicians and one's particular perspective needs to be taken into consideration, when the clinician is treating women of African Descent.

Process Questions and Considerations
1. Are there additional identities that could/should have been included in the CICM?
2. What does it mean to have a healthy core sense of self?
3. Is Colorist Identity formation continuous or static? Why?
4. Does Colorist Identity development impact the development of otheridentities, or do the other identities that are not core shape Colorist Identity?
5. Should clinicians who subscribe to Eurocentric Ideals of beauty treat African America women?

References
Akbar, N. (1984). *Chains and images of psychological slavery.* Jersey City, NJ: New Mind Productions.
Ashley, R. R., & Jung, J. (2017). # BlackBodiesMatter: Cross-Cultural Examination of Black Women's Motivation to Engage in Body Modification. *Journal of Black Studies, 48*(3), 235-255.
Banks, I. (2000). *Hair matters: Beauty, power, and Black women's consciousness.* New York, NY: New

York University Press.

Bledman, R. A. (2011). *The ideal body shape of African American college women* (Doctoral dissertation, University of Missouri--Columbia).

Burton, L., Bonilla-Silva, E., Ray, V., Buckelew, R. & Freeman, E.H. (2010). Duke University critical race theories: Colorism, and the decade's research on families of color. *Journal of Marriage and Family*: 440 - 459. DOI:10.1111/j.1741-3737.2010.00712.x

Byrd, A.D., & Tharps, L.L. (2001*) Hair story: Untangling the roots of Black hair in America*. New York, NY: St. Martin's Press.

Capodilupo, C. C. (2015). One size does not fit all: Using variables other than the thin ideal to understand black women's body image. *Cultural Diversity & Ethnic Minority Psychology, 21*(2), 268-278.

Capodilupo, C. M., & Kim, S. (2013). Gender and race matter: The importance of considering intersections in black women's body image. *Journal of Counseling Psychology.* Advance online Publication. DOI:10.1037/a0034597

Clark, K. B., & Clark, M. K. (1947). Racial identification and preference in negro children. In T. Newcomb & E. L. Hardey (Eds.), *Readings in Social Psychology* (pp. 602-611). New York: Holt.

Collins, N. L. (1996). Working models of attachment: Implications for explanation, emotion, and behavior. *Journal of Personality and Social Psychology, 71*(4), 810.

Drake, S. C., & Cayton, H. (1945). *Black metropolis.* New York: Harcourt Brace.

Egan, V., & Cordan, G. (2009). Barely legal: Is attraction and estimated age of young female faces disrupted by alcohol use, make up, and the sex of the observer? *British Journal of Psychology, 100*(2), 415-427.

Fears, L. M. (1998). Colorism of black women in news editorial photos. *Western Journal of Black Studies, 22*(1), 30.

Finzi-Smith, Z. M. (2015). *Feeding the pain: Multiple forms of discrimination, psychological functioning and eating behaviors among black women.* Unpublished Dissertation, Howard University.

Frazier, E. F. (1957). *Black bourgeoisie.* New York, NY: Free Press.

Gatewood, W. B. (1988). Aristocrat of color: South and north and the black elite, 1880-1930. *Journal of Southern History, 54*, 3-19.

Greene, B., White, J. C., & Whitten, L. (2000). Hair texture, length, and style as a metaphor in the African American mother-daughter relationship: Considerations in psychodynamic psychotherapy. In L.C. Jackson, & B. Greene (Eds.), *Psychotherapy with African-American women: Innovations in Psychodynamic Perspectives and Practice* (pp.166-193). New York, New York: Guilford Press.

Gullickson, A. (2005). The significance of color declines: A re-analysis of skin tone differentials in post-civil rights America. *Social Forces, 84*(1), 157-180.

Ha, T., Overbeek, G., & Engels, R. C. (2010). Effects of attractiveness and social status on dating desire in heterosexual adolescents: An experimental study. *Archives of Sexual Behavior, 39*(5), 1063-1071.

Haileab, L. (2018). *Shaded love and violence: Internalized colorism, femininity, depression and dating violence.* Unpublished Dissertation, Howard University.

Hill, M. E. (2002). Skin color and the perception of attractiveness among African Americans: Does gender make a difference? *Social Psychology Quarterly. 65*(1), 77-91.

Hall, C. I. (1995). Beauty is in the soul of the beholder: Psychological implications of beauty and African American women. *Cultural Diversity and Mental Health, 1*, 125-137.

Hall, R. E. (2003). Skin color as post-colonial hierarchy: A global strategy for conflict resolution. *Journal of Black Psychology, 137*, 41-53.

Hollier, C. (2018). *The influence of body dissatisfaction and self-esteem on disordered eating behaviors among female black college students.* Unpublished Dissertation, Howard University.

Hughes, M., & Hertel, B. R. (1990). The significance of color remains: A study of life chances, mate selection, and ethnic consciousness among Black Americans. *Social Forces, 68*, 1105-1120.

Imarogbe, K.A. (in press). Hair misorientation: Free your mind and your hair will follow. *Journal of Black Psychology.*

Jackson-Lowman, H. (2013). An analysis of the impact of Eurocentric concepts of beauty on the lives of African American women. In H. Jackson-Lowman (Ed.), *African American women: Living at the crossroads of race, gender, class, and culture* (pp.155-172). San Diego, CA: Cognella Academic Publishing.

Jones, S. R., & McEwen, M. K. (2000). A conceptual model of multiple dimensions of identity. *Journal of College Student Development, 41*(4).

Kambon, K. K. (1992). The African personality in American: An Africa-centered framework. Tallahassee, FL: Nubian Nation Publications.

Kerr, A. E. (2005). The paper bag principle: Of the myth and the motion of colorism. *Journal of American Folklore,* pp. 271-289.

Lakoff, R. T., & Scherr, R. L. (1984). *Face value: Politics of beauty.* Boston, MA: Kegan Paul.

Landor, A. M., & Halpern, C. T. (2016). The enduring significance of skin tone: Linking skin tone, attitudes toward marriage and cohabitation, and sexual behavior. *Journal of youth and adolescence, 45*(5), 986-1002.

Little, A. C. (2014). Facial attractiveness. *Wiley Interdisciplinary Reviews: Cognitive Science, 5*(6), 621-634.

Lynch, W. (1999).The untold "story" 1712. In W. Lynch, *The Willie Lynch letter and the making of a slave* (pp. 8-9). Chicago: Lushena Books.

Martin, J. G. (1964). Racial ethnocentrism and judgment of beauty. *Journal of Social Psychology, 63*, 59-63

Myrdal, G. (1962). An American dilemma. In *New Tribalisms* (pp. 61-72). London: Palgrave Macmillan.

Neal, A. M., & Wilson, M. L. (1989). The role of skin color and features in the black community: Implications for black women and therapy. *Clinical Psychology Review,* 9, 323-333.

Okazawa-Rey, M., Robinson, T., & Ward, J. V. (1986). Black women and the politics of skin color and hair. *Women & Therapy* 6, 89-102.

Oriowo, D. O. (2016). *Is it easier for her? Afro-textured hair and its effects on black female sexuality: A mixed methods approach.* Chester, PA: Widener University.

Parker, S., Nichter, M., Nichter, M., Vuckovic, N., Sims, C., & Ritenbaugh, C. (1995). Body image and weight concerns among African American and white adolescent females: Differences that make a difference. *Human Organization,* 103-114.

Parks, C. W., & Woodson, K. M. (2002). The impact of skin color and hair texture on mate selection: Implications for interventions with African American men and women. In E. Davis-Russell (Ed.), *The California School of Professional Handbook on Multicultural Education, Research, Intervention, and Training* (pp. 249-262). San Francisco, CA: Jossey-Bass Publishers, Inc.

Parrish, C. (1944). *The significance of skin color in the negro community.* PhD Dissertation, University of Chicago.

Patt, M. R., Lane, A. E., Finney, C. P., Yanek, L. R., & Becker, D. M. (2002). *Ethnicity and Disease, 12,* 54-62.

Poran, M. A. (2006). The politics of protection: Body image, social pressures, and the misrepresentation of young Black women. *Sex Roles, 55,* 739-755. DOI:10.1007/s11199-006-9129-5

Powell-Hicks, A. (2013). Body objectification, ethnic identity and cosmetic surgery in African-American women [ProQuest Information & Learning]. In *Dissertation Abstracts International: Section B: The Sciences and Engineering, 74,* (3-B(E)).

Sewell, C. J. (2013). Mammies and matriarchs: Tracing images of the black female in popular culture 1950s to present. *Journal of African American Studies, 17*(3), 308-326.

Robinson, T. L., & Ward, J. V. (1995) African American adolescents and skin color. *Journal of Black Psychology, 21,* 256-274.

Rooks, N. (1996). *Hair raising: Beauty, culture, and African American women.* New Brunswick, NJ: Rutgers University Press.

Russell, K., Wilson, M., & Hall, R. E. (1992), *The color complex: The politics of skin color among African Americans.* New York: Harcourt Brace Jovanovich.

Spencer, M. B. (2008). Lessons learned and opportunities ignored since Brown v. Board of Education: Youth development and the myth of a color-blind society. *Educational Researcher, 37*(5), 253.

Tummala-Narra, P. (2007). Skin color and the therapeutic relationship. *Psychoanalytic Psychology, 24*(2), 255-270.

Umberson, D., & Hughes, M. (1987). The impact of physical attractiveness on achievement and psychological well-being. *Social Psychology Quarterly*, 227-236.

Wade, T. J. (1996). The relationships between skin color and self-perceived global, physical, and sexual attractiveness, and self-esteem for African Americans. *Journal of Black Psychology, 22*(3), 358-373.

Wallace, S. A., Townsend, T. G., Glasgow, Y. M., & Ojie, M. J. (2011). Gold diggers, video vixens, and jezebels: Stereotype images and substance use among urban African American girls. *Journal of Women's Health, 20*(9), 1315-1324.

Wirth, L., & Goldhamer, H. (1944). The hybrid and the problem of miscegenation. In *Characteristics of the American Negro,* edited by Otto Klineberg, pp. 253-369. Harper and Brothers.

Woodson, K. M. (2002). *The impact of hair texture and skin color among African American men and women during mate selection on the expression of risky sexual behaviors.* Unpublished Dissertation, California School of Professional Psychology, Los Angeles, CA.

Wyatt, G. E. (1997). *Stolen women: Reclaiming our sexuality, taking back our lives.* New York, NY: John Wiley & Sons, Inc.

Wyatt, G. E., Tucker, M. B., Romero, G. J., Carmona, J. V., Newcomb, M. D., Wayment, H. A. & Mitchell-Kernan, C. (1997). Adapting a comprehensive approach to African American women's sexual risk taking. *Journal of Health Education, 28*(sup1), S-52.

CHAPTER 2.

Colorist Identity Development Across the Lifespan: Implications for Intervention and Prevention

Jannis F. Moody, Texas Southern University
Kamilah Marie Woodson, Howard University
Ashley Hill, Virginia Commonwealth University

Introduction

Family is regarded as a powerful force in the lives of Black Americans, where families function as an agent of socialization. It is oftentimes within the family unit that Black consciousness and Black pride are learned and lauded. One way that Black children are socialized is relative to racism, with the goal of countering its effects. However, at the same time, Black families can unfortunately perpetuate the internalization of colorist ideologies (Wilder & Cain, 2011). Wilder and Cain (2011) have pointed out the importance of "family ideals" with respect to self-perception and self-esteem about skin color, hair length/texture, physique, and facial features; such that the family ascribes or projects roles, expectations, and acceptance onto an individual based on appearance. By the same token, Bond and Cash (1992) have reported, irrespective of how one's skin tone compares with that of peers, being the "light child" or "dark child" may carry special significance, either favorable or unfavorable, in the context of specific family dynamics. Additional researchers have supported the notion that skin color variation can create difficulty among family members. Although there is an extensive body of revisionist literature on Black families and a growing body of scholarship on the contemporary nature of colorism, there is a dearth of literature addressing the role of Black families in relation to colorism (Wilder & Cain 2011).

Colorism within families remains as an upsetting condition that few people are ready to discuss. It is particularly troubling that color biases appear to be internalized in early life. Notably, comments about color first come from family members, later from friends and peers, then in romantic relationships, all of which shape the psychology of a Black child as it grows from infancy to adulthood (Russell et al., 1995; Woodson,

2002). Accordingly, Russell et al. (1995) posit that Black children quickly ingest the guilt, anger, jealousy, and depression generated in their families by unresolved colorist ideologies. Interestingly however, families are often unwilling to acknowledge the prejudice that exists within their own hearts, as it is upsetting, and most people have learned that it is not proper to air one's dirty laundry. While some parents do teach color biases directly to their children (Russell et al., 1992; Hill 2002) colorism often appears to be acquired passively from early exposure to racial inequalities. Many children are acutely aware of the association between color and privilege and long to share the advantages associated with whiteness (Hill 2002). Societal norms, including the ways in which children are treated and greeted can be quite harmful even when the greeting is meant to be complimentary. For example, many African Americans will greet a darker-skinned "attractive" child by saying, "What a cute dark-skinned girl. . . look at all that pretty good hair!"

By and large, colorism has a deleterious impact on early developmental processes, influencing the development of identity, sense of self, self-esteem, and self-efficacy. The way in which one sees, understands, and relates to the world around them begins to take shape within the context of relationships with primary caregivers in early childhood. Children receive and seed ideas about their identity, value, place, and purpose in the world from the messages transmitted by their family of origin or primary caregivers. Those born into family systems wherein parents or primary caregivers subscribe to colorist ideals are susceptible to early and consistent exposure to attitudes, beliefs, values, and subsequent treatment aligning with the ideologies of the color-based caste system. This exposure, particularly very early in development and with great consistency, helps to shape their perceptions of themselves; their beliefs about others' perceptions of them; beliefs about what their capabilities are; how they should expect to be treated by others; and how they should respond to the world around them, all based primarily on the value ascribed to their phenotype. Exposure to favoritism or exclusion within a family dynamic has adverse effects on children, such as issues with self-efficacy, future orientation, and even romantic relationships (Wilder & Cain, 2011). Moreover, the larger tragedy is the alternate reality that it creates and often sustains for both those victimized by discrimination, as well as those privileged by preferential treatment, thereby setting the stage for difficulty through an unremitting cycle across the lifespan (See Figure 1.)

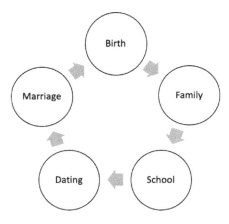

Figure 1. (Author Created)

Colorist Identity Development and the Lifespan

According to Bronfenbrenner's bioecological theory (Bronfenbrenner, 2006), one's development is shaped by the interactions between the individual and their environment, or proximal processes, "the complex reciprocal exchanges between an active, evolving human organism and its immediate external environment" (Ettekal & Mahoney, 2017). It is suggested that development is significantly impacted by these proximal processes, which consistently occur over an extended period of time, and within a specific place, at a specific time, and within a specific historical context (Bronfenbrenner, 2006; Ettekal & Mahoney, 2017). If we consider the social milieu created by the White supremist racism that predates and has been sustained beyond slavery, the attitudes, values, and beliefs endorsed thereby, and the colorism caste system it birthed, then the cycling and transgenerational transmission of this phenomenon of internalized racism makes theoretical sense.

The lens through which one sees, understands, and relates to the world is shaped by these developmental processes, thereby informing one's interactions with the world. It is plausible to expect that if a lighter-skinned Black child has been socialized within a family that subscribes to colorist ideals, that he or she may develop a sense of self-importance and grandiosity, perceiving themselves as smarter, more attractive, and/or more valuable than their darker-skinned peers. Conversely, darker-skinned children socialized within families that subscribe to colorist ideals, inundated with messages of inferiority based on phenotype, are more likely to internalize these negative messages: that they are not as smart, not as attractive, not as valuable, subsequently manifesting low self-esteem and a sense of low self-worth that are consistent with the messages of inferiority. One could argue that the internalization of colorist ideologies within one's family of origin, and systemic reinforcement by the larger social context, could position one to be an accomplice in endorsing the narrative by subconsciously engaging in behaviors that sustain the cycle. It is not unreasonable to expect that a darker-hued Black person whose experiences have fostered the internalization of the negative messages inherent in colorism would "learn" his or her place, value, and limitations, subsequently behaving in ways that would manifest the discriminatory experiences that he or she has come to expect. Conversely, it is just as reasonable to expect that a lighter-hued Black person whose experiences have fostered the internalization of colorism messages, assigning higher value to their person as a result of their more Eurocentric phenotype, would "learn" his or her place, value, and limitations, subsequently behaving in ways that would suggest expectations of privilege.

Gasman and Abiola (2015) argue that colorism was successful in suppressing and fragmenting Black communities by manufacturing social division and spurring intragroup friction, hostility, and animosity. The social division and animosity that colorism seeded in Black communities is perhaps one of the greatest tragedies resulting from these phenomena. Even those who may have escaped being indoctrinated with colorist ideals must brave the consequences of navigating a social environment that maintains the color-based caste system. The hostility among the lighter and darker hued groups created an "us" versus "them" dynamic that allows for experiences of privilege and/or discrimination, depending on group membership and context. The social dynamics are such that, despite phenotype, members of the "us" group would likely experience privilege, whereas members of the "them" group would likely experience discrimination. The literature speaks to the various lengths that many groups of lighter-skinned Blacks went in an effort to socially distance themselves from darker-skinned Blacks (Giddings, 2007; Maddox & Gray, 2002). It is not unreasonable to expect that when circumstances allow, some darker-skinned Blacks have socially discriminated against lighter-skinned Blacks in similar ways. Considering the social consequences of noncompliance with group norms, and the larger social environment's reinforcement of colorist ideologies, it is reasonable that these barriers to group reunification have been sustained.

The dynamics created by colorism influence the approach and outcomes of the developmental tasks that Erikson (Scheck, 2005) suggests unfolds over the course of the lifespan. Erikson (Scheck, 2005) argues that psychosocial development occurs in a series of eight stages across the lifespan, with each stage being marked by a developmental task and a psychological conflict. Successful resolution of each conflict yields a sense of competency, master, and, ultimately, a healthy personality. Conversely, failure to resolve the conflict or master the tasks manifests feelings of inadequacy. More specifically, the developmental implications of the internalized racism and intra-racial discrimination fostered by colorist ideologies are salient from the Preschool stage (Initiative vs. Guilt), through the Young Adulthood stage (Intimacy vs. Isolation), as one begins to engage the larger social context and seeks to develop a sense of self. The psychological implications of colorism play themselves out in one's interactions with the social environment, influencing ego identity and relationship patterns and outcomes.

The blueprint that guides our interactions with the world is established in early childhood. In Erikson's Preschool stage (3-6 years), where Initiative versus Guilt is the psychological conflict, a child begins to assert control and power over their environment. Colorism imposes restrictions on the exploration of roles and activities assigned to lighter- and darker-skinned groups in accordance with the stereotypical characteristics associated with each. At this stage, it is not unreasonable for children to be discouraged from exploring roles and relationships that violate the prescriptions of colorism. If a little lighter-hued Black girl is discouraged from choosing to wear pants as opposed to dresses, or discouraged from playing basketball as opposed to playing with dolls, because it violates the colorist stereotypes of virtue and femininity associated with lighter-skinned Black girls, then she may develop shame or begin to doubt her ability to choose.

During the School Age stage (6-11 years), where Industry versus Inferiority is the psychological conflict, children begin to compare themselves with their peers and either develop a sense of pride and accomplishment or feelings of inadequacy. Colorism imposes expectations based on phenotype, particularly around standards of beauty and intellectual capabilities. A darker-skinned Black boy academically outperforms his lighter-skinned classmates, and is only given negative feedback about his mistakes, while his lighter-skinned classmates are praised for mediocre performance. He is not selected to participate in the school spelling bee because the colorist stereotypes dictate that he cannot be as smart as, or smarter than, his lighter-skinned peers. His being denied recognition and the opportunity to experience a sense of pride, despite his academic accomplishments, may foster the development of feelings of inadequacy or inferiority. This could have implications for his future motivations.

During the Adolescence stage (12-18 years), where Identity versus Role Confusion is the psychological conflict, teens are seeking to develop a sense of self. Colorism restricts the development of a strong sense of self by limiting the role options available based on phenotype, with social consequences for noncompliance. The lighter-skinned, very attractive, popular captain of the football team chooses to take a darker-skinned girl to the prom, despite many lighter-skinned girls having expressed interest in being his date. Because colorist ideals dictate that European-like features are more attractive than African features, and his choice violates the dictates of the color caste system, he is ostracized by his teammates and friends, loses popularity with the lighter-skinned girls at school, and his parents are disappointed with him. At this developmental stage, when the sense of self can be significantly impacted by feedback from peers, the negative consequences of choosing to violate social norms can deter one from remaining true to oneself and foster confusion about one's identity.

During the Young Adulthood stage (19-40 years), wherein Intimacy versus Isolation is the psychological conflict, young adults move toward the establishment of intimate relationships. Colorism's imposition of phenotype-based standards of beauty, performance expectations, and prescriptions for social interactions can significantly impact the development of a strong sense of self in previous stages, and subsequently influence the ability to establish and maintain successful intimate relationships. For those that do not develop a strong sense of self, there may be a limited capacity to make decisions about mate selection that are not overly influenced by the dictates of colorism. Colorist ideals assign more value to European features, particularly in Black women, assigning them such characteristics as delicate, smart, kind, virtuous, gentle, and more attractive (Johnson, 2001) than darker-skinned Black women. Darker-skinned Black men tend to be associated with strength and physicality, characteristics aligning with traditional masculinity ideals. These stereotypes influence mate selection processes by limiting access to participation, based on the characteristics and value assigned to phenotype. Darker-skinned Black women may not be selected as mates because they may not be considered attractive, gentle, or kind enough, and lighter-skinned Black males may not be selected or accepted as mates because they may not be considered strong or masculine enough. The inability to establish and maintain healthy intimate relationships, particularly romantic relationships, leads to emotional isolation and loneliness. The broader implications of this dilemma are that they proliferate individualism and the dissolution of families in the Black communities.

Colorist Identity Development and Romantic Relationships

Colorist ideologies often impact the choices African Americans make while deciding whom to date and whom to marry (Corso, 2014; Okazawa-Rey et al., 1987; Parks & Woodson, 2002). Although constitutional characteristics (thoughtfulness, ambition, self-efficacy, and so on) are significant factors in relationships, it is believed that colorist ideologies have a larger influence on dating and sexual decision-making. This is significant because colorist preferences are potentially directly related to the phenotypic characteristics (skin color, hair texture/length, facial features/attractiveness, and physique) of potential offspring (Parks & Woodson, 2002). Interestingly, some Black families not only caution their children not to marry someone darker but insist the children "lighten the line" (Parks & Woodson, 2002; Russell et al., 1995), which further speaks to the cycle of colorist socialization across the lifespan. Furthermore, Black families can also be cruel in their treatment of in-laws who do not measure up on the colorist barometer; such that Blacks with lighter skin may generally be seen as more desirable marriage partners because light skin, having a historical and contemporary relationship with socioeconomic status, is a status symbol in the black community (Corso, 2014; Hughes & Hertel, 1990; Parks & Woodson, 2002).

In addition to colorist ideologies being observable in mate selection as it relates to family, colorism in romantic relationships is also heavily perpetuated by the media, where a particular aesthetic (usually lighter skin with more Eurocentric and/or racially ambiguous features) is often extolled and deemed beautiful. Though this message is not always explicit, the media has many inconspicuous ways to deliver this rhetoric. For example, lighter-skinned Black women often play more significant roles in commercials, TV shows, and movies than darker-skinned women and this preference of lighter-skinned women in the media is generally accepted (Steele, 2016). The music industry's frequent display of lighter-skinned video girls and more successful female artists further shows that the entertainment industry has been influenced by colorism as well. Given that the media is a strong socializing vehicle, second only to family, it is important to note that the media not only reifies the gendered processes that colorism implicates, but it further solidifies colorist preoccupations and consciousness among both men and women. This process seemingly reduces many Black women to feelings of inadequacy, self-loathing, and extreme alternatives to changing their phenotypic presentations, while dictating what should be considered attractive and/or suitable (Wilder & Cain, 2011). For example, Woodson (2002) noted that Black women are significantly more susceptible to colorist views because Black men more closely subscribe to Eurocentric views of beauty when choosing mates. Additionally, it was demonstrated that due to Black males' usage of colorist views when choosing mates, they are more likely to engage in risky sexual behaviors (as defined by lack of condom usage) with women who more closely align with their colorist ideals (Woodson, 2002). Many Black heterosexual males seemingly ascribe health and wellness to aesthetically pleasing phenotypic presentations as well, which has had serious implications for sexual health and other mental health disparities among African Americans.

Psychological Implications of the Internalization of Colorist Ideologies

The quality of life for many African Americans, and those to whom they are connected, has been significantly impacted, across generations (Norwood, 2014), by the implications of the color caste system on the intrapsychic functioning of those who have internalized colorist ideologies. In considering the messages seeded and cultivated by colorism during critical developmental stages, it is reasonable to expect the subsequent development of feelings of inadequacy, inferiority, and learned helplessness (Wilder & Cain, 2011). Poor self-concept, low self-esteem, and low self-efficacy, particularly for those discriminated against by the ideals, are also factors, while those privileged may be more likely to experience disillusionment, an inflated sense of self-importance, grandiosity, and expectations of preference, all of which lend themselves to increased susceptibility to psychological disorders. Clinicians working with this population are inclined to see the presentation of mood disorders, particularly depression, anxiety disorders and personality disorders, particularly narcissistic personality disorder, that are rooted in internalized colorism.

Prevention and Treatment

As with generations of old, skin color continues to shape the lives of Black women and the global Black community. Although colorism will continue to operate as long as the structure of White racism remains, what took generations to be put in place does not have to take generations to be dismantled (ABPsi, 2013; Hunter, 2007). Combating colorism can be a daunting task, as the process of colorist ideological socialization is quite complex. While Black families serve as points of origin to introduce colorism, fortunately they can also function as the mechanism for color reaffirmation and transformation. Interestingly, once the ideology of colorism is introduced, there are influential experiences that can either strengthen or shift its impact (Wilder & Cain, 2011). According to Wilder and Cain (2011), reaffirming moments occur when family members and/or events legitimize one's primary understanding of colorism, confirming the negative stereotypes and behaviors associated with normative colorism. Transformative moments occur when family members and/or events change one's primary understanding of colorism, in a positive or negative direction. In terms of intervention, maternal figures were also highlighted as having the most influence in shaping this second pattern of color socialization. Some of the ways in which maternal figures can assist in the second pattern of socialization is by identifying and exploring their biases in order to implement more affirmative ways of thinking about colorist ideologies and confronting biases, thereby challenging colorism (ABPsi, 2013; Harrell & Bond, 2006).

The Association of Black Psychologists (ABPsi) in their position paper on colorism, suggest several thoughtful tips to help promote resistance to and healing from colorism. First of all, they suggest reducing media consumption by reducing the amount of screen time and television shows that reinforce colorist ideals of beauty. Secondly, they implore individuals to remain cognizant of language to make sure the idea that complexion matters is dismantled. Additionally, they suggest abstaining from saying things like, "She is cute to be dark," or "She thinks she is cute because she is light-skinned," as these statements reinforce the idea that complexion matters, that being dark-skinned is unattractive, and that people generally base their self-concept on their complexion (ABPsi, 2013). Another tactic for fighting colorism is for parents to be on the alert for favoritism in the treatment of children in the family, social circle, classroom, or church. They posit that it is imperative that parents recognize that favoritism is harmful to children across the spectrum of children's colorist identities, and that they may struggle with issues of acceptance, identity, bullying, and so on. Moreover, ABPsi (2013) posits that it is also vital for parents to understand that the positive stereotypes associated with complexion are no more helpful than the negative ones, and that they should never put children or anyone else down about their colorist identities. Further, Black psychologists suggest that it is important to surround oneself with images of African people from different ethno-cultures and contexts— on walls at home, in the workplace, in the school, at the church, and with books, art, and magazines that present positive images of people of African heritage. Finally, they suggest that it is crucial to challenge friends and family members who make negative colorist remarks.

In addition to general interventions for adults attempting to combat colorism, there are specific developmentally appropriate interventions for children (ABPsi, 2013). First of all, parents can offset some of the colorist messaging by prominently providing images, toys, and other stimuli that depict Black men and women of all hues in spaces where the children dwell. When appropriate, parents should compliment the children in ways that suggest they are beautiful, while speaking to the uniqueness of their phenotypic presentation. It is also helpful to have the children recognize that beauty is multidimensional and multi-faceted, with their worth and value being assessed on the basis of what they do, while what they do is a reflection of their character and contribution to the community. Furthermore, having ongoing dialogues with their children about negative stereotypes through an explanation of the media's role in perpetuating them is a must! Ideally, these dialogues would occur while providing the children with the opportunity to identify negative images, with further discourse about how it makes them feel. Finally, parents should make it a point to teach children about their history and cultural heritage, as Afrocentric messages of empowerment have a positive effect on self-identity among Black children within the Black family dynamic (Wilder & Cain, 2011).

Implications for Research, Policy, and Practice

Relative to practice, clinicians must begin to query the existence of colorism/colorist identities within families. As the literature has established, colorism impacts self-esteem and sense of self; thus it would seem to be an integral part of therapy. It is important that clinicians recognize that colorist prejudice is a relative experience, such that family members can feel persecuted whether they have the ideal phenotypic presentation or not. Another important consideration would be relative to the expression of disorders such as depression and anxiety. Clinicians will need to recognize that depression and anxiety may manifest differently for African Americans (for example, in the pressure to perform) as they continue to appear high functioning in their daily lives; the clinical symptomatology may be masked by their overcompensation, which appears to be normalizing, notwithstanding their being a "wreck" on the inside. Moreover, clinicians could improve their provision of treatment by examining different types of interventions, because traditional modalities do not tend to lend themselves to the nuanced realities of African Americans. Given the sociocultural realities, African Americas could benefit from affirmation while being treated for the symptomatology. For example, experiential modalities such as the sister circles, emancipation circles, and group work create safe insular silos that allow African Americans to be affirmed, and to address, in supportive spaces, the beliefs/feelings of inferiority that fuel depression, hopelessness, and anxiety. Further, these interventions allow for the exploration of colorism through the use of culturally sensitive interventions that avow the realities of Blacks that are caused by colorist ideologies. Fortunately, emotional and psychological distress can be addressed by these adjunct interventions that facilitate healing.

With regard to research and policy, much of the literature on colorism has been anecdotal and theoretical; thus, empirical inquiry is much needed relative to measuring this construct. Also, the field could benefit from the creation of evaluation tools that measure colorist ideologies in both their internalization and externalization. In so doing, scholars will generate data that could be used to produce evidence-based therapeutic modalities and inform policy. In 2019, various states adopted the CROWN Act, which suggests these issues are being confronted by legislatures; therefore, more data are imperative.

Process Questions and Considerations

1. What might be the psychological implications of the internalization of colorist ideologies for Black males in particular?

2. Given what we know about colorism, why do you think African Americans still perpetuate colorist ideologies?

3. What intervention is necessary to break the "colorist cycle"?

4. Which is the best level upon which to intervene—with children, adults, couples, or families?

5. Once into adulthood, can colorist ideological beliefs that have been ingrained since birth be changed?

References

ABPsi. (2013). The Association of Black Psychologists on Dark Girls. Retrieved from:http://www.abpsi.org/pdf/Dark_Girls_ABPsi_ARTICLE_JUNE_23_2013_Dr%20Grills.pdf.

Bond, S., & Cash, T. F. (1992). Black beauty: Skin color and body images among African-American women. *Journal of Applied Social Psychology, 22,* 874-888.

Bronfenbrenner, U. (2005). *Making human beings human: Bioecological perspectives of human development.* Thousand Oaks, CA: SAGE.

Corso, J. (2014). Manifestations of colorism in interpersonal relationship preferences of black men. Thesis, Georgia State University, 2014. https://scholarworks.gsu.edu/aas_theses/24

Ettekal, A. V. & Mahoney, J. L. (2017). Ecological systems theory. In K. Pepler (Ed.), *The SAGE Encyclopedia of Out-of-School Learning* (pp. 239-241). Thousand Oaks, CA: SAGE.

Gasman, M., & Abiola, U. (2015). Colorism within the historically black colleges and U\universities. (HBCUs). *Theory into Practice, 55*(1), 39-45. DOI:10.1080/00405841.2016.1119018

Giddings, P. (2007). *In search of sisterhood: Delta sigma theta and the challenge of the black sorority movement.* New York, NY: William Morrow.

Harrell, S. P., & Bond, M. A. (2006). Listening to diversity stories: Principles for practice in community research and action. *American Journal of Community Psychology, 37*(3-4), 365-376.

Hill, M. E. (2002). Skin color and the perception of attractiveness among African Americans: Does gender make a difference? *Social Psychology Quarterly*, 65(1), 77-91.

Hughes, M., & Hertel, B. R. (1990). The significance of color remains: A study of life chances, mate selection, and ethnic consciousness among black Americans. *Social Forces*, 68(4), 1105-1120.

Hunter, M. (2007). The persistent problem of colorism: skin tone, status, and inequality. *Sociology Compass*, 1(1), 237-254.

Johnson, W. (2001). *Soul by soul: Life inside the antebellum slave market*. Cambridge, MA: Harvard University Press.

Maddox, K. B., & Gray, S. A. (2002). Cognitive representations of Black Americans: Reexploring the role of skin tone. *Personality & Social Psychology Bulletin*, 28, 250-259.

Norwood, K. J. (Ed.) (2014). *Color matters: Skin tone bias and myths of a post-racial America*. New York, NY: Routledge.

Okazawa-Rey, M., Robinson, T., & Ward, J. V. (1987). Black women and the politics of skin color and hair. *Women & Therapy*, 6(1-2), 89-102.

Parks, C. W., & Woodson, K.M. (2002). The impact of skin color and hair texture on mate selection: Implications for interventions with African American men and women. In E. Davis-Russell (Ed.), *The California School of Professional Psychology Handbook on Multicultural Education, Research, Intervention, and Training* (pp. 249-262). San Francisco, CA: Jossey-Bass Publishers, Inc.

Robinson, T. L., & Ward, J. V. (1995). African American adolescents and skin color. *Journal of Black Psychology*, 21(3), 256-274.

Russell, K., Wilson, M., & Hall, R. E. (1992). *The color complex: The politics of skin color among African Americans*. New York: Harcourt Brace Jovanovich.

Scheck, S. (2005). *Stages of psychosocial development according to Erik H. Erikson*. Norderstedt, Germany: GRIN Verlag GmbH.

Steele, C.K. (2016). Pride and prejudice: Pervasiveness of colorism and the animated series *Proud Family*. *Howard Journal of Communication*, 27(1), 53-67.

Wilder, J., & Cain, C. (2011). Teaching and learning color consciousness in black families: Exploring family processes and women's experiences with colorism. *Journal of Family Issues*, 32(5), 577-604.

Woodson, K. M. (2002). The impact of hair texture and skin color among African American men and women during mate selection on the expression of risky sexual behaviors. Unpublished Dissertation, California School of Professional Psychology, Los Angeles, CA.

Woodson, K. M. (2020). The colorist identity convergence model. Unpublished Manuscript.

CHAPTER 3.

Black Masculinity, Black Manhood, Black Maleness, and Colorism: An African-Centered Analysis of Responsive Manhood

Kevin Washington, Grambling State University
Steve Kniffley, Spalding University's School of Professional Psychology
Walter Stamp, Howard University

Overview

The dynamics of Black manhood can only be understood within the socio-cultural milieu from which it emerged. To apply an alien (White) analysis of Black manhood and Black masculinity is to further estrange Black men from themselves and further confound the comprehension of the true nature of Black manhood. It has been the work of oppressive Western or European scholars, such as Benjamin Rush, Herbert Spencer, Lewis Terman, G. Stanley Hall, and David Yerkes, to impose their understanding of Black people or persons of African descent utilizing a deficit model for their final analysis. This distorted perspective has had deleterious effects on Black men and their fate within society. John Henrik Clarke stated that,

> To control a people you must first control what they think about themselves and how they regard their history and culture. And when your conqueror makes you ashamed of your culture and your history, he needs no prison walls to hold you. (Clarke, 1996)

Carter G. Woodson (1933) states that when you control a man's thinking then you do not have to worry about his actions. The social control exerted upon Black men within society through imaging them as defective has been the bane of their existence in the United States and abroad. In American popular culture there has been an ongoing struggle for the image of the Black male.

Colorism, or the allocation of privilege and disadvantage according to the lightness or darkness of one's skin (Burke, 2008, p. 17), has played a significant role in how Black men are seen as well as how they see themselves in the world. The second iteration of the Mulatto Hypothesis, which was antithetical to the first postulation, advanced that lighter-skinned Blacks were more intelligent because of their genetic proximity to White people (Herskovitz, 1934). This is foundational to the notion of colorism. Wilder (2013) advances that colorism is "the unequal treatment and discrimination of individuals belonging to the same racial or ethnic minority group (for example, African Americans) based upon differences in physical features—most notably skin complexion (color) but also facial features and hair texture. This thinking seemed to have impacted the way Blacks were seen by Whites and the way Blacks saw themselves within the social setting. This view impacted the way Black men engaged in relationships as well as in socio-political activism.

Socio-Political Activism and Black Men

Eurocentric-minded researchers utilized racist metrics to determine the social importance of persons of Afrikan descent. Reuter (1917) advanced that mulattoes were superior to the full-blooded Negro because mulattoes were found to be more highly educated and to have been more politically engaged. He even stated there are "perhaps no full-blood Negroes in America today whose attainments are such as to admit them to the class of 'eminent men'," as Galton defined the term (Reuter, 1917). Much of the skewed data for Reuter's research was garnered prior to 1917 and failed to consider the socio-cultural implications that would have favored mulattoes in the U.S. For example, in Louisiana, political leadership for Afrikan Americans was in the hands of mulattoes. John Willis Menard, a mulatto, was the first African American to speak from the floor Congress and was elected to the U.S. House of Representatives in 1868, but Congress refused to seat him. P.B.S. Pinchback was the first African American elected lieutenant governor of Louisiana in 1872; his mother was a freed mulatto woman and his father was a white planter, thus making him a mulatto. These practices continued for many years and impacted the leadership of social movements and the activism of Black people in the U.S.

In 1916, Marcus Garvey sought the support of W.E.B. Du Bois at the national office of the NAACP in Harlem, located in New York City, where Garvey stated he was "unable to tell whether he was in a white office or that of the NAACP." This was due to the large number of light-skinned Blacks working in the NAACP office. Du Bois, a light-skinned Black man, retorted that Garvey was fat, black, and ugly. Unfortunately, colorism negatively impacted these two men and their organizations (Kendi, 2017). Garvey's Universal Negro Improvement Association attacked colorism among Black people, while the NAACP seemed to adhere to the tenants of the second Mulatto Hypothesis by employing lighter-skinned Blacks. The perception of credibility and colorism associated with Black men and activism extended beyond the 1930s and served to support the idea of the superiority of the mulatto.

Later in the 1950s and 1960s, a similar situation would take place between Adam Clayton Powell, Jr., a light-skinned Black man, preacher, and politician, and Dr. Martin Luther King, Jr., a brown-skinned Black man, preacher, and activist. Although they never seemed to spar publicly around skin color it was evident that colorism influenced their social impact and their level of activism. Although the two men were supportive of one another initially, their relationship eroded over time for a variety of reasons. By many, Powell was seen as more intellectually savvy and King was seen as a more hands-on activist. In actuality, it was more of the opposite. Powell, a graduate of Colgate University and Columbia University, was more of a man of streets, as he frequented nightclubs in Harlem, and King was a Morehouse College man and a graduate of Crozer Theological Seminary as well as Boston University. The academic pedigree did little to buffer King from the grip of colorism. King was seen as a nuisance that deserved to be assassinated, whereas Adam Clayton Powell, Jr. was very disruptive to the political system in Congress and died from acute prostatitis. It is imperative to note that white racist ideology, which permeates every aspect of African people's being and has influenced Black people's cognition around color, influenced how these men were treated in the public domain.

It is apparent that colorism was prevalent in the election of President Barack Obama in 2008 and 2012. He is the child of a White woman and a Kenyan (Afrikan) father. The Hip-Hop community took notice of this colorism factor. In an interview for BET in 2013, J. Cole, a self-identifying light-skinned Black man, stated the following about colorism and Black male leadership:

> That brainwashing that tells us that light skin is better, it is subconsciously in us, whether we know it or not. . . still pursuing light skin women. There are some women out there like "I don't even like light skin men" and that is fine. But Barack Obama would not be President if he were dark skin. You know what I mean? That is just truth. I might not be as successful as I am now if I was dark skin."

It is impressive that he acknowledges the potential role that colorism has played in his success and that of former U.S. President Barack Obama. In his exposition, colorism is a socio-cultural construct that impacts the way that Black wo/men relate to one another and themselves. J. Cole is insightful as to how the colorism construct may have impacted him and his trajectory within the world as a Black man. More importantly, he acknowledges how it influences activism and socio-political change.

Colorism Construct

According to Hunter (2013), white racism is a fundamental building block of colorism or skin stratification, intimating that white racist ideology and colorism are bedfellows. Hunter (2013) further states that maintenance of white supremacy in this country is predicated on the notion that dark skin represents savagery, irrationality, ugliness, and inferiority. This thinking seems to have found its way into the NAACP, as evidenced by the statements made by W.E.B. Du Bois about Garvey's appearance. The conflicting image of Black men has a long history within the U.S.

On one end of the spectrum, the image of the Black male has been constructed to portray a dumb, deviant, and dangerous individual whose only tools for relating to others are unchecked aggression and hypersexuality (Kniffley, Brown, & Davis, 2018). However, a more culturally responsive assessment of the Black man reveals an African-centered masculine ideology rooted in collectivism, spirituality, and relational/emotional attunement. This identity is grounded within the Afrikan worldview of the communal aspect of self.

There has been a schism with regards to how the Black man has been seen and treated within the context of global white superiority. There has been great admiration for the physical prowess and intellect of the Black man in America. Black men have been some of the most prominent fieldworkers and athletes, such as John Henry, Jessie Owens, Jack Johnson, and Marshall Taylor, as well as profound intellects, such as Benjamin Banneker, Elijah McCoy, Daniel Hale Williams, and George Washington Carver. (It is important to note that the majority of these men were recorded as being of a darker complexion.) Black men have been both revered and reviled by Whites within American society. This is a most schizophrenic (split-brain) way of seeing a person. Not only has the schizoid perspective been perplexing for Black men, but it has revealed a type of cognitive dissonance that seems to create a social angst for non-Blacks living in American society as it relates to how they see Black men as well as how Black men see themselves.

Drawing from W.E.B. Du Bois's concept of double consciousness, the American Black male is trapped in the middle of this continuum of Black Afrikan and Black American, with both sides pulling him to adhere to a certain ideology, set of expectations, and display of masculinity. This is an exploration into the dynamics of Black manhood from a strength-based and African-centered perspective. The authors place Black men at the center of the analysis of the essence of Black identity. This analysis will start from the beginning of Black manhood on the continent of Africa rather than within the Western context. Too often there is an attempt to understand Black manhood as Black men have sought to adjust to the ego-aggressive nature of White masculinity and European terrorism. Since Black (African) men existed before Europeans and the institution of African enslavement, then the analysis of Black manhood must extend beyond the European imposition of their fragile masculinity and racist notion of colorism.

Afrikan-Centered Manhood

It is understood within the Afrikan worldview that manhood exists within a social context and can thus be best understood within the socio-cultural context from which it evolves. Moreover, within this context, Afrikan manhood is relativistic, meaning that it must have something other than itself in existence for it to have true meaning and importance. For example, one needs woman in order for there to be man and this is true in reverse. Without the gendered other, one would simply exist as a thing. So it is with manhood. It is a construct that has real meaning within the communal context. Afrikan communalism, which is a moral doctrine that values individual rights, human dignity, and social responsibility, is a major galvanizing element of the Afrikan worldview. It suggests that everyone has an important role within their community. This communal identity can be seen in the following: One is a father because he has children; one is a healer because there are people that are sick; one is a niece because she has an aunt. John Mbiti (1990) states that the philosophical maxim for Africans is: I am because we are; we are, therefore I am. According to Nobles (2004) people engage in a sharing of experiences across groups called experiential communality. It is the idea of experiential communality that determines societies' beliefs and influences the kind of society that will be created by a people. It is within this experiential communality that we can see the full expression of manhood for Afrikan people because it is an experience of being and belonging in which a man has oneness with his family and society. It is imperative to note that colorism plays little to no role in determining the impact of experiential communality in that one's worth and value are more ascribed to them because they belong to family and community and because they exist in such.

According to many Afrikan scholars (Ani, 1994; Jackson-Lowman, 2004; Kambon, 1998; Myers 1993; Nobles, 2006; Schiele, 2000) the core tenets of an Afrikan-centered ideology are the following: (1) spirit is sacred; (2) all things are seen as spiritual; (3) all sets are connected; (4) there is a union between the sacred and the mundane; (5) life is religion and religion is life; (6) cause and effect are seen as spiritual phenomena; and (7) to attend to the mind is to attend to the spirit. These tenets lay the foundation for Afrikan-centered manhood. Describing the mutually beneficial relationship between the self and the community associated with an Afrikan-centered ideology and is captured within Afrikan American phrases such as "A big shot ain't nuttin' but a lot of little shots put together." This self-as-communal-being ideology can be seen on the continent of Afrika.

The concept of community identity has also been highlighted in Zulu phrases such as *"umuntu ngumuntu ngabantu,"* which means "a person is a person through other persons." The Shona of Zimbabwe use the phrase *munhu munhu nekuda kwevanhu* to describe a person having meaning only within the social context. The key concepts within the phrases are *Ubuntu* (Zulu) and *Unhu* (Shona), which both mean humanity within the communal context. It is not just humanity but the social construct of humanity that is being articulated with these constructs. Within the Afrikan worldview one has agency because his or her community grants such to him or her. This notion of communal identity is found throughout the Afrikan world, for it is a central aspect of being that has sustained a people for thousands of years (Washington, 2010).

Within the Afrikan context, not only is manhood a communal construct, but the demonstration of this humanity within the context of manhood is also a manifestation of a Supreme Being. To understand man within a society one must understand the ontological perspectives of a people. It is here that one gets to the essence of a man and manhood. Essence refers to the nature or constitution of something. It is the basic, invariable nature of a creation. Within an Afrikan-centered perspective the true nature of a person originates from god, the Creator. John Mbiti (1990) states that, for the Afrikan, life is religion and religion is life. The term *Zulu* means people of the heavens. If the nature of a man is within a god-referenced space then the ontology, epistemology, and axiology will speak to man's divine nature (Nobles, 2006; Washington, 2010). The intersectional experience of the Afrikan peoples can be seen in the references that various Afrikan societies have for God or the idea of the Divine and their personal divinity. Among the Akambe, the Divine is called Mumbi, meaning the Carver, or Mwatuangi meaning the Maker/Cleaver. Among the Akan, God is called Borebore, meaning the Excavator, Hewer, Carver, Inventor, Originator, or Architect, as well as Onyame, the Omnipotent One. The Zulu refer to God as uMvelingqangi, the First Creator, and as uNkulunkulu, meaning the Great Grandfather. Again, the word Zulu means people of the heavens, which suggest that man is of divine origin within the Zulu worldview. What is clearly highlighted in this short list of Afrikan names for god is the intent of Afrikan manhood or a man's existence if one is to live like god.

Within Afrikan-centered thinking, the understanding that god is the Prime Bringer into Being and is the constitution of all things has guided and continues to guide Afrikan people throughout the world (Ani, 1994, Nobles, 2015; Washington, 2010). These societies also acknowledged that the presence and power of god resided within each person and that a god-presence was needed in society. Afrikan-centered Black manhood, with an understanding of the Divine dwelling within, is believed to have contributed to the success of powerful Black men such as Pepi I, Aknaton, Thutmose, Zoser, Imhotep, Jomo Kenyatta, Kwame Nkrumah, Sekou Toure, Marcus Garvey, Franz Fanon, George Washington Carver, Percy Julian, Carter G. Woodson, Cheik Anta Diop, M.L. King Jr., George G. M. James, Nat Turner, Denmark Vessey, Boukman, Toussaint Louverture, Booker T. Washington, John Henrik Clarke, Haile Selassie, Malcolm X, Jacob Carruthers, and Asa Hillard. These Black men displayed experiential communality as they demonstrated Afrikan humanity intellectually and physically by striving to enhance the lived experiences of Black people. They are most noted for how they impacted their communities.

A communal aspect of Afrikan-centered manhood is that a conscious man exists as a reflection of the sum total of the thoughts, beliefs, and visions of all those around him (FuKiau, 2007). The conscious man, or one who is aware of his god-presence, understands that he belongs to the future and is the promise of those yet to be born. This communal understanding of the self results in the conscious man leading his life in a manner where he exercises personal and social accountability. He is first accountable to the Creator or the Divine, who allowed him to come into the event called life. He is aware that the Creator blessed the wombs of those who came before him; therefore he acknowledges that he represents the highest ideals and aspirations of the ancestors and the Divine (Nobles, 2006). The ancestors, who are intermediaries between humans and the Divine, are also the once visible but now unseen part of the community. These ancestors continue to lead and guide the conscious man through their constant contact with the Creator. Within an Afrikan-centered context, the conscious man is aware that he is the portal through which life continues. He knows that he carries the seeds of all that has ever existed and all that is come (FuKiau, 2001). This communal sense of Self gives strength and integrity to the conscious man. It is how he is able to remain conscious. He knows that he possesses the seed of antiquity and holds the future of the society within him. This responsibility is highly regarded within the tradition found in Afrikan manhood. Afrikan-centered manhood honors the past, builds in the present, and paves the way for the future.

According to Rowe and Webb-Msemaji (2004), in their *Kusudi Saba* or *The Seven Principles for (re)Defining African American Relationships*, they advance Consciousness, Character, Conduct, Collectivity, Competence, Caring, and Creed as central to understanding Afrikan-centered manhood. It is interesting that the first and last principles have a strong reference to god. The principles posit that Consciousness embodies the direct link from god, apart from which humans cannot be human; it requires demonstrating the images, interests, and intentions for reproducing the best in Afrikans (Rowe & Webb-Msemaji, 2004). The principles further assert that a Creed is a system of belief that stresses the constant and continuous relationship with god— the "Divine Spirit"; it is a knowing that god directs and inspires and is real. These elements of the Divine within man are paramount to understanding Afrikan-centered manhood (Rowe & Webb-Msemaji, 2004)

In addressing the issue of what constitutes Afrikan-centered manhood one has to contend with various attributes of god. This does not suggest that one must have a theological background to understand or to know about Afrikan manhood. Rather, it suggests that from an Afrikan-centered frame of reference all that "is" represents a reflection and extension of Divine Consciousness. John Mbiti stated that "for the Afrikan life is religion and religion is life" (1990). One need not buy into a particular religious orientation to understand Afrikan-centered manhood, because religion is a creation of man that allows man to understand and relate to god. Afrikan-centered thought holds that god is therefore greater than any religion because god is greater than any man. Rather, Afrikan-centered manhood is about knowing that one has the presence and power of the Creator within them and that once this power is brought back out into the universe one can then experience the abundance, peace and power that they seek on earth as one will experience in heaven (or life afterlife).

The Afrikan-centered worldview posits that god, and by extension, man possess the qualities of being Powerful, Peaceful, Productive, to be a Provider and a Protector. To be Patient, Knowledgeable, Righteous, Kind, Forgiving, Compassionate, and Truthful are all aspects of god. These are key elements of many traditional Afrikan religions among the Zulu, Yoruba, Akan, and others (Ani, 1994; Nobles, 2015; Washington, 2010). When the eminent scholar Dr. Asa Hilliard signed books, he would most often use Metu Neter (hieroglyphics) to express his thoughts and to write his name. A translation of his signing of some books is "I have given all life, all health, and truth like Ra (god)." This is a manifestation of Afrikan-centered manhood consciousness. Acknowledging the power and purpose of man and manhood within Afrikan-centered framework is about revealing ways for Black men to elevate the aforementioned qualities in their lives. The Eurocentric model of manhood is narrow and very destructive in many ways. It is not about living to be of communal benefit but rather it is about living as a self-serving pariah striving to impose his will on society at all costs. Afrikan-centered manhood serves the community and advances a new way of life for all. Colorism has no place within the Afrikan worldview. Out of the Eurocentric worldview one gets colorism. Wilder (2015) states that among the many consequences of America's racist legacy is colorism.

The following section provides a comparison of Eurocentric and Africentric masculinity ideologies. In addition, the following section discusses how the concept of social control (through mechanisms of legalized racism such as slavery and Jim Crow) recentered the construct of Eurocentric patriarchy as the expected masculine ideology for Black males. Lastly, the following section highlights the various psychological labels used to pathologize Black masculinity expression and performance (for example, Drapetomania).

The Decentralization of Africentricity and Black Masculinity Development

The identity conflict experienced by Black males is not a new phenomenon. From the moment the first Afrikan male stepped off a human trafficking vessel or slave ship onto American soil, his masculinity has been assaulted, subjugated, and assimilated into a Eurocentric masculine ideology (Kniffley, Brown, & Davis, 2018). According to Mukuka (2013), prior to his forced transition to America and beyond, the Afrikan male's masculinity expectation and performance encompassed the following components: (1) relational mutuality; (2) relational unity; (3) relational morality; (4) relational humility; and (5) relational generosity. Additionally, Yehduah (2015) noted that Afrikan masculinity promoted values such as community, spirituality, and respect for tradition. Furthermore, the author indicated that the sociality of selfhood and the concept of the continuity of being were also significant components of the Afrikan masculine ideology (Yehduah, 2015).

Due to the enslavement of Afrikan people, Afrikan men were not allowed to exert their manhood in a manner that supported themselves and/or their families, to protect themselves or their families, or to provide for themselves or their families. These are activities that one typically associated with men specifically and families in general. The Afrikan man's so-called "slave owners" provided for his physical needs including food, clothing, shelter, basic medical care, and employment opportunities. During the enslavement period Afrikan men made no real decisions as to what position they wanted to hold on the plantation; rather an Afrikan man was appointed to a position of labor and he was usually expected to serve in that position until death. There was no reason to consider a retirement program because the conditions under which he worked usually killed him in his youth (Byrd & Clayton, 2000).

Male-female relationships were usually determined for the enslaved Afrikans by their enslavers. Such relationships were most often established for the purpose of breeding more servants to increase the labor force and thus increase the earnings of the enslaver (Staples, 1998). Often when enslaved Afrikans were able to exercise some decisions about their relationships, there was no prolonged courtship. Rather, there were assigned or approved unions for marriages. These marriages were designed to benefit the enslaver rather than the enslaved (Guttmann, 1977).

This continued mistreatment resulted in Afrikan men developing a code of conduct for their survival. There had to be a denial of having any deep emotional feelings for any person, thus resulting in a mode of social detachment emanating from feelings of anger, hurt, fear, and unspeakable pain (Billingsley, 1993). Many times, if he had a wife, the Black man had to share her (involuntarily) with the oppressor, who would rape her at will. This resulted in children being conceived that were not of the Afrikan man's loins (Jacobs, 2001). These children would be mulatto and would often incur differential treatment from both Blacks and Whites. This contributed to several deep psychological and spiritual ruptures developing within their psyche. Europeans would value lighter-complexioned Black children and despise darker children that possessed "African" features (Wilder, 2015). Not only would the lighter-complexioned Black men be favored by their oppressors, they would often be despised by their oppressors' white children. This had a debilitating effect on the development of Black manhood. Afrikan men were unable to extend, defend, or protect their families and manifest the fullest aspect of Afrikan manhood on many levels. There are residual aspects of this trauma still haunting Black men (Kniffley, Brown, & Davis, 2018). A research study using mice by Dias and Ressler (2014) reveal that there are aspects of trauma that are passed on genetically, biologically, psychologically, and relationally. Black males are forced to contemplate deep feelings of inadequacy and inferiority that could lead to depression. Additionally, these internalized feelings are behaviorally expressed and can contribute to feelings of hopelessness and helplessness. The experience of negative internalized feelings has an external expression that can be detrimental to the longevity of Black men.

Other phenomena that occurred was that a Black man could marry the woman that he loved but he would also have sexual relations with other women for the purpose of breeding specific types of plantation workers. Many of the men reluctantly engaged with these multiple sex partners, known as breeding exercises; however, it was the price that they had to pay to be with the women that they truly loved. These breeding exercises most often occurred between the darker-complexioned Black because the lighter-complexioned Blacks were kept closer to their white parents and tormentors. In general, personal relationships were strained because of the Black man's inability to protect that which is sacred to people of Afrikan ancestry, Black family life.

The concepts put forth by the literature suggest that the enslaved Afrikan male brought with him a worldview and an expectation that the appropriate expression of masculinity would be communal in nature (via an emphasis on spirituality and relationship) and would value personhood, tradition, emotional attunement, and collective success (Nobles, 2015). However, due to the institution of enslavement, the enslaved Afrikan male was inundated with a Eurocentric conceptualization of masculinity. The Eurocentric masculinity ideology holds values of aggression, independence, sexual prowess, conquest/domination, emotional restriction, and physical/ mental toughness very highly. Under a Eurocentric masculinity ideology, a male must be able to establish his domination over others through physical means, achieve success through individual efforts, and endorse a benevolent sense of patriarchy. Many of these Eurocentric values and expectations for masculinity were in direct conflict with the Afrikan-centered masculinity ideology. However, many enslaved Afrikan males would attempt to transpose the Eurocentric masculine value system onto their own concept of masculinity as a mechanism of survival.

Emergence of Eurocentric patriarchy as the standard for masculinity ideology and performance.

To endure the atrocities of chattel slavery, with its intentional erasure of ethnic identity, culture, and language, the Afrikan male had to undergo an intense revision of his masculine ideology (Du Bois, 1903; Patterson, 1999). Emotional expression was replaced with emotional repression. Collectivism was replaced with individualistic competition with an emphasis on personal wealth acquisition, and egalitarianism with a patriarchal hierarchy. As noted by Hammond and Mattis (2005) the process of manhood reconstruction for the Afrikan male required a process of recovery, defense, and redemption. However, the accomplishment of the Afrikan male slave's manhood reconstruction in the image of Eurocentric masculinity involved a fundamental breakdown at the social and psychic levels.

Mukuka (2013) indicated that significant cultural traumas such as slavery chronically disrupted the social and psychological stability of enslaved Afrikan males. Specifically, enslaved Afrikan males were forced to reconcile their identity, psychological location, and cultural fit within a social paradigm that sought to subjugate them through dehumanizing tactics (Akbar, 1996; Wilson, 1993). According to Mukuka (2013) the cost of identity reconciliation contributed to three significant fractures of the Afrikan identity within the American context. The first fracture involved the disintegration of the Afrikan value system that emphasized nonmaterialism and personhood, communalism, and cultural traditions. Legally seen as property and a business commodity, enslaved Afrikan males were immersed in the tenets of capitalism, as their value was determined less by the qualities of their personhood (for example, generosity, relationships) and more by their ability to add to the means of production for their oppressor.

According to Mukuka (2013), the second psychic fracture for enslaved Afrikan males consisted of a hatred for their blackness in its cultural and physical forms (for example, skin color and Afrikan-centered cultural traditions). Through the creation of a differing valuation of enslaved Afrikans based on their proximity to the Eurocentric standard, enslaved Afrikan males were forced to engage in an ongoing competition for sparse social capital. The most successful enslaved Afrikan males were the ones who could demonstrate the highest level of refutation or denial of Afrikan Centered values, ideology, or traditions (for example, language, religion, cultural norms). This forced "splitting of self" from one's identity and culture as a mechanism of survival contributed to significant psychological distress and ultimately an increased fracturing of the Afrikan psyche.

Lastly, the third fracture consisted of the enslaved Afrikan male developing a negative perception of Afrikan-centered cultural ideals as unsustainable both socially and economically (Mukuka, 2013). Faced with chronic false allegations of the superiority of Eurocentric values and culture across a number of mediums (for example, popular culture, religion, literature), the enslaved Afrikan male was overwhelmed with seemingly insurmountable evidence of his inferiority. Most notably this evidence included his subjugation in chattel slavery, the intentional erasure of his history, and the argument put forth by popular culture that his enslavement was divinely inspired. The Afrikan male slave internalized these experiences and concluded that his culture and his people possessed little to no value outside of the context of generational servitude.

The intentional subjugation of a race of people required a systematic denial of their personhood. This denial of personhood involved a methodic erasure of anything that tied the enslaved Afrikan to the continent and his people including his name, language, history, and customs. Mukuka (2013) indicated that for the enslaved Afrikan male to cope with this process, his psyche underwent a significant fracturing that consisted of three main components: (1) disintegration of the Afrikan value system; (2) the development of a hatred for their Blackness in its cultural and physical forms; and (3) developing a negative perception of Afrikan-centered cultural ideals as unsustainable both socially and economically. While this psychic fracturing was experienced as an intrapsychic phenomenon with interpersonal consequences, a negative social narrative was being perpetuated in American popular culture about the Afrikan male slave. This social narrative would further reinforce the enslaved Afrikan male's perception of himself as well as the perception his community and the greater society had concerning his masculinity, expression, and performance.

Enslavement, social control, and the recentering of Eurocentric patriarchy

Several researchers have explored the institutionalization of negative stereotypes related to the Black male experience. What originally was formulated as a required justification for the enslavement of a race people evolved into a perceived factual validation for ongoing discrimination and second-class citizenship for Black individuals across more than 400 years and counting. According to various researchers and scholars, the intentional reimaging of the Afrikan male from a responsive and collectivist individual attuned to the needs of his culture and committed to the uplift of his people to a dumb, deviant, dangerous, reactionary archetype took place over the course of four unique periods.

The first period, the Period of Initial Depiction, started with the institutionalization of slavery in America and the stereotypes used to justify the mass enslavement of Afrikan people (for example, subhuman, childlike, unintelligent) (Kniffley & Brown, 2015). However, with the utilization of these stereotypes came the experience of fear by the dominant culture and the need to control the slaves mentally as well as physically. The most significant form of social control came through the media that was used to denigrate Black males via various types of print media such as flyers, leaflets, pamphlets, and newspapers, establishing a societal perception that they were more violent, more aggressive, lazy, dumb, and in all respects inferior to Whites (Baynes, 2007; Bogle, 2001; Gross & Hardy, 1926).

The media also portrayed Black males as sexual predators, and many believed they were a threat to the pureness of White women in America (Baynes, 2007; Bogle, 2001; Kniffley & Brown, 2015). The Period of Initial Depiction lasted from the beginning of slavery up until the Civil War, which played a large role in shaping society's perception of Black males.

During the second period, known as the Period of Reinforcement, Whites would continue to slander Black males by using the film industry and national radio broadcasting to sustain the perception that the Black male was dumb, lazy, a sexual predator, and dangerous (Baynes, 2007; Bogle, 2001; Kniffley & Brown, 2015). The start of these large media platforms exacerbated the negative perception of the Black male in America through their ability to reach a broader audience (Kniffley & Brown, 2015).

One of the practices used to sustain the negative perception was the growing popularity of minstrel shows and the use of "Blackface." This was one of the most prominent forms of colorism. The damage done by these shows with respect to dark-skinned men being seen as buffoons would last for generations (Hunter, 2013). Minstrel shows were stage acts, plays, and parodies that were used to entertain Whites through the imitation of Blacks. White actors/actresses imitated Blacks by dressing up to exaggerate stereotypical features of Blacks, such as their hair, lips, body types, skin tone, and so on. White men used Blackface to present and portray the Black male in a negative way (Parker & Moore III, 2014). This was known as America's first national form of entertainment. Black men were made a mockery of by White men pretending to be Black men. In 1915, the first major motion picture in the U.S. was *The Birth of a Nation* by D. W. Griffith, which was based on a book called *The Clansman* by T. F. Dixon. The basic narrative of the film and the book was the irresponsibility of Blacks and the hypersexuality and violent nature of Black men. The start of the film industry allowed these negative and stereotypical practices to spread rapidly in America and globally. From 1888 to the Civil Rights Movement, the negative perception of the Black male became more established and was constantly reinforced during this time period through different media outlets (Kniffley & Brown, 2015). The second period overlaps with the third period, which is the Period of Confusion.

The Period of Confusion is an external representation of the internal conflict facing

Black males (Kniffley & Brown, 2015). During this time, the influence of television, especially for young Black males, offered the opportunity for a differing perspective of Black masculinity. The different portrayals of Black males created significant conflict and confusion for Blacks males about the performance, perception, and expectation of their racialized masculinity. For example, although this period reflected the rise of powerful Black male leaders such as Martin Luther King, Jr. and Malcolm X that provided shining examples of positive Black manhood, Black males in their daily lives were still relegated to second-class citizenship. Unable to live up to the expectation of the "New Black male," highlighted in the form of the civil rights leaders, many Black men adopted a posture of helplessness and despair as the goals of the Civil Rights Movement were not completely realized. With the emergence of Blaxploitation films, the media contributed to these feelings by perpetuating rigid roles for Black manhood.

The final period that highlights the intersectionality between the evolution of racism and the media is the Period of Quantification, which started around the end of the Civil Rights Movement up to the present day. This last period represents the culmination of influence of the media on the perception of Black manhood. The variations of racialized media up to this point in history have significantly shaped society's perception of the Black male. This perception has contributed to significant consequences for Black men in regard to their physical safety, relationships, economic mobility, and mental health.

The current section has explored the significant distinctions between an Afrikan-centered and a Eurocentric masculinity. For example, while a Eurocentric masculinity ideology values aggression, independence, conquest/domination, and emotional restriction, the Afrocentric masculinity ideology values personhood, tradition, emotional attunement, and collective success. However, due to the institution of chattel slavery, Black males were forced in large part to abandon their Afrikan-centered values and assimilate into a Eurocentric masculine framework for the sake of survival. Additionally, the ongoing control of the Black male social narrative was consolidated over four unique periods across American social history (for example, the Period of Confusion). This phenomenon came at a significant cost for Black males psychologically in addition to their having to relinquish control of their social narrative to their captors.

The following section will discuss the labels used to capture and negatively define the Black male social narrative. Additionally, the following section will provide a discussion of how the shaping of the Black male social narrative with negative stereotypical undertones contributed to the emergence of a reactionary Black masculinity and its subsequent impact on psychological health. The section will conclude with an exploration of an alternative to reactionary Black masculinity in the form of fostering a responsive Black masculinity ideology.

Pathologizing Black masculinity

I was looking for myself and asking everyone except myself questions which I, and only I, could answer. It took me a long time and much painful boomeranging of my expectations to achieve a realization everyone else appears to have been born with: That I am nobody but myself. (Ellison, 1952)

Since the beginning of Afrikan enslavement in America, Black males have been forced to define themselves through the eyes of Eurocentric patriarchy. This often called for the envisioning of the Black self as a darker version of a White man. With some resistance, Black males were able to maintain a framework of Afrikan-centered values at the core of their Black masculinity ideology. Over time this resistance has weakened and given way to a Black masculinity ideology that mimics Eurocentric masculine standards and is malleable to the whims of popular culture and the media. This phenomenon has contributed to the experience of a chronic "searching for self" among Black males.

Instead of looking within for the answers concerning their masculine identity and following the blueprint for manhood established through relational means, Black males are discovering their manhood through the perceptions of their oppressors. Throughout history, an oppressive White patriarchy has made intentional efforts to regulate and restrict the imaging of the Black male. The Black male has been portrayed and expected to be the proverbial Coon—always happy, impulsive, and apologetic for taking up space in a White world. He has also been expected to be a Buck—hyper-aggressive, hypersexual, and athletically built, whose only purpose is to demonstrate his physical prowess on the field, on the court, or in the bedroom. During slavery, Black males who were proficient in fulfilling these roles were rewarded with their lives. In today's times, Black males are rewarded with money and fame for their strict adherence to limited masculine expressions and performance. The greater reward seems to go to lighter-skinned Black men. Notable income, educational, criminal sentencing, and perceptions of intelligence disparities exist among African American males differing in complexion (Burch, 2015).

However, many Black males have attempted to resist the pull to become complicit in stereotype perpetuation. The consequence for this resistance has been the denigration and subsequent pathologizing of their Black masculinity. For example, during institutionalized slavery in America, whenever enslaved Afrikans fought for their freedom by resisting or attempting to escape it was largely believed that they suffered from a mental illness. This belief morphed into a formal medical diagnosis via American psychiatrist Samuel Cartwright who referred to this "irrational" behavior as Drapetomania (Bynum, 1999; Guthrie, 2004, Metzl, 2009). Samuel Cartwright indicated that enslaved Afrikans experienced Drapetomania when they attempted to be more than their "authentic" self (for example, submissive and docile). An additionally diagnosis that emerged during the period of institutionalized slavery was "dyaesthesia aethiopica." This labeled was used to justify the belief that slaves were "lazy" and would only work hard if stimulated by an external force (for example, the paternalistic hand of the plantation owner).

Lastly, during the Civil Rights Movement, as Black individuals fought for equal rights and access, their efforts were oftentimes labeled as excessively angry and irrational. The psychiatric literature coined the term "Protest Psychosis" as a way to pathologize the very real struggle Black individuals were experiencing during this time period and the subsequent emotionality and demand for equality (Metzl, 2009). From slavery to the Civil Rights Movement to the present day, the racialized experience of Black individuals has been denied, dismissed, and devalued. The use of pathologizing labels provided a way to justify this phenomenon under the guise of "empirical evidence" and benevolence on the part of the majority culture. However, these labels crystalized stereotypical caricatures of the Black experience by quantifying Black individuals as unnecessarily angry and overly sensitive to imagined social ills, whose only value was perpetual servitude. This has been especially true regarding the lived experience of Black males. As a consequence of the ongoing exposure to racism/discrimination, constant relabeling of the Black lived experience by popular culture, and the institutionalization of negative Black male imagery, two forms of Black masculinity performance have emerged: reactionary masculinity and responsive masculinity.

Reactionary Black masculinity

In an effort to cope with an overwhelming exposure to racism (colorism) and discrimination at the societal, institutional, and individual level, many Black males have engaged in a more reactionary masculinity performance. Reactionary masculinity represents a social posture and a set of maladaptive behavioral skills that Black males engage in response to social situations that perpetuate negative stereotypes associated with Black masculinity. A reactionary masculinity posture values impulsivity, aggressiveness, emotional restriction, domination, and individualism. When a Black male engaged in this posture is faced with a challenge to his racialized masculinity (via the experience of racism), his actions stem from a space of striving to regain control over the situation.

The Black male attempts to control the narrative surrounding the perception of his masculinity through the means he has observed by interacting with his oppressors: denial of the impact of the situation, domination over other, and dismissiveness of others. However, by applying these lessons, the Black male is unknowingly perpetuating an even greater exaggeration of the stereotypes associated with his masculinity (for example, hyper-aggressiveness) by whites. By engaging in a Reactionary masculinity posture, the Black male becomes unwittingly complicit in his own oppression. The outcome of using a reactionary masculinity posture is a negative manifestation of Black masculinity that is inconsistent with Africentric values. It is consistent with what Akbar (1984) calls the anti-self and alien self-disorder. It is predicated on cultural misorientation (Kambon, 1998) and its behavioral correlates are learned indifference and assumed significance (Washington, 1996). The latter advances that, through a series of societal defeats and perpetual opposition, Afrikan people become indifferent to all things relevant to Afrikan or Black people while concomitantly taking on all ideas and beliefs of Europeans/Westerners as most salient to their survival. Such an identity becomes predatory upon its own people while assuming the alien ideology of European manhood. The major conflict is that because of being identified as the cultural other (Ani, 1994), the Black man will then not experience complete inclusion within White normative social structures for demonstrating the same behaviors that White men do in their expression of manhood. Black men being held on the periphery of what has become known as the dominant society creates an enduring frustration that manifests in a variety of potentially maladaptive behaviors relative to the Black community and ultimately to their health and well-being. Additionally, this posture promotes an emergence of individualism and isolation that is in direct conflict with the Black males' Afrikan-centered roots but consistent with many aspects of the European worldview. The identity conflict that the Black male experiences can potentially damage his physical and psychological health.

Responsive masculinity

Despite the constant pull to endorse and perpetuate stereotypic expressions of Black masculinity, several Black males have sought a more responsive approach to address and combat the experience of chronic racism. Responsive masculinity represents a social posture and a set of behavioral skills. This posture and skillset are used to address social contexts where Black males are pressured to engage in stereotypical norms that are consistent with a negative perception of Black masculinity. A responsive masculinity posture values thoughtfulness, assertiveness, emotional attunement, negotiation, and collectivism. When a Black male engaged in this posture is faced with a challenge to his racialized masculinity (via the experience of racism), his actions stem from a space of collective empowerment.

The Black male seeks to address the social contexts (for example, media, popular culture) that attempt to define his masculine narrative through the cultural lessons that have been passed down via his African roots. By applying these lessons, the Black male recenters the expectations concerning his Black masculinity. By engaging in a responsive masculinity posture, the Black male is able to assert his authentic racialized masculinity. The outcome of using a responsive masculinity skillset is a positive manifestation of Black masculinity. This Black masculinity expression is consistent with Afrocentric values, promotes communal uplift, and protects the Black male's physical and psychological health. This masculinity is grounded in the thought that one's manhood belongs to the community. It is a knowing that one can only be a man to the extent that there is woman and there are children. Responsive manhood takes a posture that promotes social justice and one that advances the common good of those within his community. This responsive manhood is found in the writings of Carter G. Woodson, Marcus Garvey, W.E.B. Du Bois, and others. It is found in the speeches of Martin Luther King, Jr., Malcolm X, and Huey P. Newton. It is found in the actions of the Deacons for Defense and Justice of Jonesboro, Louisiana, the Black Panther Party, Colin Kaepernick, and Malcolm Jenkins. Responsive manhood is unapologetic when it comes to confronting the ill treatment of the members of its community. It responds to the immediate issues of its people while projecting a better reality for future generations.

Responsive Masculinity and Colorism

Colorism is a social phenomenon created by popular culture to foster intragroup conflict through the elevation of a part of Black culture based on a perceived adherence to European standards and norms. Colorism is a reflection of the second psychic fracture noted by Mukuka (2013) as a representation of Black self-hatred via a false sense of colorist superiority or hyper-identification with negative Black stereotypes (for example, hyper aggressive, hypersexual). It must be acknowledged that colorism affects both Black men and Black women (Veras, 2016; Wilder, 2015). The psychic grip of colorism is noticed by members of the Hip Hop community. In 2015, Hip-Hop artists Kendrick Lamar and Rapsody released a track called *Complexion* on which they unapologetically confront colorism among Afrikan Americans. They advance the following:

> 12 years of age, thinkin' my shade too dark
>
> I love myself, I no longer need Cupid
>
> Enforcin' my dark side like a young George Lucas
>
> Light don't mean you smart, bein' dark don't mean you stupid
>
> And frame of mind for them bustas, ain't talkin. . .
>
> Let the Willie Lynch theory reverse a thousand times… (Lamar & Raleigh, 2015)

The Willie Lynch theory alludes to a plethora of divisive measures, of which colorism was one, that could be applied in an enslaver's effort to control his slaves (enslaved Afrikans). The controlling methods that would maximize profits for the enslaver (terrorist) are mentioned in a book entitled *The Willie Lynch Letter and the Making of a Slave* (2008). Lamar challenges Blacks to address colorism in a way that brings about healing for Black people because to be divided along a color caste system benefits the oppressive Whites more than it does Blacks. This position is consistent with the research literature. According to the literature, colorism has significant economic, social, legal, and educational implications for Black individuals across the skin-tone spectrum.

For example, a study by Kilien-Fisher and Crutchfield (2017) examined 68 shootings of unarmed Black males by police to determine whether skin tone may have influenced the shooting. The authors found that a higher percentage of the Black males shot and killed by police were darker-skinned, suggesting a significant vulnerability for darker-skinned Black males due to skin tone bias (that is, colorism). Additionally, as noted by Gasman and Abiola (2016), the experience of colorism has reduced Black skin tones to a litmus test for the "Blackest" individual and their perceived adherence to stereotypical Black traits.

Within the context of colorism, Black males are attempting to navigate and define their understanding of Blackness. To cope with the negative impact of colorism, the Black male who has endorsed a reactionary masculinity posture will internalize the narrative associated with his skin tone, attempt to perform the script to the best of his abilities, and contribute to the skin-tone trauma that is advanced by Landor and Smith (2019). Additionally, Black males will police the performances of other Black males around them to ensure that they "fall in line" with the colorist narratives associated with their complexion.

However, the Black male who has endorsed a responsive masculinity posture will seek to navigate through the challenges associated with colorism by consciousness raising, identity reconciliation, and community empowerment. For example, rather than blindly accepting the colorism narrative, the responsive Black male will actively interrogate the script he is expected to perform to determine its alignment with his definition of Blackness. Additionally, the responsive Black male will seek to empower his community by offering insight and engaging in collaborative skill building opportunities around the history of colorism, the ways in which colorism is reinforced both within and outside of the Black community, and the tools to navigate the potentially deleterious impact of colorism. Responsive Manhood is Woke activism that strives to break the mental bondage of Eurocentric ideology.

Research on Black families by Landor et al. (2013) found that darker-skin sons received higher quality parenting and more racial socialization promoting mistrust compared to their counterparts with lighter skin. Lighter-skin daughters received higher quality parenting compared to those with darker skin. In addition, the gender of a child moderated the association between primary caregiver skin tone and racial socialization promoting mistrust. These results suggest that colorism remains a salient issue within Afrikan American families and influence how Black men navigate the world. Such a mental hold must be addressed by responsive Afrikan manhood.

Dynamics of Black Masculinity: Healing the Warrior

True family health is contingent upon the adult family members having a strong sense of self in order to live life with purpose, and this purposeful lifestyle becomes the natural expressions of their children. They are involved in various aspects of the community. They make the necessary sacrifices for their children and their families so that all may grow up with healthy sense of self-worth. As children they learn very early that they are a part of a community that loves and supports them and that they will be held accountable for all of their actions. This accountability makes it less likely for them to make a series of bad decisions because they will think about how such a choice will affect their family. They will not have to ask others whether the behavior of choice is consistent with their purpose and direction for their lives or whether it aligns with their parents' desires, because they would have been socialized to see every aspect of their behavior as belonging to the community. This is not to imply that parental involvement will absolutely result in children who make solid decisions nor does having uninvolved parents result in delinquency. This is to suggest that the probability of having children and community members who have high self-esteem is increased as the involvement of the parents and elders is increased. The men that are connected to a Higher Spirit are more likely to provide this kind of guidance in the lives of their families because they understand how significant they are to their families and therefore reproduce the same.

Men play a vital role in the emotional, psychological, and intellectual development of children. A study by Williams (1997) using a nationally representative sample of 1,600 10- to 13-year-old youth found that children who shared important ideas with their fathers and who perceived the amount of time they spent with their fathers as excellent had fewer behavior problems and lived in more cognitively stimulating homes than their peers who did not share important ideas or view the amount of time they spent with their fathers as excellent. Father-child interactions have been shown to promote a child's well-being, perceptual abilities, and competency for relatedness with others, even at a young age (Krampe and Fairweather, 1993). This means that there must be a process to cultivate the very best that Black men have to offer the world. The stifling effects of the Eurocentric worldview must be trampled out because it has operated in a manner that is antithetical to the fullest expression of Black manhood.

The father plays an important role in the development of boys. In a study by Zimmerman (1995) using 254 African American male adolescents, boys living with both biological parents were most likely to cite their father as role models (96%), compared to only 44% of those not living with their fathers, and they were more likely to stay in school. This is true for African American males also. A survey conducted by Furstenberg (1988) with African American men revealed that men who had experienced a positive relationship with a father who cared and sacrificed for them are more likely to be responsible fathers themselves. Black men must be shown their vital role in Black family life. This is done by having men experience greater life satisfaction through self-mastery. Life satisfaction, educational attainment, occupational status, and improved mental health and psychological well-being are implicated in the idea of self-mastery (Mirowsky & Ross, 2003; Watkins et al., 2011).

Using a nationally representative sample of data on over 2,600 adults born in the inner city, Hardy et al. (1997) found that children who lived with both parents were more likely to have finished high school, be economically self-sufficient, and to have a healthier lifestyle than their peers who grew up in a broken home. Encouraging men to be involved in their children's lives is the greatest expression of Afrikan-centered manhood. Many times, institutional racism and legal systems operating from the worldview of Eurocentrism challenge healthy involvement of both mothers and fathers in the lives of Black children. Programs that promote mother-father involvement in the lives of children tend to advance an Afrikan worldview of balance found in male-female family engagement. Healthy messages about colorism and racial identity will assist Black males in challenging the negative messages associated with colorism (Azibo, 2011; Kambon, 1998, Landor et al., 2013; Landor & Smith, 2019)

If the absence of strong men in the lives of children adversely affects their emotional stability, their intellectual functioning, and their social interaction, then this suggests that men are vital in the lives of children specifically and in the community in general. So much of the contemporary literature seeks to suggest that men are not essential in the lives of their families and communities. There are sperm banks where a woman can conceive a child via artificial insemination. This suggests that the only purpose of the father is to donate sperm for ovum fertilization and not for family socialization. Artificial insemination has become a growing trend within the Afrikan (Black) community. This is another form of Black male castration. Black men must be included in their communities. Programs that consider the social construction of manhood empower young men to care for their health, and provide access to healthcare services in order to improve the health of Afrikan American men (Rich, 2000; Watkins, et al., 2010). Manhood restoration programs promise to have more of an impact on the community than simple sperm donations for the production of children.

Whereas it can be understood that some women can become frustrated with the number of game-playing boys masquerading as men that they encounter, it is imperative for women to look beyond their selfish desires to have children and seek to cultivate a solid relationship with a brother who is ready to step it up and be a man. Not all Black men are infantile males or victims of reactionary masculinity looking to take advantage of any victim (woman) that they can find, and not all woman are opportunists wanting to siphon the strength from men. Many are living beyond the confines of the European hegemonic discourse of Afrikan/Black inferiority. It must be acknowledged that this is a process and will not happen instantaneously. Colorism and European racism run deep within the psyche of Black men and society (Wilkins et al., 2012). Time for healing is needed. The greatest form of healing occurs when Black men start exhibiting responsive manhood.

Implications for Research, Policy, and Practice

The power of manhood is found in how it impacts and supports the community. There are examples of revolutionary responsive manhood throughout the Black/Afrikan world. Often these men are seen as mentally unstable because they are confronting the oppressive European/Western notion of manhood. Responsive manhood operates out of the Afrikan-centered paradigm of what is good for Afrikan people. It demonstrates the fullness of *Ubuntu* (collective humanity) and advances the liberation of Black people. Individuals seeking comfortable captivity will see Afrikan/Black manhood as making trouble. Responsive Afrikan/Black people see clearly that trouble has already been made and that it will take the efforts of men in concert with women to rectify matters. Nathaniel (Nat) Turner, Gabriel Prosser, and Dutty Boukman all embodied this emboldened notion of Afrikan/Black manhood as they struck out against their oppression and African dehumanization and colorism. Responsive masculinity honors womanhood rather than exploits it. It is the feminine that gives rise to the masculine, for all children are born of a woman. The connection gives agency to the advancement of all that is good and correct for Black people.

African responsive masculinity inspires the rebellions of Ferguson, Missouri, Sanford, Florida, Washington, DC, New York City, Chicago, Illinois, and Brunswick, Georgia. It creates a condition for a National Football Association (NFL) players' boycott to occur as Black men face being treated like boys who simply want trinkets doled out in return for the physical prowess to be a source of entertainment for the White masses. These men stand, kneel, and protest having their mothers called bitches and themselves referred to as prison inmates and servants. They protest the social injustice incurred by Black people in America. Some of the most noted Black men demonstrating Afrikan responsive manhood in the NFL are Colin Kaepernick and Malcolm Jenkins.

Afrikan responsive manhood advances the Kusudi Saba or The Seven Principles for (re)Defining Afrikan American Relationships, which advance Consciousness, Character, Conduct, Collectivity, Competence, Caring, and Creed as central to understanding Afrikan-centered manhood. It stands, builds, and elevates at all times. When Black men understand the dynamics of their warrior spirit, then they are more likely to move away from promoting misogyny and fratricide as displays of manhood. Colorism will play a less defining role in the total scope of Black manhood. Rather, a truly Afrikan-centered self will stand firm and confront the traducers in mind, body, and spirit.

Process Questions and Considerations

1. What is the challenge with labeling expressions of Afrikan manhood as hyper-aggressive?

2. What are the distinguishing elements of Responsive manhood versus Reactionary manhood?

3. How does the second iteration of the Mulatto Hypothesis impact Black Manhood within Black men's families and within their communities?

4. Identify three major tenets of Afrikan-centered Manhood. How do these tenets relate to the Kusudi Saba?

5. How were Black male and Black female relationships impacted by enslavement?

6. How did mulatto children become a strain on Black manhood and the development of Black male identity?

7. How did cultural trauma negatively impact Black male identity development?

8. According to researchers, the intentional reimaging of the Afrikan male from a responsive and collectivist individual attuned to the needs of his culture and committed to the uplift of his people to a dumb, deviant, dangerous, reactionary archetype took place over the course of four unique periods. What are these unique periods and how did they manifest into various expressions of Black manhood?

9. How has Black masculinity been pathologized and how has that contributed to the perception of the Black man in society by Whites? By Blacks?

10. What are the implications of Black men serving as Warrior Healers within the Black community?

11. What are some examples of Black men engaging in Warrior Healer behavior?

12. How are they perceived within society by Black and non-Black people?

References

Adams, J. (2014). *Black men and the stain of colorism.* https://www.ebony.com/news/black-men-and-the-stain-of-colorism-403/

Akbar, N. (1984) *Chains and images of psychological slavery.* Tallahassee, FL: Mind Productions & Associates.

Akbar, N. (1996). *Breaking the chains of psychological slavery.* Tallahassee, FL: Mind Productions & Associates.

Akbar, N. (2017). *New visions for black men.* Tallahassee, FL: Mind Productions & Associates.

Ani, M. (1994). *Yuguru: An African-centered critique of European cultural thoughts and behavior.* Trenton, NJ: African World Press.

Azibo, D. A. (2011). Commentary: On skin bleaching and lightening as psychological misorientation mental disorder. *Journal of Pan African Studies,* 4(4), 219-232.

BET (2013) J. Cole: I might not be as successful had I been dark skin

Bynum, E. B. (1999). *The African unconscious: Roots of ancient mysticism and modern psychology.* New York: Teachers College Press.

Carter, R. T. (2007). Racism and psychological and emotional injury: Recognizing and assessing race-based traumatic stress. *The Counseling Psychologist,* 35(1), 13-105.

Carter, R. T., & Forsyth, J. (2010). Reactions to racial discrimination: Emotional stress and help-seeking behaviors. *Psychological Trauma: Theory, Research, Practice, and Policy, 2*(3), 183.

Davis, R. G., Ressler, K. J., Schwartz, A. C., Stephens, K. J., & Bradley, R. G. (2008). Treatment barriers for low-income, urban African Americans with undiagnosed posttraumatic stress disorder. *Journal of Trauma and Stress.* 21(2), 218-222.

DeGruy, J. (2017). *Post traumatic slave syndrome: America's legacy of enduring injury and healing.* Portland, OR: Joy DeGruy Publications.

Dias, B. G. & Ressler, K. J. (2014). Parental olfactory experience influences behavior and neural structure in subsequent generations. *Nature Neuroscience,* 17. http://news.emory.edu/stories/2013/12/smell_epigenetics_ressler/campus.html)

Du Bois, W.E.B. (1903) *Souls of black folks.*

Elligan, D., & Utsey, S. (1999). Utility of an African-centered support group for men coping with confronting societal racism and oppression. *Cultural Diversity and Ethnic Minority Psychology, 5*(2), 156 -165.

Eyerman, R. (2001). *Cultural trauma: The formation of an African American identity.* Cambridge, UK: The Cambridge University Press.

FuKiau, K.K.B. (2007). *Simba Simbi: Hold up that which holds you up.* Pittsburgh, PA: Dorrance Publishing Co., Inc.

Furstenberg, F. F. (1988). *Good dads-bad dads: Two faces of fatherhood.* In A. J. Cherlin (Ed.), *The Changing American family and public policy* (pp.193-218). Washington, DC: Urban Institute.

Guthrie, R. V. (2003). *Even the rat was white: A historical view of psychology.* New York, New York: Pearson Publishing.

Gutman, H. G. (1977). *The black family in slavery and freedom,* 1750-1925. New York: Vintage Publishing.

Hammond, W. P., & Mattis, J. S. (2005). Being a man about it: Manhood meaning among African American men. *Psychology of Men & Masculinity,* 6(2), 114-126. http://dx.doi.org/10.1037/1524-9220.6.2.114

Hardy, J. B., Astone, N. M., Brooks-Gunn, J., Miller, T. L., & Hilton, S. C. (1997). Adolescent childbearing revisited: The age of inner-city mothers at delivery is a determinant of their children's self-sufficiency at age 27-33. *Pediatrics,* 100, 802-809.

Herskovitz, M. J. (1934). A critical discussion of the "mulatto hypothesis." *The Journal of Negro Education,* 3(3), 389-402.

Hunter, M. L. (2013). *Race, gender, and the politics of skin tone.* Routledge

Jackson-Lowman, H. (2004). Perspectives on African American mental health: Lessons from African systems. In R. Jones (Ed.), *Black psychology* (4th ed.) (pp. 599-630). Hampton, VA: Cobb & Henry Publishers.

Kambon, K.K.K. (1998). *African/black psychology in the American context: An African-centered approach.* Tallahassee, FL: Nubian Nation.

Kendi, I. X. (2017). Colorism as racism: Garvey, Du Bois, and the other color line. *Black Perspectives.* https://www.aaihs.org/colorism-as-racism-garvey-du-bois-and-the-other-color-line/

Krampe, E. M., & Fairweather, P. D. (1993). Father presence and family formation: A theoretical reformation. Journal of Family Issues. 14(4), 572-591.

Landor, A. M., et al. (2013). Exploring the Impact of Skin Tone on Family Dynamics and Race-Related Outcomes. *Journal of Family Psychology,* 27(5), 817-826.

Landor, A. M., & Smith, S. M. (2019). Skin-tone trauma: Historical and contemporary influences on the health and interpersonal outcomes of African Americans. *Perspectives on Psychological Science,* 14(4), 797-815.

Mattis, J. S. (2004). *Spirituality and religion in African American life.* In R. Jones (Ed.), Black Psychology (4th ed.), pp. 93-116. Hampton, VA: Cobb & Henry Publishers.

Mbiti, J.S. (1990). *African religions and philosophy.* Oxford: Heinemann.

Mukuka, R. (2013). Ubuntu in S. M. Kapwepwe's *Shalapo Canicandala*: Insights for Afrocentric psychology.

Journal of Black Studies, 44(2), 137-157.

Myers, L. J. (1988). *Understanding the Afrocentric worldview: An introduction to an optimal psychology.* Dubuque, IA: Kendall Hunt.

Myers, L. J., & Speight, S. L. (2010). Reframing mental health and psychological well-being among persons of African descent: Africana/black psychology meeting the challenges of fractured social and cultural realities. *Journal of Pan African Studies,* 3(8), 66-82.

Nobles, W. W. (2015). From black psychology to sakhu djaer: Implications for the further development pan African black psychology. *Journal of Black Psychology*, 4(5), 399-414.

Nobles, W. W. (2004). African philosophy: Foundations of black psychology. In R. Jones (Ed.), *Black Psychology* (pp. 47-63). Berkeley, CA: Cobb & Henry.

Nobles, W. (2015). *Island of memes: Haiti's unfinished revolution.* Baltimore, MD: Black Classic Press.

Mirokowsky, J., & Ross, C. E. (2003). *Social causes of psychological distress* (2nd ed.). Hawthorne, NY: Aldine de Gruyter.

Ojelade, I. I., et al. (2014). Use of indigenous African healing practices as a mental health intervention. The Hilliard-Jones Forum for African-Centered Psychology. *Journal of Black Psychology*, 40(6), 491-519.

Oyserman, D., Coon, H. M., & Kemmelmeir, M. (2002). Rethinking individualism and collectivism: Evaluation of theoretical assumptions and meta-analyses. *Psychological Bulletin*, 128, 3-72.

Patterson, O. (1999). *Rituals of blood.* Civitas Books.

Reuter, E. B. (1917). The superiority of the mulatto. *American Journal of Sociology,* 23(1), 83-106.

Rich, J. (2000). The health of African American men. *Annals of American Academy Political and Social Sciences,* 56(9), 149-159.

Rowe, D. M., & Webb-Msemaji, F. (2004). African-centered psychology in the community. In R. Jones (Ed.) *Black Psychology* (4th ed.) (pp. 401-421). Hampton, VA: Cobb & Henry Publishers.

Schiele, J. H. (2000). *Human services and the Afrocentric paradigm.* Binghamton, NY: The Haworth Press.

Smith, S. M., & Fincham, F. (2016). Racial discrimination experiences among black youth: A person-centered approach. *Journal of Black Psychology* 42(2), 300-319.

Speight, S. L. (2007). Internalized racism: One more piece of the puzzle. *The Counseling Psychologist,* 35(1), 126-134.

Veras, E. (2016). He's dark, dark; Colorism among African American men. Thesis, Georgia State University. https://scholarworks.gsu.edu/aas_theses/33

Washington, K. (1996). In K. Addae (Ed.). To heal a people: African scholars define a new reality. Kugichagulia Press: Columbia, MD.

Washington, K. (2010). Zulu traditional healing, African worldview and the practice of Ubuntu: Deep thought for African/black psychology. *The Journal of Pan African Studies*, 3(8), 24-39.

Watkin, D. C., Walker, R. L., & Griffin, D. M. (2010). A meta-analysis of black male mental health and well-being. *Journal of Black Psychology*, 36(3), 303-330.

Wilder, J. (2018). African Americans: Colorism in *Morrow v. IRS* litigation. *American Behavioral Scientist.* 62(14), 1978-1987.

Wilder, J-A., & Cain, C. (2010). Teaching and learning color consciousness in black families: Exploring family process and women's experiences with colorism. *Journal of Family Issues*, 32(5), 577-604.

CHAPTER 4.

Colorism in the K-12 Classroom:
Implications for Teachers of Black Students

Kamilah Marie Woodson, Howard University
Zoeann Finzi-Adams, The Chicago School of Professional Psychology
Marilyn M. Irving, Howard University
Antonio Cooper, Francis Marion University
Courtney C. Hives-Gunn, Louisiana Department of Health and Hospitals
Kathryn Aimee McFarland, IDEA Public Schools

Introduction

While students of color comprise approximately one-third of the U.S. school population, the U.S. Department of Commerce (1996) projects that, by the year 2050, African American, Asian American, and Latino students will constitute close to 55% of all U.S. students. Recent census figures indicate that children of color are the fastest growing segment of the population, currently representing 51% of all school-age children (Anyon, 1997). Of these, 15% of students enrolled in the public schools are Black (NCES, 2015). However, Black teachers represent only 7% of public school teachers, whereas more than 80% are White (NCES, 2015). Current trends in public school enrollment and teacher characteristics (National Center for Educational Statistics (NCES, 2015) indicate the overwhelming probability that Black children will experience mostly White teachers during their education. The majority of American educators are White, middle-class, and female, while the K-12 population in the United States is increasingly diverse. Currently, primarily White teachers staff schools in the United States, although the number of students of color from historically racial groups is growing rapidly (Hunter, 2016; Villegas & Lucas, 2002). Unfortunately, this reality tends to create adverse consequences for children of color, African American children in particular. Although the effects of racial discrimination in education have been widely documented, color-based discrimination, or colorism, has not been as rigorously examined in general (Hunter, 2016; Monroe, 2013), and not examined to the extent to which it relates to Black teachers teaching Black children. Thus, relatively less attention has been directed toward specific within-group stereotypes and stratifications that may influence the educational process. Colorism, which has been defined as a form of intragroup stratification that subjectively ranks individuals according to skin color tones, asserts the belief that a person's skin tone impacts how a person is both perceived and treated by others. For example, people who "look white" may receive preferential or prejudicial treatment from persons both within and outside their own ethnic group. Although present across any number of ethnic groups, specifically those that have been stereotypically disenfranchised, colorism most commonly has been associated with American Blacks. Internalized colorism, both in terms of skin color and hair texture, has been noted in the extant literature as having both distant (historic) and direct connections to the self-concept and self-esteem of African Americans (Woodson, 2002). Current literature has also linked attractiveness and body image to self-esteem for African Americans, which also speaks to colorist ideologies (Hill, 2002).

In the educational process, the effects of colorism may manifest in various ways, including inter-student conflicts or stratifications (that is, peer isolation or bullying based on colorist ideologies); differential teacher-student expectations (that is, lowered academic expectations); differential teacher-student treatment (that is, preferential treatment of fairer skinned students and/or less lenient discipline practices for darker-skinned students). Indeed, several researchers have highlighted disparities in school discipline practices across ethnic groups. However, questions remain as to whether similar disparities exist within ethnic groups, particularly as it relates to colorism. Colorism also may affect student learning, given the established links between school performance and low self-esteem/self-efficacy, which is impacted by colorism. As such, it is imperative for teachers and teacher trainers to gain a more thorough understanding of the significance, impact, and implications of colorism in the classroom, especially in terms of enabling teachers to identify it and foster learning environments that combat its effects. Hunter (2016) further supports this notion by positing that it is crucial to understand the dynamics of colorism in schools as it operates as a subsystem of structural racism. Colorist trends are exacerbated by stereotypical notions of superiority, moral character, and attractiveness in social interaction (Keith & Monroe, 2016) and because beauty is associated with perceived intellectual capabilities, behavioral evaluations, and likeability, light-complexioned people may receive signals that they are smart, capable, and more welcome in social spaces than dark-complexioned individuals. Therefore, implications of colorism may plausibly be found in sectors such as academic tracks, student leadership positions, and teacher recommendations for student opportunities

(Keith & Monroe, 2016).This chapter will discuss the development of colorism in children, the impact of colorism in the classroom relative to teachers and students. It provides implications for teachers of diverse populations, and will introduce a colorism model for use in the preparation of teachers and those who educate African American students.

Colorist Identity Development in Children

There are several ways that African American children are socialized about their phenotypic presentation. They are socialized by their family, their classmates, the media, their teachers, and by society in general (see Figure 1). Beginning in childhood, African American children form an identity attached to skin complexion, their level of attractiveness, hair texture/length, and physique. This "colorist identity" is largely shaped by their parents and other family members. Values about skin color, hair texture, facial features and body types (Woodson, 2020) are conveyed to children as they come out of the womb. According to Russell et al. (1992),

> Many Black families can barely disguise their anxious concerns about the color and features of a newborn. Following routine inquiries about the baby's sex, weight, and health, most relatives will immediately want to know, "What's he or she looks like?"—a veiled request for information about the skin color and features (p. 94).

Comments about color, first from family members and later from friends, peers, and society (Woodson, 2020) shape the psychology of a Black child as he/she grows from infancy to adulthood (Russell et al., 1992). Russell et al. (1992) further state, "Black children quickly absorb the guilt, anger, jealousy, and depression generated in their families by an unresolved color complex" (p. 95) Unfortunately, however, Black mothers, aunts, and grandmothers have been found to be the voice of colorist prejudice and the most influential in color identity formation (Parmer, Arnold, Natt, & Janson, 2004).

Parmer, Arnold, Natt, and Janson (2004) argue that African American families' views on skin color are shaped by their history of oppression and enslavement, in which they often adopt Eurocentric values of beauty and attractiveness. These values of beauty can be variable and not just contingent on complexion, as colorism is multifaceted. Simultaneously, the internalization of oppressive views toward beauty often translates into expressing that light skin is more advantageous and beautiful than dark skin (Parmer et al., 2004; Woodson, 2002). At times, colorist messages may be explicit (that

Colorism in African American Students Model

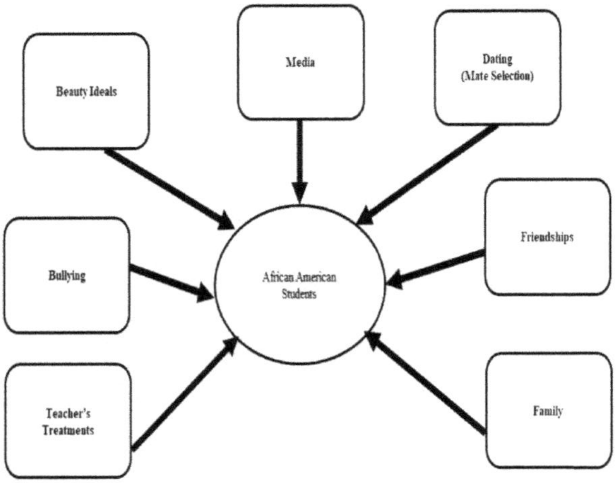

Figure 1. (Author Developed)

is, using demeaning terms to refer to dark skin) or implicit (for example, cautioning children to stay out of the sun for fear of becoming too dark) (Wilder & Cain, 2011), while in other instances colorism can be unspoken. Further, it is important to note that colorist ideology formation may be more profound in families that have heterogeneous skin complexions, body types, facial features, and hair textures where sharp contrasts can be found (Wilder & Cain, 2011).

Again, beyond skin tone, colorism as defined in this chapter also refers to attitudes surrounding Black hair texture, physique, and attractiveness within the Black family. Because of colorist prejudices enforced during slavery, recognizably Afrocentric features such as "kinky" hair have been demeaned in American society. Even within the Black community, hair is often segregated into two distinct categories, "good" and "bad" hair. "Good Hair" refers to African American hair that is usually described as soft or wavy or hair that has Eurocentric features, while "Bad Hair" is "nappy," hard to manage, and tightly curled. In childhood, African Americans learn the stereotypes and biases that are attached to their hair textures (Parmer et al. 2004; Woodson, 2002), with this knowledge having a more profound impact on African American girls. The unspoken pressure among Black females and in the Black family to chemically alter their hair or wear artificial hair is best illustrated in Chris Rock's documentary,

Good Hair. Likewise, the unpleasant childhood hair experiences of African American mothers are frequently passed down to their daughters (Parmer et al., 2004). Seemingly, in response to the generational trauma relative to hair texture and length, in order to shield their daughters from those negative experiences, African American mothers may pressure them to conform to Eurocentric ideals through straightening and chemically altering their natural hair textures, or adding extensions (weaves) and partial wigs. Maternal figures have also been known to pinch the noses of little girls and/or restrict their food intake to influence levels of attractiveness relative to facial features and physique (Poran, 2006).

Colorism and Parenting

Colorist ideology within African American family dynamics affects how children view themselves as well as parents' parenting patterns; such that these colorist messages to African American children may negatively impact self-identity. Colorist ideologies have been thought to also impact parental expectations and the quality of parenting, especially if the child has the disfavored phenotypes and/or shunned paternity. It is, however, important to note that the opposite may be true when the darker-skinned child is favored over lighter-skinned children, recognizing that context plays a significant role that is less likely to be found in colorism literature. Moreover, interestingly, colorism's role in parenting may sharply differ depending on the gender of the child. In a quantitative study analyzing how skin tone affects parenting styles, Landor et al. (2013) measured the interaction of skin tone and the quality of parenting, where parenting was assessed on levels of warmth, attention, and styles of discipline. Researchers found that African American daughters with lighter complexions were favored and received a "better quality of parenting" than their darker-skinned counterparts (Landor et al., 2013). In contrast, African American sons with darker skin reported receiving more preferential treatment from their parents than males with fairer skin (Landor, 2013). This study suggests that this difference may occur because parents may be trying to protect their children from the racist attitudes of society (Landor et al., 2013). Darker-skinned African American males, in particular, experience a high level of racism because they are stereotyped as criminal, delinquent, and violent. Unlike sons, African American daughters with light skin are traditionally thought to be advantaged in American society. Further, Black parents may favor their light-skinned daughters in an attempt to instill a sense of entitlement to promote success. Unfortunately, African American parents who express colorist prejudice may inadvertently generate feelings of inadequacy among children without the favored skin tone and/or hair texture (which again could be a departure from the prevailing societal preferences) despite attempts to protect their children (Landor et al., 2013). This colorist ideological indoctrination is so remarkable because the students are developing their racial identities and are still maturing and developing cognitively. In addition to being socialized by the family, young people, as we know, are quite impressionable and are equally, if not more, influenced by the social aspects of community (including media).

Colorism in the Media and Social Engagement

The media heavily perpetuates colorism, where light skin is often deemed beautiful, though this message is not always explicit, as the media has many inconspicuous ways of delivering this rhetoric. For example, during childhood, young girls often aspire to emulate fantasy characters such as queens and princesses. The Walt Disney Corporation has saturated the media with images of leading characters who are often of European American decent, or who have Eurocentric features, which serves to propagate Eurocentric beauty ideals. Additionally, lighter-skinned Black children, or racially ambiguous children often play more significant roles in commercials, TV shows, and movies than darker-skinned children, and this preference of lighter-skinned children in the media is generally accepted (Steele, 2016). The music industry's frequent display of lighter-skinned video girls and more successful female artists shows it has been influenced by colorism as well. Jacobs, Levine, Abney, and Davids (2016) discuss the gradual skin lightening of famous artists such as Beyoncé, Rihanna, and Nicki Minaj. Further, outside of American pop culture, lightening one's skin by bleaching is also glorified in many Jamaican song lyrics (Charles, 2011). Sadly, children and young adults are the main consumers of these images and music and are heavily influenced.

Social media also propagates colorist beliefs. In 2010, African American comedian Kevin Hart posted tweets that started viral debates and outrage among Black Americans. Kevin Hart stated, "#hands down light-skinned women usually have better credit than a dark-skinned women …broke *** hoes…lol." As Hart later tweets ". . . I'm joking jeeeez." there is some underlying truth to his "joke" (Harrison, 2015), given that lighter-complexioned individuals often benefit from an elevated socioeconomic status (Keith & Monroe, 2016). Similarly, Williams (2016) cites an example on Twitter where there was a preponderance of support for #TEAMLIGHTSKIN and #TEAMDARKSKIN. Regrettably, children who are on social media are exposed to this type of discourse. Further, children also tend to be impacted by social media models and often try to emulate what they see. For attention and status, they often post provocative photographs, and their self-worth and self-esteem are then inextricably linked to the number of likes and followers they have.

Manifestation of Colorism in the Classroom Among Students

In addition to cyberspace interactions, in-person peer interactions also matter a great deal in schooling experiences (Hunter, 2016). For example, when electing a homecoming queen, choosing a date for prom, electing class representatives, and choosing class superlatives, peer status is highly influenced by colorist definitions of beauty, lighter-skinned privilege, in particular (Fergus, 2009; Hunter, 2016). This tends to be so because people routinely attribute other positive traits (like competence or integrity) to individuals they perceive as physically attractive (Hunter, 2016). Ascribing to these beliefs and attitudes can be very detrimental to the well-being of the children. For example, those who have positive social capital based on their phenotypic privilege can be targeted in the same ways as those who do not. There are instances of social isolation, teasing, taunting, rumor spreading, bullying, and even assault (Hunter, 2016). These behaviors are often documented in the literature relative to girls, but less so for boys, though clinicians anecdotally recognize that it does exist. This is also an issue relative to dating, and having "crushes" and close interpersonal relationships. Colorist ideologies impact who is deemed datable or even likable, which fuels conflict and creates power differential (Keith & Monroe, 2016).

Colorism and Bullying

Though there are many theories related to how a person can develop an inflated or lower self-esteem, one phenomenon that is infrequently mentioned is the impact of colorism on self-concept. Considering that both bullying and colorism have a hierarchy of power, it is possible that colorism may influence bullying behavior in school settings. For instance, students who are afforded preferential treatment because of their phenotypic attributes may have an inflated sense of self-worth, which may result in engaging in bullying behaviors. Similarly, students who have endured within-group discrimination may either engage in bullying behavior in an effort to exert power in ways that are within their control, or they may become the victim of bullying behavior because of their lower self-esteem. Conversely, those who are deemed most attractive and/or privileged may become targeted and mistreated by their peers. Bullying can be caused by increased narcissism or and/or decreased self-esteem, which is dependent on environmental factors and the composition of the students within the school and home environments.

Bullying has become a widespread and serious problem within the school systems of the United States. Though there are multiple definitions of bullying, the central theme of most definitions is an imbalance of power that is intended to cause repeated harm over time to another person or group (Department of Health and Human Services, 2019). There are several methods of bullying that perpetrators tend to utilize. The most common form of bullying is verbal harassment. This is when the perpetrator uses name-calling and teasing as a way of exerting their power. Insults such as "Blackie, half-breed, glow-worm, bald-headed, nappy-headed," and so on tend to be used when the verbal harassment is fueled by colorist ideologies. Social exclusion is another method of bullying that is often utilized by female perpetrators. This is when a person purposely excludes others from social events, spreads rumors about another person in effort to damage them socially, or maliciously breaks up the friendships of others. This can often be observed with African American adolescents with regard to groups that are similar in one or more physical characteristics, such as a group of darker-skinned girls excluding the lighter-skinned girls, or just the opposite, the lighter-skinned girls excluding or exhibiting cruelty to darker-skinned girls. Physical violence is also a method of bullying that, until recently, has most commonly been utilized by males. It involves hitting, punching, and physically harming others in effort to exert power. African American female adolescents have become increasingly more violent, and the number of exclusions of girls from school for fighting and physical assaults has increased tremendously. Colorism is likely at play, and one could argue that the perpetrators and victims are unaware of the underlying issues or motivation for their strife and/or conflicts. Further, the final type of bullying that is becoming an increasingly severe problem is cyberbullying. This occurs when bullies utilize the Internet, cellular phones, and other forms of digital media as a means for causing harm (Department of Health and Human Services, 2019). Many schools limit children's access to their personal cellphones during school hours. However, cyberbullying often occurs after hours. Students make mean-spirited posts about each other, take pictures with the significant others of their friends to promote jealousy, make denigrating comments on each other's posts, make posts that show others that they were excluded from various outings and/or activities (Department of Health and Human Services, 2019). The consequences of bullying are widespread. Bullying not only affects the victims but also has psychological implications for the bully and those who witness the bullying. Children who have been victims of bullying are at a higher risk of depression and anxiety, are at increased risk of suicide, are more likely to have health concerns, may suffer from decreased academic achievement, are likely to be truant or drop out of school, and are at a high risk of violently retaliating against their perpetrator (Department of Health and Human Services, 2019). These consequences become even more pronounced for African American children who have unresolved colorist complexes.

Unfortunately, children who are bullies are likely to have a life trajectory that includes substance abuse, destructive behavior, premature sexual behavior, criminal convictions, and domestic abuse (Department of Health and Human Services, 2019). Similarly, children who witness bullying are more likely to suffer from depression and anxiety, have increased substance abuse, and are increasingly likely to be truant—many outcomes that have unfortunately been associated with African American children.

Colorism and Dating

For African American adolescents with unresolved colorist ideologies, dating can also be challenging. Black females are significantly more susceptible to colorist views because Black males more closely subscribe to Eurocentric views of beauty when choosing mates (Woodson, 2002). Hunter (2016) underscores this by stating that boys and girls experience some key differences in color-based discrimination, particularly related to ideals of physical attractiveness and criteria for status among peers. Darker-skinned girls are more likely to experience negative teasing and name-calling. For same-sex attracted African American adolescents, the same can be observed, where individuals with Eurocentric features are deemed most attractive and more desirable. This has implications for dating satisfaction, as those individuals who feel less desirable may find themselves in situations where they are participating in nonconsensual open relationships, unable to acquire a partner, or are even the survivors of dating violence (Haileab, 2018). Woodson (2002) further found that due to Black males' usage of colorist views when choosing mates they are more likely to engage in risky sexual behaviors (as defined by lack of condom usage) with females who were more closely aligned with their colorist ideals. Accordingly, it should be noted that when Black females, who find themselves in relationships with someone they deem ideal, often tend to relax their boundaries, are susceptible to mistreatment, and are less inclined to advocate for themselves if they have internalized negative colorist ideals relative to themselves.

Children, depending on their age, come to school having had a variation of the aforementioned types of colorist socialization incidents, which prime them for a particular set of experiences with their teachers. This suggests there is a need for teachers to not only be skilled in pedagogical and didactic approaches, but to also have an advanced level of competency in the culture of African American children, so as not to "do more harm." Ideally, competencies in colorist ideologies would be acquired either in preservice teacher training programs, and/or in the professional development activities at the school district level. Embedded in those skills trainings should also be lessons and experiential components that allow teachers, both African American and others, to explore their own colorist socialization experiences that may manifest in the classroom while relating to and teaching their Black students.

Manifestations of Colorism in the Classroom Among Teachers

The majority of children's time in school is spent in a classroom interacting with teachers. For this reason, understanding the manifestation of colorism in the classroom is vital (Hunter, 2016). In line with colorist ideologies, the halo effect, which is the propensity to allow positive evaluation about one trait in a person and to influence the appraisal of other aspects of that person's characteristics, such as intelligence, kindness, and likeability can be observed. For example, African American children who are perceived as attractive (often lighter-skinned) may seem more attractive because of colorist/racialized standards of beauty, thus engendering strong teacher expectations. The reverse is also likely true, as teachers may have lowered expectations if the African American student is perceived (consciously or unconsciously) as unattractive (Hunter, 2016; Keith & Monroe, 2016). Accordingly, children who are not perceived as intelligent, likeable, or attractive are often treated more harshly when they misbehave, and their behaviors are often considered intentional rather than being given the "benefit of the doubt." Attractiveness is often linked to integrity and competence (Hunter, 2016). Previous studies have well documented teacher expectations and implicit biases.

Teacher Expectations and Implicit Biases

According to Staats & Patton (2013), McKown and Weinstein (2002) affirmed the role of teacher expectancy effects on the achievement of African American students, using a sample of 561 elementary school children. The researchers studied whether students' ethnicity played a role in their susceptibility to teacher expectancy effects. By conceptualizing teacher expectations as the degree to which teachers over- or underestimated achievement compared to the students' actual academic performance, McKown and Weinstein (2002) found that African American children are more likely than Caucasian children "to confirm teacher underestimates of ability and less likely to benefit from teacher overestimates of ability" (McKown & Weinstein, 2002, p. 176; Staats & Patton, 2013).

Although the aforementioned study addresses race, the colorism in education literature suggests that racism and colorism are interlocking systems of discrimination (Keith & Monroe, 2016); thus, the findings seem applicable. The aforementioned examples speak to implicit bias and discrimination relative to the children being African American or children of color, suggesting that the students' phenotypic presentation inspires bias and prejudicial treatment by their teachers on an even deeper level. Keith and Monroe (2016) assert that when African Americans and other students of color fare comparably well within their ethno-racial group, they tend to have lighter complexions. Hunter (2016) also underscores this notion by stating that skin-color bias, often an implicit or unconscious bias, affects many school level interactions among teachers, students, and families (Burton, Bonilla-Silva Ray, Buckelew & Freeman, 2010). Implicit negative associations and appraisals may arise outside of their conscious awareness, such that these associations may not necessarily align with individuals' openly held beliefs or even reflect stances one would explicitly endorse. Thus, teacher training is paramount! When teachers are not aware of the schemas and biases that they or their students hold, the occasion is set for seriously adverse consequences.

Consequences of implicit biases and lower expectations

The implicit biases held by teachers, which affect the expectations they hold for students, have negative consequences for African American students in the classroom. If African American students are taught by teachers who do not believe in their full potential, these subtle biases can accumulate over time to create a deficient educational context that fails to prepare students to become fully thriving, contributing members of society (Keith & Monroe, 2016; Staats & Patton, 2013). Holding lower standards for Black students is particularly disheartening given the fact that research suggests that holding students to higher standards benefits students and actually improves grades and test scores (Staats & Patton, 2013). Additionally, teachers' beliefs, attitudes, expectations, and biases have been cited as a major factor in the overrepresentation of Black children within special education placements. Many teachers, both Black and other, develop negative views of the behaviors of Black students, particularly Black male students, because of their high physical activity, which frequently lands them in special education classes (Staats & Patton, 2013). Lloyd Dunn first called the problem of the overrepresentation of Black students in special education programs to the attention of the education community in 1968 (Hunter, 2016.) Despite 50 years of awareness of this problem, this pattern has obstinately persisted. Teacher prejudices, racial bias, expectations, and differential treatment remain active and alive (Bondy & Ross, 1998; Hunter, 2016).

Combating Colorism Through Culturally Relevant Pedagogy, Curricula, and Training

Teachers should be advocates of students regardless of their skin color or race. Unfortunately, African American students are expelled from school or sent to detention more than other students, and many teachers expect the misbehavior of African American students as if it were the norm. One way to address the deficiencies in school systems and to increase the academic achievement of minority students (specifically African American students) is through culturally relevant pedagogy. Culturally relevant pedagogy can be defined as, "instructional practices that build on the premise that the way students learn differs across cultures" (Reis and Kay, 2007). When a teacher takes time to understand a student's background, culture, and family circumstances, and uses these characteristics as strengths to build upon, the student is more likely to succeed. Research also suggests that a teacher's knowledge and skill in working with culturally and linguistically diverse students may impact student success (Au & Raphael, 2000; Cummins, 1996; Gay, 2000; Ladson-Billings, 1994). Further, teachers who understand their students' cultures and backgrounds are better able to design instruction that best meet their needs. In order to maximize learning opportunities for students, teachers must gain knowledge about the (colorist) cultures represented in the classrooms, and then translate this knowledge into instructional practices (Gay, 2000; Ladson- Billings, 1994; Villegas, 1991). When teacher educators ignore (colorist) cultural differences in their classrooms, students' fears and sense of isolation increase, resulting in poor literacy, failure, and high dropout rates. For both ethical and practical reasons, it is incumbent upon our educational systems to focus on teaching culturally relevant pedagogy that includes the nuanced ethnic and racial identities of African American children.

Until all teachers have an understanding of, and a deep respect for, the intra-group diversity of Black children, Black children will lag behind in achievement. All teachers, including African American teachers, must have high expectations of Black children's abilities regardless of their phenotypic presentation. They must also have a willingness to learn both about themselves and about the best practices with their students. Although African American children tend to have very well-developed ideas and beliefs about their appearance long before they begin attending school, their self-concept and self-esteem are often shaped and reified by school experiences. Therefore, with proper knowledge and skills, teachers have the opportunity and responsibility to create corrective emotional experiences when they are aware of the negative schemas and scripts held by their students. Insight into Black students' cultural style and colorist socialization helps teachers understand their students' behaviors and core sense of self. Further, when teachers are aware of students' learning styles, show respect for their intrapsychic experiences, and have high expectations for all of them, greater student achievement will occur!

Implications for Research, Policy, and Practice

The scholarship on race and educational outcomes is voluminous, yet little attention is devoted to the place of colorism in education (Keith & Monroe, 2016). As such, researchers could advance the literature by conducting studies at the school district level to yield data that could inform colorism/implicit bias in teacher trainings and professional development workshops. Conducting colorism research with the children could also provide useful data that would inform both group and individual prevention/ interventions with students. While conducting informative research is imperative, another important area to address is relative policy. For example, there should be carefully developed diversity policies centered around the recruitment of teachers and preservice teacher training of teachers of children of color. It would be ideal to hire teachers who have experience and competency, while actively "policing and training" other teachers when competence is missing and/or waning. Morell (2010) underscores this idea by stating, as the curriculum and pedagogy are analyzed to meet the needs of elementary and secondary students, that the same should be done with teacher education programs so that they respond to the experiences and knowledge of all students in the classroom. Moreover, educators must do a better job of screening for the disposition necessary for teaching a culturally diverse student population. Preparation for teaching in a diverse classroom, one that is diverse in many ways—ethnically, culturally, socioeconomically—as well as other forms of diversity, ought to be integral parts of all preservice teacher training programs. (Morell, 2010). Additionally, perhaps there could be a policy developed that would allow for "school auditing" to examine the "real time" interplay of colorism and education in the school setting. Further, in terms of curricula and programming, discussions of racism and colorism should occur regularly where appropriate. Finally, from the practice/praxis lens, the student-teacher relationship is a critical factor in student achievement, especially for Black students (Steele & Aronson, 1995; Woolley & Grogan-Kaylor, 2006). As such, teachers, who set and communicate high standards and communicate high expectations will help advance the success of their students' achievement.

Process Questions and Considerations

1. What would be the best way to get through to the teachers who are resistant to buy into colorist cultural competency?

2. Given the socialization that children receive prior to school, can teachers help? If so, how?

3. Given the socialization that some teachers have received, can their perceptions and unconscious biases change?

4. How should the university preservice teacher training programs address these phenomena?

5. What interventions could be useful at the school and district or state level?

References

Anyon, J. (1997). *Ghetto schooling: A political economy of urban educational reform.* New York: Teachers College Press.

Au, K. H., & Raphael, T.E. (2000). Equity and literacy in the next millennium. *Reading Research Quarterly,* 35(1), 170-188.

Bondy, E., & Ross, D. (1998). Confronting myths about teaching black children: A challenge for teacher educators. *Teacher Education and Special Education,* 21(4), 241-254.

Burton, L., Bonilla-Silva, E., Ray, V., Buckelew, R., & Freeman, E. H. (2010). Duke University critical race theories: Colorism, and the decade's research on families of color. *Journal of Marriage and Family,* 440-459. DOI:10.1111/j.1741-3737.2010.00712.x

Center for Research on Education, Diversity and Excellence (CREDE). (2002). http//:crede.berkeley.edu

Charles, C. (2011). Skin bleaching and the prestige complexion of sexual attraction. *Sexuality & Culture,* 15(4), 375-390. DOI:10.1007/s12119-011-9107-0

Charles, C.A.D. (2011). The derogatory representations of the skin bleaching products sold in Harlem. *Journal of Pan African Studies,* 4(4), 117-141. Retrieved from http://search.ebscohost.com/login.aspx?direct=true&db=aph&AN=65721065&scope=site

Cooper, P. (2003). Effective white teachers of black children: teaching within a community. *Journal of Teacher Education,* 54 (5), 413-427.

Cummins J. (1996). Negotiating identities: Education for empowerment in a diverse society. Ontario, CA: California Association for Bilingual Education.

Department of Health and Human Services. (2019). What is bullying? Retrieved from https://www.stopbullying.gov/bullying/what-is-bullying

Fergus, E. (2009). Understanding Latino students' schooling experiences: The of skin color among Mexican and Puerto Rican high school students. *Teachers College Record, 111*(2).

Finzi-Smith, Z. M. (2015). Feeding the pain: Multiple forms of discrimination: Psychological functioning and eating behaviors among black women. Unpublished Dissertation, Howard University

Frisen, A., Jonsson, A., Persson, C. (2007). Adolescents' perception of bullying: Who is the victim? Who is the bully? What can be done to stop bullying? *Adolescence, 42*(168).

Gay, G. (2000). *Culturally responsive teaching.* New York: Teachers College Press.

Haileab, L. (2018). Shaded love and violence: Internalized colorism, femininity, depression and dating violence. Unpublished Dissertation, Howard University

Hall, R. E. (2003). Skin color as post-colonial hierarchy: A global strategy for conflict resolution. *Journal of Black Psychology,* 137, 41-53.

Harrison, M. S. 2010. Colorism: The often undiscussed "ism" in America's workforce. *The Jury Expert, 22,* 67-72.

Howard, T. C. (2001). Powerful pedagogy for Black students: A case of power teachers. *Urban Education,* 36, 179-202.

Hyland, N. (2005). Being a good teacher of black students? White teachers and unintentional racism. The Ontario Institute for Studies in Education of the University of Toronto. *Curriculum Inquiry, 35*(4), 429-459.

Hunter, M. (2016). Colorism in the classroom: How skin tone stratifies African American and Latina/o students. *Theory into Practice, 55*(1), 54-61. DOI:10.1080/00405841.2016.1119019

Keith, V., & Monroe, C. (2016). Histories of colorism and implications for education, *Theory into Practice, 55*(1), 4-10. DOI:10.1080/00405841.2016.1116847

Irvine, J. (1990). *Black students and school failure: Policies practices and prescriptions.* New York: Greenwood.

Jacobs, M., Levine, S., Abney, K., & Davids, L. (2016). Fifty shades of African lightness: A bio-psychosocial review of the global phenomenon of skin lightening practices. *Journal of Public Health in Africa, 7,* 552.

Ladson-Billings, G. (1994). The dreamkeepers: Successful teachers for African American children. San Francisco: Jossey-Bass.

Landor, A. M., Simons, L. G., Simmons, R. L., Brody, G. H., Bryant, C. M., Gibbons, F. X., Granberg, E. M., et al. (2013). Exploring the impact of skin tone on family dynamics and race-related outcomes. *Journal of Family Psychology,* 27(5), 817-26. DOI:10.1037/a0033883.

Lee, V. E., Smith, J. B., Perry, T. E., & Smylie, M. A. (1999). Social support, academic press, and student achievement: A view from the middle grades in Chicago. *Improving Chicago's schools: A report of the Chicago Annenberg research project.* Chicago, IL: Consortium on Chicago School Research.

McGee, E., Alvarez, A., & Milner, H. R., IV. (2016) Colorism as a salient space for understanding in teacher preparation. *Theory into Practice, 55*(1), 69-79, DOI:10.1080/00405841.2016.1116882

McKown, C., & Weinstein, R. S. (2002). Modeling the role of child ethnicity and gender in children's differential response to teacher expectations. *Journal of Applied Social Psychology, 32*(1), 159-184. Retrieved from: http://onlinelibrary.wiley.com/doi/10.1111/j.1559-1816.2002. Tb01425.x/abstract

Monroe, C. R. (2013). Colorizing educational research: African American life and schooling as an exemplar. *Educational Researcher, 42,* 9-19.

Morell, J. (2010). Teacher preparation and diversity: When America pre-service teachers aren't white and middle class. *International Journal of Multicultural Education, 12*(1), 1-16.

Nakray, K. (2018). The global beauty industry, colorism, racism and the national body. *Journal of Gender Studies, 27*(7), 861-863, DOI:10.1080/09589236.2018.1521117

National Center for Educational Statistics. (2015). *National Center for Educational Statistics.* Washington, DC: U.S. Department of Education.

Parmer, T., Arnold, M., Natt, T., & Janson, C. (2004). Physical attractiveness as a process of internalized oppression and multigenerational transmission in African American families. *Family Journal, 12*(3),

230-242. DOI:10.1177/1066480704264345

Reis, N., & Kay, S. (2007). Incorporating culturally relevant pedagogy into the teaching of science: The role of the principal. *Electronic Journal of Literacy Through Science, 6*(2), 54-57.

Russell, K., Wilson, M., & Hall, R. (1992). *The color complex: The politics of skin color among African Americans.* New York: Anchor.

Steele, C. K. (2016). Pride and prejudice: Pervasiveness of colorism and the animated series *Proud Family. Howard Journal of Communication, 27*(1), 53-67.

Steele, C., & Aronson, J. (1995). Stereotype threat and the intellectual test performance of blacks. *Journal of Personality and Social Psychology, 69,* 797-811.

Tummala-Narra, P. (2007. Skin color and therapeutic relationship. *Psychoanalytic Psychology, 24*(2), 255-270.

U.S. Department of Commerce (1996) Current population reports: Populations projects of the United States by age, sex, race, Hispanic origin: 1995 to 2050.

Villegas, A. M. (1991). Culturally responsive pedagogy. Washington, DC: ERIC *Clearinghouse on Teacher Education.*

Villegas, A. M., & Lucas, T. (2002). *Educating culturally responsive teachers: A coherent approach.* Albany, NY: State University of New York Press.

Wilder, J., & Cain, C. (2011). Teaching and learning color consciousness in black families: Exploring family processes and women's experiences with colorism. *Journal of Family Issues, 32* (5), 577-604.

Williams, J. Retrieved from Http//watercoolerconvos.com/2016/07/18/jesse-williams-zendaya-and-our issues with colorism.

Woodson, K. M. (2002). The impact of hair texture and skin color among African American men and women during mate selection on the expression of risky sexual behaviors. Unpublished Dissertation, California School of Professional Psychology, Los Angeles, CA.

Woodson, K. M. (2020). The colorist identity convergence model: A re-conceptualization of colorism among black women. Unpublished Manuscript.

Woolley, M. E., & Grogan-Kaylor, A. (2006). Protective family factors in the context of neighborhood: Promoting positive school outcomes. *Family Relations, 55,* 95-106.

Chapter 5.

Colorism and Racial Politics at Historically Black Colleges/Universities (HBCUs)

Naomi M. Hall-Byers, Winston-Salem State University
Danielle D. Dickens, Spelman College
Anna K. Lee, North Carolina A&T State University
Maya Corneille and Sinead N. Younge, Morehouse College

Introduction

Discussing colorism is difficult and can be uncomfortable for some. It can be especially daunting to tackle the "secret shame" of colorism at some of the most beloved Black institutions in America. However, it is necessary if progress is to be made. This chapter is written by a community psychologist and four social psychologists of different shades/hues, who are all faculty at different historically Black colleges/universities (HBCUs) across the southern region of the United States. Three of the five authors also attended an HBCU for their undergraduate studies, and one attended an HBCU for doctoral studies. This chapter focuses on colorism and its history with some HBCUs, racial politics, and how both may manifest in privileges afforded to groups of individuals who attend or work at these institutions, and how they are related to topics that engage some students in the classroom.

Brief History of Colorism

Colorism and racism are not synonymous, yet they are intertwined. Racism is a system of practices and ideologies that privilege certain groups of people over others, based on the construct of race. Although race is a social construct, racism is predicated upon the idea that there are biologically-driven hierarchies among racial groups that make certain groups (for example, those who identify as White) superior over others (for example, those who identify as people of color). Colorism is prejudicial attitudes and discrimination based on skin tone that privileges individuals with lighter skin complexions over their counterparts with darker skin complexions (Hunter, 2007).

Thus, colorism can be seen as an extension of how racism operates within people of color. In many parts of the world, people who have lighter skin complexions are given opportunities over those with darker skin complexions, even within the same racial and/or ethnic group. Colorism is not confined to racial or ethnic group identification but centered on skin tone and other racialized phenotypical characteristics such as hair texture, nose shape, fullness/thinness of lips, and eye color (Reece, 2018). Colorism is often gendered and plays a complementary role to classism. Skin tone has often been used to determine who is beautiful in society, thus affecting colorism among women more than men (Norwood, 2015). Colorism is prominent in parts of South and Southeast Asia, Latin America, and Africa. Skin tone and color, in many of these countries, has historically been associated with class, such that those who had darker skin were more likely to be poor, and thus treated as inferior. Because those who were lighter were believed to be from a higher class, they were also deemed to be not only beautiful, but also superior. While the authors acknowledge that colorism is a global phenomenon, the emphasis of this chapter is on Black people and their experiences in the United States. "Black" is used as an inclusive term for individuals of African descent or the term "African American." Additionally, the focus is on colorism and racial politics on some HBCU campuses located within U.S. territories.

Pulitzer Prize winning novelist Alice Walker is often credited with coining the postmodern term "colorism" in 1983 with her book, *In Search of Our Mothers' Gardens: Womanist Prose*. Walker states that

> . . . unless the question of colorism—in my definition, prejudicial or preferential treatment of same-race people based solely on their color—is addressed in our communities, and definitely in our Black sisterhoods, we cannot, as a people, progress. For colorism, like colonialism, sexism, and racism, impedes us. (Walker, 1983, p. 291)

In the U.S., colorism was the result of the historical practices of slave-owning Whites that divided Blacks by complexion (Dhillon-Jamerson, 2018). The roots of colorism for Black individuals in the U.S. began with chattel slavery and the perpetuation of the myth of White supremacy. While slave masters devised ways to keep enslaved people in bondage, skin tone emerged as a way to create, and sustain, a system of hierarchy on the plantation. The darker-skinned enslaved people were not given the same "privileges" of lighter-skin enslaved people. For instance, working in the house instead of outside in the fields was deemed a "privilege." Plantation owners and workers showed preference for individuals who were either mixed race or lighter-skinned. Blacks who were of lighter complexion were also thought to be better suited for intellectual and skilled labor, whereas darker complexioned Blacks were thought to be better suited for manual labor (Johnson, 2001; Neal & Wilson, 1989). These misconceptions were mostly perpetuated by slave owners who desired their progeny to have "better" treatment, despite remaining in bondage. The manufacturing of this intra-racial competition helped to create the long-lasting complex relationship that Blacks in the U.S. have with each other around complexion and hair texture. This complex, yet unfortunate, relationship was and is still seen on the campuses of many HBCUs.

Colorism at HBCUs

HBCUs were established for the purpose of educating formerly enslaved people, and most were established after the Civil War through the year 1964. However, three institutions were created prior to the Civil War: 1) Cheyney University of Pennsylvania (1837); 2) Lincoln University (1854); and 3) Wilberforce University (1856). In 2017, there were 102 HBCUs, both private and public, in 19 states, the District of Columbia, and the U.S. Virgin Islands. Most of the institutions are located in the Southern region of the United States. Many of the older HBCUs were established by, and/or supported by, Black churches. For example, Wilberforce University was initially established in 1856, but temporarily closed its doors in 1863 due to the outbreak of the Civil War. In March 1863, a bishop in the African Methodist Episcopal church negotiated the purchase of the land and buildings and reincorporated the university in July of the same year. The American Missionary Association (AMA) and the Freedmen's Bureau helped to establish numerous HBCUs such as Hampton University (formerly Institute), Fisk University, and Dillard University. The Freedmen's Bureau was an agency established in 1865 to provide assistance to the formerly enslaved Blacks and impoverished Whites in southern states and Washington, D.C. Additionally, a second Morrill Act of 1890 required former Confederate states to either prove that race was not used as an admission criterion, or to designate a land-grant institution for non-White students. There were 70 colleges and universities created from this act, and as a result, 19 HBCUs were founded (APLU, n.d.).

HBCUs were created to educate and uplift Blacks, however, there was still a pervasive practice of discrimination within the institutions. In the book, *Blacks in College,* Fleming (1984) identified the "Black Ivy League" which were eight elite HBCUs that educated the "upper echelon" of Blacks in the United States. There is some debate about the exact composition of what schools comprise the Black Ivy League, however, those most noted are Howard University (Washington, DC), Fisk University (Tennessee), Spelman College (Georgia), Morehouse College (Georgia), Hampton University (Virginia), Dillard University (Louisiana) Clark College (now merged as Clark-Atlanta University in Georgia), and Tuskegee University (Alabama). These institutions were believed to have attracted Blacks of higher socioeconomic status and contributed to the establishment of the Black bourgeoisie and skin tone discrimination, as lighter-skinned Blacks frequented these institutions (Gatewood, 2000).

As noted, most HBCUs were church affiliated and adopted church tenants including moral development and community service; however, other cultural practices were also transmitted to HBCUs. In *The Black Bourgeoisie,* by E. Franklin Frazier (1957), the seminal sociologist described that many Black churches still subscribed to exclusion based on complexion or hair texture. Many churches practiced the brown paper bag and/or comb test as admission criteria. The brown paper bag test was an exercise where a person's skin tone was matched to a brown paper bag. If the skin tone matched, or was lighter, admission was granted. A fine-toothed comb was used in the hair, and if it did not pass "with ease," the person could not attend the church. As one will read in the next section, these frivolous standards of beauty were used to determine which Black individuals were "worthy" of admittance to elite organizations and institutions, church congregations, and in leadership positions. Skin tone, according to Russell-Cole, Wilson, and Ronald (2013), is believed to be the most important and contentious attribute among Blacks. Mathews and Johnson (2015) noted that colorism erodes the framework of cultural identity, inclusion, mobility, and social acceptance.

In his 1930 commencement speech at Howard University, W.E.B. Du Bois revisited his debates with Booker T. Washington on vocational/industrial training versus liberal arts education (Foner, 1970). In his speech Du Bois explored and enumerated the aims of educating the formerly enslaved and their children in the *new* social and economic *South*; however, he bemoaned the current state of the Negro college in not doing enough to liberate the Black community. In a 1933 commencement speech at Fisk University, Du Bois provided a critique of what he referred to as "a university of the air," the type of institutions that provide "culture for the cultured" (Douglas, 2019, p. 69). Du Bois went on to assert that Black colleges and universities should embrace their African past and affirm their distinctive identities. Part of embracing African identity is to practice forms of resistance against White supremacy, including the notion that proximity to Whiteness included the physical embodiment of "White" or "European" characteristics.

These speeches and accompanying writings are evidence that Du Bois began revising his thesis on the "Talented Tenth," which many continued to use as a justification for social stratification as the role of HBCUs in training newly freed Negroes to assimilate into a new social and economic reality.

Respectability Politics

Respectability politics are established rules by which people from marginalized groups police their own members' behaviors to be more in alignment with dominant values (Harris, 2014). Higginbotham (1993) coined the term "politics of Black respectability" and defined it as the promotion of cleanliness, polite manners, self-restraint, sexual purity, and frugality to disrupt negative perceptions of Black people. Black American institutions (for example, family, church, schools) create and maintain the guidelines of respectable behavior of Black Americans. It is suggested that the interracial dynamics between Black and White people have shaped White people's perceptions of how Black people should comport themselves (Obasogie & Newman, 2016).

Historically, respectability politics served as a survival mechanism to mitigate experiences of racial discrimination. As such, due to the popular media images of Black people as being lazy and uneducated, Black leaders aimed to dismantle these stereotypes against Black Americans through success and achievement. This notion was deeply rooted in the HBCUs' history to uplift and empower the Black community through education and academic achievement (Albritton, 2012). Thus, early respectability politics challenged racist imagery of Black people by cultivating an "opposite" image—for example, a successful Black citizen (Obasogie & Newman, 2016). Furthermore, research has shown that those who endorse respectability politics may be more likely to alter the way they talk and behave in order to fit in or to accommodate others, which is referred to as identity shifting (Dickens, Womack, & Dimes, 2019).

Research has demonstrated that Black people engage in shifting behaviors in predominantly White settings to mitigate the negative consequences associated with discrimination (Dickens & Chavez, 2018; Jones & Shorter-Gooden, 2004). In some instances, Blacks may also alter the way they talk and behave in predominantly Black environments, such as HBCUs. For instance, the same stereotypes associated with Blacks that were socially constructed in the dominant White culture are internalized within the Black community and shape how Black people believe they should behave (Dickens, 2014).

These ideologies of respectability politics are reinforced on the campuses of HBCUs. To begin, there remains a divide between HBCU administrators and Black youth activists who are committed to combating social and political issues impacting the Black community. In 2017, Bethune Cookman University's students booed and turned their backs on Betsy DeVos, U.S. Secretary of education and the invited 2017 commencement speaker. This incident engendered discussions about how Black students should act in Black communities, in order for White people to feel comfortable. Additionally, HBCUs maintain strict codes of conduct, and if students disobey these that may lose certain privileges or may be subject to expulsion (Ihle, 1992). Guy-Sheftall and Cole (2003) insist that though all HBCU students are subject to campus rules, HBCUs have more restrictive rules for Black women that are guided to "protect" them and develop them into respectable women. In an article in Mic (Dionne, 2013), one HBCU student stated:

> Black female students are encouraged to conform to an unattainable ideal of Black womanhood, even at HBCUs. We're supposed to be dainty, quiet and dedicated to uplifting the community like Alabama State University alum Rosa Parks. We're forbidden from twerking. We're given strict curfews. We're told to wear pearls and stockings because that's what ladies do.

Moreover, Hampton University's MBA program had a policy banning cornrows and dreadlocks. In 2007, the then new president of Paul Quinn College in Texas, Michael Sorrell, discussed his newly implemented dress code stating that, "historically Black colleges have a history of expecting a certain level of dress as a way of preparing the students to combat the stereotypes which we know we all face" (Sorrell, 11/7/2007). Hence, HBCU campuses may dictate students' expressions through dress codes, thus creating a discriminatory climate for sexual freedom and homosexuality (Harper & Gasman, 2008; Njoku, Butler, & Beatty, 2017). It is important to note that HBCUs, similar to Predominantly White Institutions (PWIs), have dress codes; however, the enforcement of the dress codes often receives more attention at HBCUs. Respectability politics is still occurring at HBCUs, and HBCU faculty, staff, and leadership should work toward embracing all forms and expressions of Blackness.

Faculty Advancement and Leadership

Another way in which colorism and respectability politics has been upheld at HBCUs is through the hiring of administration and faculty. Researchers have posited that HBCUs have contributed to the Black bourgeoisie that was undergirded by skin-tone bias (Gatewood, 2000; Taylor, 2009). Many of the early HBCU administrators and faculty were White (Albritton, 2012; Anderson, 1988). It was not until the Great Depression, when funding and resources for HBCUs became limited, that HBCUs began hiring more Black administrators and faculty. After the Civil War, most Black people who received some manner of a "formal" or "informal" education were those who were often the offspring of White slave owners and, in turn, had more proximity "privilege" and resources (Gasman & Abiola, 2016). Additionally, many elite Black organizations had color tests that prospective members had to pass to gain membership into the organizations (Hall, 2008). Consequently, Blacks with lighter complexions were among the earliest Black HBCU leaders and educators.

However, there is evidence that stratifications based on skin tone are shifting. While there are no published studies on the topic of colorism among HBCU faculty, it appears that HBCUs employ Black faculty, across different skin tones, more than most non-HBCU institutions. Black tenured faculty constitutes 4.7% of the total number of tenured faculty in the U.S. HBCUs house a substantial proportion of Black faculty. Many faculty at HBCUs attended an HBCU (Collins, Davis, & Hilton, 2013). There are nearly twice as many Black tenure-track and tenured faculty at HBCUs in comparison to Black faculty at PWIs, due to the greater service demands and experiences of discrimination as a Black faculty member at a predominantly White institution (Butner, Burley, Marbey, 2000). Thirty percent of HBCU presidents are women in comparison to 25% at PWIs. Despite the lack of evidence for systemic colorism among HBCU faculty and leadership, colorism has traditionally been most pronounced among HBCU students including sororities/fraternities, homecoming queens, and student government positions (Giddings, 2007; Taylor, 2009).

Student Manifestations of Colorism at HBCUs

Though historically Black colleges have been lauded for their work as sites of resistance (Douglas, 2012), colorism is perpetuated throughout the HBCU student body culture. Many HBCUs require students to take courses in the African American experience, and some require psychology majors to study Black psychology. HBCU curricula often contain values and perspectives that are meant to challenge racism and white supremacy (Margolis, 2001). Many of these courses teach students from an African-centered lens about the history of colonization and its impact on internalized racism, internalization of European beauty ideals, and colorism, and thereby offer students a way to contextualize their experiences with colorism and develop new

107

modes of resistance.

Though these courses exist to teach students about skin color politics, colorism is pronounced within extracurricular activities, which play an important role in the experience of many HBCU students. Consequently, HBCUs' strong connection to traditions such as sororities and fraternities, and Homecoming Courts may perpetuate the legacy of colorism (Tindall, Hernandez, & Hughey, 2011). It is suggested that extracurricular activities served as a site for skin-tone discrimination on HBCU campuses (Gasman & Abioloa, 2016). As mentioned previously, colorism is gendered and often linked to class. In the context of HBCUs, colorism is identifiable in student organizations such as fraternities and sororities, homecoming queen competitions, and student leadership positions (Giddings, 2007; Taylor, 2009). As such, the Black sorority movement began at an HBCU in the early 1900s. Black sororities and fraternities provide students with the opportunity to learn about service and to build networks that extend beyond their college years. However, the history of colorism and classism as determinants of inclusion and exclusion within these organizations (Tindall, Hernandez, & Hughley, 2011) may persist in harmful ways, particularly for those who are excluded. Kerr (2006) suggests that darker-skin women were historically more likely to be members of Zeta Phi Beta Sorority Inc. or Delta Sigma Theta, Inc., and lighter-skin women were more likely to be members of Alpha Kappa Alpha Sorority Inc. While these practices may not be explicit, vestiges of these beliefs persist in campus organizations including sororities, fraternities, student government organizations, and homecoming courts.

As it relates to homecoming courts, these groups offer students the opportunity to represent their institution and provide leadership. Historically, most of the HBCU homecoming courts were lighter-skinned and were often selected by presidents of HBCUs who were more likely to be White women or men (Taylor, 2009). Yet, during the Civil Rights Movement and the Black Power Movement, ideas of Blackness were embraced and it changed the dynamics of skin color respectability politics on HBCU campuses (Gasman & Abioloa, 2016). Consequently, it was during the Civil Rights Movement that some Black Studies programs were being established at HBCUs. A new form of "Blackness" was being embraced and HBCU students took pride in their darker skin tones and natural hair, while alternatively some lighter-skinned Black people felt subject to questions about their authentic Blackness (Hunter, 2008; Piper, 1992). Today, students who are elected to homecoming courts become visual representations of the types of characteristics that the student body values. Taylor (2009) conducted interviews with Howard University students who pursued leadership roles on campus, such as homecoming court, and believed that their loss was due to their skin being too light or too dark. Moreover, in *Ebony* Magazine's *2018-2019 HBCU Homecoming Queens,* it highlights queens across 66 HBCUs. Though all of the queens ranged in different skin colors, it is interesting to note that less than ten of the women wore their hair in a non-straightened hair style, which is an example of texturism. Texturism, known as colorism in the natural hair community, is described as a preference for a certain type of natural hair such as loose curls, while ignoring other hair types such as kinky curls (Blay, 2016; Shepherd, 2018).Currently, while there may be less skin color-based discrimination in the selection of HBCU queens, there appear to be expectations regarding hair aesthetics. Black Americans' internalization of bias and favor for lighter skin, "European" features and "good hair" has been in the Black community for generations (Wilder, 2010). These findings illustrate the nuanced ways in which colorism and skin tone have significant implications for Black women. Because of the power of these representations to produce internalization of ideas about leadership, beauty, and worth (Jackson-Lowman, 2013), HBCUs should work to ensure that the legacy of colorism does not persist in these opportunities.

Influence of Mass Media

Mass media perpetuates colorism in our society and impacts HBCU students' understanding of skin color in various contexts: social settings, employment, and interpersonal relationships. Media is represented in many different forms including: television shows, webcasts, movies, websites, and social media platforms such as Instagram and Twitter. In the many courses that the authors teach, there are frequent discussions regarding topics trending on social media that are about the Black community. There is a lack of scholarly research on colorism and media and very little that explores these issues with respect to students at HBCUs. However, Black people are a significant portion of media consumers. Black college students in particular heavily use social media including Twitter and Instagram. Coyne, Padilla-Walker, and Howard (2013) noted that one of the most salient features of emerging adulthood (which includes college students) is the extensive use of media. On average, college students spend close to half of the day using some form of media. Current college students have unprecedented access to media through technological advances. With the amount of time college students spend accessing media, researchers claim they are "media saturated" (Vandewater, Rideout, Wartella, Huang, Lee, & Shim, 2007) and Black students spend more time utilizing media than other groups (Matabane & Merritt, 2014). Scholars have documented the connection between socialization and media exposure, particularly television (Hall & Smith, 2012; Tynes & Ward, 2009). Although emerging adults have greater access to a wide variety of Black images in the media than past generations, when the content of the media exposure presents a picture that has phenotypical characteristics closer to European standards of beauty are preferred, it can lead to students engaging in social comparison.

Social Comparison

At some HBCUs, courses in Black psychology are offered or required as part of the general education curriculum. In addition, other popular courses include those that focus on media such as social media. In both of these courses the topic of colorism is frequently brought up by students as an issue within the Black community. Students often engage in social comparisons based on content they view on their social media platforms. This is reflected via the continued popularity of Twitter hashtags such as #TeamLightSkin and #TeamDarkSkin. For example, in a study investigating colorism on Twitter, the authors suggest that hashtags such as #TeamLightSkin and #TeamDarkSkin demonstrate that America is neither post-racial, nor post-colorism (Williams, 2016). It is argued in various blogs and op-eds that in many cases posts demean darker-skinned African Americans whereas lighter-skinned African Americans are praised heavily. As noted by Dunlap-Fowler (2015) in her post entitled, *Colorism and Social Media*, many of the posts using these hashtags focused on attraction and hypersexualization based on skin complexion. Women who posted under #TeamLightSkin were often deemed highly desirable and attractive in comparison with those who displayed #TeamDarkSkin. Psychological research supports the notion that people deemed attractive benefit from the halo effect, a cognitive bias perception that people are thought to be smarter and friendlier based on characteristics such as appearance (Hatfield & Sprecher, 1986). For Black men posting under the hashtag, issues of attraction and hypersexualization were replaced with degrees of aggression, masculinity, and authenticity. Lighter men were still deemed attractive and desirable; however, they were not perceived to be as masculine or "authentically Black" as darker men. Additionally, there were still more negative associations with darker-hued men than their lighter counterparts.

Television

In a study examining television viewers' emotional discomfort with a crime story and perceptions and memorability of a perpetrator and victim, participants were exposed to a White, lighter-skinned Black, medium-skinned Black, or a darker-skinned Black perpetrator (Dixon & Maddox, 2005). Results indicated that those who self-reported as heavy television news viewers were more likely than lighter viewers to feel emotional discomfort after being exposed to the darker-skinned Black perpetrator. Furthermore, heavy news viewers also had favorable perceptions of the victim when the perpetrator was Black, regardless of skin tone. Results also indicated that all participants, regardless of prior news exposure, found the perpetrator more memorable when the perpetrator was a darker-skinned Black male.

Music

While a variety of musical genres contain references that could be interpreted as colorism, rap music has been a consistent source of gendered colorism for decades. Why is this relevant to HBCUs? Because Black emerging adults are frequent and consistent consumers of rap music and fervent supporters of rappers and Hip-Hop culture. Rap music and rappers have a global presence and influence and are major contributors to the discourse surrounding complexion and hair texture preference. Research on rap lyrics and colorism have found that rap lyrics perpetuate the stereotype that lighter complexions are the ultimate standard of beauty. In a research study exploring the ways in which rap music covertly or overtly transmits skin-color related messages to African American female adolescents, results demonstrated three themes including: 1) preferences for women with lighter complexioned skin; 2) unfavorable messages about or exclusion of women with darker complexioned skin; and 3) use of skin color nicknames (Maxwell, Abrams, & Belgrave, 2016). Three classic examples of lyrical content glorifying lighter-complexioned women are:

• Lil' Boosie shouting out "redbones and caramels" on his 2007 classic, *Wipe Me Down*

• Gucci Mane proclaiming he liked "yellow everything" including "yellow bones" on his 2009 song, *Lemonade*

• Lil' Wayne rhyming about "beautiful Black women, I bet that bitch look better red" on his 2010 track, *Right Above It*

While there are numerous examples of rappers in the 1980s and 1990s who perpetuated skin tone and hair texture preference in their songs, more recent songs seem to be more overt and this content seems to have exploded in the 21st century. Additionally, all one has to do is attend any event on the "Yard" (campus) of an HBCU to hear these songs in heavy rotation. Other songs that ascribe positive attributes to women who look "exotic" or refer to people by colorist labels by both male and female rappers are also guaranteed to be requested.

Many rappers do not talk about skin-tone beliefs and practices within the Black community, but one can infer someone's partner preferences by looking at their dating histories. Others make their partialities known through interviews and/or the use of social media. For instance, in 2016 rapper/producer Kanye West (Yeezy) tweeted about an upcoming casting call for "multiracial women only" for his fashion show. This caused quite a bit of backlash on Black Twitter for its implications about who is deemed beautiful, attractive, and worthy to be in the Yeezy show. However, one must remember Kanye is the same rapper who warned Black women to be aware because "he'll leave yo' ass for a White girl." Another example of rappers directly expressing their preference happened in the summer of 2017. Kodak Black, a darker-skin rapper from Florida stated his feelings about the attractiveness of a well-known Black actress. He stated ". . . she straight. . . but I don't really like Black girls like that." He went on to say, "I love Black, African-American women; it's just not my forte to deal with a darker-skin woman. I prefer them to have a lighter complexion than me. #MyPreference #FuckYou" (Grapevine, 2017).

A content analysis study examining rap videos revealed that the men and women in those videos differ in their appearance, with more Black women appearing to have Eurocentric features (Conrad, Dixon, & Zhang, 2009). For example, Kanye West's video for his song *Power* presents a surreal visual display of a Black man at the center of the video with a bevy of women rotating around and below him. The vast majority of the women in the video fit a certain aesthetic that is closer to White than Black.

Internalized colorism

As Generation Z students (born between 1996 and 2010) enter HBCUs, faculty find themselves addressing colorism with students continuously. While the representations of colorism may look different than when the authors were in college, the issue is still as pervasive now as it was then. Because colorism is an internalized system of hegemonic control within the Black community, preference for lighter-skinned Blacks is widely accepted in the media produced for Blacks (Steele, 2016).

As noted, colorism at HBCUs often presents itself in student organizations. Classic examples of portraying colorism in an HBCU context can be seen in movies, such as *School Daze*, and TV shows such as *A Different World*. For example, in Spike Lee's

School Daze, comparisons were specifically made between sororities and fraternities based on skin tone and hair texture. In the film, he illuminates the skin color bias that existed and continues to persist in some Black sororities. The "Wannabees" were lighter-skinned women who came from middle- or upper-class families and were representations of European standards of beauty. The "Jigaboos" were darker-skinned women who, primarily, came from working-class families, were not interested in assimilating, and were proud of their African features. One of the most seminal moments in the film is a scene in Madame Re-Res Beauty Salon where the Wannabees and Jigaboos sing about good or bad hair in the song "Straight and Nappy." The opening verse, sung by the Wannabees says:

> Don't you wish you had hair like this
>
> Then the boys would give you a kiss
>
> Talk about nothin' but bliss
>
> Then you gonna see what you missed

Toward the end of the song, the Jigaboos say:

> Don't you ever worry 'bout that
>
> Cause I don't mind being Black
>
> Oh with your old mixed up head
>
> I ain't ever gonna be your friend

This contrast is indicative of the HBCU experience for some students. Even though *School Daze* was released in 1988, this debate about "good" or "bad" hair is still happening on HBCU campuses across the nation. While students attending HBCUs may not encounter the same level of racial tension and discrimination as they would on a PWI, these campuses are not exempt from these issues. Student perceptions and experiences on college campuses are integral to their success both in school, and post-college years (Museus & Quaye, 2009). Coming to a university and expecting to be embraced for simply being Black is not the experience that all students have. A *Los Angeles Times* article (Kaleem & Lee, 2019) interviewed current and former HBCU students about their experiences on campus. While they were overwhelmingly positive, one alumna who identified as mixed race indicated that while she enjoyed her time at her HBCU, she felt the effects of colorism on campus. She felt "judged because of the color of my skin—like I'm not Black enough." Some students relied on the media to guide their expectations of college life at an HBCU.

A Different World, a spin-off of *The Cosby Show*, was one of the first introductions to life on an HBCU campus for many mainstream viewers. Both shows are believed to have influenced a generation of students to consider, and attend, HBCUs. They depicted personal and professional success and fulfillment as a result of their experiences at HBCUs. Tackling controversial issues on primetime television is not new, but issues that are as pertinent in the Black community such as colorism was ground-breaking back in 1991. Some may remember the episode "Mammy Dearest" where Kim, a darker-skinned working-class student who roomed with Whitley Gilbert, a lighter-skinned, upper-middle-class self-proclaimed Southern belle. Whitley was in charge of creating an art exhibit and decided to focus on Black women in history. The exhibit included stereotypical "Mammy" items and Kim, along with other friends, expressed discomfort with the representations. During the episode, one sees Kim and Whitley come to terms with their own beliefs and experiences with colorism.

Other recent television shows have tackled colorism, such as *Dear White People*, a show about Black students at a PWI, have also tackled this issue, along with *Grownish*, a spinoff of *Blackish*, a show about a group of students of color at a PWI. *Blackish* tackled colorism in the episode entitled "Black Like Us." Diane, Jack's twin and the youngest daughter, comes home with school photographs that are unflattering because the photographer did not adjust the light for Diane's darker complexion. This incites a heated conversation among the parents, but Diane wants to move on. Junior, the oldest son in the family, mentions that he thinks the family has complexion issues and recites some of the jokes that other family members have said over the years about him being the lightest person in the family. The grandmother, Ruby, notes that "light-skins don't have problems." Diane describes her experiences as the darkest member of the family, the frequent micro-aggressions she deals with based on her appearance, and how she is aware that society believes lighter skin is better.

Other noteworthy contributions to the conversation about colorism include the documentaries *Dark Girls* (Berry, Berry & Duke, 2011) and *Light Girls* (Berry, Berry, & Duke 2015). Both documentaries address the issue of colorism globally. Colorism is also present in reality TV shows. Lifetime's *Married at First Sight* once featured a Black man speaking about his preferences for a mate. Not only did he mention weight, but commented that he does not want to marry a woman darker than his "butterscotch" color (The Grio, 2018). The films and television shows mentioned help document colorism in the U.S. and help spark the conversation with students—they find the content relatable and engaging. It is important to provide relevant content about colorism and racial politics for fruitful discussions with students inside and outside of the classroom. It is equally important, if not more important, for vested HBCU faculty to engage students in strategies that critically examine the persistent messages that support and perpetuate colorism and its negative effects.

Resisting

Although considerable research has focused on the persistence of colorism among Black Americans, there are demonstrated efforts to resist and contest the perpetuation of colorism within the Black community. Social connotations associated with darker skin still tend to be negative, especially for Black women. In a qualitative study examining colorism, self-esteem, and resiliency among darker-skinned Black Americans, the experiences of darker-skinned Black American women varied significantly between them and other Black women (Pearson-Trammell, 2010). As such, findings suggested that protective factors such as familial support, social support, and faith were especially valuable in the rejection of a negative self-image and the internalization of a positive self-image. Support from primary caregivers during childhood and adolescence was also found to be key in the establishment of a healthy self-esteem despite being negatively impacted by colorism. Furthermore, the authors suggest that creating a community and social support network of those who did not perpetuate colorism was positively associated with resilience (Pearson-Trammell, 2010). Resiliency included actively resisting colorism's influence through educating oneself on the history of oppression and internalized oppression within the Black American community. A quantitative study conducted with 93 young Black women (aged 18-23) attending an HBCU investigated how colorism affects their daily lives (Mathews & Johnson, 2015). Results reveal that women who identified as having a darker complexion reported higher incidences of colorism and agreed that society devalues their tone more than those who are lighter. However, when asked if, given the opportunity to change to a lighter hue, they stated they would remain the same color. Creating an environment where the whole person is affirmed, not just one characteristic, can solidify a strong sense of self that will follow both men and women throughout their lives.

Another way in which the Black community can resist colorism is by deconstructing the language surrounding skin color. Historically, the color language in Black American culture has positive words associated with lighter skin tone, such as "bright" and "sexy red," while negative words such as "chocolate" and "tar baby" are used to describe darker skin tone (Parrish, 1946). Furthermore, Wilder (2010) conducted focus groups examining internalized scripts about color among Black women and found that many shared how they are impacted by the predominant stereotypes of lighter-skinned girls as pretty and darker-skinned girls as ghetto, which mirror the ideology from previous generations. Additionally, Wilder and Cain (2011) explored the influence of families on the development and maintenance of colorist consciousness among Black women. The researchers found that while some of the Black women's families were responsible for instilling judgmental thoughts about skin tone, others expressed how their families taught them to embrace and celebrate all hues of Blackness. Those who were exposed to language and behaviors that promoted positive attributes of both lighter and darker skin did not discriminate against others based on skin tone.

As we discussed earlier, media can be used to perpetuate colorism but it is also used as a tool of resistance. A search on Twitter using the terms "colorism" and "HBCUs" reveals a large number of tweets condemning the continuation of colorism on HBCU campuses. On Instagram, a search of #colorism results in over 55,000 posts. These posts include messages such as, "It's ok to love your light skin. You're not embracing White supremacy. You were born with that skin color. You're embracing yourself. #selflove" and "If you're dark-skinned, you don't have to brighten your selfies, Love— you are gorgeous just the way you are." This suggests that social media may serve as an impactful intervention tool to combat colorism. Additionally, there are rappers who have spoken out about colorism in the music industry and the media. For example, Wale (a Nigerian-born rapper), Rapsody (rapper from North Carolina), and J. Cole (biracial rapper from North Carolina) have all discussed the impact of colorism on their success.

Implications for Policy, Research, and Practice

HBCUs are uniquely positioned to develop the strategies most beneficial for creating resilient young people who actively resist colorism. HBCUs can analyze patterns of treatment of individuals within classroom spaces, organizations, and leadership and implement action plans to address patterns of inequities. Past research suggests that awareness of colorism and preferential preference for lighter skin may influence sense of belonging and acceptance in a predominately Black or in a predominately White setting (Awad et al., 2015).

Additionally, HBCUs have the faculty, students, and expertise to expand the work of developing curricula designed to educate people about the diversity of Black/African contributions across the Diaspora and to educate students and faculty on the history of colonization, internalized oppression, and colorism. As such, HBCU students in programs or majors involving social justice, criminology, sociology, and so on should have lessons/courses about colorism incorporated into their degree plan (Gasman &

Abiola, 2016). Also, HBCUs can invite speakers to campus to discuss the issue and colleges can have film discussions about colorism (Gasman & Abiola, 2016).

Faculty at HBCUs need to engage in more research and scholarship regarding colorism. Many of the studies are based on older generations, and/or utilize older representations in media. As Matane and Merritt (2014) noted, present-day youth and emerging adults have different perspectives and lived experiences than those from previous eras. Much of the published literature examines the perceptions and experiences of Black women, as they seem to bear the brunt of colorism. However, colorism is not a "woman" problem. More research on the perceptions, socialization, and experiences of Black youth and men is needed. While it may be difficult to accept, skin color and hair texture still matter in the U.S. HBCUs can combat colorism and respectability politics by embracing all types of Blackness. In doing so, HBCUs can create the next generation of educators and leaders poised to disrupt the legacy of colorism.

Process Questions and Considerations

The authors leave you with five questions to process about colorism and racial politics at HBCUs:

1. Are respectability politics still serving as a survival mechanism to mitigate experiences of racial discrimination? If not, what purpose are they serving for Black students attending HBCUs?

2. In what ways can HBCUs counteract media's conceptualizations of colorism?

3. What are some practical strategies that faculty, staff, and administrators at HBCUs can use to resist the continued perpetuation of colorism on campus?

4. Is it truly possible to "embrace all types of Blackness" on HBCU campuses, and how would that look in terms of formal and informal policies?

5. Why is it important that HBCUs provide spaces to resist colorism?

References

Albritton, T. J. (2012). Educating our own: The historical legacy of HBCUs and their relevance for educating a new generation of leaders. *The Urban Review*, 44(3), 311-331. https://doi.org/10.1007/s11256-012-0202-9

Anderson, J. D. (1988). *The education of Blacks in the south*, 1860-1935. Chapel Hill, NC: The University of North Carolina Press.

Association of Public and Land Grant Universities (n.d.). *1890 Universities*. Retrieved from: https://www.aplu.org/members/councils/1890-universities

Awad, G. H., Norwood, C., Taylor, D. S., Martinez, M., McClain, S., Jones, B. & Chapman-Hilliard, C. (2015). Beauty and body image concerns among African American college women. *Journal of Black*

Psychology, 41(6), 540-564. https://doi.org/10.1177/0095798414550864

Berry, D. C. (Producer), Berry, D. C., & Duke, B. (Directors) (2011). *Dark girls* [Motion picture documentary]. Los Angeles, CA: Urban Winter Entertainment.

Berry, D. C., Duke, B., Berry, D., & Duke, B. (2015). *Light Girls* [Motion Picture]. Chatsworth, CA: Urban Winter Entertainment & Duke Media.

Blay, Z. (2016, January 05). Let's talk about colorism in the natural hair community Retrieved September 14, 2017, from Huffington Post: http://www.huffingtonpost.com/entry/lets-talk-about-colorism-in-the-natural-haircommunity_us_566df1dfe4b011b83a6ba4f0

Butner, B. K., Burley, H., & Marbley, A. F. (2000). Coping with the unexpected: Black faculty at predominately white institutions. *Journal of Black Studies, 30*(3), 453-462.

Collins, E., Davis, C. H., & Hilton, A. A. (2013). The relevance of Historically Black Colleges and Universities in preparing Black educators and teachers. *eJEP: eJournal of Education Policy.* Retrieved from http://nau.edu/COE/eJournal/_Forms/Fall2013/CollinsHunterDavisandHilton/

Conrad, K., Dixon, T. L., Zhang, Y. (2009). Controversial rap themes, gender portrayals and skin tone distortion: A content analysis of rap music videos. *Journal of Broadcasting & Electronic Media, 51*(1), 134-156

Coyne, S. M., Padilla-Walker, L. M., & Howard, E. (2013). Emerging in a digital world: A decade review of media use, effects, and gratifications in emerging adulthood. *Emerging Adulthood,* 1, 125-137. DOI:10.1177/2167696813479782

Dhillon-Jamerson, K. K. (2018). Euro-Americans favoring people of color: Covert racism and economies of white colorism. *American Behavioral Scientist, 62*(14), 2087-2100.

Dickens, D. D. (2014). *Double consciousness: The negotiation of the intersectionality of Identities among academically successful black women* (Unpublished dissertation). Colorado State University, Colorado.

Dickens, D. D., & Chavez, E. L. (2018). Navigating the workplace: The costs and benefits of shifting identities at work among early career US black women. *Sex Roles, 78*(11-12), 760-774. https://doi.org/10.1007/s11199-017-0844-x

Dickens, D. D., Womack, V. Y., & Dimes, T. (2019). Managing hypervisibility: An exploration of theory and research on identity shifting strategies in the workplace among black women. *Journal of Vocational Behavior,* 113, 153-163. https://doi.org/10.1016/j.jvb.2018.10.008

Dionne, E. (2013). *College taught me that as a black woman, I had to wear pearls.* Retrieved December 1, 2019. https://www.mic.com/articles/73491/college-taught-me-that-as-a-black-woman-i-had-to-wear-pearls

Dixon, T. L., & Maddox, K. B. (2005). Skin tone, crime news, and social reality judgments: Priming the stereotype of the dark and dangerous black criminal. *Journal of Applied Social Psychology, 35*(8), 1555-1570.

Douglas, A. J. (2019). *W.E.B. DuBois and the critique of the competitive society.* Athens, GA: The University of Georgia Press.

Douglas, T.R.M. (2012). HBCUs as sites of resistance: The malignity of materialism, western masculinity, and spiritual malefaction. *The Urban Review, 44*(3), 378-400.

Dunlap-Fowler, W. (2015, January). *Colorism and social media.* Retrieved from:https://medium.com/@WhitneyDunlapF/colorism-and-social-media-24e0948d1287

Fleming, J. (1984). *Blacks in college: A comparative study of students' success in black and white institutions.* San Francisco, CA: Jossey-Bass.

Foner, P. S. (Ed.). (1970). *W.E.B. DuBois speaks: Speeches and addresses 1890-1963.* Pathfinder Press.

Frazier, E. F. (1957). *Black bourgeoisie.* Glencoe, IL: Free Press.

Gasman, M., & Abiola, U. (2016). Colorism within the historically Black colleges and universities (HBCUs). *Theory into Practice, 55*(1), 39-45. https://doi.org/10.1080/00405841.2016.1119018

Gatewood, W. B. (2000). *Aristocrats of color: The educated Black elite,* 1880-1920. Fayetteville, AK: University of Arkansas

Giddings, P. (2007). *In search of sisterhood: Delta sigma theta and the challenge of the black sorority movement.* New York, NY: William Morrow.

Grapevine (2017, June 27). *Dark skinned black women should be relieved that Kodak Black doesn't like them.* Retrieved: https://thegrapevine.theroot.com/dark-skinned-black-woman-should-be-relieved-that-kodak-1796460765

Grio (2018, July 16). *Color struck Black man on "Married at First Sight" angers fans, "I don't prefer women who are darker than me."* Retrieved from: https://thegrio.com/2018/07/16/color-struck-black-man-on-married-at-first-sight-angers-fans-i-really-dont-prefer-women-that-are-darker-than-me/

Guy-Sheftall, B., & Cole, J. B. (2003). *Gender talk: The struggle for women's equality in African American communities.* New York: Random House.

Hall, H. R., & Smith, E. L. (2012). "This Is Not Reality . . . It's Only TV": African American girls respond to media (mis)representations. *The New Educator 8*(3), 222-42.

Hall, R. E. (1992). Bias among African Americans regarding skin color: Implications for social work practice. *Research on Social Work Practice, 2*(4), 479-486.

Harper, S. R., & Gasman, M. (2008). Consequences of conservatism: Black male undergraduates and the politics of Historically Black Colleges and Universities. *The Journal of Negro Education, 77*(4), 336-351.

Harris, F. C. (2014). The rise of respectability politics. *Dissent, 61*(1), 33-37.

Hatfield, E., & Sprecher, S. (1986). *Mirror, mirror: The importance of looks in everyday life.* Albany, NY: State University of New York Press.

Higginbotham, E. B. (1993). The politics of respectability. *Righteous discontent: The women's movement in the Black Baptist church, 1880-1920,* 185-230.

Hunter, M. (2008). The cost of color: What we pay for being Black and brown. In *Racism in the 21st Century* (pp. 63-76). New York, NY: Springer.

Hunter, M. (2007). The persistent problem of colorism: Skin tone, status, and inequality. *Sociology Compass, 1*(1), 237-254.

Ihle, E. L. (1992). *Black women in higher education: An anthology of essays, studies, and documents* (Vol. 2). Taylor & Francis.

Jackson-Lowman, H. (2013). An analysis of the impact of Eurocentric concepts of beauty on the lives of African American women. *African American women: Living at the crossroads of race, gender, class, and culture,* pp. 155-172.

Johnson, W. (2001). *Soul by soul: Life inside the antebellum slave market.* Cambridge, MA: Harvard University Press.

Jones, C., & Shorter-Gooden, K. (2004). *Shifting: The lives of black women in America.* New York, NY: Harper Collins.

Kaleem, J., & Lee, K. (2019, April 22). *We asked for your experiences at Historically Black Colleges. These are your stories.* Los Angeles Times. Retrieved from: https://www.latimes.com/nation/la-na-hbcu-reader-experiences-20190422-story.html

Kerr, A. E. (2005). The paper bag principle: Of the myth and the motion of colorism. *Journal of American folklore, 118*(469), 271-289.

Kerr, A. E. (2006). *The Paper Bag Principle: Class, colorism, and rumor and the case of Black Washington, DC.* Univ. of Tennessee Press.

Margolis, E. (2001). *The hidden curriculum in higher education.* Routledge.

Matabane, P. W., & Merritt, B. D. (2014). Media use, gender, and African American college attendance: The Cosby effect. *Howard Journal of Communications, 25,* 452-471.

Mathews, T. J., & Johnson, G. S. (2015). Skin complexion in the twenty-first century: The impact of colorism on African American women. *Race, Gender & Class, 22*(1-2), 248-274.

Maxwell, M. L., Abrams, J. A., Belgrave, F. Z. (2016). Redbones and earth mothers: A contemporary exploration of colorism and its perception among African American female adolescents. *Psychology of Music, 44*(6), 1488-1499.

Museus, S. D., & Quaye, S. J. (2009). Toward an intercultural perspective of racial and ethnic minority college student persistence. *The Review of Higher Education, 33*(1), 67-94.

Neal, A. M., & Wilson, M. L. (1989). The role of skin color and features in the Black community: Implications for Black women and therapy. *Clinical Psychology Review, 9*(3), 323-333.

Njoku, N., Butler, M., & Beatty, C. C. (2017). Reimagining the Historically Black College and University (HBCU) environment: Exposing race secrets and the binding chains of respectability and other mothering. *International Journal of Qualitative Studies in Education, 30(8)*, 783-799.

Norwood, K. J. (2015). "If you is white, you's alright. . . " Stories about colorism in America. *Washington University Global Studies Law Review, 14*, 585-607.

Obasogie, O. K., & Newman, Z. (2016). Black Lives Matter and respectability politics in local news accounts of officer-involved civilian deaths: An early empirical assessment. *Wisconsin Law Review*, 541- 574.

Parrish, C. H. (1946). Color names and color notions. *The Journal of Negro Education,* 15(1), 13-20. https://www.jstor.org/stable/2966307

Pearson-Trammell, N. (2010). *Colorism, self-esteem, and resiliency: A qualitative study of dark skinned African American women.* California Institute of Integral Studies.

Piper, A. (1992). Passing for white, passing for black. *Transition* (58), 4-32.

Reece, R. (2018). Genesis of U.S. colorism and skin tone stratification: Slavery, freedom, and Mulatto-Black occupational inequality in the late 19th century. *The Review of Black Political Economy, 45*(1), 3-21.

Russell-Cole, K., Wilson, M., & Ronald, E. H. (2013). *The color complex: The politics of skin color in a new millennium.* New York, NY: Anchor Books.

Shepherd, J. M. (2018). Don't touch my crown: Texturism as an extension of colorism in the natural hair community. Thesis. Texas State University. Retrieved from https://digital.library.txstate.edu/handle/10877/7886

Sorrell, M. (2007, November 7). HBCU President enforces strict dress code. (M. Martin, Interviewer). *National Public Radio News.* Retrieved from https://www.npr.org/templates/story/story.php?storyId=16069645.

Steele, C. K. (2016) Pride and prejudice: Pervasiveness of colorism and the animated series "Proud Family." *Howard Journal of Communications, 27,* 53-67

Taylor, B. (2009). Color and class: The promulgation of elitist attitudes at black colleges. In M. Gasman & C. Tudico (Eds.), *Triumphs, troubles, and taboos: Historically Black Colleges and Universities.* New York, NY: Palgrave Press.

Tindall, N. T., Hernandez, M. D., & Hughey, M. W. (2011). Doing a good job at a bad thing: prevalence and perpetuation of stereotypes among members of historically black sororities. *Oracle: The Research Journal of the Association of Fraternity/Sorority Advisors, 6*(2).

Tynes, B., & Ward, L. M. (2009). The role of media use and portrayals in African Americans' psychosocial development. In H. A. Neville, B. M. Tynes, & S. O. Utsey (Eds.), *Handbook of African American Psychology* (pp. 143-158), Thousand Oaks, CA: SAGE.

Vandewater, E. A., Rideout, V. J., Wartella, E. A., Huang, X., Lee, J. H., & Shim, M. (2007). Digital childhood: Electronic media and technology use among infants, toddlers, and preschoolers. *Pediatrics, 119,* e1006-e1015.

Walker, A. (1983). *In search of our mothers' gardens: Womanist prose.* San Diego, CA: Harcourt Brace Jovanovich.

Wilder, J. (2010). Revisiting color names and color notions: A contemporary examination of the language and attitudes of skin color among young black women. *Journal of Black studies, 41*(1), 184-206. https://doi.org/10.1177/0021934709337986

Wilder, J., & Cain, C. (2011). Teaching and learning color consciousness in black families: Exploring family processes and women's experiences with colorism. *Journal of Family Issues, 32*(5), 577-604. https://doi.org/10.1177/0192513X10390858

CHAPTER 6.

Shedding Light on African American Colorist Legacies in Education

P. Quick Hall, African American Education and Research Organization
K. Melchor Quick Hall, Fielding Graduate University

> Admittedly, there is a grave danger in bringing up the question of hair and skin color
> when we need more than anything else to become united and are finally moving in that
> direction. . . . But we cannot become truly unified until we sift out the problem. Although
> I do not subscribe to the belief that slavery and colonialism left us dehumanized (far from
> it!), I do believe, however, that in the area of color-consciousness, we have been brutally
> scarred.
>
> Ann Cook, *Black Pride? Some Contradictions*, pp. 151-152

Cook highlights both the danger and the high stakes in an essay about colorism in
education. There is the risk, with so much to be done in a white supremacist U.S.
education system, that this conversation will somehow distract White folks from their
responsibility to dismantle racism in an educational system that serves "Whites only."
At the same time, there is the dire need to sift through the intra-communal rifts within
the African American communities that threaten to destroy us.

Some people within the African American community might see this chapter
as an airing of our dirty laundry—sometimes described as "African Americans'
pernicious, persistent dirty little secret—colorism, color-conscious, color-struck, color
complex" (Golden, 2004, p. 7). In this chapter we aim to make explicit the connection
between color and power. We do this by discussing the relationship between color,
educational status, and privileges, which impacts economic (and other) opportunities.
This conversation about intra-racial colorism, which occurs "when a member of one
racial group makes a distinction based upon skin color between members of her own
race" (Jones, 2000, pp. 1498-1499), is engaged from the perspective of two generations
of Black female educators.

We believe that our work must address colorist hierarchies. As Farah Jasmine Griffin
wrote, "The issue of colorism, of distinctions based on grade of hair and keenness

of features, tears at the very fabric of who we are as a people" (Griffin, 2001, pp. 220-221). (Use of the term *grade* to differentiate hair textures reflects the hierarchical characterization of this variation.) In this chapter, we suggest some piecemeal mending, following the quilting tradition that has been so important to African American culture and tradition. To start, we contextualize our perspectives through our joint and individual histories.

We Are Family: Education and Intentions

We are two Black women with doctorates, a mother and daughter, who constitute the fourth and fifth generations of college-educated African Americans in our family line. The benefits related to this educational privilege have been social and material. In many ways, our family resembles Lawrence Otis Graham's (1999) *Our Kind of People: Inside America's Black Upper Class*. Both of us were born in Washington, DC, where we were, for at least a short period of time, part of the Black elite invitation-only "Jack and Jill" children's organization, which required selection of upper-middle-class Black women to join the mothers' club. Our mothers are lighter-skinned—some would say almost passably White were it not for their features and hair. Although we were born in the nation's capital, we both spent significant portions of our childhood in North Carolina, where we were privileged by our more northern origins as well as by access to and association with the elite Pinehurst Country Club, where our (also fair-skinned) father (or grandfather in the case of the daughter) golfed once Blacks were allowed on the course. In short, we both grew up in a "Negroland. . . where residents were sheltered by a certain amount of privilege and plenty" (Jefferson, 2015, p. 3).

For much of our lives, we have been educators. The mother, now retired from teaching, founded a nonprofit organization, African American Education and Research Organization (AAERO), which she now leads as president of the Board of Directors. AAERO was designed to transfer the benefits of her privileged background to other African Americans through the dissemination of informal teachings that are an integral part of climbing the Black (and sometimes White) elite social ladder. The daughter works at a predominately White, graduate-only university, supervising doctoral students. Our first schools and teachers were all Black, and our PhD-granting institutions were predominately White. We have experienced the contrast between "education as the practice of freedom and education that merely strives to reinforce dominance" (Hooks, 1994, p. 4). Our early experiences in Black schools were aimed at socializing free Black people, who were not subordinate to White people in any way. Our later experiences

123

at White schools were structured without any attention to the rich Black educational legacies that informed our early years, and in ways that reinforced racial hierarchies (i.e., White dominance and Black subordination).

At the same time, we have been socialized to understand the particularities of Black women's educational status. The mother co-author has maternal and paternal aunts and grandmothers who attended the historically Black, all-women's Bennett College in North Carolina. These four college-educated women, in addition to numerous cousins, embodied what it meant to be among the Black, female, educated elite. In order to understand this history, we provide some context from the city where both co-authors were born, Washington, DC. We start with the color politics of DC's historically Black Howard University, the alma mater of the mother in this co-authoring pair and her father.

The Capital of Color Consciousness: DC's Howard University

When Marita Golden wrote about a mulatto or lighter-skinned Black elite that spanned U.S. cities, she described DC as "the 'capital' of colorism" (Golden, 2004, p. 42). In spite of the characterization of DC as "Chocolate City" because of its predominately Black population, colorist social norms enforced by lighter-skinned Blacks had a tremendous impact on African American life and education in the city. Howard University's students were described as "the future polite society of NAACP cocktail parties" (Wallace, 2015, p. 8). In this way, the city acted as a hub for national race politics. The university was "a beacon in and builder of the Washington and national Black community" (Golden, 2004, p. 46). Both co-authors of this article have had experience as students and employees at Howard. We are familiar with the notoriously color-coded fraternities and sororities that shaped so much of social life on campus. Although neither of us joined a sorority, our status as light (and light brown) women of educational privilege meant that we need not worry about the networks that would land us in the right internship, job, or marriage. We were aware of colorist politics and entered with the power and status to navigate them as we chose. This historical significance of skin color privilege (as paired with other forms of privilege) is critical to understanding our perspectives and the stories we share in our personal narratives. Before engaging our personal narratives, we want to acknowledge a long history of educational privilege experiences by lighter-skinned Black (and especially mulatto) people.

From Mulatto to Light-Skinned Black Skin Color Privilege

In contemporary discussions of predominately White institutions, or PWIs, and historically Black colleges and universities, or HBCUs, the prior existence of a three-tier system (described below) that included mulattoes, or lighter-skinned Blacks, is sometimes overlooked. However, the privilege of lighter-skinned Blacks can be linked to earlier privileges of a mulatto class and "the early division between house slaves and field slaves and the fact that, due to the status of their White fathers, some light-skinned slaves were granted greater educational and professional opportunities" (Jones, 2000, pp. 1527-1528). According to Jones (2000, p. 1515), "The origin of colorism is inextricably linked to the way in which colonial legislatures responded to this question because one of the more distinguishing features of mulattoes, or mixed-race individuals, was skin tone ." Often this moment in history is rushed over, but this three-tier system of Whites, Mulattoes, and Blacks was important to the investment in and development of educational systems that were later simply described as Black (for example, historically Black colleges).

> One of the most important areas in which mulattoes received superior treatment to darker-skinned Blacks was in education. Mulattoes formed preparatory schools and colleges that denied access to persons who were too dark. Many historically Black colleges and universities established in the nineteenth century also discriminated on the basis of color in their admissions process. Not only were educational institutions segregated by color, but their curricula differed as well. In schools attended by mulattoes, students received a liberal arts education. By contrast, darker-skinned Blacks were taught in schools and programs that focused primarily on vocational learning. This focus on training in practical skills reinforced the placement of darker-skinned Blacks into lower-paying, less-skilled positions (Jones 2000, p. 1516).

Linking racism and colorism, Hunter (2005) described how "communities of color themselves are divided into quasi-racial hierarchies. Without a larger system of institutional racism, colorism based on skin tone would not exist. Colorism is part and parcel of racism and exists because of it" (Hunter, 2005, p. 7). To be clear, colorism was an important extension of violence against African Americans, designed to extend the privileges of White parents to their mulatto children.

> As one of the violent mechanisms of social control that whites exercised against African Americans, sexual violence, including rape, was part of the beginning of the skin color stratification process itself. This violent method of social

control produced two important effects. The first and most obvious result was the creation of racially mixed children by white fathers and [B]lack mothers. The second more long-term effect was the creation of a color hierarchy through systematic privileging of light-skinned African Americans over darker-skinned African Americans (Hunter, 2005, pp. 17-18).

In different parts of the country, this question of the status and privilege of the mulatto class was initially answered in different ways: "In the North and in the Upper South, mixed-race persons shared the same status as Blacks under the one-drop rule. In the Lower South, distinctions within the Black population based upon mixed-racial heritage and skin color were made routinely" (Jones, 2000, p. 1509). Under the one-drop rule, a drop of Black blood meant that an individual had the legal status of being Black. In the Lower South region of the U.S., which extended from parts of North Carolina to the Gulf of Mexico, some mulattoes owned slaves. Even when there were not cases of ownership, discrimination was commonplace: "Fearing that Whites would associate them with the poorer, darker-skinned newly freed slaves, some mulattoes in the Lower South began to discriminate actively against those who were darker than themselves and to socialize exclusively with other mulattoes" (Jones, 2000, p. 1510). However, even after the solidification of a Black-and-White, two-category system, social entitlements continued to be distributed on the basis of color differences.

Mulattoes and lighter-skinned Blacks have had educational and professional advantages. Initially, this was an important part of how mulatto individuals distinguished themselves as "educated, multilingual parlor entertainers" (Robinson and Group, 1970, p. 206), or in "less onerous indoor positions as domestics or artisans" (Jones, 2000, p. 1507). Early educational advantages were vocational in nature: "Opportunities for manumission, less violent treatment by overseers, less stressful work tasks, access to education, and opportunities for skilled labor are all examples of the privileges that lighter-skinned [B]lack children often received" (Hunter, 2005, p. 19). Years later, Whites interpreted;

> . . . the emergence of this light-skinned African American leadership as confirmation that white blood and lineage was superior to [B]lack. Many whites saw the notable success of mixed-race and light-skinned people as evidence that only those with "white blood" had the capacity to lead (Hunter, 2005, p. 20).

As more formal educational opportunities became available to Blacks, there continued to be separation between mulattoes (and lighter-skinned Blacks) and darker-skinned Blacks in a range of social and professional contexts:

In the post-Civil War era, the growing class of light-skinned Freedmen found itself poised to lead the now free African American population. Many Freedmen served as leaders of local business, church, and civic, organizations. They were able to take up positions of leadership more easily than many other African Americans because they had been free and often economically established for years. (Hunter, 2005, p. 20)

More importantly, lighter-skinned Blacks used this "leadership" to create forms of distinction within Black communities in the post-Civil War era: "In order to distinguish themselves from the darker-skinned masses, these mulattoes established separate communities in which skin color served as the key to access" (Jones, 2000, p. 1515). Although today many people think of HBCUs as educational institutions that offer opportunities to Black people who were unable to attend White institutions, their colorist practices were significant.

Lighter-skinned Blacks' educational privilege is rooted in intentional separation from darker-skinned Blacks, supported by the broader racist context. Certainly, that understanding should shift how we understand the historic role of HBCUs: "Education was a primary vehicle for entrance, and, due to the preferential treatment afforded light-skinned [B]lacks in the mission schools and [B]lack colleges established after the Civil War, skin color serves as a foundation for the emerging [B]lack middle class (Okazawa-Rey, Robinson & Ward 1987, p. 93).

As with the country's unresolved legacy of racism, this colorist history continues to inform educational and economic opportunities: "Blacks with lighter skin tones also fare better educationally and economically than darker Blacks. Indeed, since the 1960s, most Blacks elected or appointed to prominent governmental positions have had light skin" (Jones, 2000, p. 1520). Further, it has been shown that "lighter-skinned African American women are rewarded with more resources and more status than are darker-skinned women" (Hunter, 2005, p. 12). With this knowledge of the history and the ongoing consequences of colorist practices, there are important implications for African American women who benefit from light-skin privilege. This essay considers the specific experiences of two African American women—a mother and daughter—who aim to shift educational practices in ways that will change the course of this colorist legacy.

Mother's Story of Color and Education

I write about colorism from the perspective of a 70-year-old African American woman with light skin, and long, somewhat nappy gray hair. My appearance has defined my relationships with people and shaped the opportunities I have had. Equally important is the way my values, self-esteem, and essential character have been influenced by the messages of my childhood. I recall my childhood as a comfortable life surrounded by African Americans who took care of me and the other children in our Black neighborhood, attending Black schools and our Black Episcopal church. Our family even had a house at a Black beach. I spent most of the summers there with my grandmother and mother; the men—my father and grandfather— came for short periods when they were not working. Both my father and maternal grandfather were medical doctors who were self-employed.

Most of the families I knew had a narrow range of complexions, rarely darker than the milk chocolate tone of the spectrum. I remember the one person in my fifth and sixth grade classes whose skin was nearly black—darker than anyone else I knew. I don't recall conversations or explanations of advantages and disadvantages related to skin color. As I tried to make sense of what I observed, I made a few decisions about relationships. Somehow I came to associate masculinity with darker skin. I remember hearing men described as "tall, dark, and handsome." Eventually I realized that this description was being applied to White actors. Women were described as attractive if they had "fair" skin. In my family and social groups, most African Americans had light complexions. There seemed to be an assumption that people whose skin tone was similar to or close to mine felt superior to other Black people. I did not make that assumption, at least not consciously. I was struggling with a need to be accepted and liked, despite the ways in which I was different from many of my peers. (I am an "only child" and grandchild of medical doctors and teachers.)

By the time I was 14 years old, I was trying to understand how African Americans related to one another and to be intentional about my interactions. At age 16, I was "presented to society" with an "at home" reception and at a debutante ball in Washington, DC. None of the people I knew in my hometown were presented to society in formal "at home" receptions. My mother asked some of my friends to serve as hostesses for my "coming out" event. The girls she chose had light skin and curly hair.

My socialization was informed by my mother's indoctrination as a student at Palmer Memorial Institute. There she was taught by Dr. Charlotte Hawkins Brown, author of *The Correct Thing to Do—To Say—To Wear*. From my family I learned the means by which Black people of my class maintained our status and privileges. Exclusivity was the key. Although it was possible to acquire wealth by various means, access to exclusive groups was by invitation only, and people with dark skin were less likely to be invited. I was not allowed to attend social events for which tickets were sold. The cotillions in which debutantes sold tickets to earn scholarships were not as prestigious as the kind for which all expenses were paid by the members. My godfather "presented" me at the cotillion held by his exclusive DC men's club. There were no scholarships and all expenses were paid by the hosts.

When I entered Howard University, I found "my kind of people" in the majority. I had relatives and friends in Washington, DC who helped me feel comfortable. I was not prepared, however, for the Black Power Movement, which peaked during my freshman year. Blackness was being defined by economic status and oppression—dark skin, poverty, and racism—of which I knew little. My response was to be quiet and hide behind assertive, confident Black men. This was in sharp contrast to the leadership I had exercised in high school as president of the student council and treasurer of the Black state association of student governments. I had written for the newspaper at North Carolina's Governor's School, which I attended the summer before my senior year. But this was before "Black Power." At Howard I questioned my legitimacy as a Black person. I did not want to associate with the bourgeoisie that dominated sororities, and I was intimidated by the activists who seemed of one accord. Sororities and fraternities at Howard were associated with skin color stereotypes. As nothing in my socialization had made me value relationships with women, I minimized their importance until much later in life.

In my naïve effort to undermine classist behavior and find my place in the evolving Black community, I sought and built relationships with peers "outside" the acceptable boundaries. Ultimately, I married a man who embodied many of the attributes that I had been trained to avoid. He also had a combination of less visible characteristics that enabled some people of his darker skin complexion to overcome some of the disadvantages of colorism. In much the same way as Black people have deceived their oppressors during periods of enslavement (for example, surreptitiously learning to "read, write, and cipher") my husband had mastered the art of "reading" people like me. A popular fraternity leader and social activist from Georgia, this tall athletic man with dark brown skin had a reputation that caused a dormitory matron to warn freshman girls to avoid this "scoundrel." He and I met one another's needs in ways mirrored in other Black couples of our generation—partners chosen with contrasting skin tones reflecting what Djamba and Kimuna (2014) refer to as "status exchange."

This union made possible and necessary a kind of informal education within our family, as our children made sense of the consequences and implications of skin color in and beyond our household. We had two children—a son and a daughter—who were a shade of brown that is right in the middle of our lighter and darker shades. This means they developed a different understanding of color, inheritance of color advantage and/or disadvantage, and educational legacies. In the section below, my daughter contextualizes her racialized, colorist, and gendered educational experience in the context of my family's lighter skin.

Shedding Darkness on Mother's Light: Inheriting Skin Privilege

In August 2019, I pulled into a gas station with my grandmother in the passenger's seat of my car. My grandmother is much lighter than I and has white hair. From a distance, she might even appear White. The White man at the pump across from mine asked if I worked in health care. This was not the first time I've been mistaken for my grandmother's employee. In fact, I have used that perception to navigate sections of North Carolina where Confederate flags fly frequently. My mother is closer to my grandmother's complexion. In spite of that, because of my mother's experiences in segregated communities, she never imagined that anyone would "mistake" her for White. I recall, as a child, an incident when a classmate asked me who the White woman was who was picking me up from school. When I told my mother, she insisted that the child was poorly educated, knowing nothing of Black features. Carole Brown wrote, "It never ceases to amaze me that I am mistaken by my own. White people I can forgive their ignorance, but Blacks I cannot" (Brown, 1970, p. 234). My mother still finds it hard to imagine that some African Americans have difficulty identifying lighter-skinned Black people. As her browner daughter, however, I have witnessed the look of recognition when my entry into a room has answered (unspoken) questions about my mother's race. My mother's complexion has opened doors that were closed on my father's side of the family. Further, it is clear to me that the educational privilege on my mother's side is inextricably linked to skin color privilege, or colorism.

As a young woman, I benefited from accelerated classes and elite social groups. Although I was a Jack and Jill dropout, and never had a cotillion as my mother did, I knew more about Black elite culture than many—maybe all—of my friends, some of whom had never heard of such an event. The pressure (from my maternal grandparents more than from my mother) for me to participate in Black elite social events came after a move back to DC after eight years in Durham. From the events I attended, it was clear to me that the social gatherings were a project in prospective mate matching:

> [The cotillion] introduced these young women in a formal way to the men of their
> class, the young men who because of birth, family, status, skin color, achievement,
> would be suitable mates. And it confirmed that these young women, for the same
> reasons, were acceptable (Golden, 2004, p. 44).

I never encountered anyone in these social environments who reminded me of my father, and I was not interested in what seemed to me superficial encounters.

Too often discussions about colorism end with the mating game. Especially when talking about women, narrowly defined gender-appropriate discourse leads one to believe that women should be primarily concerned with mating. "Isn't that why these attractive Black women are in college anyway? Aren't they preparing to be good helpmates to the doctors and lawyers they will marry?" However, we cannot ignore the fact that because of gendered discrimination in the workplace, it has been important to marry up if one wants to succeed, and often marrying up meant marrying lighter. If we dig into the roots of these superficial mating discussions, we will find underlying issues of economic security and survival.

While, indeed, there is evidence that lighter-skinned African Americans "marry higher status spouses" (Hunter, 2005, p. 13-14), that is just the tip of the iceberg. It is important not to stop there, but instead to understand the more profound implications of colorism.

> It's about access, as one of my former students reminds me when recalling his
> days at Princeton; he tells me that the Black students there were either biracial or
> light-skinned. It's about the diversity trainer for several major corporations telling
> me that she feels ambivalent because she benefits from light-skinned privilege
> and says that it's sad but true that Whites simply feel more comfortable around
> lighter-skinned Blacks. . . . it's about opportunity, as I remember reading an article
> in *Essence* about African American actresses and the dearth of opportunities in
> Hollywood and how one dark-skinned actress was told by a White producer that
> she wouldn't find much work because she was "nigger black" (Golden, 2004, pp.
> 116-117).

Yes, skin color privilege, even among African Americans, is about opportunity—every type of opportunity imaginable. There is evidence to suggest that the "preference for whiteness" results in an intra-racial wage gap that favors light-skinned Blacks (Goldsmith, Hamilton & Darity, 2007, p. 725). This finding demonstrates that although the U.S. legal structures may have conformed to the one-drop rule, the *de facto* hierarchy that is responsible for allocating benefits based on skin color continues to function in a three-tiered system: "[A]mong [B]lacks in the United States, lightness—possessing white characteristics as measured by skin shade—is rewarded in the labor market" (Goldsmith, Hamilton & Darity, 2007, p. 729). Education, social status, race, color, gender are interrelated factors of oppression that work together in what Patricia Hill Collins (2009) has called a matrix of domination.

Thus, we find that African Americans who have lighter skin experience a host of benefits, including that they "earn more money, complete more years of education, live in more integrated neighborhoods, and have better mental health" (Hunter 2005, p. 2). One study found that:

> . . . for every increment of lightness on the color scale, income increases by $673 annually. . . . The consequence of this finding is that a woman described as very light brown earns over $2,600 more per year than a woman of similar background who is described as very dark brown (Hunter, 2005, p. 44).

In this way,

> . . . A person's relative lightness determines whether she can access the benefits associated with a particular class. This phenomenon occurred in the post-Civil War era when elite mulattoes created social and political organizations into which access was granted or denied based upon one's skin color regardless of one's actual socio-economic class (Jones, 2000, p. 1528).

This trend continues today, as I embody the educational privilege inherited on my mother's side.

Having studied mathematics at a prestigious liberal arts college, I went on to earn a master of science degree in computer and information sciences, a master of arts degree in international communication, and a PhD in international relations. I have no student debt because my mother's family used their understanding of educational systems, including how racial wealth gap disparities could (and should) be used to make a case for scholarships, as well as accumulated wealth to help me navigate the system with numerous scholarships and no shame. My father did not participate in any of the decision-making that determined where I would attend school or how I would fund it. My mother and I continue to collaborate on grant applications to fund research by and about African Americans.

Research on educational disparities is clear:

> For African American women, skin color is a statistically significant predictor of education. For every additional gradation of lightness (on a 5-point scale) educational attainment increases by one-third year. That means that the lightest

woman has more than one entire year of additional education when compared to a darker-skinned woman with similar background characteristics (Hunter, 2005, p. 42).

In one study, "not knowing one's mother's education level was a strong predictor of a respondent's own educational attainment, lowering the education level by 1½ years" (Hunter, 2005, p. 43). Not only do I know that my mother has a doctorate, I also know the strong legacy of educational attainment on this side of the family. Although I have a paternal aunt, great aunt, and grandmother who earned undergraduate degrees, I do not have additional information about any such legacy on my father's side.

The color of African American educational legacies in the U.S. began with privileges extended to a mulatto class and continues today in various forms. (My mother's doctoral dissertation was about tracking along racial lines in North Carolina public schools.) This legacy of colorism has, in a sense, lightened our mark: "The Negroes who had managed to pull off the most amazing feats of achievement (Massachusetts Senator Edward Brooke; Supreme Court Justice Thurgood Marshall), those we referred to as 'Negro Firsts,' were usually light-skinned" (Golden 2004, p. 8). I am part of that legacy, benefitting from my mother's light-skin privilege in its educational, social, and material dimensions.

The question for me is what can be done to shift this legacy in a direction that aims at (anti-colorist) justice. If we do not attend to the material realities of colorism, then we will never effectively address the racism in this country. As an example, if African Americans receive reparations, it will close the gap between privileged lighter-skinned Blacks and Whites, yet potentially widen the gap between lighter- and darker-skinned Blacks. There are (and have always been) many ways to undermine the efforts of African Americans working collectively in the name of racial justice that engages issues of colorism. In response to these obstacles to justice, we need many responses. Given our similar, yet different, experiences coming from two generations of the same family, my mother and I have unique approaches to this work. In the section below, she outlines her ideas.

Mother Applying Lessons of Liberatory Teaching in Informal Education

Now retired from academic life, I focus on informal education. (Informal education includes activities in camps, libraries, science centers, children's museums, at home, and other venues not specifically designated as schools.) Most salient is the role of family members in the socialization of children. Home environments, including those that offer home-schooling, reflect values by the presence (or absence) of books, music, videos, television, games, and other materials of varying quality and cultural orientations. Colorism is typically so pervasive that adult learners must unlearn deeply rooted values that are instilled during childhood and reinforced by every segment of U.S. life. We understand the contexts and content of our prior schooling as steeped in overt and subtle messages of White supremacy and light-skin superiority.

The African American Education and Research Organization (AAERO) seeks to engage African Americans in experiences that reflect the best of what we know about teaching and learning. As we engage and support students as interns and volunteers with this nonprofit organization, we affirm a commitment to inclusion, affirmative action and equity. This means (1) acknowledging our own color attributes, and the elements for which skin color is a proxy; (2) remembering our prior education contexts, and recalling the race and complexions of teachers, administrators and leaders in various roles; (3) recalling the distribution of students in classes and categories with different value; (4) being aware of the ways in which colorism may interfere with or distort learning; and (5) being conscious of our goals and motives for engaging in educational activities. Education to satisfy curiosity may be different from that which is motivated by a need for respect, or an objective associated with career advancement. Our understanding of how perceptions and values related to skin color influence our motives, goals and actions is critical to the health and well-being of Black people. Our interactions now must (1) raise awareness of the origins, historical development and implications colorism in contemporary education; (2) acknowledge our own colorist identities and experiences, and assist others in doing so, particularly in educational settings and activities; (3) acknowledge prior patterns of opportunity and distribution of benefits, and disrupt current and future behaviors that reinforce colorism; and (4) use our privilege to benefit the community. While we emphasize implications for practice, the need for evaluation research is critical. It is essential that practices in schools and informal education settings be evaluated to document their efficacy as means to change the culture and sustain equitable educational practices.

Daughter Leveraging Skin Privilege for an Anti-Colorist Education

We know that Black history (and her-story) has resulted in the privileging of stories of lighter-skinned Blacks. Even the "Black is Beautiful" days of people reciting James Brown's "Say it loud! I'm Black and I'm proud!" did not change the entrenched color politics of the country.

Remembering those days I recall that even then the female icons of the movement, Civil Rights to Black Power, were light-skinned Angela Davis, Rosa Parks, Coretta Scott King, Kathleen Cleaver, and Elaine Brown, who headed the Black Panthers for a time. Righteous sisters. My sisters. But Fannie Lou Hamer was too black and too angry and too country to achieve the icon status her sacrifice and hard work should have earned her. (Golden, 2004, p. 14)

Many of us know Fannie Lou Hamer, but fewer of us know Claudette Colvin:

Colvin, pregnant, poor, and unmarried, had been thrown off a Montgomery bus weeks before Rosa Parks took her now-famous stand, but because Colvin did not fit the image of a respectable, middle-class citizen—because she was not a "lady"—her case was passed over by those who were looking for an opportunity to test the segregation laws and launch a public campaign. (Ransby 2003, pp. 292-293)

Parks also had lighter skin than Colvin. That light skin, and all the related privileges, contributed to "the genteel, ladylike demeanor that Rosa Parks exhibited, which made her an ideal candidate to personify respectable [B]lack resistance in Montgomery in 1955" (Ransby, 2003, p. 292). That history is an important part of how we should read, redirect, and refocus Black history when we have the opportunity to teach it. Further, if we are to take to heart all the ways that lighter-skinned privilege has impacted Black education, we will do much more than add darker-skinned footnotes to the accomplishments of lighter-skinned "Firsts." As a start, I suggest that Black educators consider implementing the following:

1. Ensure diverse color representation in reading and educational materials. In questioning the "whiteness" of the curriculum of my faculty colleagues, I have made a collage of the authors represented in their required readings. Often, the entire group of authors is White. Just as that is unacceptable, so is teaching only texts of African Americans who represent a mulatto class, in terms of their historical privilege. African American educators should ensure that they are not teaching only the stories of lighter-skinned Black people. In general, we should ensure that the "people of color" included in our syllabi are not only the lightest (in terms of skin color) representatives of their respective groups. Since racist and colorist structures have limited the early publications of darker-skinned (especially female) African Americans, the negritude movement can provide rich sources from the Caribbean and the African continent as starting points. These sources do not always provide a good gender balance and may require embracing

multilingual sources that speak to experiences across the Black Diaspora. Elsewhere, I write about the importance of radical multilingualism in liberatory, feminist adult education (Hua and Hall forthcoming)

2. Include visual and narrative representations across the color spectrum in text, video, photographic, and other artistic materials. Because so many documented "Firsts" are lighter-skinned Blacks, we sometimes have to do our homework in order to tell a fuller story. We might have to learn more about the Montgomery bus boycotts, as an example, in order to post images of the people, such as Claudette Colvin, who came before the "Firsts." Just as our (virtual or physical) classrooms have racially diverse images linked to our areas of study, we should also ensure that there is color diversity among the African Americans who are seen and read in our courses.

3. Use color privilege (that is, proximity to whiteness) to redefine/expand notions of diversity and insist upon a broader color continuum in decision-making bodies (for example, nonprofit boards, curriculum design teams, and so on) and as part of diversity initiatives. Many White organizations prefer Black people who are not African American (or other people of color) to engage them in diversity work. If and when lighter-skinned African American people (or other people of color) find themselves in these positions, they should use that access to force a reckoning with the country's native darker citizen, so that the story of (darker) African Americans does not continue to be marginalized, even in so-called diversity work. Thus, there must be an intentional effort to counter this exclusion from educational and professional organizations and associations.

This list is simply a starting point, but it intends to address colorism with (1) inclusion of darker-skinned authors and writers; (2) more representation of the stories and images of darker-skinned people; and (3) greater power in education governance by darker-skinned people. AAERO was created to redistribute educational privilege among African Americans who may not have had access to the privileges of my family, in which I represent the fifth generation of a terminal degree (MD or PhD) graduate. The organization is attentive to the need for intentional and explicit responses to colorist injustices in the African American community. Further, as Black women educators, who have benefitted from the formal and informal education provided by other Black women, we understand and take seriously the impact that African American women can have on reversing the impact of colorism. We must battle this injustice alongside our anti-racism work: "Since colorism is a by-product of the effects of racism and sexism which underlie our social foundation, we as [B]lack women must continue to engage in activities aimed at social reconstruction. We as [B]lack women must become agents for social change" (Okazawa-Rey, Robinson & Ward, 1987, p. 101). That is the work of AAERO, and that is the daily work of my mother and me in our efforts to create a more livable world for Black women and girls.

Process Questions and Considerations:

1. When you look at leaders in your community, where do they fall on the color line?

2. In your community, does there seem to be a difference in the relationship between skin color and status, based on gender?

3. What could you do to raise awareness of colorism in your peer group?

4. What changes would you like to see to undo the effects of colorism in your peer group?

5. How could you use your understanding of colorism to improve the work you do in your occupation?

References

Collins, P. H. (2009). *Black feminist thought: Knowledge, consciousness, and the politics of empowerment.* New York: Routledge.

Cook, A. (1970). "Black Pride? Some Contradictions." In T. C. Bambara (Ed.), *The Black women: An anthology* (pp. 149-161). New York: Penguin Books.

Djamba , Y. K., & Kimuna, S. R. (2014). Are Americans really in favor of interracial marriage? A closer look at when they are asked about black-white marriage for their relatives. *Journal of Black Studies* 45(6), 528 -544.

Golden, M. (2004). *Don't play in the sun: One woman's journey through the color complex.* New York: Doubleday.

Goldsmith, A. H., Hamilton, D., & Darity, Jr., W. (2007). From dark to light: Skin color and wages among African-Americans. *The Journal of Human Resources 42*, 701-738.

Graham, L. O. (1999). *Our kind of people: Inside America's black upper class.* New York: HarperCollins Publishers.

Griffin, F. J. (2001). "Ironies of the saint": Malcolm X, black women, and the price of protection. In B. Collier-Thomas and V. P. Franklin (Eds.), *Sisters in struggle: African American women in the civil rights-black power movement* (pp. 214-229). New York: New York University Press.

Hooks, B. (1994). *Teaching to transgress: Education as the practice of freedom.* New York: Routledge.

Hua, L., & Hall, K.M.Q. (forthcoming). Radical feminist transgressions in teaching/learning. In I. Nusair & B. Shaw (Eds.), *Feminist Collaborations: Intersectional and Transnational Teaching & Learning.*

Jefferson, M. (2015). *Negroland: A memoir.* New York: Pantheon Books.

Jones, T. (2000). Shades of brown: The law of skin color. *Duke Law Journal* 49(6), 1487-1557.

Okazawa-Rey, M., Robinson, T., & Ward, J. V. (1987). Black women and the politics of skin color and hair. *Women & Therapy 6*(1-2), 89-102.

Ransby, B. (2003). *Ella Baker & the black freedom movement: A radical democratic vision.* Chapel Hill, NC: The University of North Carolina Press.

CHAPTER 7.

Colorism and Life Satisfaction of Professional
African American Men

Sarah J. Stewart, Livingstone College
Kamilah Marie Woodson, Howard University

Introduction

African American men experience racism and colorist discrimination in their daily lives, in society and in corporate America in particular, which appears to have a direct impact on their mental health and life satisfaction. According to Blake (2020),

> There was a time that I thought if White America saw more examples of successful black men, that things would change. I thought that having a president like Barack H. Obama would shift something in America. Perhaps it did for some. But it was astonishing how the fearful gaze of White America transformed even Obama into another black male threat who was lynched online or labeled "Primate in Chief."

Often, African American men have been subjected to stereotypes that perceive them to be violent, womanizing, and lazy (Cornelius, 2012), which also seems to impact their sense of self and overall functioning. Rodriguez (2008) found that African American men have an increased likelihood of being discriminated against, and he noted that black men are more likely to be treated with less respect and be perceived as less smart than other people. Most recently, in an article published by *Medium*, African American employees at Facebook spoke out about their experiences with racism, sexism, micro- and macro-aggressions while working at Facebook, which was not only provocative, but important. Similarly, NBA, NFL, and NASCAR drivers have all taken a stand (and at times a knee) to highlight the transgressions against Black men regardless of social standing and/or socio-economic status. The kinds of information yielded from the exercise at Facebook and the declarations by various professional athletes speak to the inability to escape racism even in the "upper echelon" of society.

Racism in the United States is alive and ever present. The unfortunate killings of Ahmaud Arbrey, George Floyd, Rayshard Brooks (most recently), and a host of other infamous killings at the behest of the police (active and retired) underscore the need for attention to race relations in this country in 2020. Similarly, in June of 2020, there were two African American men found hanging from trees in California. Although disturbing and obviously racial motivated, there are many "conservative" individuals who suggest racism is a thing of the past, and that because enslavement occurred centuries ago, Black people need to move on. Fortunately, the aforementioned travesties have reignited the Black Lives Matter Movement all over the world, in hopes of promoting understanding and reform. Thus, these anecdotal accounts suggest that racism is very much a part of society and has many tributaries, colorism being one of them. Racism and colorism are interwoven, as one seemingly begets the other. Racism can be defined as a system of practices and/or ideological positions that privilege certain groups of people over others, based on race. By and large, racism is predicated upon the idea that there are biological hierarchies among racial groups that make certain groups superior over others, usually Caucasians, although race is a socially fashioned concept. While colorism can be defined as prejudicial and/or discriminatory attitudes and practices based on skin color and other phenotypic presentations commensurate with Caucasian features that advantage one group of individuals over another based on those phenotypes. Therefore, colorism can be best understood as a derivative of racism with very similar psychological corollaries.

A study of the impact of skin color on professional African American males is not only important for scholarly research, but also to improve mental health practices and institutional policies that affect professional African American males. Understanding the impact of experiences as a result of skin color on Black men will inform researchers, practitioners, students, parents and policymakers regarding: (1) future research on skin color and African American male identity development; (2) programs to enhance the mental health of African American men; (3) techniques for decreasing the negative impact skin color may have in educational and professional settings; (4) factors that protect against racism and discrimination that can help African American male students and professionals acquire certain skills to reduce the effects of racism and discrimination have on their psychological well-being; (5) future research studies and literature on the impact that skin color has on African American males and their development; and (6) informing practice by aiding college counseling centers, students, corporations, and other organizations that work closely with African American males in helping this population obtain the competencies necessary to successfully and comfortably transition into environments where they may be judged by their skin complexion.

Overall, the rationale for this research is twofold: first, the need to stimulate future research studies on skin color, African American male identity development, and life satisfaction of African American men; and second, the need to understand the factors that protect against racism and discrimination that can help African American men acquire skills that can reduce the effects of racism and discrimination. This study takes a post-positivist worldview and uses a mixed methods research approach to understand the impact colorism has on the African American male's psychological well-being and the influence of families.

Literature Review

Professional African American Men

Since the doors of the corporate world have been opened to African American men, there have been various opportunities for growth relative to career development. However, African Americans still encounter overt and covert racism and disparate treatment in corporate America, which often significantly affects the ascension and overall career development of African American men in particular. Similarly, Black men, like Black women, experience discrimination that is related to their history and social position in society (*Harvard Law Review*, 1991). African American professional men encounter gendered racism, which includes and is not limited to negative stereotypes and oppression, because they are "Black men" (Mutua, 2008). Further, research studies have found that African American men experience unscrupulous gendered racism during the hiring process; for example, there is usually an unfounded belief that African American men lack the "soft skills" that have been found essential for a minority individual working in a predominately White environment. The soft skills being cited are broadly referred to as motivational skills and interactional skills (Cornileus, 2012). Research concluded that African American men have less of a chance of getting into occupations requiring hiring levels of "soft skills," which affects their career development. Moreover, employers refuse to extend the same equal employment opportunities they extend to Black women and the law does not extend the same protections for race as it does with gender. Reasons for this experience are best explained by the fact that African American men are the least represented in white-collar environments, as compared to White males. The *Harvard Review* study made some provocative statements regarding African American men in corporate environments:

There are several possible ways to explain the discrimination against black men.

Differences in cultural styles often lead employers to conclude that black men have attitudes and personal characteristics that conflict with a predominantly white social atmosphere. Many black men—although certainly not all—are more verbally direct, expressive, and assertive than white men, who provide the standard against which black male behavior is measured (pp. 756-757).

These findings were further supported by Kirschenman, Moss, and Tilly (1996) as they reported that African American men have recently filed more lawsuits than women of color, reflecting their unique experiences with racism, lack of opportunity, and social position in American society. To understand and examine the experiences of African Americans, a universal approach to describe and understand their career development has been used in many studies (Cornileus, 2012). Cornileus (2012) conducted a study examining the impact racism has on the career development of African American men in corporate America, and found that African American men experience both repressive and facilitative structures. As such, repressive structures were defined as social rules and practices that constrain the career development of African American men, while facilitative structures outlined social rules and practices that enable African American men to circumvent racism and advance in their career development. The four repressive structures consisted of the following: (1) stereotypes of African American men; (2) subjective and divergent career development practices; (3) differentiated opportunities for the acquisition of sociopolitical capital; and (4) changing priorities in workplace diversity. The participants identified being labeled as an "angry Black man" as a common stereotype. Additionally, many participants stated that they downplay their smarts such as educational background and experiences, because they face more scrutiny if their credentials surpass those of their White counterparts.

There were five facilitative structures were found. They are: (1) the ability to build and leverage key relationships; (2) bicultural strategies; (3) self-efficacy and personal agency; (4) education and continuous learning; and (5) spirituality and purpose. It was also noted that to navigate the racist work environment, most participants identified the ability to build and leverage key relationships as an approach to combat the racist environment. Secondly, bicultural strategies were identified to help African American men cope with double consciousness. Thus, results confirm the need for further research on career development that emphasizes cultural constructs. One of the more recognized theories used to study professional African American men is the Social Cognitive Career theory or SCCT (Lent, Brown, & Hackett, 1994, 2000). Social cognitive career theory assumes that a person's inputs and background contextual factors shape one's learning experiences and later become an aspect of an individual's self-efficacy. According to Lent, Brown, and Hackett (1994, 2000), individual factors such as gender, ethnicity, and other personal factors that may influence career development are defined as a person's inputs. Further, a person's inputs also influence background contextual factors and proximal contextual factors. Background contextual factors are variables that influence a person's career interest. Proximal factors continually affect a person's academic and career development and self-efficacy beliefs (Wright, McGovern, Boo, & Vannatter, 2014). SCCT has been used to study under-represented populations, as it provides a framework to consider many different factors. A study conducted by Lent, Brown, Sheu, Schimdt, Brenner, Gloster, and Teistman (2005) tested the utility of SCCT on women and students at a historically Black college and concluded that women do not differ from men in healthy levels of self-efficacy, interests, goals, and outcome expectations. Although SCCT has been used to understand career interest and choices of African American female engineering students, this model does not emphasize the impact of racism and discrimination that may affect the career development of African American men. Hence, the importance in examining the impact that racism, discrimination, and colorism has on career development choices and theories of African American males, as well as other people of color.

Effects of Colorism on African American men

The social construct of colorism has a long-standing history and has had deleterious consequences on the African American community in general, with a particularly strong impact on the psychological health of African American men. Colorism seems to impact their levels of depression, the development of stereotypes, racial identity development, and their experiences of discrimination. Additionally, colorism also seems to impact the educational and economical outcomes of the African American community. The literature on colorism and the work environment has suggested that darker- skinned African American men experience more discrimination than lighter-skinned African American men. For example, in the Civil War, lighter- skinned African American men in the army were considered to be better-skilled workers and were selected as lieutenants and sergeants (Hochschild and Weaver, 2007) more often than their darker-skinned counterparts. Shilpa (2006) found that lighter- skinned Black males with only a bachelor's degree and average work experience were considered more appealing in interviews than darker-skinned African American males with an MBA and above-average managerial experience. Thus, Shilpa (2006) concluded that skin color was more relevant than the educational level and occupational background of African American males. Overall, lighter-skinned Black men seem to have better job prospects, are seen to be more attractive, and often appear to be less threatening to their White coworkers. Similarly, Uzogara, Abdou, and Jackson (2014) examined whether skin tone matters in different contexts, specifically, among other African Americans as well as outside their racial group. The results were consistent with the historical context of colorism. The authors found that light-skinned men consistently received the best treatment from Whites, while dark-skinned men consistently received prejudicial treatment from Whites. Further, past studies have suggested that social economic status can be a catalyst for skin color discrimination.

Therefore, in this study, professional African American men are being assessed to control for the potential confound of socioeconomic status. Interestingly, a few research studies have suggested that there may be an ideal skin color for African Americans that may neutralize the effects of within-group discrimination and discrimination from the majority group. Although a lighter skin is preferred, individuals with medium skin seem to be more attractive to other African Americans and those medium-complexioned men tend to utilize this skin color identity for protection (Hall, 1992; Holtzman, 1973). Moreover, the skin color of African American males has also been known to be impactful in the criminal justice system, as research in this area has yielded data suggesting that there is a strong relationship between skin color and severity of punishment/sentencing. Further, another point of interest is relative to the fact that African American men have stereotypes about each other that are shared between them in the African American community. For example, darker-skinned African American man may say, "You cannot trust a light- skinned brother." Thus, these past and present experiences of skin tone discrimination still affect the lives of African American men today, especially in the workplace and in predominately White settings.

Colorism and Psychological well-being

Some studies have focused on discrimination and its effect on psychological distress such as anxiety and depression, while other research has examined the components of self-concept and life satisfaction. Literature on this topic has suggested that being treated poorly or being discriminated against contributes to reduced levels of self-esteem, self-efficacy, racial identity, and other related life-satisfaction factors. Chaudoir, Earnshaw, and Andel (2013) posit that mental and psychological health outcomes were worse for individuals with "unconcealable stigmas" (in this case, dark skin color) than for those who were able to "conceal" (having a lighter skin tone). Further, literature on life satisfaction and discrimination has suggested that there may be a distinct difference between the effects of discrimination being directed at an individual as a function of their group membership versus discrimination directed at a group as a whole. Crosby (1984) further suggested that members of minority groups often identify less personal discrimination and over-identify group discrimination, because it is less threatening. Additional research has also suggested that this may be a protective self-preserving mechanism used by African Americans to limit their experience with psychological distress; as such, the notion of group suppression or group discrimination does not lead an individual to think about rejection on a personal level.

Theoretical Framework

To investigate the impact of colorism on professional African American men, the African American Male Theory (Bush & Bush, 2013) was utilized. This framework provides the foundation for understanding the interrelationship among the following variables: bicultural competence, racial identity, depression, and psychological well-being. This unified theoretical framework illuminates different levels of identity, how they interact as a barrier to racism in professional environments, and how they promote the life satisfaction of African American males. Brewer and Gardner (1996) suggested that if we acknowledge the different levels of identity, we will find that it signifies different perspectives for interpreting social reality; as such, collective identity theory becomes a comprehensive theory for understanding variability within, as well as between, individuals.

The African American Male Theory (AAMT) is a multidisciplinary approach to theorizing the experiences of some African American boys and men. AAMT concepts are built upon the African worldview, as well as Bronfenbrenner's ecological system model (1986) and posit that some African American males exist in a symbolic and bidirectional relationship with other individuals, concepts, and phenomena. Bronfenbrenner's ecological human development model conceptualizes human development and suggests that it is necessary to consider an individual's entire environment to understand the human development process. Therefore, Bronfenbrenner's model consists of interconnected environmental systems, which include microsystems, mesosystem, ecosystem, macrosystem, and chronosystem (Bronfenbrenner, 1986). AAMT is comprised of six tenets:

1. Individual and collective experiences, behaviors, outcomes, events, and

phenomena of African American men and boys are best analyzed using an ecological approach. The purpose of the first tenet is twofold: First, African American Male Theory includes instructional systems and structures in its conceptualization because these systems and structures often shape and influence African American males' experiences with various environments (for example, school, neighborhood, social communities) and relationships with others. For instance, the historical tension between the African American community and police may directly or indirectly shape an African American male's emotional, physical, mental, and environmental development. Secondly, AAMT includes all five parts of Bronfenbrenner's Ecological Model; however, it divides the microsystem into two parts, the inner and outer microsystem. The inner microsystem contains an individual's personality, biology, and beliefs, while the outer microsystem contains interactions with family, peers, and the school environment. In addition, AAMT suggests that the mesosystem is a link between the inner microsystem, the outer microsystem, and the subsystem of the mesosystem. The subsystem of the mesosystem contains an individual's spirituality, internalized thoughts and feelings, and unconscious information (Bush & Bush, 2013).

2. There is something unique about being male and of African descent. This tenet attempts to acknowledge the unique events and circumstances African American males experience. The unique experiences may include negative within-group situations (for example, colorism) and outer group experiences (for example, racisms). The second tenet further emphasizes the creation of specialized educational programs, workshops, community partnerships, and other social supports to assist African American males to process their experiences.

3. There is a continuity and continuation of African culture, consciousness, and biology that influence the experiences of African American boys and men. This tenet suggests that the research on African American males should consider aspects of African culture that still exist in the upbringing of African American males. Not incorporating African cultural principles affects the way African American males conceptualize themselves and their development.

4. African American boys and men are resilient and resistant. This fourth tenet suggests that African American males are born with resilience and self-determination. It posits that resilience is in both the inner and outer microsystem and in the subsystems of the mesosystems. Resiliency can be interpreted as

resistance, which is a tool used to resist White mainstream culture.

5. Race and racism, coupled with classism and sexism, have a profound impact on every aspect of the lives of African American boys and men. The fifth tenet acknowledges racism and sexism as factors in society and how they affect African American men.

6. The focus and purpose of study and programs concerning African American boys and men should be the pursuit of social justice. The premises of the theory are to undermine the history of oppression by investigating and exploring systems, policies, and institutions that continue to affect African American males, and to strive for social justice for African American males (Bush & Bush, 2013). Finally, the study strives for social justice.

These six tenets help capture the overall experiences, behaviors, events, actions, and environmental and historical situations that may have influenced the lives of African American men.

Methodology

The design for this study was a mixed method, concurrent, nested research design. Participants were recruited via online methods and social networks such as Facebook groups, LinkedIn, African American fraternities, other professional networks, and email list servers. After the data were collected, a raffle for two $100.00 Visa gift cards was offered as an incentive for participating in the study. The study included 172 participants who ranged in age from 22-65. Participants identified as single, in a committed relationship, married, separated, divorced, widowed, or other. Participants resided throughout the United States, living in the Mid-Atlantic, Midwest, Southern, and Western regions of the country. Inclusion criteria for participants included self-identification as African American, graduated from a four-year college or university. Survey Monkey was used to design and host the online self-report measures. Measures used in the study consisted of four self-report measures: the Bicultural Self-Efficacy Scale (David, 2009), the Satisfaction with Life Scale (Diener, Emmons, Larsen, & Griffin, 1985), the Multi-dimensional Inventory of Black Identity (MIBI; Sellers, Rowley, Chavous, et al., 1997), the Skin Color Assessment Procedure (Bond & Cash, 1992), and the Internalized Colorism scale adapted from the Weight Bias Internalization Scale (WBIS; Durso & Latner, 2008).

Results

Question 1:

A multiple regression analysis was conducted, and the results indicated that African American men who identified with Bicultural knowledge and Attitudes at 21% (F [6,161] =7.0; p<.001) and with positive racial identity reported higher levels of life satisfaction. The total variance explained by the model was 14% (F [6,160]=4.4; p<.001). It is important to point out that racial salience is context- specific, whereas centrality refers to a person's stable attitude toward their race.

Question 2:

To analyze the relationship between life satisfaction and colorism, a Pearson correlation was carried out. The results indicated a small, negative inverse relationship between internalized colorism and life satisfaction, meaning that high levels of internalized colorism are associated with lower levels of life satisfaction (r=.-217, n=170, p<.0005).

Question 3:

A two- way ANOVA analysis was conducted to answer Question 3. The results indicated that when we ignore whether the participant was light-, medium-, or dark-skinned, professional occupation influenced the life satisfaction of professional African American men. In addition, when we ignored the professional occupation, the skin color of participants did not influence their life satisfaction. A post-hoc comparison using the Tukey HSD test indicated that mean scores for engineering occupations (M=27.3, SD=5.7) were significantly different from educational occupations (M=22; SD=6.8). Other occupational groups did not differ. Upon further analysis, the interaction effect between skin color and professional occupation was statistically significant (F [10,154]=1.98, p=.038), indicating that the effect of professional occupation on life satisfaction is different for light-skinned Black men in law occupations.

Summary of Findings

The findings of this study are as follows:

1. African American men who identify with Bicultural knowledge and attitudes and identify with positive racial identity reported higher levels of life satisfaction.

2. Higher levels of internalized colorism are associated with lower levels of life satisfaction, which is an inverse relationship.

3. The main effect when we ignore whether the participants were light-, medium-, or dark- skinned indicates that professional occupation influences the life satisfaction of professional African American men.

4. The interaction effect between skin color and professional occupation was statistically significant. Thus, the effects of professional occupation on life satisfaction are different for light-skinned Black men in law-related occupations.

Discussion

The main purpose of this chapter was to document the impact that colorism, bicultural competence, and racial identity have on the life satisfaction of professional African American men. Of note, *professional* was defined as completing a degree from a four-year college/university and at least one full year of working experience. The findings from this inquiry are a bit provocative, while at the same time they support the existing literature. The data in this study give rise to information that could be useful in the creation of interventions with professional African American men.

Racial identity and bicultural competence Endorsement

The first finding suggests that racial identity and bicultural competency subscales predicted a positive endorsement of life satisfaction for African American professional men, which is similar to the conclusion of Pierre and Mahalik (2005) linking racial identity with positive life satisfaction for African American men. The private regard subscale of racial identity and the positive attitude and knowledge subscales of the bicultural scale make the strongest contribution to explaining the life satisfaction of professional African American men. The private regard subscale and racial centrality on the Multidimensional Inventory of Black Identity (MIBI) have been assessed to determine how specific aspects of identity help in coping with racism and discrimination, suggesting that professional African-American men who acquire knowledge about other cultures, endorse positive attitudes about other cultures, and view their own culture favorably are satisfied with their lives. Additionally, Phinney, Lockner, and Murphy (1990) suggest that some African-American males need to resolve two primary issues/conflicts that result from their marginalized status in society: (1) society's prejudicial attitudes; and (2) developing and adopting differing sets of values, one for the dominant culture and the other for the African-American culture. Research studies on racial identity have found that racial identity can be a barrier to racism, and because colorism is a form of racism, one could assume that racial identity can also be a buffer for colorism. The findings of this study found that not only can racial identity improve life satisfaction of professional African American men, but bicultural characteristics or competencies may serve as a buffer as well. In this study, biculturalism was conceptualized as professional African American males' sense of belonging and understanding of mainstream corporate American and African American culture. W.E.B. Bois coined the term "double consciousness" to describe the struggle to navigate two worlds simultaneously. The pressure to constantly juggle "two worlds" may lead individuals to experience racial battle fatigue. However, with strong connection to African American culture and bi-cultural characteristics such as a positive attitude toward other cultures and knowledge of mainstream American culture, professional African American men may be able to increase their life satisfaction and use these competencies as a buffer from White racial ideology.

Internalized Identities and Life Satisfaction

The second finding was that internalized discrimination is negatively correlated with life satisfaction of professional African American men, whereby as experiences of discrimination increases, life satisfaction of professional African American men will decrease. Thus, African American men who endorsed or identified with more internally discriminative ideas of their culture may have less life satisfaction. Although there is a small correlation between colorism and life satisfaction, the relationship is weak between the two variables; thus, more research is needed to understand what accounts for the low correlation between the variables. This research finding suggests that some professional African American men have internalized negative aspects or characteristics of African American culture, which is affecting their life satisfaction in a negative way. A report by the Surgeon General on the various ways racism and discrimination affect the mental and physical health of minorities states: (1) internalization of negative racial images and stereotypes that harm self-worth (2) institutional racism, and (3) racism and discrimination that are stressful events, which directly lead to psychological distress (U.S. Department of Health & Human Services; DHHS, 2001). The correlation found in this study may be related to the various ways in which the participants had internalized racism or discrimination in the past. The results of this finding expose two limitations in the analysis. First, a different scale to measure internalized colorism or discrimination is needed. Currently, there is no inventory or reliable scale that can measure the internalization of racist experiences. Crosby (1984) suggests that members of minority groups often identify less with personal discrimination and over-identify with group discrimination, as it is less threatening. Secondly, the language used to describe internalized colorism varies between "internalized racism," "skin tone bias" and "appropriated racial oppression." As a relativistic social construction, internalized colorism may influence how a person identifies with racism and discrimination experiences.

Impact of Colorism on Law and Criminal Justice Occupations

The last finding is that occupations such as medicine and engineering will increase the life satisfaction of professional African American men. In addition, those who identify their skin color as light or medium endorsed higher levels of life satisfaction than darker- skinned African American men. Using two-way between-groups (ANOVA), the findings indicate that the influence of occupation on life satisfaction is different for light-, medium-, and dark-skinned African American professional men. African American men who identify as medium- skinned endorsed higher levels of life satisfaction across all professional occupations, compared to light-skinned and dark-skinned African American men. These findings are congruent with past research and historical references that suggest certain privileges are afforded to African-Americans with lighter complexions and distinctly different socio-economic group (Breland, 1998; Edwards, 1972; Graham, 1999; Keith &Herring, 1991; Hughes & Hertel, 1990; Seltzer & Smith, 1991).

Remarkably, there may be an ideal skin color for African Americans that may neutralize the effects of within-group discrimination and discrimination from the majority group. Similarly, most participants in this study indicated their skin color to be a medium skin tone. Perhaps it could be assumed that there is an ideal preference for medium skin as opposed to light or dark skin. These findings are also consistent with other studies (Coard, Breland, & Raskin, 1999) that have found individuals with medium skin fare better in life than African-Americans at either end of the skin color spectrum, that light skin is preferred, and individuals with medium skin seem to be more attached to other African-Americans and use their identity for protection. Further analysis broke down the initial findings even further by looking at occupations by specific skin color. Across skin colors, African American men in educational occupations endorsed similar life satisfaction levels, and light-skinned African American men in engineering occupations reported the highest levels of life satisfaction. Further research should seek to understand why certain professions report having a higher life satisfaction. A possible reason for this could be that some professions require African American men to be more visible than others. In this sample, there could have been more variability in education, pay, and job requirements, especially in law occupations that could contribute to the lower levels of life satisfaction for professional African American men.

Implications for Policy, Research, and Practice

Implications for Human Resource Development and Diversity Training (Policy)

Human resource departments and industrial/organizational psychologists can begin to examine unconscious skin tone bias in the workplace, by recognizing the influence of White racial ideology, as it reinforces power and privilege within organizational structures. Research has shown that darker-skinned employees across various ethnic backgrounds may receive lower salaries and are less likely to acquire leadership roles. Banerji (2006) concluded that light-skinned Black male employees with a bachelor's degree and typical work experience were preferred over their dark-skinned counterparts who have an MBA. Many diversity trainings focus on discrimination, sexism, racism and ageism, but there are minimal trainings that discuss the color discrimination and privilege within organizations (Sims, 2009). Aguilar and Woo (2000) suggest having employees examine their pre-conceptions and biases, discuss discomfort and acknowledge social inequalities that exist in the organization, by rethinking human resource development models such as the Critical Human Resource Development (HRD), which addresses issues of power, privilege and inequities in the workplace. Using HRD may provide organizations a platform for discussions on skin tone biases.

Implications for African American Male Identity Development

The results of this study also have implications for theories that address development of African American men. First, these results suggest that skin color and internalized colorism may affect the masculine identity theory. African American male identity development is an under-researched topic, and studies conceptualize African American identity by Euro-American standards. Racial identity theorists such as William Cross, Janet Helms, and Robert Carter support the need for African Americans to affirm things that are noticeably Black, especially skin color; therefore, further research, solely devoted to African American male development, is needed.

Implications for Practice

The results of this study have serval implications for the assessment and treatment of African American men. First, skin color and internalized colorism exist and may be something African American male clients struggle with and may have an adverse impact on their racial identity, gender identity, and worldview. With this knowledge, clinicians may provide a space in therapy for their clients to address racial concerns; thus, exploration of psychological and emotionally internalized ideologies can be recognized. This information may be helpful in the conceptualization and treatment of their clients. College counseling centers and employers can better understand the anxieties people of color may have in asserting themselves in interviews, career choices, and the workplace. Further research is needed in this area to provide evidence and more information for clinicians to provide more comprehensive treatment plans and treatment to their male clients of color. Bell (2018) suggest that career counselors use an existential psychology approach, as it may allow Black male clients to explore and find meaning in their career as they face racism, discrimination, micro and macro-aggressions in the workplace. It appears that many participants learned about skin color through verbal and non-verbal interactions with their families and other social learning environments. It is vital that mental health professionals, especially those working with families of color, be made aware of the messages they may be communicating to their children about skin color. Clinicians working with African American men should be particularly conscious of this issue. It may become a topic of discussion regarding romantic relationships and friendships, as teens may experience trauma about being excluded from certain groups or as romantic partners, because of their skin color. Moreover, the results seek to reduce racism and discrimination experienced by African American men. The importance of affirmative action on college campuses and work settings may be reinforced by understanding the unique experiences (educational, familial, and social) of Black men and how they shape their readiness to compete at higher educational institutions. With tense race relations existing between the African American community and its White counterparts, especially regarding black men and law enforcement, the results of this study can promote an understanding of the Black experience, while providing a context in which African American men can understand and respect one another.

Implications for Research

Future research should examine the social structures of organizations, to determine and ensure that their mission and goals regarding diversity, inclusion and equity are aligned. Organizational, Industrial Psychologists and researchers should conduct both qualitative and quantitative research on the impact colorism/skin tone bias has on promotional trends, salaries, and job satisfaction, in order to acknowledge that colorism is a real phenomenon in the workplace and has real life implications for employees. Likewise, vocational counselors may also need to be aware of the impact certain career choices may have on their client's life satisfaction. Further, research is required on how bi-cultural competencies are developed in minorities, especially African Americans, as previous research has shown that bi-cultural competencies can serve as a buffer from various forms of racism and discrimination. Finally, future research should investigate internalized forms of racism and how they impact an individual's life satisfaction, especially in law enforcement fields. Conclusions from various studies in this area may provide some insight into police shootings of unarmed Black men and women and provide new ways to train law enforcement, especially African Americans as law enforcement officers.

Summary and Conclusion

The purpose of this study was to explore the impact colorism has on professional African American men. The results of this study suggest that racial identity, bi-cultural competence, internalized colorism, and depression influence the life satisfaction of professional African American men. Specifically, the intersection between skin color and professional occupation of African-American men influences the life satisfaction of professional African American men; however, the strongest predictor in this interaction is professional occupation and African American men having light skin and in law-related professions experience the lowest levels of life satisfaction. In contrast, African American men who were medium- skinned or darker- skinned experienced higher levels of life satisfaction across all occupations. The findings contradict the literature on colorism, which concludes that having a lighter skin leads to more educational, social and career opportunities, and ultimately higher levels of life satisfaction. As Smith, Hung and Franklin (2011) found that as educational attainment increases, the more exposure to racism, microaggression and Black misandry an African American man must cope with. In sum, racism, colorism, and micro-aggressions are frequent and common experiences that affect the life satisfaction of professional African American men. It would be short-sighted and callous for researchers, professional organizations and educational intuitions to not address them.

Process Questions and Considerations

1. How might colorism affect African American men working in law enforcement?
2. Should bicultural competency skills be taught to African American men to reduce

discrimination?

3. Why is it important for mental health professionals and vocational counselors to discuss colorism with their African American male clients?

4. The theory of life satisfaction may not incorporate the life factors that are important to African Americans. What are the factors that should be considered when conceptualizing the life satisfaction of African American men?

5. How should colorism be addressed at organizations, institutions of education and the workplace? Who should be responsible for training and educating employees on the impact of colorism?

References

Aguilar, V., & Woo, G. (2000). Team teaching and learning in diversity training for national service programs. *New Directions for Adult and Continuing Education*, 87, 63-71.

Banerji, S. (2006) Study: *Darker-skinned black job applicants hit more obstacles.* Diverse Education.com article6303.

Bell, T. (2018). Career counseling with black men: Applying principles of existential psychotherapy. *The Career Development Quarterly, 66*, 162-175. DOI:10.1002/cdq.12130.

Blind, F.B. (2019). Facebook empowers racism against its employees of color. Retrieved from https: medium. com/@blindfb2020/facebook-empowers-racism-against-its-employees-of-color-fbbfaf55ab76

Borrell, L. N., Kiefe, C. I., Williams, D. R., Diez-Roux, A. V., & Gordon-Larsen, P. (2006). Self-reported health perceived racial discrimination, and skin color in African Americans in the CARDIA study. *Social Science & Medicine, 63*, 1415-1427.

Breland, A. M. (1998). A model for differential perceptions of competence based on skin tone among African Americans. *Journal of Multicultural Counseling & Development, 26*(4), 294-312.

Brewer, A. M. (1998). The relationship among gender role conflict, depression, hopelessness, and marital satisfaction in a sample of African American men (Doctoral dissertation, Kent State University, 1998). *Dissertation Abstracts International, 59,* 3049.

Brewer, M. B., & Gardner, W. (1996). Who is this "we"? Levels of collective identity and self-representations. *Journal of Personality & Social Psychology, 71*(1), 83-93.

Brown, L.E.C. (2009). "If you're black, Get back!" The color complex: Issues of skin-tone bias in the workplace. *Ethnic Studies Review, 32*(2), 120-130.

Bronfenbrenner, U. (1986). Ecology of the family as a context for human development: Research perspectives. *Developmental Psychology, 22*(6), 723-742.

Bush, V. L., & Bush, E. C. (2013). Introducing African American Male Theory (AAMT). *Journal of African American Males in Education, 4*(1), 6-17.

Bynum, M. S., Best, C., Barnes, S. L. & Burton, E. L. (2008). Private regard, identity protection and perceived racism among African American males. *Journal of African American Studies, 12*, 142-155. DOI 10.1007/s12111-008-9038-5.

Cash, T. F., & Duncan, N. C. (1984). Physical attractiveness stereotyping among black American college students. *Journal of Social Psychology, 122*, 71-77.

Carter, R. T., Williams, B., Juby, H. T., & Buckley, T. R. (2005). Racial identity as mediator of the relationship between gender role conflict and severity of psychological symptoms in black, Latino and Asian Men. *Sex Roles, 53,* 473- 486. DOI:10.1007/s11199-005-7135-7

Centers for Disease Control and Prevention. (2010). Current depression among adults—United States, 2006 and 2008. *MMWR, 59,* 1229-1235.

Chaudoir, S. R., Earnshaw, V. A., & Andel, S. (2013). "Discredited" versus "discreditable": Understanding how shared and unique stigma mechanisms affect psychological and physical health disparities. *Basic and Applied Social Psychology, 35,* 75-87. DOI:10.1080/01973533.2012

Cheatham, H. E. (1990). Africentricity and career development of African Americans. *The Career Development Quarterly*, 38(4), 334-347.

Coard, S. I., Breland, A. F., & Raskin, P. (2001). Perceptions of preferences for skin color, racial identity, and self-esteem among African Americans. *Journal of Applied Social Psychology, 31*(11), 2256-2274.

Cornileus, H.T. (2012). "I'm a black man and I'm doing this job very well": How African American professional men negotiate the impact of racism on their career development. *Journal of African American Studies, 17*(4), 444-460.

Crosby, F. J. (1984). The denial of personal discrimination. *American Behavioral Scientist, 27,* 371-386. DOI:10.1177/000276484027003008

Cross, W. E., Jr. (1995). The psychology of nigrescence: Revising the Cross model. In J. G. Ponterotto, J. M. Casas, L. A. Suzuki, & C. M. Alexander (Eds.), *Handbook of multicultural counseling* (pp. 93-122). Thousand Oaks, CA: SAGE Publications.

Cross, W. E., Jr., & Vandiver, B. J. (2001). Nigrescence theory and measurement: Introducing the Cross Racial Identity Scale (CRIS). In J. G. Ponterotto et al. (Eds.), *Handbook of Multicultural Counseling*, 2nd edition (pp. 95-130). Thousand Oaks, CA: SAGE.

Cross, W. E., & Vandiver, B. (2001). Nigrescence theory: Current status and challenges for the future. *Journal of Multicultural Counseling and Developing, 29* (3), 201-213.

Diemer, M. A. (2007). Two Worlds: African American Men's Negotiation of Predominately White Educational and Occupational Worlds. *Journal of Multicultural Counseling and Development, 35,* 2-14.

Diener, E., Emmons, R. A., Larsen, R. J., & Griffin, S. (1985). The Satisfaction with Life Scale. *Journal of Personality Assessment*, 49, 71-75.

David, E.J.R., Okazaki, S., & Saw, A. (2009). Bicultural self-efficacy among college students: Initial scale development and mental health correlates. *Journal of Counseling Psychology,* 56, 211-226. DOI:10.1037/a0015419

Donnay, D. A., & Borgen, F. H. (1999). The incremental validity of vocational self-efficacy: An examination of interest, self-E=efficacy, and O=occupation. *Journal of Counseling Psychology, 46*(4), 432-447.

Du Bois, W.E.B . (1903, 1965 ed.). *The souls of black folk.* London: Longmans, Green and Co. Ltd.

Durant, T. J., Jr., & Louden, J. S. (1986). The black middle class in America: historical and contemporary perspectives. *Phylon, 47*(4), 253-263.

Elligan, D., & Utsey, S. (1990). Utility of an African American support group for African American men confronting societal racism and oppression. *Cultural Diversity and Ethnic Minority Psychology, 5,* 156-165.

Feagin, J. R. (1992). The continuing significance of racism: Discrimination against black students in White colleges. *Journal of Black Studies, 22,* 546-578.

Feagin, J. R., & Sikes, M. P. (1994). *Living with racism: The black middle-class experience.* Boston: Beacon.

Goldsmith, A. H., Hamilton, D., & Darity, D. (2003). *Skin-tone discrimination and economic outcomes, shades of discrimination.* In *Skin Tone and Wages, American Economic Review, 96*(2), pp. 242-245.

Greer, T. M., & Chwalisz, K. (2007). Minority related stressors and coping processes among African American college students. *Journal of College Student Development, 48,* 388-404.

Hall, R. (1992). Bias among African Americans regarding skin color: Implications for social work practice. *Research on Social Work Practice,* (2), pp. 479-86.DOI:10.1177/104973159200200404.

Harvard Law Review. (1991). Invisible man: Black and male under Title VII. *Harvard Law Review, 104*(3), 749-768.

Hill, M. (2000). Color Differences in the socioeconomic status of African American men: Results of a longitudinal study. *Social Forces, 78*(4), 1437-1460.

Hochschild, D., & Weaver, V. (2007). The skin color paradox and the American racial order. *Social Forces, 86*(2), 643-670.

Holtzman J. (1973). Color caste changes among black college students. *Journal of Black Studies*, (4)92-101.

Kirschenman, J., Moss, P., & Tilley, C. (1996). "Soft" skills and race: An investigation of black men's employment problems. *Work and Occupations, 23*(3), 252-76. DOI:10.1177/0730888496023003002

Lacy, D. A. (2008). The most endangered Title VII plaintiff: exponential discrimination against African-American males. *Nebraska Law Review, 86*(3). Retrieved October 1, 2008, from http://ssrn.com/abstract0984552.

LaFromboise, T., Coleman, H.L.K., & Gerton, J. (1993). Psychological impact of biculturalism: Evidence and theory. *Psychological Bulletin, 114*, 395-412. DOI:10.1037/0033-2909.114.3.395.

Lavrakas, P. (2008). *Encyclopedia of survey research.* Thousand Oaks, CA: SAGE.

Lent, R. W., Brown, S. D., & Hackett, G. (2000). Contextual supports and barriers to career choice: A social cognitive analysis, *The Journal of Counseling Psychology,47*(1), 36-49.

Lent, R. W., Brown, S. D., Sheu, H.-B., Schmidt, J., Brenner, B. R., Gloster, C. S., & Treistman, D. (2005). Social cognitive predictors of academic interests and goals in engineering: Utility for women and students at historically black universities. *Journal of Counseling Psychology, 52*(1), 84-92. DOI:10.1037/0022- 0167.52.1.84

Major, B., Quinton, W. J., & McCoy, S. K. (2002). Antecedents and consequences of attributions to discrimination: Theoretical and empirical advances. In M. P. Zanna (Ed.), *Advances in experimental social psychology, 34,* pp. 251-330). New York, NY: Academic Press.

Matthews, D. D., Hammond, W., Nuru-Jeter, A., Cole-Lewis, Y., & Melvin, T. (2013). Racial discrimination and depressive symptoms among African-American men: The mediating and moderating roles of masculine self-reliance and John Henryism. *Psychology of Men & Masculinity,* 14(1), 35-46. DOI:10.1037/a0028436.

Neville, H. A., Heppner, P. P., Peter, J., & Thye, R. (2004).The relations among general and race-related stressors and psychoeducational adjustment in black students attending predominantly white institutions. *Journal of Black Studies, 34*(4), 599-618.

Owen. D., Lacey, K., Rawls, G., & Holbert-Quince, J. (2010). First-generation African American male college students: Implications for career counselors. *Career Development Quarterly, 58*(4), 291-300.

Pascoe, E. A., & Richman, S.L. (2009). Perceived discrimination and health: A meta-analytic review. *Psychological Bulletin, 135*, 531-554. DOI:10.1037/a0016059

Pitcan, M., Taylor, J. P., & Hayslett, J. (2018). Black men and racial microaggressions at work. *The Career Development Quarterly,66*(4), 300-314.

Phinney, J. S., Lochner, B. T., & Murphy, R. (1990). Ethnic identity development and psychological adjustment in adolescence. In Arlene Rubin Stiffman and Larry E. Davis (Eds.), *Ethnic issues in adolescent mental health* (pp. 53-72). Newbury Park, CA. SAGE.

Peirre, M. R., & Mahalik, J.R. (2005). Examining African self-consciousness and black racial identity as predictors of black male psychological well-being. *Cultural Diversity and Ethnic Minority Psychology, 11*(1), 28-40.

Pelzer, D. L. (2016). Creating a new narrative: Reframing black masculinity for college men. *The Journal of Negro Education, 85*, 16-27.

Pieterse, A., & Carter, R. (2007). Examination of the relationship between general life stress, racism-related stress, and psychological health among black men. *Journal of Counseling Psychology, 54*, 101-109.

Rodriguez, M. (2008). Perceived discrimination: Multiple measures and the intersections of race and gender. *Journal of African American Studies, 12*, 348-365.

Ryff, C. D. (1 January 1989). Happiness is everything, or is it? Explorations on the meaning of psychological well-being. *Journal of Personality and Social Psychology, 57*(6) 1069-1081. DOI:10.1037./0022-3514.57.6.1069.

Salmans, S. (1997). *Depression: Questions you have—answers you need.* People's Medical Society.

Schmitt M. T., Branscombe, N. R., Postmes, T., & Garcia, A. (2014). The consequences of perceived discrimination for psychological well-being: A meta-analytic review. *American Psychological Association, 140*(4), 921-948.

Seaton, E. K., Caldwell, C. H., Sellers, R. M., & Jackson, J. S. (2010). An intersectional approach forunderstanding perceived discrimination and life satisfaction among African American and Caribbean black youth. *Developmental Psychology, 46*(5), 1372-1379.

Seaton, E. K., Lopez, A. M., Yip, T., & Sellers, R. M. (2012). Racial discrimination and racial socialization as predictors of African American adolescents' racial identity development Using LatentTransition Analysis. *Developmental Psychology, 48*(2), 448-458.

Sellers, S., Neighbors, H. W., & Bonham, V. L. (2011). Goal-striving stress and the mental health of college-educated black American men: The protective effects of system-blame. *American Journal of Orthopsychiatry, 81*(4), 507-518

Shilpa, B. (2006). *Darker-skinned black job applicants face more obstacles. Diverse issues in higher education, 23*(16), 20.

Sims, C. (2009). The impact of African American skin tone bias in the workplace: Implications for critical human resource development. *Online Journal of Workforce Education and Development, III*(4), 1-17.

Smith, W., Hung, M., & Franklin, J. D. (2011). Racial battle fatigue and the miseducation of black men: racial microaggressions, societal problems, and environmental stress. *Journal of Negro Education, 80*(3), 63-82.

Taylor, E. (1998). A primer on critical race theory. *The Journal of Blacks in Higher Education, 19,* 122-124.

Thomas, D. A., & Gabarro, J. J. (1999). *Breaking through: the making of minority executives in corporate America.* Boston: Harvard Business School Press.

Toossi, M. (2006). A new look at long-term labor force projections to 2050. *Monthly Labor Review* (pp. 19-39). Washington, DC: U.S. Department of Labor.

Utsey, S. O., Ponterotto, J. G., Reynolds, A. L., Cancelli, A. A. (2000). Racial discrimination, coping, life satisfaction and self-esteem among African Americans. *Journal of Counseling and Development, 78,* 72-80.

Uzogara, E., Lee, H., Abdou, C. & Jackson, J. S. (2014). A comparison of skin tone discrimination among African American men: 1995 to 2003. *Psychology of Men and Masculinity, 15*(2), 201-212.

Williams, D. R., Neighbors, H. W., & Jackson, J. S. (2003). Racial/ethnic discrimination and health: Findings from community studies. *American Journal of Public Health, 93,* 200-208. DOI: 10.2105/AJPH.93.2.20/0

Wright, P., McGovern, K. P., Boo, J. N, & Vannatter, A. W. (2014). Influential factors in academic and career self-efficacy: Attachment, supports, and career barriers. *Journal of Counseling & Development, 92,* 36-46.

CHAPTER 8.

Brown and Bullied Around: The Relationship between Colorism and Workplace Bullying for African Americans/Blacks

Leah P. Hollis, Morgan State University

Introduction

Since the 1990s, academic scholars have been examining workplace bullying and its impact on organizations and individuals (Bassman, 1992; Einarsen, Raknes, & Matthiesen, 1994; Resch & Schubinski, 1996). More contemporary studies have considered workplace bullying in various work environments such as higher education and health care (Faucher, Cassidy, & Jackson, 2015; Hollis, 2015; Lever, Dyball, Greenberg & Stevelink, 2019; Piotrowski, & King, 2016; Rainford, Wood, McMullen, & Philipsen, 2015; Sauer & McCoy, 2017). Researchers have also examined how workplace bullying has a negative impact on employees' health in terms of depression, insomnia, anxiety, and suicidal ideation (Antoniou & Daliana, 2018; Conway, Hogh, Balducci, & Ebbesen, 2018; Hollis, 2019a; Einarsen & Nielsen, 2015). Other social and behavioral approaches analyze how intersectionality is directly related to the workplace bullying that Black women experience (Hollis, 2018); and how gender and race alter or intensify the workplace bullying experience (Attell, Brown, & Treiber, 2017).

Regardless of the focus on health, environment, race, or gender, workplace bullying occurs when someone with more power harasses and belittles someone with less status, fewer resources, or the capacity to initiate change. Typical workplace bullying emerges from an abusive boss or leader. A leader's tacit acceptance with no interventions also enables bullying (Hollis, 2019). Over time, bullied employees mentally disengage, which results in diminished and costly ineffective work productivity. Workplace bullying contributes to dysfunctional organizations and decreased work productivity (Colligan & Higgins, 2006) with 16% of bullied employees leaving the organization (Hollis, 2015). Giga, Hoel, and Lewis (2008) estimate that over 200,000 employees in the United Kingdom have left organizations due to workplace bullying, resulting in a loss of 100 million days' productivity. Consequently, workplace bullies trigger an expensive job search to replace the employees who resigned to escape the tyrant (Coetzee & van Dyk, 2018; Hollis, 2015; Nabe-Nielsen, et al., 2017).

Some researchers consider that workplace bullying is a product, not the precipitator, of the dysfunctional organization (Hodson, Roscigno, & Lopez 2006). When organizations do not follow their own rules and policies, have a rampant turnover in leadership positions, or even have leaders who refuse to hold the bullies accountable, workplace bullying behaviors can infest the organizational culture (Hodson, Roscigno, & Lopez, 2006). As a result, those employees who are lower on the organizational chart are least equipped to protect themselves within a chaotic and mismanaged organization that allows for workplace bullying. Within the historical traditions that assign privilege to people with lighter skin, a person with a lighter skin complexion may hold jobs with advanced status.

As noted by several researchers who study colorism (Egbeyemi, 2009; Hunter, 2007; Kerr, 2005), those with darker skin often do not advance as quickly as lighter-skinned counterparts. In short, darker-skinned colleagues would also not readily have the organizational power and privilege offered to lighter-skinned colleagues. In considering workplace bullying, power differential, and colorism, I was inspired to examine the impact of colorism for African Americans/Blacks who face workplace bullying. My research has confirmed that workplace bullying occurs due to intersecting elements such as race, gender, and sexual orientation. Colorism would also contribute to the frequency of workplace bullying. Hence, the intersection of colorism, power, and career ascendance is deserving of further analysis.

Theoretical Framework

Colorism, that is, bias against a person because of skin tone and complexion, historically emerges from the vestiges of slavery. Such ideas were proliferated globally through the colonial imperialism of the time. Those with darker complexions were considered physically stronger, brutish in fact, and more suited for harsh fieldwork. In contrast, those with lighter complexions were considered more fragile and suited for housework. Hall (2018) noted that the British developed and imposed a color-based racial hierarchy. Given that the British Empire at one time expanded to the four corners of the globe, it undoubtedly imposed its biased and colorist discrimination onto the global community (Lloyd, 1984; Newsinger, 2013). The color bias systematically blankets society because of the indelible expectation that those with lighter skin presumably are more acceptable, attractive, and privileged (Burton, Bonilla-Silva, Ray,

Buckelew, & Hordge Freeman, 2010). These colorized systems have governed social clubs, access to employment, and even family dynamics. In turn, such systems have created another series of barriers for darker-skinned people seeking social mobility and self-determination.

Though human slavery is universally outlawed, the colorized discriminatory values still pollute ideologies regarding acceptable skin color. For example, during my recent tour of Havana, Cuba in October, 2019, our tour group of African American scholars heard the tour guide almost brag about the practice of racial mixing between owners and slaves. The practice in Cuba was for white slave owners to visit their plantations in the summer to coerce and engage in sexual relationships with Black women slaves, believing that sex with a slave made the White slave owner stronger and more virile. Lighter-skinned slaves were the product of White male slave owners having sexual relations with their African women slaves, often forcibly. The result of raping African slaves created generations of racially mixed slaves or "mulattoes" who were more valuable in the slave trade, as their appearance aligned with European features in build, hair, and eye color (Johnson, 1999).

Mulattoes at the time considered themselves better than their darker-complexioned counterparts (Toplin, 1979). Similar to contemporary colorist practices that hire lighter-skinned people in highly traveled tourist areas, mulattoes had more employment opportunities in urban areas such as Charleston, Atlanta, and New Orleans. These tourist areas were distinctively more affluent than impoverished agricultural districts (Toplin, 1979).

Egbeyemi (2019) argued that colorism is a phenomenon deserving of more attention, which not only affects who is deemed acceptable but also influences socioeconomic status. Because White slave owners systematically favored lighter-skinned slaves, these owners allowed the lighter-skinned slaves to learn how to read and write (Hunter, 2007). This preference was also related to slave owners being the fathers of racially mixed children, therefore creating a preference for mix raced and lighter-skinned slaves (Parks & Woodson, 2002). Such preference led to lighter-skinned slaves receiving less arduous work assignments. Lighter-skinned slaves received minimal education, better clothes, and better food. As a result, this group led to the emergence of Black teachers, artists, and religious leaders in the African American community when slavery was abolished (Egbeyemi, 2019). The different educational levels along color lines also produced a system in which lighter skin is preferred, more educated, and more employable. To this point, Kerr (2006) confirmed that during the Reconstruction years of the late 1880s,

60% of mulattos could read while only 20% of brown and darker-skinned Blacks could read (Egbeyemi, 2019).

The preference for lighter-skin people remained embedded throughout the culture and was at times co-opted to redefine the Black community. *Ebony Magazine* featured Lena Horne on the cover repeatedly as a new model for Black women (Williams, 2009). Using a more socially acceptable lighter-skinned Black woman, who was also a visionary in her own right, *Ebony* publisher John H. Johnson reframed Black womanhood in his landmark magazine. Being a "normal" girl, a pretty girl was the message recast to distance Blacks from the darker-skinned and unsavory Mammy and Jezebel images (Williams, 2009). *Ebony Magazine* was creating distance from the hypersexualized and aggressive Jezebel stereotype, and the bossy yet expert domestic Mammy figure (Brown, White-Johnson, & Griffin-Fennell, 2013; Sewell, 2013). Though Johnson's *Ebony Magazine* was revolutionary at its inception, the images in his magazine still informed this general longing for African Americans/Blacks to be lighter-skinned (Glenn, 2008). Henceforth, the media images continually perpetuate colorized expectations of acceptability; music videos, movies, and social media have bolstered these expectations that still affect the Black population.

Colorism within the Black community continues to have an impact on family status and wealth. Hunter (2007) confirmed that lighter-skinned women "married up" to men with higher-paying jobs and more social prestige (Egbeyemi, 2019). Similarly, Goldsmith, Hamilton, Darity, Jr. (2007), and Burton, Bonilla-Silva, Ray, Buckelew, and Hordge Freeman (2010) further documented employment inequities where darker-skinned people have lower-paying positions. In the UCLA Law Review, Banks (1999) also confirmed that darker skin has detrimental effects on economic ascendance, while white or lighter-skin people have advantages in employment. In the employment arena, Banks (1999) insisted that the legal system truly embraced colorism as a protected marker instead of redirecting legal complaints on colorism to racial discrimination.

Lighter-skinned women also had greater access to educational opportunities and employment opportunities. Such intersecting personas that include European blood and appearance created society's preference for lighter-skinned Black women to the detriment of darker-skinned women, who typically must disproportionally shoulder such bias at work and in their own communities (Hollis, 2018). These historical and contemporary colorist attitudes yield the need to empirically examine colorism in the workplace.

For this study, the goal was to examine the extent of the systematic color bias for African Americans/Blacks in employment. These structural problems, which have been manifest over 500 years, have infiltrated global thinking on skin color. Hence, to reply to one of the respondents in this study who commented, "Didn't realize this was still a thing," I borrow from Bonilla-Silva (2009), who solidified the point that such racialized and colorized systems are pervasive and remain intact, informing a color-coded value judgment on people of color.

The Color of Power

A society subscribing to Eurocentrism and a preference for lighter skin has assigned power to those with such attributes. The power dynamic remains critical to considering the cross-section of workplace bullying and colorism. The historical power differential along color lines has denigrated many while hoisting a few lighter-skinned people to heights of acceptance, yielding socioeconomic gains for them. The hegemonic culture perpetuates colorist bias and prejudice regarding skin tone. Blacks and whites alike, indoctrinated with this bias, subscribe to such discrimination even in raising respective families and setting social expectations.

The power dynamic informs unjust behaviors at work and school. Bullying, whether in the homeroom or the boardroom, is based on a power differential. Those who have power abuse it to the detriment of those without power (Hollis, 2018). In the colorism context, those of darker skin might be perceived to have physical power, strength, and endurance, but intellectual power, gentility, access, and financial power is often granted to lighter-skinned individuals. Consequently, those with European features have been and continue to be elevated with more social power.

These behaviors and imperialist expectations not only have empowered lighter-skinned individuals through the centuries, but have also diminished the self-esteem and perception of potential power for those with darker skin. As Lewis, Noroña, McConnico, and Thomas (2013) stated, even darker-skinned people endure a historical trauma regarding color, attractiveness, and acceptability, being taught, "if you're Black, step back. . . " A culture divided by color lines that run deep is integral to our social systems, inclusive of family structures. Not only do we collectively remain victims of such bias, we consciously or unconsciously perpetuate these colorist systems (Burton et al., 2010).

Purpose Statement

Employment scholars continue to proclaim a need to further examine employees' experiences and potential marginalization (Espino & Franz, 2002; Klonoff & Landrine, 2000; Ruggs et al., 2013). Marir and Mitra (2013) examined colorism in the workplace as a global problem. In a recent study, when faced with choosing a lighter-skinned or a darker-skinned employment candidate, Whites chose the lighted-skinned candidate with a bachelor's degree over the darker-skinned candidate with a master's degree (Harrison & Thomas 2009; Marir & Mitra, 2013).

Colorism in the African American/Black community stems from the slavery traditions where those with lighter skin were considered more demure and appropriate for housework, while darker slaves were relegated to heavy and arduous fieldwork. Those with fairer skin can be more readily accepted by White/Anglo society and historically have better access to jobs, financial freedom, and social ascension (Goldsmith, Hamilton, & Darity Jr, 2006; Hughes & Hertel, 1990). In contrast, darker-complexioned African Americans/Blacks have faced ostracism by both white communities and Black communities and assigned harsher and lower-paid work assignments.

Though the 1964 Civil Rights legislations explicitly prohibit discrimination based on color, Harris (2008) and Banks (2009) stated that the legal system does not seriously consider colorism as a problem in the workplace, but instead assigns such discrimination and harassment to race only. With these historical factors infiltrating the contemporary workplace, I have empirically analyzed how colorism for African American/Black employees, regardless of the work sector, may have an impact on their work experiences. Therefore, the purpose of this study was to examine whether colorism is a factor in which African Americans/Blacks endure workplace bullying.

Research Methods
Data Collection

During the last week of October 2019, I disseminated a 12-question instrument through SurveyMonkey Audience. I also sent the survey to African American/Black colleagues, regardless of industry. LinkedIn was a vital component in the respondent recruitment process. I posted the link to the survey in groups such as Black Enterprise, higheredjobs.com, the American Association for Access, Equity and Diversity, two different Black alumni associations, and the International Black Doctoral Network. Further, with over 3,500 LinkedIn contacts, I randomly choose 175 African American/ Black contacts and emailed them directly to request their participation. The recruitment message also asked potential respondents to circulate the instrument link to their friends. The Survey Monkey platform estimated that respondents needed three minutes to complete the 12-question survey. With Survey Monkey Audience, LinkedIn online groups, direct email, and the snowball process in which respondents also recruited colleagues via email, I would be unable to determine a response rate. However, when I considered my last seven years of conducting survey research, this recruitment period was the only one in which only one round of dissemination was required to achieve the target sample. Typically, the data collection period minimally occurs over a 12-week period instead of the 10-day period used to collect n=158 completed responses (Hollis, 2017). Initially, I did not make the decision for a 10-day data collection period; the study seemed to have considerable appeal to potential respondents who completed the instrument without a second or third reminder. Further, over 20 respondents wrote to me directly to ensure that they received the findings.

With regard to instrument development, I had conducted a literature review to consider colorism among African Americans/Blacks before developing the tool. Such practice is consistent with recommendations to have a clear understanding of the literature before developing the instrument. As a member of the African American community, I would have some preconceived bias about colorism; however, the survey questions that appear in the appendix were presented in a neutral fashion to support the validity of the study. Demographic information could inform future analysis regarding age, gender, and colorism, yet these factors are outside the scope of this initial study on colorism and workplace bullying. The instrument format not only gathered respondents' information regarding color, but respondents were also given the opportunity to provide other insight in the final open-ended question (Hollis, 2017). These comments were used in qualitative content analysis to confirm or challenge the statistical findings.

I specifically disseminated the instrument to African Americans/Blacks only regardless of career or title; therefore, 100% of the sample identifies within the African American/Black race. To address colorism, I asked participants to identify with a skin complexion. In short, color bands a, b, and c are the darker complexions, with d and e as the lighter complexions (See Table 1).

Research Questions

RQ1 Are African Americans/Blacks with darker skin complexions more likely to report workplace bullying than African Americans/Blacks with lighter skin complexions?

H1 African Americans/Blacks with darker skin complexions are more likely to report workplace bullying than African Americans/Blacks with lighter skin complexions.

Table 1

Real Skin Tones from SchemColor https://www.schemecolor.com/

A- Russet or darker,

B- Peru,

C- Fawn,

D- Apricot,

E- Navajo White or lighter

55% of respondents choose Russet or darker; 22.5% chose Peru; 14 % choose Fawn; 7% choose Apricot, and under 1.5% choose Navajo White or lighter.

RQ2 Are African Americans/Blacks with darker skin complexions more likely to report vicarious workplace bullying than African Americans/Blacks with lighter skin complexions?

H2 African Americans/Blacks with darker skin complexions are more likely to report vicarious workplace bullying than African Americans/Blacks with lighter skin complexions.

Findings

Females comprised 70% of the sample and males comprised 30% of the sample. The ages of the sample ranged from 18 years of age to 60 years and over, while the median age range (37%) was at 40-49 years of age. Over 56% of the sample was from the Northeast and Mid-Atlantic states, but with representation from the Southeast 17%, Midwest 14%, Southwest 7%, Pacific Northwest 3%, and West 3%.

The reported prevalence of workplace bullying among the African American/ Black respondents was 67% (106/158 who answered this question) who reported being affected by workplace bullying. Also, 57% (90/158) of the sample has been affected by vicarious workplace bullying—that is, when the bully sends a subordinate to conduct the bullying. When compared to the general population of American workers, this sample reported a prevalence of workplace bullying double the prevalence of 37% that Namie and Namie reported for the general American workforce (2009).

The data were coded in a binary format, with Yes=1 and No=2. For those reporting Russet/Peru complexions, 71% (87/122) reported experiencing workplace bullying in the last two years. For those reporting Fawn, Apricot, or Navajo White, 53% (19/36) reported experiencing workplace bullying in regard to colorism, N=158 of those who answered this question. A Chi-square analysis, with the use of IBM SPSS version 25, confirmed H1, African Americans/Blacks with darker skin complexions are more likely to report workplace bullying than African Americans/Blacks with lighter skin complexions. Participants with a darker complexion (Russet and Peru) are more likely to experience workplace bullying at a statistically significant level (X2 [2, N=158]=4.32; p=.038). See Table 2.

Table 2

Colorism and Workplace Bullying

	1= Yes	2= No	Total
Fawn Apr Nave (lighter)			
Count	19	17	36
Exp Count	24.2	11.8	36
RUS PER (darker)			
Count	87	35	122
Exp Count	81.8	40.2	122

To address the second research question, I used the Chi-square analysis to determine whether color was a significant factor in respondents' reporting vicarious bullying. In this form of workplace bullying, the bully sends a subordinate to inflict the abuse (Hollis, 2019). For those reporting Russet or Peru complexion, 59% (73/122) reported experiencing vicarious workplace bullying in the last two years; those reporting Fawn Apricot or Navajo White complexion, 47% (17/36) reported experiencing vicarious workplace bullying. A Chi-square analysis confirmed that participants with a darker complexion (Russet and Peru) have a somewhat direct relationship with experiencing vicarious workplace bullying; however, this occurrence is not at a statistically significant level. Therefore, H2—African Americans/Blacks with darker skin complexions—are more likely to report vicarious workplace bullying than African Americans/Blacks with lighter skin complexions is not rejected (X2 [2, N=158] =1.80; =.179). See Table 3.

The final question of the instrument, "Are there other comments you can offer about complexion and workplace experiences?" collected 51 open-ended comments. This optional question was not a factor in determining whether the respondent completed the survey; yet the data from this option provided enough data for a qualitative content

Table 3

Colorism and Vicarious Workplace Bullying

	1= Yes	2= No	Total
Fawn Apr Nav (lighter)			
Count	17	19	36
Exp Count	20.5	15.5	36
RUS PER (darker)			
Count	73	49	122
Exp Count	69.5	52.5	122

analysis (Hsieh & Shannon, 2005). From the 51 respondents, two themes emerged. The central theme related to colorism hurting one's career path. The second theme related to the notion that hard work and expertise can transcend colorism in the work environment. Of the respondents who left open-ended comments, 18 of 51, or 35%, reinforced that the element of color, beyond racism, is a detrimental factor in their careers. Please see comments regarding colorism from respondents' own words, and Table 4.

Table 4

Respondents in their own words about colorism on the job

Respondent #5: I think that I am "more" accepted because my skin color is medium and NOT darker.

Respondent #15: I was denied a promotion at my previous job twice; the promotion was given to persons with lighter complexion, who had less experience than me as well as less education.

Respondent #21: In my opinion, my darker complexion causes others to act cautiously in speaking about racial issues in my presence. My colleagues appear more comfortable with lighter skinned Blacks.

Respondent #28: Yes, whereas I have not been bullied, it is evident that my skin color holds me back for promotion. My supervisor (she is white) just got her master's degree after five years of being the supervisor whereas I have had a master's degree for 19 years and have also earned my PhD. The AA principals who have been hired in our district are all fair skinned.

Respondent #32: Given my complexion, education, and experience, I have encountered many white or fair skinned females that have felt intimidated by me. This has resulted in my being exposed to workplace bullying, character assassination, and wrongful termination.

Respondent #49: The darker an African American man is, the more exceptional he must [be on the job].

Respondents' comments corroborate the Chi-square results, that colorism remains a hurtful practice that adversely affects the African/American community. Consistent with the historical writings about darker skin and diminished employment opportunities, this contemporary study illustrates that colorism is not fading as a traditional practice. Instead, these problems still hurt careers and respective earning power for those subjected to this bias.

Implications for Practice, Research, and Policy

The complex system of color prejudice continues to subjugate people based on their skin complexion instead of their contributions to the community. Further, just as United States researchers focus on workplace bullying and tend to consider it as a litigious matter (Hollis, 2017a), legal scholars and practitioners can also push for colorism to be taken seriously as a protected status under the 1964 Title VII legislation. Further, the literature on workplace bullying confirms that abusive work conditions can severely damage employees' health. With the aforementioned health concerns about anxiety, depression, and insomnia related to workplace bullying, more research is needed to empirically confirm the impact on the African American/Black community. With these concepts in mind, please see the following recommendations for research, policy, and practice.

Research

1. Colorism is a discriminatory practice that affects the global community; future study could examine how colorism contributes to workplace bullying for the Asian and Hispanic/Latinx community.

2. Future studies could examine how workplace bullying from colorism has an impact on the health and wellness of those disproportionately affected by color prejudice on the job.

3. Educational researchers who study the primary and secondary grades can conduct phenomenological and ethnographic studies to determine whether the school setting supports and perpetuates colorism bias.

Practice

4. As colorism is woven into our social structures, family counseling with a licensed Black psychologist or therapist could address the ills of color bias and curtail this type of bias in young people's formative years.

5. Parents and family members should consider how color is discussed in the home

and embrace inclusive conversations about color instead of allowing teasing about color if that is occurring.

6. Organizations can hold exit interviews for departing employees. These exit interviews can include questions about the organization's cultural competency, inclusive of questions about colorism.

Policy

1. Organizations should have training for EEO and human resources staff to recognize and address colorism instead of conflating colorism with racism.

2. Employment climate studies, whether in industry, government, or education, should include questions to unmask colorist practices that may taint the work environment.

3. Title VII anti-discrimination policies should explicitly note colorism as an issue separate from racism and that colorism specifically is also prohibited.

Conclusion

Scholastic voices throughout the Diaspora call for analytical and activist progression to end White privilege and the corresponding property rights that Whites often maintain in access, education, and employment (Curry, 2009). Colorism, as one of the vestiges of American slavery, embraces that ripple of White privilege, granting lighter-skinned African Americans/Blacks favor, even if that favor was forced upon them through nonconsensual relations. Curry continued in his analysis that diminishing racism requires more than polite congeniality and good manners (2009). Colorism, as a derivative of racist practices, may favor the lighter over the darker, but also turns one against the other. Therefore, the dominant culture literally bred into Black communities remains a divisive element in Black communities, Black families, and Black employees. Competitive conversations about who has "good hair," or "lighter eyes" divide a community against itself while that same community struggles for equality within the very White community that infiltrated it.

Colorism and all of its alienating baggage should be unpacked in the Black community, faced directly to address the truths of its origins, and then healed within the Black community. The Black community faces grander social economic challenges in housing, politics, employment, and health care than to be divided among itself over color and bloodlines. As this study confirms, those with darker skin are still less favored than lighter-skinned Blacks, and therefore become targets by workplace bullies more frequently. As noted earlier, these colorized practices not only hurt people within a community's social structures, but these practices illegally harm darker-skinned peoples' socioeconomic ascendance and self-determination. Further, workplace bullying is directly related to health issues such as insomnia, depression, anxiety, and substance abuse. In acute cases, aggressive work behaviors lead to suicidal ideations. These factors reasonably contribute to darker-skinned people's coping with more emotional and psychological challenges resulting from workplace trauma. For these aforementioned reasons, colorism is a critical yet still understudied workplace phenomenon.

Repelling someone based on color not only denies that individual opportunities, but it also denies society the benefit of that expertise and innovation. With international communities transforming into a more beige and brown world given the minority/majority status—that is more Black and Brown children than White children were born after 2015—this colorism remains an urgent dynamic that needs to be dismantled. For the race to continue its progress, all members need to shed any possible negative self-images associated with colorism (Pearson-Trammell, 2010) and instead unite with resilience to oppose colorist ideologies that hurt the entire Black community. To echo the famed words of Martin Luther King, Jr., it is the content of our character, not the color of our skin, which should be the central focus (King & Pascoe, 1969).

Process Questions and Considerations

1. Have you or someone close to you ever faced colorism in employment? If so, how was it handled?

2. This research addresses colorism in the Black/African American community. How do Asian and Latin communities deal with colorism?

3. Do you think colorism affects men and women differently on the job? Regardless of your answer, please explain your position.

4. How has colorism affected your career choices or work behaviors? Please give an example.

5. Why do you think colorism is not as enforced as other illegal Title VII behaviors such as racism and sexism?

References

Antoniou, A. S., & Daliana, N. (2018). Depression and suicidality as results of workplace bullying. *Dialogues in Clinical Neuroscience & Mental Health, 1*(2).

Attell, B. K., Brown, K. K., & Treiber, L. A. (2017). Workplace bullying, perceived job stressors, and psychological distress: Gender and race differences in the stress process. *Social Science Research, 65*, 210-221.

Banks, T. L. (2009). Multilayered racism: Courts' continued resistance to colorism claims. In E. N. Glenn

(Ed.), *Shades of difference: Why skin color matters* (pp. 213-222). Palo Alto, CA: Stanford University Press.

Banks, T. L. (1999). Colorism: A darker shade of pale. *UCLA Law Review, 47,* 1705.

Bassman, E. S. (1992). *Abuse in the workplace: Management remedies and bottom line impact* (p. 77). Westport, CT: Quorum Books.

Brown, D. L., White-Johnson, R. L., & Griffin-Fennell, F. D. (2013). Breaking the chains: examining the endorsement of modern Jezebel images and racial-ethnic esteem among African American women. *Culture, Health & Sexuality, 15*(5), 525-539. https://doi.org/10.1080/13691058.2013.772240

Bonilla-Silva, E. (2009). Racism without racists: color-blind racism and the persistence of racial inequality in the United States (2nd ed.). Boulder, CO: Rowman & Littlefield.

Burton, L. M., Bonilla-Silva, E., Ray, V., Buckelew, R., & Hordge Freeman, E. (2010). Critical race theories, colorism, and the decade's research on families of color. *Journal of Marriage and Family, 72*(3), 440-459.

Coetzee, M., & van Dyk, J. (2018). Workplace bullying and turnover intention: Exploring work engagement as a potential mediator. *Psychological reports, 121*(2), 375-392.

Colligan, T. W., & Higgins, E. M. (2006). Workplace stress: Etiology and consequences. *Journal of Workplace Behavioral Health, 21*(2), 89-97.

Conway, P. M., Hogh, A., Balducci, C., & Ebbesen, D. K. (2018). Workplace bullying and mental health. *Pathways of Job-related Negative Behaviour,* 1-27.

Curry, T. J. (2009). Will the real CRT please stand up—the dangers of philosophical contributions to CRT. *Crit, 2,* 1.

Egbeyemi, A. (2019). Shedding light on colorism: How the colonial fabrication of colorism impacts the lives of African American women. *Journal of Integrative Research & Reflection, 2*(2), 14-25.

Einarsen, S., Hoel, H., Zapf, D., & Cooper, C. L. (2011). The concept of bullying and harassment at work: The European tradition. *Bullying and Harassment in the Workplace: Developments in Theory, Research, and Practice, 2,* 3-40.

Einarsen, S., & Nielsen, M. B. (2015). Workplace bullying as an antecedent of mental health problems: a five-year prospective and representative study. *International Archives of Occupational and Environmental Health, 88*(2), 131-142.

Einarsen, S., Raknes, B. R. I., & Matthiesen, S. B. (1994). Bullying and harassment at work and their relationships to work environment quality: An exploratory study. *European Journal of Work and Organizational Psychology, 4*(4), 381-401.

Espino, R., & Franz, M. M. (2002). Latino phenotypic discrimination revisited: The impact of skin color on occupational status. *Social Science Quarterly, 83,* 612-623.

Faucher, C., Cassidy, W., & Jackson, M. (2015). From the sandbox to the inbox: Comparing the acts, impacts, and solutions of bullying in K-12, higher education, and the workplace. *Journal of Education and Training Studies, 3*(6), 111-125.

Giga, S. I., Hoel, H., & Lewis, D. (2008). The costs of workplace bullying. *University of Manchester Institute of Science and Technology, 8.*

Glenn, E. N. (2008). Yearning for lightness: Transnational circuits in the marketing and consumption of skin lighteners. *Gender & Society, 22*(3), 281-302.

Goldsmith, A. H., Hamilton, D., & Darity Jr, W. (2006). Shades of discrimination: Skin tone and wages. *American Economic Review, 96*(2), 242-245

Goldsmith, A., Hamilton, D., & Darity, W. A. (2007). From dark to light: Skin color and wages among African Americans. *Journal of Human Resources, 4,* 701-738.

Harrison, M. S., & Thomas, K. M. (2009). The hidden prejudice in selection: A research investigation on skin color bias. *Journal of Applied Social Psychology, 39,* 134-168.

Hall, R. E. (2018). The globalization of light skin colorism: From critical race to critical skin theory. *American Behavioral Scientist, 62*(14), 2133-2145.

Harris, A. P. (2008). From color line to color chart: Racism and colorism in the new century. *Berkeley J. Afr.-Am. L. & Pol'y, 10,* 52.

Hodson, R., Roscigno, V. J., & Lopez, S. H. (2006). Chaos and the abuse of power: Workplace bullying in organizational and interactional context. *Work and occupations, 33*(4), 382-416.

Hollis, L. P. (2015). Take the bull by the horns: Structural approach to minimize workplace bullying for women in American higher education. Oxford, England: Oxford Forum on Public Policy.

Hollis, L. P. (2017a). Workplace bullying in the United States and Canada: Organizational accountability required in higher education. *Comparative Civilizations Review.* 76 (76), Available at: https://scholarsarchive.byu.edu/ccr/vol76/iss76/13

Hollis, L. P. (2018). Bullied out of position: Black women's complex intersectionality, Workplace bullying, and resulting career disruption. *Journal of Black Sexuality and Relationships, 4*(3), 73-89.

Hollis, L. P. (2019). The abetting bully: Vicarious bullying and unethical leadership in higher education. *Journal for the Study of Postsecondary and Tertiary Education, 3,* 1-18. https://doi.org/10.28945/4255

Hollis, L. P. (2017). Crafting an online instrument to conduct research on workplace bullying. *European Journal of Educational Research, 6*(1), 105-111. DOI:10.12973/eu-jer.6.1.105

Hollis, L. P. (2019a). Something to lose sleep over? Predictive analysis of black men's and white men's insomnia issues due to workplace bullying in higher education. *Journal of Black Sexuality and Relationships, 5*(4), 1-19.

Hollis, L. P. (2017a). Workplace bullying in the United States and Canada: Organizational accountability required in higher education. *Comparative Civilizations Review, 76*(76). Available at: https://scholarsarchive.byu.edu/ccr/vol76/iss76/13

Hollis, L. P. (2018). Bullied out of position: Black women's complex intersectionality, Workplace bullying, and resulting career disruption. *Journal of Black Sexuality and Relationships, 4*(3), 73-89.

Hsieh, H. F., & Shannon, S. E. (2005). Three approaches to qualitative content analysis. *Qualitative health research, 15*(9), 1277-1288.

Hughes, M., & Hertel, B.R. (1990). The significance of color remains: A study of life changes, mate selection, and ethnic consciousness among black Americans. *Social Forces, 68,* 1105-1120.

Hunter, M. (2007). The persistent problem of colorism: Skin tone, status, and inequality. *Sociology Compass, 1*(1), 237-254.

Johnson, W. (1999). *Soul by soul.* Cambridge, MA: Harvard University Press.

Kerr, A. E. (2006). *The paper bag principle: Class, colorism, and rumor and the case of black Washington.* Knoxville, TN: University of Tennessee Press.

Kerr, A. E. (2005). The paper bag principle: Of the myth and the motion of colorism. *Journal of American Folklore,* 271-289.

King, C. S., & Pascoe, L. (1969). *My life with Martin Luther King, Jr.* (p. 91). New York: Holt, Rinehart and Winston.

Klonoff, E. A., & Landrine, H. (2000). Is skin color a marker for racial discrimination? Explaining the skin color-hypertension relationship. *Journal of Behavioral Medicine, 23,* 329-338.

Lever, I., Dyball, D., Greenberg, N., & Stevelink, S. A. (2019). Health consequences of bullying in the healthcare workplace: A systematic review. *Journal of Advanced Nursing, 75*(12), 3195-3209.

Lewis, M. L., Noroña, C. R., McConnico, N., & Thomas, K. (2013). Colorism, a legacy of historical trauma in parent-child relationships: Clinical, research, and personal perspectives. *Zero to Three, 34*(2), 11-23.

Lloyd, T. O. (1984). *The British Empire* (pp. 1558-1983). Oxford, UK: Oxford University Press.

Marira, T. D., & Mitra, P. (2013). Colorism: Ubiquitous yet understudied. *Industrial and Organizational Psychology, 6*(1), 103-107.

Nabe-Nielsen, K., Grynderup, M. B., Conway, P. M., Clausen, T., Bonde, J. P., Garde, A. H., . . . & Hansen, Å. M. (2017). The role of psychological stress reactions in the longitudinal relation between workplace bullying and turnover. *Journal of Occupational and Environmental Medicine, 59*(7), 665-672.

Namie, G., & Namie, R. (2009). *Bully at work: What you can do to stop the hurt and reclaim your dignity on the job.* Napersville, IL: Sourcebooks, Inc.

Newsinger, J. (2013). *The blood never dried: a people's history of the British Empire.* London, England: Bookmarks.

Parks, C. W., & Woodson, K. M. (2002). The impact of skin color and hair texture on mate selection. *California School of Professional Psychology Handbook of Multicultural Education, Research, Intervention, and Training, 249.*

Pearson-Trammell, N. (2010). *Colorism, self-esteem, and resiliency: A qualitative study of dark skinned African American women.* California Institute of Integral Studies.

Piotrowski, C., & King, C. (2016). The enigma of adult bullying in higher education: A research-based conceptual framework. *Education, 136*(3), 299-306.

Rainford, W. C., Wood, S., McMullen, P. C., & Philipsen, N. D. (2015). The disruptive force of lateral violence in the health care setting. *The Journal for Nurse Practitioners, 11*(2), 157-164.

Real Skin Tones (n.d.) Retrieved from https://www.schemecolor.com/real-skin-tones-color-palette.php

Resch, M., & Schubinski, M. (1996). Mobbing-prevention and management in organizations. *European Journal of Work and Organizational Psychology, 5*(2), 295-307.

Ruggs, E. N., Law, C., Cox, C. B., Roehling, M. V., Wiener, R. L., Hebl, M. R., & Barron, L. (2013). Gone fishing: I-O psychologists' missed opportunities to understand marginalized employees' experiences with discrimination. *Industrial and Organizational Psychology: Perspectives on Science and Practice, 6,* 39-60.

Sauer, P. A., & McCoy, T. P. (2017). Nurse bullying: Impact on nurses' health. *Western Journal of Nursing Research, 39*(12), 1533-1546.

Sewell, C. (2013). Mammies and matriarchs: Tracing images of the black female in popular culture, 1950s to the present. *Journal of African American Studies, 17*(3), 308-326. https://doi.org/10.1007/s12111-012-9238-x

Toplin, R. B. (1979). Between black and white: attitudes toward southern mulattoes, 1830-1861. *The Journal of Southern History, 45*(2), 185-200.

Williams, M. E. (2009). Meet the real Lena Horne: Representations of Lena Horne in Ebony Magazine, 1945-1949. *Journal of American Studies, 43*(1), 117-130.

CHAPTER 9.

Coloring Identity: The Impact of Colorism on the Racial Identity of Black and Latinx Individuals

Patricia S. Dixon and Josephine M. Almanzar
Florida School of Professional Psychology at National Louis University

Colorism has the potential to greatly impact identity development among Black and Latinx individuals. More specifically, colorism is a type of microaggression that is systemically embedded across all entities of American society. This systemic racism contributes to Black and Latinx individuals receiving an ascribed identity that may disrupt the development of an achieved identity and ultimately hinder the process and progression of psychological well-being. The field of psychology requires a greater understanding of the concept of colorism and the impact on racial identity development in order to promote healthy development among Black and Latinx individuals.

Eurocentric standards of beauty have long plagued the lives of racial and ethnic minorities. These standards, including characteristics such as lighter skin, slim figures, and straight hair, have served as a breeding ground for generations of racist ideology, one of which is colorism. Colorism is the system that grants privileges and opportunities to those who possess lighter skin complexion, while inflicting microaggressions and discrimination against those of darker complexion. Colorism is a unique microaggression that is produced by a racist society that is perpetuated both outside of and within one's own racial and ethnic groups. Consequently, the idea of a positive racial identity trajectory poses an issue when those of darker complexion do not feel accepted by those of lighter complexion; although these light and dark individuals may be a part of the same racial group, there becomes an added obstacle to the experience of in-group belonging. Historical ideologies of racism and Eurocentrism have enabled colorism to continue to operate today and negatively influence identity development and psychological well-being, group belonging, and overall quality of life.

Colorism begins the moment a woman gives birth; often, immediately after the birth of a Latinx or Black infant, some people begin to inquire about their skin color.

Common themes of questions that may arise regarding skin color may include "Did they come out dark?" and "How dark are they?" or more specifically, "Are they Black?" In addition, some people may attempt to predict the skin color of the infant by checking the skin behind their ears or the end of the fingernails. In any case, an ascribed identity is created when skin color and other physical features are utilized by others as a demographic description to assume the child's experiences, preferences, and overall identity.

Skin color is one of the most identifiable dimensions of race, making it an important tool in the racial and ethnic socialization in early childhood. Kenneth Clark and Mamie Clark (1947) conducted one of the first studies regarding racial differences, attitudes, and preferences among Black children of various skin colors. Their research found that decisions of racial preference occur at an early age, and regardless of skin color; some of the children tended to prefer the White doll and reject the Black doll (Clark & Clark, 1947). Building on the Doll Study, Teplin (1976) investigated the racial and ethnic preferences of White, Black, and Latinx school-age children by using photographs. Results showed that some Latinx children expressed a preference for photos of their in-group significantly less than Black and White children and, instead, endorsed a preference for photographs of White children. Teplin hypothesized three explanations from her findings. The first suggests that some Latinx children have a negative self-concept or low self-esteem. The second explanation is that some Latinx children did not recognize the photographs of the Latinx children as being part of their ethnic group. Finally, Teplin's third explanation was that some Latinx children may not be accustomed to viewing inanimate representations of other Latinx children. Another consideration of Teplin's hypothesis is that some Latinx children are exposed to representations of other Latinx children, but those representations are mostly children of lighter skin. Therefore, when some Latinx children are presented with images of darker-skinned Latinx children, they may reject such images due to a preference for Eurocentric features that have been internalized from an early age.

Identity development is the way an individual's attitudes and behavior become influenced due to the relationship they establish with a particular reference group (Greenwald, 1988). Erik Erickson proposed that social and historical factors affect the formation of the ego identity, which in turn affects the nature of personality. The process of identity development is a critical task for adolescents, specifically between the ages of 12 and 18 (Akos & Ellis, 2008). More specifically, it is during this time that individuals form their self-image and integrate ideas about themselves with what others think of them. Erickson believed that failure to achieve cohesive identity results in an identity crisis. In youth populations, this identity crisis will exhibit in the form of confusion and may transition into adulthood. Thus, failure to establish a strong sense of self-identity may result in later difficulties in education, career, and interpersonal relationships (Schultz & Schultz, 2005).

Although all adolescents have a process for developing their identity, for minorities there are added layers to the identity development process. Racial and ethnic minorities have an added task of developing an understanding of what it means to be a part of their racial minority group (Howard, 2018). This task of identity development for racial and ethnic minority children is different from that of their White counterparts in that most White children do not have to go through a process of racial socialization. Therefore, most White children are not burdened by this added layer of identity development. Helms (1990a) described racial identity as "A person's sense of a collective or group identity based on one's perception that he or she shares a common racial heritage with a particular racial group." However, racial identity development for adolescents of color is often subjected to experiences of colorism, which significantly disrupt healthy identity development, particularly for Black and Latinx adolescents.

In our current culture, as it relates to dark skin, the ascribed identity for people of color often has negative connotations. Aside from processing an ascribed identity, identity development also includes developing an avowed identity, or an identity that we claim and create ourselves. While ascribed identity is based on both physical features and stereotypes, avowed identity is comprised of the group affiliations that the individual is most intensely connected to (Antony, 2016). Finally, an achieved identity is when a person reaches a point in life where they have embraced a true sense of self (Makros & McCabe, 2001). Thus, with early experiences of colorism comes the lifelong challenge of balancing the ascribed identity and the avowed identity, and ultimately attaining a healthy resolution through an achieved identity.

Most of the current racial and ethnic identity models are in some form or fashion indicative of movement into an achieved racial identity. However, the question is: What is the impact of colorism on attaining that achieved racial identity? People of color are varied and unique, with various extrinsic and intrinsic differences. These extrinsic differences, such as skin tone, have not fully been explored as they relate to racial identity, nor have intrinsic differences, such as how one feels about their skin color. Therefore, the question remains: What is the impact of skin color and tone on the racial identity of Black and Latinx individuals? There is a need to begin incorporating a conceptualization of colorism in our understanding and definition of racial identity development.

Identity developed based on an individual's relationship to a particular group and the way one perceives others' perceptions of that group is the core aspect of racial identity. As it relates to Black people, racial identity is described as a set of principles drawn from one's culture and history. These principles provide specific guidelines to help establish a worldview, objectives, and future actions on the basis of race-based information (Nkruma, 1970). Regarding the racial and ethnic identity of Latinx individuals, marginalization and assimilation can become negative risk factors for mental and emotional well-being; however, satisfaction with one's ethnic identity may serve as a protective factor (Pew Research Center, 2019). Therefore, the development of the racial and ethnic identities of Black and Latinx individuals has the potential to impact self-perception and psychological health.

Over the past several decades, there has been a great deal of interest in researching and understanding racial identity development. Many models have been proposed for racial identity development among people of color (Burlew & Smith, 1991; Cross, 1971; Helms, 1990; Milliones, 1980; Sellers, Smith, Shelton, Rowley, & Chavous, 1998; Worrell, Mendoza-Denton, Wand, 2019). Four major conceptualization approaches have been identified for understanding racial identity among Black people: developmental, Afrocentric, group-based, and measures of racial stereotype (Burlew & Smith, 1991). In this chapter, we will examine the racial identity development model for the Black, Latinx, and multi-racial American population, while also taking a look at multi-dimensional models of racial identity.

The Nigrescence model, or the process of becoming Black, is a common approach in the conceptualization of Black racial identity development, and has been used by several researchers to approach Black racial identity and measures (Cross, 1971, 1978, 1991; Cross, Parham, & Helms, 1991; Helms,1990a; Milliones, 1973, 1980; Thomas, 1971). For instance, Thomas (1971) and Cross (1971) provided the groundwork for many of the developmental racial identity measures (Burlew & Smith, 1991). The basic notion behind these models is that a healthy Black identity is associated with a stronger identification with Black culture; whereas, an over-identification with White culture leads to unhealthy ways of resolving identity issues related to living in a discriminatory society.

For example, Thomas (1971) proposed a five-stage process in which Black Americans have a devalued sense of self and an increased dependence on White society for self-definition. These five stages include withdrawal, testifying, information-processing, activity, and transcendental. Stage one, withdrawal, refers to the individual taking the first step away from the White definition toward a new Black identity. Stage two, testifying, is characterized by addressing anxiety about becoming a self-defined Black person. Stage three, information-processing, is the process of acquiring knowledge about one's Black heritage and the Black experience. In stage four, activity, the individual is involved in activities that provide the opportunity for communion within the Black experience. Finally, the fifth stage, transcendental, encompasses the experience of being relatively free of conflict regarding issues of race, age, sex, and social class.

Thomas's model of racial identity development rests upon the notion that when Black individuals define themselves on a White or Eurocentric standard of acceptability, they experience confusion and struggle with their sense of self-worth. To overcome this confusion and lack of self-worth, the Thomas model proposes that Black individuals dissent from the perceived White standard of worth and, in turn, embrace a newly defined racial identity regarding what it means to be Black. When encompassing the concept of colorism in the Thomas model, there becomes an added complexity in the development of a positive Black racial identity: Those with a darker complexion are identified as being even further from the acceptable White societal prototype of beauty and worth. Therefore, those of darker skin may experience additional challenges in gaining a sense of positive racial identity and unity with mankind.

Colorism may impact the experience of each stage of the Thomas model. The complexion of Black individuals likely influences how they navigate through stage 1, the withdrawal stage; those with darker skin may feel a closer connection with the Black community, while those with lighter skin may experience conflicting feelings about how much they belong to the Black community. In addition, those who have a lighter complexion may find greater difficulty in breaking away from the White group due to feeling more accepted by those who are White. When exploring how colorism may impact the navigation through stage 2, testifying, depending on the complexion of the individuals' skin color, Black individuals may struggle with feelings of belonging. For instance, skin complexion may influence one's thought process as to whether they have a right to self-proclaim being Black, raising the question: How dark does one have to be to understand the experience of being Black? Stage 3 of the Thomas model, information-processing, has similar implications related to colorism: If individuals are discovering knowledge that does not resonate with their experience of being Black, perhaps because they are of lighter complexion, it may cause distress or confusion regarding group belonging. As a result, different skin complexions have the potential to impact individuals' personal experiences of being Black. Finally, stage 4, the activity stage, may be experienced differently based on skin color, as skin color may be a determining factor in inclusion versus exclusion for Black individuals.

Cross (1971) posited that African Americans go through five stages to fully develop a Black identity (pre-encounter, encounter, immersion/emersion, internalization, and internalization-commitment). Cross (1991) later revamped this model and describes the five stages believed to be experienced by African Americans as they develop their racial identity as: 1) pre-encounter: minimizing the significance of race and largely assimilating to the dominant culture; 2) encounter: an experience that promotes a personal interpretation of the African American condition; 3) immersion/emersion: the process of withdrawing from the dominant culture and developing pride in Blackness; 4) internalization: proactive Black pride; and 5) internalization-commitment: the ability to maintain Black pride while also maintaining a connection to the dominant culture.

Like Thomas's model of racial identity, skin color and colorism can significantly impact how individuals navigate racial identity development in Cross's model. For example, the majority of the literature has demonstrated how those of darker skin are treated more negatively than those with lighter skin, implying the likelihood that lighter skin individuals may remain in the pre-encounter stage longer than those of darker skin. Moreover, those of darker skin may be subjected to significantly more distressful experiences during the encounter stage, which may impact psychological well-being. On the other hand, the immersion/emersion stage may pose unique difficulties for those with lighter skin; they may experience self-doubt as they question whether they truly belong in their racial group compared to those of darker skin. Additionally, there may be perceived differences of favoritism in the way those of lighter skin are treated, resulting in individuals of darker skin being less accepting. Skin color and colorism may not have a significant impact on the internalization and internalization-commitment stages.

The Afrocentric conceptualization of racial identity presumes that when African Americans develop a racial identity consistent with an African worldview, they will have a more optimal and healthier state (Burlew & Smith, 1991). This approach takes the notion that individuals who are more Afrocentric in their orientation experience less dissonance from the inevitable conflict between their orientation and the natural order of self (Baldwin, Brown, & Rackley, 1990). Theorists who conceptualize from this framework posit that the Black personality is comprised of two core components: the African self-extension orientation and African self-consciousness (Baldwin, 1984). The most widely used Afrocentric measure of identity is the African Self-Consciousness Scale (Baldwin, 1984). This measure was derived from Baldwin's Afrocentric Theory of Black Personality, which describes the healthy Black personality as encompassing three characteristics. First is having a strong biogenetic propensity to affirm African American life. The second is placing a high priority on the survival of African American institutions and culture. The third characteristic is participation in activities that promote the survival, dignity, worth, and integrity of African people.

When examining the concept behind the Afrocentric models of racial identity, there is the notion that Black individuals who have an orientation that is more reflective of an African worldview experience healthier psychological outcomes. However, what does this mean in the context of skin color? One unique aspect of colorism is that it is a form of discrimination embodied by both the White population as well as those representing ethnic minorities. Therefore, there is a question regarding the experience of individuals who are Black, but do not physically have the appearance of those who are of African descent. In other words, what is the experience of the Black individual who, in every way, self-identifies as Black and would like to be connected to their African roots yet due to not neatly meeting the criteria of Black physical appearance and features? Although the Afrocentric models of racial identity development reflect Black individuals having a more African centered worldview, they do not take into account the additional complexities in development when considering one's skin tone and ascribed identity. For instance, when we consider the impact of skin color on embracing an African worldview, conflict between navigating and attaining group belonging and coping with an ascribed identity may arise; the extent of experiencing a sense of belonging to a group may depend on their skin tone. This, in turn, may impact their ability to feel more connected to their African roots. More specifically, when compared to darker-skin Blacks, some lighter-skin Blacks may have more difficulty connecting to their African roots.

Another proposed conceptual framework of racial identity is the group-based approach. This framework assesses an individual's affiliation or allegiance with their racial group. Measures that fall under this approach tap into the presence or absence of a sense of affiliation with one's racial group, one's evaluation of one's self and others as members of that group, and a commitment to the objectives of a specific movement or activist organization within the African American community (Burlew & Smith,

1991). The group-based approach differs from the developmental approach in that it is not a stage model, and differs from the Afrocentric approach in that the African-centered orientation is not a necessity. Two examples identified in Burlew and Smith's (1991) research of measures using the group-based approach are Banks's (1970) Black Consciousness Scale (BCS), and Wilderson's (1979) Black Awareness Scale. Both scales effectively measure an individual's alliance and coalition with their racial group.

According to Newman and Newman (1976), the major developmental task in early adolescence is achieving a group identity by exploring and understanding group dynamics. Given that group belonging is an experience salient to cultural identity, this developmental task may be especially important for adolescents from minority racial and ethnic groups. Gillen-O'Neel et al. (2015) explored the development and perception of ethnic and racial identity among multi-ethno-racial adolescents compared to their mono-ethno-racial peers. Results showed that the participants did not indicate that their ethno-racial identification varied depending on the context, challenge the notion that multi-ethno racial groups experience racial and ethnic passing and code-switching. Thus, more research is needed to clarify to what extent multi-ethno racial individuals exhibit passing and code-switching behaviors to attain group belonging, and how skin color impacts the group in which one feels a sense of belonging. Furthermore, examining racial identity and group belonging in African American adolescents through a model may reflect important implications as they explore their identity and define their role in society.

The fourth identified framework for understanding racial identity is the racial stereotyping approach. This approach assesses the degree to which individuals internalize negative images and stereotypes regarding their racial group. This approach differs from the developmental approach in that it does not assess the degree to which an individual considers race important to the self-concept. Measures that utilize this approach, such as Taylor's (1972) Nationalization Scale and Matthews and Prothro's (1966) Racial Stereotype Index, examine individual perceptions of their racial group, and assess stereotypic attitudes historically held by Whites toward Blacks (Burlew & Smith, 1991). For instances, scales my incorporate statements such as "African Americans are more ignorant than Whites" and ask participants to respond in agreement or disagreement. Other similar scales include the Cultural Mistrust Inventory (Taylor & Terrell, 1991) and Stephen and Rosenfield's (1979) Racial Attitude Scale (Burlew & Smith, 1991).

The literature on skin tone among racial and ethnic minority groups has shown that darker-skin individuals are perceived and treated more negatively than their lighter-skin counterparts. This societal bias may be attributed to observers evaluating darker skin as being more closely representative of the negative cultural stereotypes of that racial and ethnic group (Hunter, 2007). The awareness of the devalued status of darker skin in minority groups may reveal a negative effect on the quality of life and psychological well-being of Black Americans and other minority groups. For example, studies have shown that Hispanics of darker skin were found to be at risk of economic, educational, and other societal disadvantages (Painter, Wassink, & Bateman, 2015; Saperstein & Penner, 2012). In regard to health risk, Perreira, Wassink, and Mullan (2019) found that skin color affected all self-reported races and ethnicities; however, Hispanics of darker-toned skin had greater BMIs, higher odds of obesity, and poorer self-reported health than lighter-toned Hispanics.

One common theme throughout the literature is the impact of intersecting identities, such as race, class, and gender, on the experiences and psychological effects of colorism (Wilder & Cain, 2011). For instance, the literature revealed that depressive symptoms are reported at higher levels for Latinx women of African descent, compared to individuals who identify as European Americans and African Americans (Ramos, Jaccard, & Guilamo-Ramos, 2003). Moreover, some Latinx immigrant participants with darker skin tended to have more negative self-perceptions. These negative self-perceptions include feeling less attractive, having a desire to change their skin color to be lighter, and having lower self-esteem compared to U.S.-born participants with darker skin (Telzer & Vazquez Garcia, 2009). One of the greatest areas in which we may discover the impact and intersection of colorism and ascribed identity is for those who identify as multi-racial.

The Latino/a American Identity Development Model (LAIDM) proposed by Ruiz (1990), is based on five stages of ethnic identity development: casual, cognitive, consequence, working through, and successful resolution. LAIDM was created based on research from counseling sessions related to the identity formation of Chicano, Mexican American, and Latinx college students (Bernal et al., 1987; Garcia, 1982; Keefe & Padilla, 1987; Phinney & Rotherman, 1987; Rodriquez & DeBlassie, 1983). The LAIDM is grounded on the following premises:

(a) that marginality correlates highly with maladjustment (LeVine & Padilla, 1980); (b) that both marginality and the pressure to assimilate can be destructive to an individual (LeVine & Padilla, 1980); (c) that pride in one's own ethnic identity is conducive to mental health (Bernal, Bernal, Martinez, Olmedo, &

Santisteban, 1983); and (d) that during the acculturation process, pride in one's own ethnic identity affords the Hispanic more freedom to choose (Bernal et al., 1983) (Ruiz, 1990).

Although this model reflects the ethnic identity development of Latinxs, it does not take into consideration the experiences of racial development that may be occurring concurrently and influencing one another. Moreover, the focus on Mexican Americans in research is aligned with the current demographics of Latinxs in the United States. In 2017 the Pew Research Center reported that out of the 58,838,000 people identified as Hispanic, 36,634,000 identified as Mexican (Pew Research Center, 2019). Although fruitful findings have stemmed from research on the experiences of Mexican Americans and how they may respond to the racial order of the U.S., more research is needed to reflect the ethnic development experiences of Latinxs from various countries of origin.

Group membership is an integral part of cultural identity and its development. The literature reflects Latinxs having cognizance of the dominant racial hierarchy and stigma of blackness in the United States, resulting in an avoidance of identifying as part of the Black racial group (Stokes-Brown, 2012). For example, in 2014, the first nationally representative survey of Latinx adults in the U.S. was conducted; in this survey, one-quarter of all U.S. Latinxs self-identify as Afro-Latinx, Afro-Caribbean, or of African descent with roots in Latin America. However, when explicitly asked to report race, only 18% identified as being racially Black and 39% reporting being racially White (Pew Research Center, 2016). There is uncertainty about how these percentages reflect skin tone.

The process of being included or excluded from the Black and White line in the U.S. is twofold; one must self-identify as part of the in-group, and the group must also identify one as a part of that group. The latter may carry more weight when gaining membership and may be exercised by the group in power more to maintain the status quo (Frank, Akresh, & Lu, 2010; Sanchez, Good, & Chavez, 2011). Thus, although some Latinxs may classify themselves as White, it tends to be when that group comes to view them as such that the racial boundary has broadened (Roth, 2016). Skin color may impact the experience of group membership and exclusion of Latinxs, and how they believe American society perceives them. For example, those with darker skin tones may not have the option of classifying themselves as White or are more likely to experience group exclusion compared to their lighter-skin counterparts. Ho, Chin, and Kteily (2017) explored whether and how Black and White Americans utilize hypodescent (also known as the "one drop rule")—the labeling of a biracial individual with their minority racial status as opposed to their majority racial status—when categorizing biracial Black and White individuals. They found that Black participants were more likely to expand their racial group to include biracial individuals compared to White participants.

Many Latinx individuals have difficulty navigating the dichotomous Black and White racial order in the U.S. Some Latinx find themselves opting out of the Black and White group and identifying with a separate group entirely. Hiltin, Brown, and Elder (2011) explored respondents' self-identification to race and ethnicity when presented with similar questioning found on the Census. This study found that participants' responses to ethnicity and race changed when given the option to identify as "Other"; participants leaned toward reporting that they were White more often when they were not given the option to endorse "Other" as their race (Hiltin, Brown, & Elder, 2011; Stokes-Brown, 2012). Although participants tend to endorse a White racial classification, the option to classify as Other may shed light on the dichotomous nature of the U.S. racial order evolving. Additionally, given that the Black racial group and the Latinx ethnic group are both considered minority groups in the U.S., more research is needed on how hypodescent is applied to Afro-Latinxs.

The conflict between self-identification and identity ascribed may result in racial and ethnic confusion and psychological distress, particularly when skin color is taken into consideration. Vargas and Stainback (2015) examined the relationship between racial contestation and group closeness among Latinx, Asian, Black, and White participants. Racial contestation is defined as an experience when an individual's racial self-classification does not coincide with how others perceived them racially. The research found that Latinxs endorsed experiencing some level of racial contestation more than the other three groups. In addition, on average, individuals who reported experiencing racial contestation felt less of an affective connection to other members of their self-identified group (Vargas & Stainback, 2015). Afro-Latinx, being ethnically Latinx and racially Black, may experience racial contestation at a higher rate, resulting in feeling rejected, invalidated, and experiencing a greater disconnect between themselves and their ethnic group.

Latinx may engage in various coping strategies to evade psychological distress associated with negative experiences when attempting to attain group belonging. Racial passing involves the internalization of Eurocentrism and lighter skin as a reference point, and the "racial denial and active attempts to be perceived (by self and others) as White, or at least, non-Black" (Greene, 1992). Code switching is the attempt to alter one's racial and ethnic expression and identity based on social cues (Navarrete-Vivero & Jenkins, 1999). Fundamentally, racial passing and code-switching have been shown to be methods of survival to avoid imminent harm and discrimination. However, these experiences may also be used in more implicit circumstances to gain access to power and privilege, and acceptance into the majority or in-group, and to alleviate psychological and identity crises (Root, 1996). One the other hand, the detection of racial passing and code-switching by others may result in being perceived as untrustworthy and inauthentic, which may impact to what extent group membership can be attained and group boundaries expanded (Albuja, Sanchez, & Gaither, 2018).

The focus on research related to racial passing and code-switching has primarily been on the experience of African Americans navigating environments that are majority White, reiterating the dichotomous racial lens of the U.S. The increase in racial and ethnic diversity in the U.S. has started to pave the way to research shedding light on the experiences of other minority groups and their relationship with racial passing, code-switching, and group belonging. For Latinx, suppressing ethnic markers such as language, accents, and tradition may create a perceived opportunity to avoid discrimination and be accepted into a group. This process is reflected in the consequences stage of the Latino/a American Identity Development Model and may result in a lack of ethnic identification and the parting of one's group (Ruiz, 1990; Dawson & Quiros, 2014). Racially, Latinx may attempt to lighten their skin by avoiding the sun, by skin bleaching, straightening or chemically altering naturally curly hair, or altering their appearance surgically to be aligned with Eurocentric features (Dawson & Quiros, 2014).

In 1937, Evertt Stonequist introduced the first model of biracial identity development, the Marginal Person Model. In this model, biracial identity was conceptualized as being linked to two worlds but not truly belonging to either one, leading to exacerbated feelings of identity confusion, low self-esteem, and reduce group belonging. Walker S. Carlos Poston, viewed Stonequist's model as one founded in deficit, as its basic design compared Black minority samples to a White majority sample as a reference point of identity development. Therefore, Poston (1990) proposed the Biracial Identity Development Model (BRIDM) in response to the rise of self-identified biracial and multi-racial people in the U.S., and to provide a different perspective to the identity development of this population. BRIDM's five stages, personal identity, choice of group categorization, enmeshment/denial, appreciation, and integration, assume that the biracial identity develops healthily and that multiple factors influence identities, such as family and peer influences. Along with a similar philosophy, Maria Root (1990) proposed four resolutions for resolving otherness that outline potentially positive outcomes of the tensions of biracial identity: acceptance of the identity society assigns; identification with both racial groups; identification with a single racial group; and identification as a new racial group. Although these perspectives on biracial identity development yield a more positive formation and outcome, there are some limitations to their generalizability. For example, these models are based on the experiences of biracial people who were White and Black, White and Asian, or White and Latinx, leaving the experiences of those who are not mixed with White, such as those who are Latinxs of African descent, unaccounted for. In addition, a large portion of the literature defines a biracial identity as having two monoracial parents of different races, such as having a White mother and an Asian father. Given the history of racial mixing in Latin America, Poston's definition of a biracial identity does not fully encompass the blended identity of Afro-Latinxs.

Harris (2017) found that multi-racial students on college campuses often felt that they were automatically labeled with an ascribed monoracial identity by their peers, and endorsed shared themes of invalidation and lack of acknowledgment of their ethnic and racial identity. This monoracial ascribed identity is often based on the physical features someone presents with, reinforcing the impact of skin color as a major tool for labeling racial identity. Thus, further evaluation of how ascribed identity and skin color impact an individual's racial identification is necessary. In addition, students also reported difficulty feeling that they belonged at their respective campuses due to resources and spaces being structured for monoracial students (Harris, 2017). The tendency to associate multi-racial people with one racial category may be viewed as a micro-aggression called monoracism. Johnston and Nadal (2010) defined the experience as "a social system of psychological inequality where individuals who do not fit monoracial categories may be oppressed on systemic and interpersonal levels because of underlying assumptions and beliefs in the singular, discrete racial categories." Further research is needed to explore these mixed messages and micro-aggressions regarding ethnic and racial identity, as well as the variables that may serve as a protective factor for Afro-Latinx well-being and belonging.

When exploring group belonging, many multicultural individuals may experience cultural homelessness. Cultural Homelessness, a theoretical framework proposed by Navarrete-Vivero and Jenkins (1999) is characterized as "repeated experiences of rejection by multiple groups, feelings of not belonging to any group, struggles to attain membership within the desired group(s), and the felt need to find a cultural home among multicultural individuals." Navarrete and Jenkins (2011) found that participants of multi-racial status endorsed higher feelings of cultural homelessness compared to monoracial participants. On the other hand, they found that participants of multiethnic status endorsed lower feelings of cultural homelessness compared to monoethnic participants. Given these findings, researchers proposed that the influence of racial mixing in the U.S. has a different and more negative effect for those who are racially but not ethnically mixed (Navarrete & Jenkins, 2011). In addition, contrary to ethnicity, race is a construct that involves visible physical features that are difficult to change, resulting in multi-racial individuals feeling alienated and invalidated by a self-identified group. For instance, for Afro-Latinxs, the physical feature of having darker skin may elicit a higher feeling of cultural homelessness. This may suggest the need for more research to provide clarity on cultural homelessness and its relationship with skin color among multicultural individuals. This may begin with examining racial identity through more multidimensional lenses.

Researchers began to examine racial identity using a multi-dimensional model approximately 20 years ago. One of the first multi-dimensional models assessing Black racial identity was the Multi-dimensional Model of Racial Identity (MMRI). This model conceptualizes racial identity by integrating African Americans' self-concepts and the qualitative meanings individuals attribute to being members of this racial category (Sellars, Smith, Shelton, Rowley, & Chavous, 1998). The MMRI considers social, historical, and economic factors that have impacted the development of racial self-concept (Sellers et al., 1998). The MMRI defines racial identity in African Americans as "the significance and qualitative meaning that individuals attribute to their membership within the Black racial group within their self-concepts" (Sellers et al., 1998). The MMRI maintains four testable assumptions: 1) identities are both situationally influenced as well as stable to the properties of the person; 2) individuals have several different identities that are hierarchically ordered; 3) individuals' perceptions of their racial identity are the most valid indicator of their identity; and 4) there are individual differences in the qualitative nature of the meaning individuals ascribe to being a member of the Black racial group. The MMRI proposes four dimensions of racial identity which include racial salience, racial centrality, racial regard, and racial ideology. Racial salience refers to the relevance individuals attribute race to their self-concept. Salience is a dynamic concept that varies among individuals, can change from one event to another, and has major implications for the way individuals interpret various situations. The second dimension of the MMRI, racial centrality, refers to how individuals define their sense of self, particularly regarding race. While salience is dynamic, centrality is relatively stable across situations. The third dimension, racial regard, refers to how positively or negatively one feels about their race. This dimension is further broken down into two dimensions of private and public regard. Private regard is how one feels about being an African American, and how that individual feels toward African Americans. On the other hand, public regard is an individual's perceptions of the level of positive or negative feelings others have toward African Americans. Given the historical discriminatory practices against those of darker skin, continued research and consideration is needed on the impact of colorism in healthy racial identity development across multiple factors. For example, when examining public regard, accounting for the influence of skin color may shed light on different outcomes and perspectives regarding an individual's perceptions that others have toward African Americans. Finally, the fourth dimension of the MMRI, racial ideology, addresses an individual's beliefs, opinions, and attitudes regarding the way members from the African American group should act. This dimension is further broken down into four ideological philosophies: 1) nationalist, which stresses the unique Black experience; 2) oppressed, which identifies similarities between African Americans and other minority groups; 3) assimilation, which emphasizes similarities between African Americans and all Americans; and 4) humanist, which emphasizes similarities among all humankind.

Another example of a multi-dimensional model is the Minority Identity Development Model (MIDM). Atkinson, Morten, and Sue (1998), created MIDM based on five-stages—conformity, dissonance, resistance and immersion, introspection, and synergetic articulation and awareness—to capture the person-environment or psychosocial process that is implicit in earlier models of racial identity development (Renn, 2008). Thus, the five stages of MIDM not only highlight how an individual feels toward themselves and their identity, but also how they view others within their group, other minority groups, and the dominant group (Atkinson, Morten, & Sue, 1998). Although this model does not provide applicability toward the unique developmental experiences that occur in any specific racial and ethnic group, it is a foundational tool that takes into consideration the internal and external processes of development. Thus, as both Black and Latinx are identities that are marginalized in the U.S., exploring racial and ethnic identity development through its double minority status may yield informative insight on the identity development of Afro-Latinxs. Currently, there is some research that examines the experience of individuals who have multiple marginalized identities, however more research is needed to examine specifically the experience of two racially marginalized identities (Balsam, Molina, Beadnell, Simoni, & Walters, 2011).

Although these multi-dimensional models take a more in-depth look at various factors that contribute to racial identity, the question remains how these models account for skin color throughout the various aspects of identity development. There is so much complexity to living in a society that is embedded with broken systems in which everyone in society plays a role as both a product and a participant. This broken society has birthed beliefs about what it means to be an individual of dark complexion. Society has created an ascribed identity in which those of dark skin are considered less than, undesirable, and ultimately bad. This in turn impacts the way those of darker complexion will feel about themselves. This in turn will impact the way darker individuals feel about what it means to be a part of their racial or ethnic group. The potential disruption of identity development that results from colorism has been largely under-examined and underestimated. Colorism influences the ascribed identity people assign others. Although the major theories of racial identity encompass some level of the role skin color may play on the development of racial identity, none of them directly explore the consequences of colorism.

Colorism is not a new concept in our society. Colorism has had an impact on people of color in the past and continues to have implications in the present. In order to avoid the pervasive negative consequences of colorism in the future, it is imperative that the concept be further understood in the context of identity development. The multigenerational impact of colorism has important implications for how Black and Latinx people feel about themselves, what they believe others may think about them, and ultimately how they navigate through life. There is a responsibility that needs to be upheld to better understand the depth of the impact of colorism, if there is any hope for resolving and eliminating the impact on the youth of tomorrow.

Therefore, as it relates to implications for clinical practice, it is imperative for clinicians to address racial identity from multiple perspectives. This entails going beyond the simple identification of someone's racial or ethnic identity. There is a need to explore what it means to be a part of one's identified racial group. Even more, it is important to examine both the intrinsic and extrinsic factors that contribute to how someone identifies. It is important to examine whether an individual is basing their identity on how others perceive them versus how they perceive themselves. This is the distinction between achieved versus ascribed identity.

Process Questions and Considerations

1. How does skin tone impact how someone racially identifies?

2. How might skin tone contribute to achieved versus ascribed identity?

3. How does skin tone impact group belonging?

4. What is the relationship between skin tone and the experience of cultural homelessness?

5. What is the relationship between belonging to multiple marginalized racial groups, skin tone, and racial identity?

References

Akos, P., & Ellis, C. M. (2008). Racial identity development in middle school: A case study for school counselor individual and systemic intervention. *Journal of Counseling & Development, 86,* 26-33.

Antony, M. G. (2016) Exploring diversity through dialogue: avowed and ascribed identities, *Communication Teacher, 30*(3), 125-130. DOI:10.1080/17404622.2016.1192663

Albuja, A. F., Sanchez, D. T., & Gaither, S. E. (2018). Fluid racial presentation: Perceptions of contextual "passing" among biracial people. *Journal of Experimental Social Psychology, 77,* 132-142.

Atkinson, D. R., Morten, G., & Sue, D. W. (Eds.). (1998). *Counseling American minorities* (5th ed.). McGraw-Hill.

Baldwin, J. A. (1979). Theory and research concerning the notion of Black self-hatred: A review and reinterpretation. *Journal of Black Psychology, 5*(2), 51-77.

Baldwin, J. A. (1984). African self-consciousness and the mental health of African Americans. *Journal of Black Studies, 15*(2), 177-194.

Baldwin, J. A., Brown, R., & Rackley, R. (1990). Some background and behavioral correlates of African self-consciousness. *Journal of Black Psychology, 17*(1), 1-17.

Balsam, K. F., Molina, Y., Beadnell, B., Simoni, J., & Walters, K. (2011). Measuring Multiple Minority Stress: The LGBT People of Color Microaggressions Scale. *Cultural Diversity & Ethnic Minority Psychology, 17*(2), 163-174.

Bernal, G., Bernal, M. E., Martinez, A. C., Olmedo, E. L., & Santisteban, D. (1983). Hispanic mental health curriculum for psychology. In J. C. Chunn II, P. J. Dunston, & F. Ross-Sheriff (Eds.), *Mental Health and People of Color: Curriculum Development and Change* (pp. 64-93). Washington, DC: Howard University Press.

Bernal, M. E., Knight, G. P., Organista, K., Garza, C., & Maez, B. (1987). The young Mexican American child's understanding of ethnic identity. In P. C. Martinelli (Ed.), *First symposium on ethnic identity: Conceptualization and measurement of Mexican American ethnic identity in the social sciences* (pp. 10-17). Tempe, AZ: Arizona State University, Hispanic Research Center.

Burlew, A. K., & Smith, L. R. (1991). Measures of racial identity: An overview and proposed framework. *Journal of Black Psychology, 17,* 53-71.

Clark, K. B., & Clark, M. P. (1947). Racial identification and preference in Negro children. In T.M. Newcomb and E.L. Hartley (Eds.), *Readings in social psychology* (pp. 169-178). New York: Holt.

Clark, R., Dogan, R. R., & Akbar, N. J. (2003). Youth and parental correlates of externalizing symptoms, adaptive functioning, and academic performance: An exploratory study in preadolescent blacks. *Journal of Black Psychology, 29,* 210-229.

Cross, W. E., Jr. (1971, July). The Negro-to-Black conversion experience. *Black World,* 13-27.

Cross, W. E., Jr. (1978). The Thomas and Cross models on psychological nigrescence: A literature review. *Journal of Black Psychology, 4,* 13-31.

Cross, W. E., Jr. (1991). *Shades of Black: Diversity in African American identity.* Philadelphia: Temple

University Press.

Cross, W. E., Jr., Parham, T. A., & Helms, J. E. (1991). The stages of black identity development: Nigrescence models. In R. L. Jones (Ed.), *Black psychology* (3rd ed.), (pp. 319-338). Berkeley, CA: Cobb & Henry.

Cross, W. E., Parham, T. A., & Helms, J. E. (1998). Nigrescence revisited: Theory and research. In R. L. Jones (Ed.), *African American identity development: Theory, research, and intervention* (pp. 3-71). Hampton, VA: Cobb & Henry.

Dawson, B., & Quiros, L. (2014). The effects of racial socialization on the racial and ethnic identity development of Latinas. *Journal of Latina/o Psychology, 2*(4), 200-213.

Frank, R., Akresh, I. R., & Lu, B. (2010). Latino immigrants and the U.S. racial order: How and where do they fit in? *American Sociological Review, 75*(3), 378-401. https://doi.org/10.1177/0003122410372216

Garcia, J. A. (1982). Ethnicity and Chicanos: Measurement of ethnic identification, identity, and consciousness. *Hispanic Journal of Behavioral Sciences, 4,* 295-314.

Gillen-O'Neel, C., Mistry, R. S., Brown, C. S., Rodriguez, V. C., White, E. S., & Chow, K. A. (2015). Not excluded from analyses: Racial meanings and identification among multiracial early adolescents. *Journal of Adolescent Research.* DOI:10.1177/0743558414560626

Greene, B. A. (1992). Racial socialization as a tool in psychotherapy with African American children. In L. A. Vargas & J. D. Koss-Chioino (Eds.), Working with culture: Psychotherapeutic interventions with ethnic minority children and adolescents (pp. 63-81). San Francisco, CA: Jossey-Bass.

Greenwald, A. G. (1988). A social-cognitive account of the self's development. In Sanders Thompson, V. L., & Akbar, M. (2003). The understanding of race and the construction of African American identity. *The Western Journal of Black Studies, 27*(2), 80-88.

Harris, J. (2017). Multiracial college students' experiences with multiracial microaggressions. *Race Ethnicity and Education, 20*(4), 429-445. DOI:10.1080/13613324.2016.1248836

Helms, J. E. (1990a). *Black and white racial identity: Theory, research, and practice.* New York: Greenwood Press.

Helms, J. E. (2007). Some better practices for measuring racial and ethnic identity constructs. *Journal of Counseling Psychology, 54*(3), 235-246.

Hitlin, S., Brown, J., & Elder, G. (2011). Measuring Latinos: Racial vs. ethnic classification and self-understandings. *Social Forces, 86*(2), 587-611.

Ho, A., Kteily, N., & Chen, J. (2017). "You're one of us": Black Americans' use of hypodescent and its association with egalitarianism. *Journal of Personality and Social Psychology, 113*(5), 753-768.

Howard, J. (2018). That's not something we have to discuss: Interrupting silences about multiracial students in teacher work. *Urban Review, 50*(4), 693-712.

Hunter, M. (2007). The persistent problem of colorism: Skin tone, status, and inequality. *Sociology Compass, 100006*(10), 237-254. DOI:10.1111/j.1751-9020.2007.00006.x

Johnston, M. P., and Nadal, K. L. 2010. Multiracial microaggressions: Exposing monoracism in everyday life and clinical practice. In D. W. Sue (Ed.), *microaggressions and marginality: Manifestation, dynamics, and impact* (pp. 123-144). New York: Wiley & Sons.

Keefe, S. E., & Padilla, A. M. (1987). *Chicano identity.* Albuquerque, NM: University of New Mexico Press.

LeVine, E. S., & Padilla, A. M. (1980). *Crossing cultures in therapy: Pluralistic counseling for the Hispanic.* Monterey, CA: Brooks/Cole.

Makros, J., & McCabe, M. P. (2001). Relationships between identity and self-representations during adolescence. *Journal of Youth and Adolescence, 30*(5), 623-639. https://doi.org/10.1023/A:1010404822585

Milliones, J. (1980). Construction of a black consciousness measure: Psycho-therapeutic implications. *Psychotherapy: Theory, Research and Practice, 17,* 175-182.

Navarrete-Vivero, V., Jenkins, S. (1999). Existential hazards of the multicultural individual: Defining and understanding cultural homelessness. *Cultural Diversity and Ethnic Minority Psychology, 5*(1), 6-26.

Navarrete-Vivero, V., Jenkins, S. (2011). Cultural homelessness, multi-minority status, ethnic identity development, and self-esteem. *International Journal of Intercultural Relations, 35,* 791- 804.

Newman, P. R., and Newman, B. M. (1976). Early adolescence and its conflict: Group identity versus alienation. *Adolescence, 11*(42), 261-274.

Nkrumah, K. (1970). *Class struggle in Africa.* London: Panaf Books.

Painter II, M. A, Holmes, M. D., & Bateman, J. (2015). Skin tone, race/ethnicity, and wealth inequality among new immigrants. *Social Forces, 94*(3), 1153-1185.

Perreira, K. M., Wassink, J., & Harris, K. M. (2018). Beyond race/ethnicity: Skin color, gender, and the health of young adults in the United States. *Population Research and Policy Review, 38*(2), 271-299.

Pew Research Center. (2016). *Afro-Latino: A deeply rooted identity among U.S. Hispanics.* Washington, D.C. Retrieved from: https://www.pewresearch.org/fact-tank/2016/03/01/afro-latino-a-deeply-rooted-identity-among-u-s-hispanics/

Pew Research Center. (2019). *Facts on Latinos in the U.S.* Washington, D.C. Retrieved from: https://www.pewresearch.org/hispanic/fact-sheet/latinos-in-the-u-s-fact-sheet /

Poston, W. (1990). The biracial identity development model: A needed addition. *Journal of Counseling & Development, 69,* 152-155.

Ramos, B., Jaccard, J., & Guilamo-Ramos, V. (2003). Dual ethnicity and depressive symptoms: Implications of being black and Latino in the United States. *Hispanic Journal of Behavioral Sciences, 25,* 147-173.

Renn, K. A. (2008). Research on biracial and multicultural identity development: Overview and synthesis. *New Direction for Student Services, 123,* 13-21. DOI:10.1002/ss.282

Rodriquez, A., & DeBlassie, R. R. (1983). Ethnic designation, identification, and preference as they relate to Chicano children. *Journal of Non-White Concerns, 11,* 99-106.

Root, M.P.P. (1990). Resolving "other" status: Identity development of biracial individuals. *Women and Therapy, 9,* 185-205.

Root, M.P.P. (1996). *The multiracial experience.* Thousand Oaks, CA: SAGE.

Roth, W. (2016). The multiple dimensions of race. *Ethnic and Racial Studies, 39*(8), 1310-1338.

Ruiz, A. S. (1990), Ethnic identity: Crisis and resolution. *Journal of Multicultural Counseling and Development, 18,* 29-40. DOI:10.1002/j.2161-1912.1990.tb00434.x

Sanchez, D. T., Good, J. J., & Chavez, G. (2011). Blood quantum and perceptions of black-white biracial targets: the black ancestry prototype model of affirmative action. *Personality and Social Psychology Bulletin, 37*(1), 3-14.

Saperstein, A., & Penner, A. M. (2012). Racial fluidity and inequality in the United States. *American Journal of Sociology, 118*(3), 676-727.

Sellars, R. M., Smith, M. A., Shelton, J. N., Rowley, A. J., & Chavous, T. M. (1998). Multidimensional model of racial identity: A reconceptualization of African American racial identity. *Personality and Social Psychology Review, 2*(1), 18-39.

Schults, D. P., & Schults, S. E. (2005). *Theories of personality* (8th ed.), (pp. 219-248). Belmont, CA: Thompson, Wadsworth Publication.

Smith, L. R. (1991). Measures of racial identity: An overview and proposed framework. *The Journal of Black Psychology, 17,* 53-71.

Stokes-Brown, A. (2012). America's shifting color line? Reexamining determinants of Latino racial self-identification. *Social Science Quarterly, 93*(2), 309-332. Retrieved from www.jstor.org/stable/42864073

Stonequist, E. V. (1937). *The marginal man: A study in personality and culture conflict.* New York, Chicago: Charles Scribner's sons.

Taylor, A. Z., & Graham, S. (2007). An examination of the relationship between achievement values and perceptions of barriers among low-socioeconomic status African American and Latino students. *Journal of Educational Psychology, 99*(1), 52-64.

Taylor, J., & Tomasic, M. (1991). Taylor's measures of dysphoria, anxiety, anger, and self-esteem. *Handbook of tests and measurements for black populations*, 295-305.

Telzer, E. H., & Vazquez Garcia, H. A. (2009). Skin color and self-perceptions of immigrant and U.S.-born Latinas: The moderating role of racial socialization and ethnic identity. *Hispanic Journal of Behavioral Sciences, 31*(3), 357-374. https://doi.org/10.1177/0739986309336913

Teplin, L. A. (1976). A comparison of racial preference among Black, Anglo and Latino children. *American Journal of Orthopsychiatry, 46*, 702-709.

Thomas, C. S. (1971). *Boys no more*. Beverly Hills, CA: Glencoe Press. In Burlew, A. K.

Vargas, N., & Stainback, K. (2015). Documenting contested racial identities among self-identified Latina/os, Asians, blacks, and whites. *American Behavioral Scientist, 60*(4), 442-464.

Wilder, J., & Cain C. (2011). Teaching and learning color consciousness in black families: Exploring family processes and women's experiences with colorism. *Journal of Family Issues, 32*(5), 577-604. DOI:10.1007/s11199-009-9706-5.

Worrell, F. C., Mendoza-Denton, R., Wand, A. (2019). Introducing a new assessment tool for measuring ethnic-racial identity: The Cross Ethnic-Racial Identity Scale–Adult (CERIS-A). *Assessment, 26*(3), *404-418.*

CHAPTER 10.

Colorism in Ghana, West Africa: Examining the Impact of Colonialism with Afrikan perspectives

Kevin Washington, Grambling State University
Kamilah Marie Woodson, Howard University
Nana K.O. Gyesie, Baltimore City Community College
Dwayne M. Bryant and Janicia Dugas,
San Jose Unified School District in California

Introduction

The discovery of Afrika by the Europeans was a fortunate incident in the history of the Europeans and a most tragic incident in the history of Africans. The Afrikans who encountered Europeans had no clear understanding of the European mind then and have no clear understanding of the European mind now (Clarke, 1996). These two peoples met at the crossroads of history at a time when they could have complimented one another; they could have changed the world by forming a partnership. Instead one chose to subdue the other and traffic them as slaves. The results of this decision reverberate throughout the world until this day (Clarke, 1996). Every Eurocentric social institution conspires with Eurocentric historiography to handcuff and incarcerate Afrikan consciousness, to justify and facilitate the subordination and exploitation of Afrikan peoples (Wilson, 2014). Afrika has always been the prize of the nations that discovered and beheld its potential and its possibilities. It has always had and still has things that other people want, cannot do without, and don't want to pay for (Clarke, 1996). Most people who lust after Africa and its richness know more about Afrika's potential than may Afrikans themselves (Clarke, 1996). According to Utsey, Abrams, Opare-Henaku, Bolden, and Williams (2014), in the conquest of Ghana, European colonizers had the goal of establishing dominance and developing wealth for the countries from which they came. Unfortunately, colonialism destroyed Afrikan communities, incited the degradation of Afrikan culture, and instilled a belief in White supremacy (Igboin, 2011). These White supremist beliefs seem to permeate the mentality and worldview of Ghanaians today, resulting in behaviors that edify and support the colonial master and his institutions (Igboin, 2011; Utsey et al., 2014).

The remnants of the indoctrination, if you will, are still observable today. John Henrik Clarke (1996) suggests that he would be happy to say that after slavery and the effects of its aftermath, we are free of this dilemma of self-identity and misguided direction, but in fact quite the contrary is true. He suggests that we (Afrikans) seem to be in the same dilemma now, more tragically and deeper than ever. Dubois (1961) speaks further to this travesty, by stating,

"It is a particular sensation, this double-consciousness, this sense of always looking at one's self through the eyes of others, of measuring one's soul by the tape of a world that looks on in amused contempt and pity." He further states, ". . . one ever feels his two-ness in America, a Negro; two souls, two thoughts, two reconciled strivings; two warring ideals in one dark body, whose dogged strength alone keeps it from being torn asunder" (p. 16). This double consciousness, if you will, can be observed in Ghanaians, as many of the people of Ghana have seemingly subscribed to Eurocentric aesthetics and ideologies, and have attributed value to them. These values are often observable with regard to phenotypic presentation, marriage preferences, education, and religious symbols/practices, to name a few.

Omnipresence of European Symbolism (Religion)

Despite the long period of European rule and domination in Ghana, there is a dearth of empirical studies that have examined the psychological residuals of colonialism on the personality and behavior of Ghanaians (Utsey et al., 2014). According to Utsey et al. (2014) colonialism exists in the Ghanaian psyche with regard to religion. For example, the Twi expression *Wu yi Nyame a Obroni na eba* ("the Whiteman is next to god") exemplifies the deification of the colonial master (Europeans) in Ghanaian culture (Prah, 1992; Utsey et al., 2014). Interestingly, pictorial representations of a White Jesus can be seen on billboards all over the country. Viewing this image daily and repeatedly can certainly reinforce the idea of White supremacy, as the depiction of Jesus in a White or Eurocentric presentation is inextricably linked to salvation. Akbar (1996) further supports this notion as he suggested that to see god in others (Caucasians) to the exclusion of oneself (Ghanaians) sets the stage for psychological harm (Utsey et al., 2016). Utsey et al., (2014) further state that the process by which Ghanaians internalize notions of White supremacy has received some empirical attention in the psychological literature, such that, a replication of the Clark Doll Study conducted by Mahama, Danquah, and Wan (2009) found that Ghanaian boys from lower socioeconomic status expressed a preference for the White doll. Seemingly where there has been colonization and racial subjugation, colorism is an expressed and salient vestige. Colorism seems to be an unrelenting intricacy of racism and a direct descendent of colonialism.

Colonialism and Colorism in Ghana

A colonial mentality is a broad multidimensional construct that refers to personal feelings or beliefs of ethnic or cultural inferiority (David & Okazaki, 2006; Utsey et al., 2014). Utsey et al. (2014) posit that a colonialized mentality can manifest in the following ways: (1) depreciation of the self; (2) denigration of the culture or body; (3) discriminating against less acculturated in-group members; and (4) abiding both historical and contemporary oppression (Nadal, 2011). Understandably, the literature on racism suggests that this form of internalized oppression has an adverse effect on ethnic identity development and psychological functioning and is also associated with maladaptive behaviors (Utsey et al., 2014). Therefore, this "colonial mentality" appears to rest at the core of the expression of colorist ideologies in Ghana. Moreover, those who develop admiration for the colonizer's culture tend to not only develop a dislike for the indigenous culture but are also discriminatory against persons who have physical characteristics associated with the indigenous culture (for example, being dark-skinned) (Utsey et al., 2014). As such, similar to African Americans in the United States, skin color and hair texture play a significant role in the lives of Ghanaians. Specifically, many Ghanaians' feelings about beauty, value, and attractiveness are directly related to marriage and life outcomes, and many have resorted to skin bleaching to better approximate Whiteness (Fokuo, 2009).

Skin Bleaching

In 1992, various Afrikan governments launched a campaign to prevent people from using skin-bleaching products that have been known to cause irrevocable damage to skin cells and, more alarmingly, skin cancer (Asante, 2016). Those countries were South Africa, Ghana, Nigeria, and Ivory Coast. Although the governments of these countries have tried to prevent people from using skin bleaching products, the sociocultural pressures, privileges, and material benefits associated with being lighter-skinned are widely apparent and supported (Asante, 2016; Fukuo, 2009). Asante (2016) also asserts that even in countries where there are few White inhabitants, the influence of whiteness and its inseparable tie to capitalism can be seen in the higher status that is placed on lighter skin (Asante, 2016). The numerous skin-whitening products, as well as the advertising for them in Ghana, send clear colorist messages about identity, beauty, and social standing. They tend to equate health and "body success" with lighter skin. Further, whiteness/lighter skin is perceived as such an important commodity that some Ghanaians risk their health to achieve it (Hunter, 2007) despite the injurious effects of excessive bleaching (Utsey et al., 2014.) In Ghana, the practice of skin bleaching among Ghanaian women is related to assumptions that lighter skin is preferred and can be used specifically as social capital for marriage and possibly other aspects of life (Fokuo, 2009; Utsey et al., 2014). These phenomena are observable in African American culture as well, as lighter-skinned African American women are more privileged in the areas of education, income, and spousal status than their darker-skinned counterparts (Haileab, 2018; Hunter, 1998, 2002).

Colorism and Marriage

Scholars suggest that the lived experiences that surface from colorism are gendered (Hill, 2002; Hunter, 1998; Ozakawa-Rey, Robinson, & Ward, 1987), such that skin color, along with other correlated characteristics such as hair texture, facial features, and body types have "more bearing" on the lives of women (Hill, 2002) than men. Thus, the association between skin color and physical attractiveness is significantly stronger for women than men, in general. However, in Ghana the reverse is also true, with Ghanaian men, by and large, possessing an exaggerated preference for lighter-skinned women (Fokuo, 2009). Fokuo's (2009) research argues that, for many Ghanaian women, feelings concerning beauty, attractiveness, and their marriage marketability are partially determined by the lightness of their skin, which causes some women to believe that skin bleaching is a necessity. Accordingly, colorism researchers posit that skin color is more important as a predictor of self-esteem among women than among men and lighter skin tones are positively related to higher self-esteem (Thompson & Keith, 2001). These findings are not surprising, given the societal value placed on female beauty and the ways in which the pursuit of beauty is gendered. Again, Mahama, Danquah, and Wan (2009) found that Ghanaian boys from lower socioeconomic status expressed a preference for the White doll (Utsey et al., 2014), suggesting the preference for lighter skin relative to Ghanaian children develops through early socialization and colorist indoctrination and is sustained into adulthood. This nuanced perspective of "gendered" colorism further suggests that dating/courting for Ghanaian women can be rather precarious.

Ghanaian women often get married to increase their social status; they are not only considered adults within the society, but being married allows them to escape the stereotypes of unmarried women (Fokou, 2009). Thus, marriage is an important avenue for Ghanaian women to gain status within the community (Fokou, 2009). Given the societal pressures toward being married, it makes sense, however unfortunate, that women in this culture feel the need to resort to such extreme measures as skin bleaching to be considered eligible and/or suitable for marriage. In Ghanaian society, like most others, beautiful women are able to obtain social standing and reverence based solely on their physical appearance. Sadly, for many Ghanaian women, beauty is synonymous with possessing a lighter skin complexion, often unattainable, which further attests to the power and persistent nature of White supremacy and privilege in Ghana (Fokuo, 2009) and speaks to the potential psychological challenges these colorist ideologies evoke.

Psychological Impact of Colorism

Cultural patterns and linguistic expressions suggest that remnants of internalized colonialism exist in the Ghanaian psyche. For example, having a "double consciousness" can have serious psychological ramifications for Ghanaians. As stated by Utsey et al. (2014), the inability to literally become like the colonizer robs the person of the ability to be authentic, leaving him or her with feelings of anxiety (Memmi, 1965). Researchers suggest, on the other hand, however, that the internalized shame of a person's culture may increase the experience of anxiety and depression, and that this paradox may occur because the adoption of colonial values is likely coupled with condemnation of the self (Utsey et al., 2014). This incongruence tends to saddle the person with a profound sense of disappointment and denunciation when unable to approximate the colonizer despite repeated attempts. Further, Utsey et al. (2014) suggest that being torn between the indigenous culture and the colonizer's cultural values relegates the person to a posture of self-loathing and/or even shame. Fortunately, prominent Black scholars and others have developed robust theoretical frameworks that not only provide contextualization to the aforementioned colorist phenomena, but also yield suggestions for deprograming and liberation.

Theoretical Framework and Intervention from an Afrikan Liberation Perspective

The proper healing of a people is difficult if not impossible without a correct understanding of those peoples' experiences and their worldview. This is very true with respect to the healing of the psycho-spiritual disruption and the ancillary lingering psychological effects of what has been called the transatlantic slave trade encountered (Maafa) by Afrikan people in America, throughout the Afrikan Diaspora, and among continental Afrikans as well. Given the uniqueness of this multifaceted attack on Afrikan people, a distinct psychology of healing is implicated because psychic disruption is unique. More importantly, the worldview that Afrikan people generally operate from is distinct from that of Europeans (Myers, 1993). Dr. Linda James Myers makes the distinction by positing the following:

Sub-Optimal/European

       a. Control/mastery over Nature

       b. Survival of the Fittest

       c. Dichotomy/Competition

       d. Separateness-independence

       e. Individualism

       f. Uniqueness-Differences

Optimal/Afrikan

       a. Oneness/Harmony with Nature

       b. Survival of the Group

       c. Synthesis/Cooperation

       d. Corporateness-interdependence

       e. Groupness

       f. Sameness-Commonality

With this major difference in paradigms, it is important to note that culturally relevant healing frameworks will facilitate the psychic trauma repair of Afrikan people, both continental and Diasporan. Such an approach will consider Afrikan people's experiences, while maintaining strict consideration of their worldview. Moreover, such a distinct psychology of healing will be consistent with the unique psychology of Afrikans in general, as it will be sensitive to the essence and ethos of Afrikanity. Implications for continental Afrikans, as shown by a unique Afrikan worldview is evident; there are concepts that metaphysically speak to connection and interdependences through life forces. For example, there are constructs that speak to this: the Akan concept of *Ntoro*—personality life-force transmitted through the father's sperm, which spiritually bonds the child to the father, and *Mogya*—blood/bloodline though the mother, which supposes that the physical body that comes from the mother, through to the Zulu concept of *Ukufa KwaBantu* (the metaphysical illnesses/challenges of the Black people).In all Afrikan people of the Afrikan Diaspora this is seemingly evident and relevant.

Although similar, it is often suggested that one cannot apply a monolithic perspective for the totality of people of the Afrikan continent and that largely the application of the unifying Afrikan-centered thought is an Afrikan American enterprise, whereas the Afrikan-centered scholarship advanced by Asante and others evolved out of an African American experience in North America, and out of critical scholarship and research of continental Afrikan societies with many indigenous African thinkers engaged in the discourse. Khoza (2005) advances that an African value system that means humanness or being human is a universal worldview characterized by such values as caring, sharing, compassion, communalism, communocracy and related predispositions. Jomo Kenyatta (1965) stated that nobody is an isolated individual. . . that one's uniqueness is a secondary fact about him, and that first and foremost one is several people's relative and contemporary. This fact is the basis of one's sense of moral responsibility and social obligation, as it attests to the communal aspects of self. This recognition of the communal identity of the Afrikan self is found throughout the Afrikan world and it has been a galvanizing aspect of a sense of being, which has resulted in the sustained presence of Afrikan people for thousands of years (Washington, 2010). Many Afrikan-centered scholars (Ani, 1994; Jackson-Lowman, 2004; Kambon, 1998; Myers 1993; Nobles, 2006; Schiele, 2000) advance the following as the core tenets of an Afrikan-centered ideology, emanating from an Afrikan worldview: (1) spirit is sacred; (2) all things are seen as spiritual; (3) all sets are connected; (4) there is a union between the sacred and the mundane; (5) life is religion and religion is life; (6) cause and effect are seen as spiritual phenomena; and (7) to attend to the mind is to attend to the spirit.

Convincing many contemporary continental Africans that there is an Afrikan-centered thrust that more or less applies to all people of Afrikan descent is challenging; however, the presence of such is undeniable. Continental Afrikans have a lived experience of their worldview; thus, their familiarity with their experiences is akin to trying to tell a fish what water is. Afrikans of the Diaspora, many of whom may be guilty of having a highly idealized perspective of Afrika, have had an opportunity to coexist with Europeans and have a clearer sense of the contrasting elements of the Afrikan and European worldviews. It is this living with and among persons of European descent that allowed W.E.B. Dubois (1961) to advance the aforementioned construct, double consciousness. One sees clearly how he is not European but is not clear about his native identity. Afrikan-centered scholars give voice to this paradoxical identity crisis by identifying the distinct elements of the Afrikan worldview. It is this worldview that can assess the challenges that Africans have with colorism in Ghana and throughout the Afrikan Diaspora.

On Western Psychology (Mental Health)

The necessity of an Afrikan-centered modality of psycho-spiritual healing is most justifiable when one considers elements of Western thought that have facilitated and continue to facilitate some aspects of the psychological disruption of persons of Afrikan ancestry (Myers, 1998). The maintenance of various cultural ethnic groups is often facilitated through culturally structured thought or the *utamawazo* (Ani, 1994). Additionally, the cultural survival imperative informs the *utamawazo* of the evolving needs of the people (Welsing, 1991). Further, Western cultural thought is normalized and stabilized through European behavioral sciences. The discipline of Western psychology is a major cultural vehicle that Europeans employ to maintain their culturally structured thought as well to advance their worldview (Kambon, 1998; Wilson, 1993). It must be acknowledged that the field of Western psychology is an extension and product of the European worldview through their culturally structured thoughts about the universe (Ani, 1994). Western behavioral scientists have assisted Western cultures with organizing their people's behavior within the desired context of their European cultural imperative. Behavioral scientists have advanced diagnosis and treatment of human behavior consistent with European cultural thought and desire (Akbar, 2003; Guthrie, 2004; X, C. et al., 1975). Those who do not fit within their cultural paradigm will become labeled as the other or outcaste and they become the cultural other (Ani, 1994). Thus, Western "mental health" practices are disruptive to the Afrikan spirit essence found within Afrikan humanity. Moreover, this worldview would not see colorism as an anomaly because the European thought thrives on being admired as the greatest. However, for Afrikan people to identify with their oppressor to be validated, is a sign of mental unrest when applying an Afrikan-centered analysis.

The Call for Spirit Alignment

People's perception of themselves governs their actions and dictates their destiny. Afrikan people have received consistent misinformation about themselves and their status within the world. This misinformation has created what Dr. Kambon (1998) calls Misorientation to Afrikan orientation. This occurs when persons of Afrikan descent engage in anti-Afrikan, racially disempowering and self-destructive behaviors. The behavioral correlates of this are learned indifference and assumed significance (Washington, 1996). This occurs when persons of Afrikan descent become disinterested

201

is cultural, racial and ethnic beliefs as well as values and artifacts of Afrikan people. Subsequently they began to operate from the position that what is a part of the European populations is reality and is the most salient cultural, racial and ethnic artifacts to which one needs to aspire to attain. This observable when Afrikan people buy into colorism. Although Ghanaians take pride in being an Akan, Asante, Fante, Twi, Ga, Ewe. . . one can see the ever-presence of a European image of Jesus, a taste for European cultural styles of dress, education, a propensity for skin bleaching, and having the accoutrements of success that are associated with Europeans, while simultaneously having a disdain for Indigenous Afrikan religion, culture, and beliefs. Many posit that what is European is modern and what is traditionally Afrikan is outdated and should be shunned. This unfortunately leads to an internal disavowing of that which is Afrikan and contributes to psycho-spiritual distress. Preferably, shifting from being a diminishment of another's reality to operating with the context of our own understanding and knowledge is ideal. Furthermore, behavioral scientists familiar with the Afrikan conceptualization of self will likely be most instrumental in this process, as there is, based on this paradigm, an interconnectedness.

Afrikan Cultural Considerations

Among the Zulu of South Afrika there is a concept for disorders called *ukufa kwabantu* that means "illnesses of the Bantu or Black people." It suggests that there are certain disorders that only occur to Black people who operate in or are a part of an indigenous Zulu worldview. It is within the context of culture that proper mental health diagnosis and treatment of Afrikans should occur. Afrikan terms such as *abaphansi basifulathele*—ancestral protection withdrawal (Zulu), *akom ko*—without spirit (Akan), *sikere folo*—to act without spiritual connection (Bamana), and *elenini*—spirit defilement (Yoruba) are advanced. All of these terms imply that the invisible realm of the human experience is most impactful to the visible aspect of being. They suggest that spirit must be attended to in order to have a peaceful community. Thus, we advance spirit alignment rather than mental health. To place a European image of deity is a psycho-spiritually misaligned moment for Afrikan people, because no one would dare revere their tormentor as the symbol of humanity and high culture. The enslavement of Afrikan people (Maafa) took place at the hands of Europeans and was indeed a horrific event for people of Afrikan descent. To identify with one's oppressor as a progenitor of humanity represents a psycho-spiritual distortion of reality. Unfortunately, scientific content suggesting that Afrikans were inferior to Europeans has been advanced for years.

The founder of psychology in America, G. Stanley Hall, asserted that the "Negro" was an adolescent race experiencing a stage of incomplete development (Guthrie, 2003). In this he advanced that there was really nothing that could be done to bring these people to the standards of Whites because they were a "whole historical layer less than Whites." With such psychology how could Afrikan people be viewed as having any value or worth? It is important to note that, out of this thinking, psychology was born. Similar biased "quasi-science" has provided the background for the recent mental conditioning of Afrikan (Black) people in general. As such, the socio-cultural belief in European superiority, which was extended and defended by Westernized religion, and science that posits the defamation of the Afrikan character, has had some deleterious psychological effects on Afrikan people globally. Moreover, the Western construct of "mental health" is anemic in addressing the psycho-spiritual essence and spirit alignment of Afrikan/Black people; thus, an Afrikan-centered model of healing is needed, which could help address the dynamics of colorism in Ghana and throughout the continent.

Afrikan-Centered Ideology

A major strength of the Afrikan-centered ideological core was the fortification of spiritual values that allows Afrikan people to be resilient in the face of adverse situations. To a varying degree, success in life results from a strong value system, which includes belief in self, industrious efforts, desire and motivation to achieve, religious beliefs, self-respect and respect for others, responsibility toward one's family and community, and cooperation. Therefore, family, blood kin and extended kin, are very important to people of Afrikan descent (Hill, 2003). Of note, various kinship relationships have been essential to the survival of Afrikan people through enslavement and remain today. Extended kin and kinship networks have historically managed to contradict psychological isolation and poverty and have been recognized as an alternative means of provision. This system of kinship is a carryover from Afrika, which was adapted to the system of enslavement, which disrupted Afrikan family life. Family members were often sold to different plantations to create confusion and reduce the likelihood that a solid Afrikan identity would be maintained (Stewart, 2007). The process failed because the common Afrikan ethos is about the survival of the group. Afrikans maintained this ethos irrespective of the conditions under which they had to survive (Nobles, 1986). Ghanaian scholar-researcher Gyekye (1996) posits that there is a social communal aspect to family that is expansive. The communal values of group identity/solidarity, interdependence, and mutual aid all promote a sense of well-being for the family and its members. This ethos and worldview are different from the Eurocentric worldview in many ways. Thus, we acknowledge the need to strengthen the Afrikan core through spirit alignment and the increase in the positive perception of our Afrikan/Black identity. High racial and ethnic identity has been found to be associated with positive psychological well-being (Lloyd & Williams, 2017).

Spirit (Afrikan Self) Expression as a Source of Strength

The current Afrikan cultural expression has been the major source of strength for the survival of Afrikan people in the midst of these aforementioned forces of the European hegemonic onslaught. Afrikan/Black psychology acknowledges that the ideological core of Afrikan people is not monolithic, but the ways of being are consistent across tribes, societies, countries, and other arbitrary borders. The anchoring element of this Afrikan/Black psychology is the Afrikan philosophical communal self (Mukaka, 2013). The key components of this Afrikan psychology are that Spirit is ever-present, all is connected, family is sacred, and the community is essential. Additionally, a philosophical manifestation of these components is found among the Zulu, who advance a philosophical construct called *Ubuntu*. *Ubuntu* speaks to the idea that all things are interrelated through one Spirit, indivisible wholeness. For example, if anyone in the community does wrong, then the entire community will be impacted. *Ubuntu* alludes to profound humanness—one that respects the humanity of others. *Ubu* refers to being, while *ntu* refers to universal/unifying life force. It has been this ideological construct as well as the culturally structured thought that have sustained Afrikan/ Black people thus far. Admittedly, there has been a strong desire to survive; however, the chosen survival behaviors must be closely examined. The overidentification of Afrikan people in Ghana and throughout the Continent with European culture is an indication of a psychic disruption that interferes with the full manifestation of the Afrikan ideological core. Hence, the psychic events of Afrikan enslavement altered the manifestation of the Afrikan ideological core, which must be examined before the proper healing paradigm can be advanced.

African/Black people continue to experience forms of racial discrimination and harassment as well as deprivation, disenfranchisement, dehumanization, despiritualization, and disidentification with African culture, which is an indication of the multiple dimensions of African trauma. Furthermore, the term Post (Persistent) Enslavement Systemic Trauma (PEST) is posited in an effort to describe a specific dimension of the African trans-generational trauma. One of the ways that this trauma manifests, is through the belief that white skin in prettier and that European culture is the highest form of modernity. Within this context of PEST, the emphasis is placed on the systemic trauma that has residual effects upon the self-perception of African/Black people. Not only does this systemic trauma influence the names that African/Black people give their children, but it impacts the schools that they attend, the clothes that they wear, the style that wear their hair in, as well as foods they eat, without recognition of how all of this impacts their sense of self. This includes their physical bodies, their minds, their perceptions of reality and their relationships with themselves and others as well as their notion of what it means to be human. The effects of this trauma are trans-generational, and sadly impacts the psychological well-being of African/Black people.

As it relates to PEST, the first portion of the term alludes to "post (persistent) enslavement" which is a period of time that is beyond the physical enslavement. It is being noted here that the Maafa or what is often called the Trans-Atlantic Slave Trade impacted the continent of Afrika by invading the continent and forcibly extracting millions of its inhabitants and dispersing them all over the world. The hundreds of years of barbaric actions of the Europeans against the inhabitants of Afrika has had a lasting impact on the continent and its's people. Unlike "post traumatic" which suggest that one is in a period that is beyond the trauma, "post (persistent) enslavement" refers to a period beyond physical enslavement.

Colorism is readily present in current Afrika. It is understood that enslavement takes on many forms and that the mental (psycho-spiritual) form is more violent in many ways than the physical form; however, the mental (psycho-spiritual) period of enslavement represents a different season of the trauma process and thus requires a slightly different approach to healing. Here, it is important to acknowledge the physical and spiritual assaults, because they are easily identifiable, and they have been most instrumental in solidifying the stronghold of the mental (psycho-spiritual) enslavement structures though repetition of physical brutality. Therefore, this is where the notion of "persistent" becomes a salient part of the conversation. Because the psycho-spiritual disruption continues to manifest in various ways both psychologically and physically, one must acknowledge that Afrikans are in a various era of trauma, and that the primary purpose of the physical brutality was to cause psychic disruption. Thus, the post physical enslavement serves as the point where the psycho-spiritual disruption takes place. Further, it is important to note that the many descendants of the oppressors continue the agenda of the psychic disruption of Afrikan people through police brutality and other forms of physical and psychological terror/violence. It is this disruption that healers seek to repair. Therefore, the notion of Afrikan Liberation Psychology or Afrikan Centered Spirit Alignment Model seems most befitting.

Afrikan Trauma Cycle

Agyei Akoto and Akua Akoto (2000) assert that given the current fragmentation of Afrikan society (continental and Diasporan), healing or the return to order and balance is a major concern. They further state that healing, whether of the individual person or of the nation, is as much a spiritual matter as it is physical and socio-political issue. The Akotos talk about the need for a Re-Afrikanization process that will reveal the healing of Afrikan people. What is most striking, however, is their usage of the idea of a "Historical Spirocycle" that examines the Afrikan challenges through the lens of an Afrikan reality, not as a European interpretation. The historical spirocycle is akin to the earth's tilt on its axis in its movement around the sun, which in turn influences the four seasons that we experience. A description of the cycle is as follows. The earth has two solstitial points and two equinoctial points. The solstitial points are where the stream of Afrikan history (a) most approximates the order and balance of the ancients, and (b) that moment where it is most remote form that order and balance. The solstitial points represent Maat (point of origin and divine order) and Isfet (point of maximal disorder and chaos). Further, there is a counterclockwise progression that enters into Ogoyne or divergence followed by Maafa or Destruction. Then, Maafa (destruction) ends at Isfet (chaos) and then begins the season of Khepera (convergence) followed by the fourth season of Kuroka (reconstruction) which leads to Maat (divine order). The Akotos use the History Spirocycle to also discuss the transition, from the Nile Valley Civilization to the present, and this framework can be applied to a discussion about the proper healing paradigm for Afrikan/Black people. The paradigm ultimately examines the Afrikan notion of what it means to be human (Maat), the cycles of movement away from that idea of self, and then healing during Isfet (chaos) that creates movement back toward Maat (divine order).

Afrikan Psychology (Spirit Healing/Alignment) Kuroka

Afrikan Psychologists/Healers and those truly empathic as it relates to Afrikan issues, can facilitate the healing of Afrikan people. Their knowledge into the workings of the minds/spirits of Afrikan/Black people places them in an ideal place to accurately orient the thinking of the people. Their system of healing will be consistent with the culturally structured thought (utamawazo) of the Afrikan/Black people thus allowing them to create culturally appropriate paradigms for true healing of Afrikan/Black people. Since Healers are exactly where the greatest amount of damage took place, they have the potential of being efficient in the healing process, while drawing upon the knowledge of the ancestors.

Spirit Alignment and Afrikan Structured Thought

The Psycho-Spiritual Alignment (*Ubuntu*) model must be grounded in the Afrikan Structured thought which holds that spirit is central to every aspect of being. It must take account that individual work must include the family, and the family work must include the community, and the community work must hold the individual accountable. John Mbiti advanced the following Afrikan philosophical existential statement: "I am because we are; we are, therefore I am." Therefore, the therapeutic model must embrace that philosophy. The work should occur on the individual, family and community levels. This will call for a stretch from the Western mental health model which tends to focus on each person and issues as a separate component. The Afrikan Centered (*Ubuntu*) model acknowledges that the person does not exist without the community and that the community affects the person, just as the person affects the community. Additionally, true Afrikan Spirit (Psyche) healing must pull all of these factors together as such, the overall goal of the Afrikan Centered (*Ubuntu*) healing paradigm for each person is to:

a. Achieve Spiritual Alignment

b. Strive for Afrikan renormalization, and

c. Attain Afrikan Self-Authentification

The outcomes are:

a. Increased self-love

b. Enhanced self-understanding

c. Greater self-efficacy

d. Spiritual alignment

e. Interpersonal normalization, and

f. Afrikan Self "Authentification."

A major goal is to assist Afrikan/Black people with healing from trans-generational trauma caused by the Maafa. If spirit is central, then the model must seek to align spirit with essence. Among the Yoruba this is called Ori-Ire or alignment of head (spirit) with destiny (being). There also must an effort to renormalize Afrikan people back to what it means to be Afrikan. The European structured thought sought to move and eradicate the Afrikan knowledge of self and to adopt a European way of being superior to that of the Afrikan. Ndabaninigi Sithole (1959) said of the Portuguese *assimilado*, "The African is taught under the *assimilado* system, to think of himself as a Portuguese in Portugal, not as an Afrikan. The Portuguese policy aims at killing the Afrikan within and at replacing him with a Portuguese." The same could be said for every encounter of Afrikans with Europeans. The re-normalization and "authentification" is to re-establish within the spirit (psyche) of Afrikan people what truly means to be Afrikan. Out of this, Afrikans will be able to embrace and celebrate themselves while living life with full power, passion, and purpose.

Implications for Research, Policy and Practice

Internalized cultural shame is apparent in the Ghanaian culture. Examples of this internalized cultural shame can be noted in the many depictions of a Caucasian representation of Jesus throughout Ghana, as well as the abuse of skin lightening products. It is important to note however, that bleaching is not a practice imposed on the Ghanaian community by the Western world. Now although, Ghana's interaction with Europeans, Afrikan Americans, Lebanese, biracial individuals and even the influential nature of bleaching advertisements encourages the practice of skin bleaching, it is Ghana's longstanding social structure that maintains it (Fukuo, 2009). Utsey et al. (2014) support this point as they state the sociopolitical structure of Ghana may inadvertently support an acrimonious cycle through its adherence to the norms set by the colonial masters and there by validate the negative cognitions and perceptions associated with the colonial mentality. Therefore, from a sociopolitical perspective, it would appear that the Ghanaian government has a civic responsibility to intervene on a deeper level by imposing its will to ensure that these practices do not continue, and that the anti-Afrikan beliefs change. First of all, the government can impede advertisement by requiring the removal of the billboards and signs, as they are a constant socializing agent causing psychological harm both conscious and subliminal. As an aside, while removing the skin bleaching signs, they can also sanction the positioning of religious paraphernalia, to counter the effect of the White presentation of Jesus. Secondly, also from a policy perspective, more strict rules relative to the importation and distribution of skin lightening products can be enforced. Perhaps if access to these products is restricted and/or the circulation of them is criminalized, a decline in their usage may be observed. Another policy that could be beneficial to the Ghanaian community could be instituted in the educational system. Required lessons about colorist ideologies and the dangers of skin lightening can be taught from a developmental perspective to intervene with the children, while they are developing their cultural ideas beliefs and perspectives about themselves. Further, the government can sponsor public service announcements and affirming campaigns that promote self-love and cultural appreciation.

Research is also an avenue that can assist in combatting the colorist ideologies that exist among Ghanaians. Scholars can conduct both qualitative and quantitative studies that yield data that can be utilized in developing evidence-based prevention and intervention strategies. More studies like those done by Utsey et al. (2014) should be conducted that address the impact of colonization and its resulting manifestations. For example, the aforementioned practice of skin lightening, is one such vestige that should be extensively explored. Specifically, there is a need for more studies that directly ask Ghanaian women why they bleach their skin. Fukuo (2009) suggests that in so doing, the data may yield findings that suggest that the women are not trying to be white, they like being Afrikan, but just want to be lighter-skinned Africans (Fukuo, 2009.) Studies could also query Ghanaian men to obtain a better understanding of why they tend to prefer lighter-skinned women. Thus, the many nuances relative to skin bleaching behaviors seemingly have yet to be fully uncovered empirically. Anecdotally however, the intricacies of the practice of skin lightening and the subscriptions to colorist ideologies can be expressed and explored in the context of therapy.

Clinicians working with individuals from the Ghanaian culture may first want to familiarize themselves with colorist ideologies from the point of view of how and why they are aparent in Ghanaian culture today. Although similar to other countries where there are Afrikans who have remnants of colonization, Ghanians have a very unique expression of the residue of their historical past and European influence. Consequently, clinicians may want to intervene from a Critical race theory paridigm as it offers what is most often referred to as counter-narratives but we refer to as corrective narratives as a means of recognizing and legitimizing the perspectives of the oppressed and marginalized, even when they are unaware. The utilization of corrective narrative emphasizes centering the personal discourse within context of the person rather that within that of the forces of oppression. Given that power and privilege undergird this theory, clinicians can work to help individual clients in therapy, and in the community, through workshops and presentations, to develop counter-narratives/corrective narratives to combat colorist ideologies there by curbing skin-lightening product use, and overall self denigration among women, in particular. Clinicians may also want to target Ghanaian men to help them understand and own the part they play in the perpetuation of the skin bleaching behaviors and cultural shame. Centering the understanding of what it means to be human within an Afrikan context for a person of Afrikan decent allows for the inherit strengths to be identified and enhanced. This strength-based perspective can facilitate clinicians with supporting clients work through their feelings of inferiority or ambivalence about what it means to be Afrikan. Perhaps psychoeducation and/or therapy groups could address these issues and promote psychological healing. Further, clinicians may want to incorporate his or her understanding and assessment of the clients level of internalized colorism/racism in their diagnostics to ensure that they take a more holist approach to understanding the full sociocultural context of their clients, as this understanding may be the root cause of the expressed psychopathology.

Process Questions and Considerations

1. What is your understanding of colorism in Ghana?

2. In what ways do colorist ideologies manifest in Ghana?

3. In what ways have colonization and slavery impacted slavery in modern times?

4. Are there differences in how colorism manifests in Ghana when compared in the United States?

5. How has globalization aided and/or hindered the spread of colorism across the world?

6. How has social media and access to technology globally impacted the development of colorist ideologies?

7. How do the theories of African personality support the next steps of combating colorism globally?

8. There have been several periods in history whereby there has been intentional movement to support people feeling good about "the skin they're in." Project forward. . . what would such a movement look like 10 years from now?

References

Akbar, N. (1996). Breaking the chains of psychological slavery. Tallahassee, FL: Mind Productions.

Akoto, K. A. & Akoto, A. N. (2000). *The Sankofa Movement and the reality of war.* Washington, DC: Oyoko InfoCom.

Ani, M (1980). *Let the circle be unbroken: The implications of African spirituality in the Diaspora.* New York: Nkonimfo Publications.

Ani, M. (1994). *Yuguru: An Afrikan-centered critique of European cultural thoughts and behavior.* Trenton, NJ: African World Press.

Asante, M. K. (1992). *Kemet, Afrocentricity, and knowledge* (3rd printing). Trenton, NJ: Africa World Press.

Asante, G. (2016). Glocalized whiteness: Sustaining and reproducing whiteness through "skin toning" in post-colonial Ghana, *Journal of International and Intercultural Communication.* DOI:

10.1080/17513057.2016.1154184

Clarke, J. H. (1996). *Critical Lessons in Slavery and the Slave trade.* Native Sun Publishers.

David, E.J.R., & Okazaki, S. (2010). Activation and automaticity of colonial mentality. *Journal of Applied Social Psychology, 40,* 850-887.

DeGruy, J. (2017). *Post traumatic slave syndrome: America's legacy of enduring injury and healing.* Portland, OR: Joy DeGruy Publications.

DuBois, W.E.B. (1961). *The souls of black folk: Essays and sketches.* Chicago, IL: A. C. McClurg.

Fokuo, J. K. (2009). The lighter side of marriage: Skin bleaching in post-colonial Ghana. *African and Asian Studies, 8,* 125-146.

Guthrie, R. V. (2003). *Even the rat was white: A historical view of psychology.* New York, New York: Pearson Publishing.

Gyekye, K. (1996). *African cultural values: An introduction.* Philadelphia: Sankofa Publishing Company.

Gyekye, K. (1995). *An essay on African philosophical thought: The Akan conceptual scheme* (Revised ed.). Philadelphia: Temple University Press.

Haileab, L. (2018). *Shaded love and violence: Internalized colorism, femininity, depression and dating violence.* Unpublished Dissertation, Howard University.

Hill, M. (2002). Skin color and the perception of attractiveness among African Americans: Does gender make a difference? *Social Psychology Quarterly, 65*(1), 77-92.

Hill, R. B. (2003). *The strengths of black families.* Lanham, MD: The University Press of America.

Hunter, M. (1998). Colorstruck: Skin color stratification in the lives of African American women. *Sociological Inquiry, 68,* 517-535.

Hunter, M. (2002). "If you're light you're alright." Light skin color as social capital for women of color. *Gender and Society, 16*(2), 175-193.

Hunter, M. (2007). The persistent problem of colorism: Skin tone, status, and inequality. *Sociology Compass, 1,* 237-254.

Igboin, B. O. (2011). Colonialism and African cultural values. *African Journal of History and Culture, 3,* 96-103.

Jackson-Lowman, H. (2004). Perspectives on Afrikan American mental health: Lessons from Afrikan systems. In R. Jones (Ed.), *Black psychology* (4th ed.) (pp. 599-630). Hampton, VA: Cobb & Henry Publishers.

Kambon, K.K.K. (1998). *African/Black psychology in the American context: An African-centered approach.* Tallahassee, FL: Nubian Nation.

Lloyd, B. A., & Williams, B. V. (2017). The potential for youth programs to promote African American youth's development of ethnic and racial identity. *Child Development Perspectives, 11*(1), 29-38.

Mahama, S., Danquah, A. N., & Wan, M. W. (2009). Doll choice in young children: Representing self through skin color. *Ghana International Journal of Mental Health, 1,* 107-119.

Mbiti, J. S. (1990). *African Religions and Philosophy.* Oxford: Heinemann, 108.

Memmi, A. (1965). The colonizer and the colonized. Boston, MA: Beacon Press

Myers, L. J. (1993). *Understanding an Afrocentric worldview: Introduction to an optimal psychology* (2nd ed.). Dubuque, IA: Kendall/Hunt Publishing Company.

Myers, L. J. (1998). The deep structure of culture: Relevance of traditional African culture in contemporary life. In J. D. Hamlet (Ed.), *Afrocentric visions: Studies in culture and communication.* Thousand Oaks, CA: SAGE.

Mukuka, R. (2013). Ubuntu in S. M. Kapwepwe's Shalapo Canicandala: Insights for Afrocentric Psychology. *Journal of Black Studies, 44*(2), 137-157.

Nadal, K. L. (2011). *Filipino American psychology: A handbook of theory, research, and clinical practice.* Hoboken, NJ: Wiley.

Nobles, W. W. (2004). African philosophy: Foundations of black psychology. In R. Jones (Ed.). *Black Psychology* (pp. 47-63). Berkeley, CA: Cobb & Henry.

Nobles, W. W. (1986). *African psychology: Toward its reclamation, reascension, and revitalization.* Oakland: Black Family Institute.

Nobles, W.W. (2015). From black psychology of sakhu djaer: Implications for the further development of a pan African black psychology. *Journal of Black Psychology, 41*(5), 399-414.

Ozakawa-Rey, M., Robinson, T. L., & Ward, J. V. (1987). Black women and the politics of skin color and hair. *Women & Therapy, 6,* 89-102.

Prah, K. K. (1992). *Capitein: A critical study of an 18th century African.* Trenton, NJ: African World Books.

Stewart, P.S. (2007). Who is kin? *Journal of Human Behavior in the Social Behavior, 15,* 163-181.

Thompson, M. S., & Keith, V. M. (2001). The blacker the berry: Gender, skin-tone, self-esteem and self-efficacy. *Gender & Society, 15,* 336-357.

Washington, K. (1996). In K. Addae (Ed.), *To heal a people: Afrikan scholars define a new reality.* Columbia, MD: Kugichagulia Press.

Washington, K. (2010). Zulu traditional healing, Afrikan worldview and the practice of Ubuntu: Deep thought for Afrikan/black psychology. *The Journal of Pan African Studies, 3*(8), 24-39.

Wilson, A. N. (2014). *The falsification of Afrikan consciousness.* Brooklyn, New York: Afrikan World InfoSystems.

Utsey, S. O, Abrams, J. A., Opare-Henaku, A., Bolden, M. A., & Williams, O. (2014). Assessing the psychological consequences of internalized colonialism on the psychological well-being of young adults in Ghana. *Journal of Black Psychology.* DOI:10.1177/0095798414537935

X (Clark), C., McGee, D. P., Nobles, W. and X (Weems), L. (1975). Voodoo or IQ: An introduction to African psychology. *Journal of Black Psychology, 2,* 9-29.

CHAPTER 11.

DARK CURRENTS: Caste, Conflict, and Cosmetics in India: Colorism as a Reflection of Privilege and Power

David Blake Willis, Fielding Graduate University
J. Rajasekaran, CM Centre, Madurai, South India

"Amma (Mother) how is that you are so fair? How come I am so dark?"
She laughs, "Go on with you—who can be so beautiful as you?"
But when she hears that her daughter has attained puberty, she goes on to say,
"Ahh, we, too, have a Black one."
Crestfallen, her teen-aged daughter now knows the problem
of finding a marriage partner for someone like her, a darker woman.
(Ambai, 1992)

Color North and South: Historical Roots of Colorism in India

The power of sacred rivers, a perennial theme throughout South Asia, suggests dark currents flowing throughout the societies of the Subcontinent. Colorism in South Asia has historical roots which reflect these dark currents, with the flow of privilege, power, and colonialism revealing themselves in stories of dominance and degradation.

The roots of colorism in South Asia go deep indeed. Not only is there an intricate connection with Hinduism and caste, but modern and postmodern talk around color permeates South Asia—India, Pakistani, Bangladeshi, Nepali (a somewhat different story when it comes to color), and Sri Lankan society, from marriages to movies and beyond. As the many stories of colorism of one of the world's great civilizations are narrated, they also reveal the current dynamics of color prejudices in South Asia, of how colorism is deeply tied to caste and colonialism; of the resistance movements of the darkest Indians; of the popularization of color issues through the media, especially in movies and on television; and of the hope for an alternative, perhaps that of mixing, as a possible new color vision.

The primary context of this chapter on colorism is South Asia, India, and nearby countries. We begin with a discussion of the major cultural divisions in the Subcontinent between the Dravidians and the Aryans, which has a direct, divisive, and complex relationship to colorism. The standard depiction of color in South Asia, for example, is one of the dark people of the South, Dravidians, and the "fair" people of the North, to use the standard parlance in India about skin color. The reality is of course more complicated, with dark people in the North and fair people in the South as well, but these geographical stereotypes hold strongly for South Asians. What is perhaps less understood is how different these two peoples are, with Dravidians from a completely different language and cultural family from the Indo-Europeans of North India. Dominant and dominating views of color are complex and revealing for each of these two major culture areas. (We note that one can find "fair" or dark people anywhere in India).

Standards of beauty are less clear about what is often called "fairness" in South Asia, however. While it is true that outsiders, whether Aryans, Mughals, Persians, or English and their "fair" skin have been associated with power and dominance, there has also always been an alternative view of darkness and power. This is particularly seen through the principle Hindu gods Shiva, also called *Nilakanta* (blue-throated), and *Krishna* (clearly darker and also referred to as "the dark one," as the word means "black" in Sanskrit) as imbued with great power (Figures 1, 2, and 3). At the same time, other gods, *Rama* and his consort goddess *Sita* (Figure 4), for example, are usually seen as fair, even to the point of looking Western European in some depictions.

Figure 1. Nilakanta, Lord Shiva (Wikimedia Commons)

Figure 2. Shiva and Family (Wikimedia Commons)

Figure 3. Krishna (By Nil.Pawaskar, Wikimedia Commons)

Figure 4. Rama and Sita with Brother Lakshmana (Wikimedia Commons)

Ironically, of course, Rama is an incarnation of Vishnu, who is often depicted as darker as well (Figure 5). The nemesis of Rama and Sita, the ten-headed god-king Ravana (Figure 6), who lives in Lanka (Sri Lanka), is clearly dark and seen by some in South India as the Dravidian resistance to the "fair" Aryan invasions (Basham, 1975, p. 69). While Valmiki's *Ramayana* (5th to 1st century BCE) implies fair skin for the protagonists from the north and sees Ravana as a dark demon, the Tamil version of the *Ramayana* by Kambar (9th century CE, Ibid., p. 304, p. 308) has a different view of this anti-hero, who in some ways becomes a hero (Richman, 1991). Moreover, South India has what may be a majority of goddesses in the Hindu pantheon, many of whom are fierce gods who are dark themselves such as Mariamman, the smallpox goddess (Mines, 2005). Beauty is in the eye of the beholder, and these South Indian visions of color and resistance have found their way into the political struggles of the 20th century in India in ways both novel and powerful, including for the favorite god of the Tamils, Murugan, son of Shiva (Clothey, 2007).

Figure 5. Vishnu Surrounded by His Avatars (Tumblr.com)

Southern Nights: Beauty of Another Color

Despite the hegemony of Aryan visions of "fairness," there is another vision of color in South Asia, not of North India, but of the South, which presents a more complex set of visions around colorism. Both gods and goddesses in South India, including

Figure 6. Ravana, early 19th century (British Museum)

protective deities like *Iyyanar* and *Karuppasamy*, as well as the various *Amman Sakthi* or Mother goddesses, who are seen as darker compared to Vishnu's consort *Lakshmi*, the goddess of Wealth, who is usually depicted as pure white.

A key text for understanding color in India early on is *Paripatal*, the earliest Sangam poetry collection, fixed between the second and seventh century CE (Sarangapani, 1984; Shulman, 2016). Sangam literature is regarded as the fountainhead of Tamil culture, and three key words frequently appear in this ancient poetry: *Vaigai* (the river of the ancient city of Madurai), *Tirumal* (an earlier god seen as dark and soon identified with Vishnu), and *Murugan* (the son of Shiva). There is no mention of Brahminical associations, although many Sanskrit words are found in the *Paripatal*. In fact, there is an underlying stratum of Dravidian words in Sanskrit as well, as David Shulman has pointed out, indicating a reciprocal melding earlier on than has been thought.

Alagar (Vishnu) is derived from the Tamil word for beautiful or handsome and indicates a dark visage, as opposed to the fairer-skinned Sanskritized version of Vishnu and his incarnations found elsewhere. Early Sangam literature such as the *Tholkappiam* and the *Tirukkural* also see black and red as portraying anger (Paramasivam, 2001, p. 127), and one of the principal deities of South India is the all-powerful dark Dravidian goddess Meenakshi of Madurai (Saivam.org, ND).

Of the ancient Dravidian village gods remaining after the influence of Sanskirtization, *Karuppasamy* (literally, the "dark god") and his variants are among the most celebrated in rural South India. During the Nayak rule in Madurai in the

16th century, the fairer-skinned Telegu Nayaks from what is now Andhra Pradesh had become the rulers of Madurai. They met with great resistance from a dark caste called Kallars as they were going to their favorite hunting ground in the Alagar Mountains, and the road that led toward Alagar Kovil was known as *Kallar Naadu* (Kallar Country). The Nayaks made peace with the Kallar community by building a temple for the guardian deity Karrupasamy outside the Eastern wall of the Sundaraja Perumal Temple at Alagar Kovil. It was made to appear that anyone coming to worship Vishnu had to stop by the shrine of Karuppasamy first to get permission from Karuppasamy as the *Kaaval Deivam* or guardian deity of Vishnu.

During the important *Chitirai* Festival in April-May, when Alagar comes to Madurai, a drama is enacted at the Tallakulam Karrupasamy Temple. A small group of men in black traditionally oppose the entry of Alagar by saying that "he is not our god." Looking at the bronze statue, they say, "What is this? Our god is black in color, but this god is white." Finally, it was negotiated that he would wear dark attire throughout the Kallar country—that is, all the way from Alagarkoil to Tallakulam, where he is stationed under the protection of Karrupasamy. The next morning when he leaves, he changes the color of his attire, according to the decision of the Brahmin priests.

He is also not just Alagar but *Kalalagar*, which means he belongs to the Kallars, according to oral tradition. We note here that the Kallars prefer a new moon day to get on with their ostensible profession of robbery (DuBois, 1816, 2006, p. 18), which they were proud of (only after the British came to India were the Kallars labelled a "Criminal Tribe"). A dark night, with their dark skin smeared with castor oil, is seen as the best time to work, so dark colors are worshiped by them. The Kallars, however, cannot hope to compete with the power and dominance of the Brahmins who brought their visions of a hierarchical society, also partly based on color, to larger questions of political and social order through the caste system.

Brahmins, Sahibs, and the Institution of Caste and Color

One of the first imperial influences on South Asia was through Aryanization from North to South India brought by Brahmins and their concepts of an ordered universe, which first appear during the early Sangam Era (0-300 CE). This also brought concepts of color, with fairer skin being associated with power. The capacity and access to education, languages, and mathematics of the Brahmins is a key fact of South Asian civilization. South Indian Brahmins have deeply influenced the world through their concepts of zero, binaries, algorithms. The many South Indians working in the Silicon

Valley are an indication of this even today and include Google's CEO Sundar Pichai, a South Indian Brahmin. We might note, too, that Indians are also the richest immigrant group in the United States.

From the early to medieval history of South India, Brahmins have increasingly had power. The immediate success of Brahmins during the early days of English colonialism was of course not only because of their ability with numbers but also their facility with languages. Learning the Sanskrit Vedas by heart resulted in a powerful ability to interact with other areas in society under the British. The Brahmins had often been the intermediaries as well between the Mughals as Persian-speaking rulers, with Persian as the language of the courts and bureaucracies before the British. Moreover, the Brahmins brought their ideas about color to their discourse with the powers that were in India. How and where did they do this?

One of the most important color distinctions in India has thus arisen from the caste system (*varna-asrama*) brought by the Brahmins and laid down in the sacred text by Manu the Lawgiver (see Hinduwebsite.com, Manusmriti: The Laws of Manu Introduction, 2000). To have power is, again, often correlated with color (Dirks, 2001; Dumont, 1981), though not always in modern South India as we shall see below. The caste system, a complex set of traditional rules and duties that governs social relations in India, and which is breaking down (or at least transforming today to some extent), has exerted enormous influence on the notion of colorism in the South Asian context. Interestingly enough, the original documents speaking authoritatively on *caste* (a Portuguese word) use the word *varna*, which literally means color in Sanskrit.

The *Manu-smriti*, the seminal "Code of Conduct" for Indian society, dated 1250-1000 BCE, sees *varna* as the preordained, ordered arrangement of society, the caste hierarchy which mirrors the color gradations of social rankings. This ordering of society was mentioned, too, by Al-Biruni in 1048 (Lorenzen, 2005, p. 75) and the Abbe DuBois in the 18th century (1816, 2006). Along with it, one of the most important aspects of colorism in India as well as the surrounding countries is the way in which color matches hierarchical caste status, something reflected in class, power, and wealth. Purity and pollution are a significant part of this, with elaborate codes of conduct that continue to be enacted in the society in subtle and not-so-subtle ways. The pursuit of a "fair" bride or bridegroom through arranged marriage is a key aspect of family relations throughout South Asia even today.

In an eloquent essay on colorism that includes a survey on "fairness" (n=100), Neha Mishra notes her belief that Indian history also offers some answers to these questions, with the arrival of Europeans after the 15th century signaling a new kind of dominance in the social hierarchy (2015). Coming as traders and then as colonizers, first the Portuguese, then the Dutch, English, and the French, it was not lost upon the peoples of India that these foreigners who would come to rule South Asia had fair complexions (not unlike the Mughals before them). As Mishra and Hall put it in a later essay (2017):

> Being subject to a succession of white(ish) overlords has long associated light skin with power, status and desirability among Indians. Today, the contempt for brown skin is embraced by both the ruling class and lower castes and reinforced daily by beauty magazine covers that feature almost exclusively Caucasian, often foreign, models.
>
> Colonialism in India was predicated around what has been called "Sahib Culture," the idea that white colonials were to be honored and respected as the top of the power structure. *Sahib* is a Hindi word showing great deference and honor to someone who is at the top of the social hierarchy. These White Sahibs and later their *Memsahibs* (British women) were given special treatment throughout India, something which we saw as late as the 1970s with railway station Waiting Rooms marked "For Europeans Only."

British ideas about color meant that fairer-skinned Indians, and of course Anglo-Indians who were the offspring of British and Indian unions from the late 1700s, were favored for jobs. Of course, part of this is also language, since their mother tongue was essentially English. They were and are partly British, and many in the past did indeed have fair skin. The Abbe DuBois, a French missionary who commented extensively on Indian society in the 18th century, of course frequently commented on caste in South Asia, and Mishra's detailed essay mentioned above cites many relevant examples from Vedic Aryans onwards (2015).

Black is Beautiful: The *Dravidar Kazhagam* Movement and 20th-Century India

One of the most powerful political movements of 20th-century India, and one deeply associated with the color black, was the *Dravidar Kazhagam* (the alliance of Dravidians) founded by E.V.R. Periyar (Figure 7) and associated with the Indian Independence Movement (Diehl, 1977). Periyar had a history of performing dramas called *Kimayana*, with Ravana as the hero played by the actor M. R. Radha, contrary to the traditional depiction of a dark and evil Ravana. Ravana has 10 heads because he is a devotee of Shiva and cannot be killed (the 10 heads also represent 10 different kinds of knowledge and skills). Like Jimi Hendrix playing the American national anthem *The Star-Spangled Banner,* the image of Ravana as a counter-culture hero who has been misunderstood is a strong one. One of the early cinematic depictions of Ravana as the dark hero was in the movie *Sampoorna Ramayanam* (1958). In the Indian context it is the South against the North, with overtones of color.

Figure 7. E.V. Ramasamy ("Periyar") with C.N. Annadurai, Tamil Political Leaders, 1946 (Blogspot)

The Indian leaders of the independence movement, government, and industry in the 19th and 20th centuries were dominated by fair-skinned people, mostly Brahmins. The *Dravida Kazhagam* (DK) and Periyar opposed this dominance, railing against Brahminical power. This is an old line of resistance, as we have noticed above, by Dravidian Southerners against cultural incursions and what has been called Sanskritization from the North. The (DK) and Periyar chose black and red as the colors of their politics, indicating changing attitudes about color from the 1950s onward. DK workers were also called *karuppuchattaikaran*, those who wear black shirts. Since that time, black and red have been the colors of Tamil Nadu southern political parties which inherited the mantle of the DK and which have been alternately as the DMK and AIADMK, ruling in that southern state since the 1970s. In Hinduism, of course, black is, however, also associated with death or bad luck, in contrast with saffron which is considered auspicious. We note here the American Black Power Movement of the Black Panthers, Malcolm X, Angela Davis, Eldridge Cleaver, Bobby Seale, and others which celebrate Blackness as Beautiful.

In India, the concept of color continues to change. It is no longer about aesthetics

221

and cosmetics alone. Black, when worn as a shirt, is taken as a protest against the dominance and oppression of the yellow-orange saffron color used by fundamentalist Hindu groups. For protests, the only color that is used is black, most recently with the massive protest struggle around *Jallikattu* in Tamil Nadu, a bull-chasing sport (the goal being to catch the hump of a large Brahman bull) and then the protests against the Hindutva politics of dominance of the Narendra Modi Government after 2014, culminating in the CAA, Citizenship Amendment Act, and NPR, National Population Registry. The power and unity that the color black brings to Dravidian or protest crowds when everyone is in black is an impressive display of resistance and a demand for a new view of color. (White, we might add, represents death, as seen in the traditional dress of widows, all-white without adornments and to be avoided by brides).

Unfortunately, throughout the Subcontinent and even in Southern India, job selection, not to mention marriageability (which we will discuss below) has reflected prejudices about skin color, too. From the late 18th century, fairer-skinned people have been selected for many prominent jobs, including Customs and Excise, Post and Telegraphs, the Forestry Department, railways, the hospitality industry, office reception, telephone operators, stenographers, kindergarten teachers, and more recently, airline flight attendants and check-in counter employees. Front-line workers who interact with the public are seen as the face of the company, school, or job, thus requiring an image of higher status. This preference is of course about more than just color, notably with the railways and the ease of communication in English being critical for the operation of certain vocations.

The origins of the Anglo-Indian community, who numbered over two million at the time of Indian Independence in 1947, are from a blending of Indian women and British men said to have had its origins in a policy promulgated by the English colonialist Robert Clive during the Carnatic Wars of the 1750s for British soldiers to have children with local women. It was thought that language and trust could then be better established between the colonizer and the colonized, with the symbolism of fairer skin yet another marker of dominance. These struggles with color in India began to transform in the public eye with push-back from cinema actors in South India from the 1960s.

Being Black in Indian Cinema: The Elevation of Dark Skin as Power in South India

In 1963 a controversial film appeared in South Indian Tamil cinemas titled *Naanum Oru Penn*: "I Am Also a Woman (Though I Am Dark)." The film highlighted the clear prejudices rife then as well as now in Indian society concerning "fair" or dark skin. Starring the actress Vijayakumari and directed by A. C. Tirulokchandar, the film directly challenged the idea that fair is beautiful. Originally a Bengali play, *Naanum Oru Penn* concerns two brothers living with their landlord father who wants to marry his sons to fair-skinned partners. One of the brothers, Rajendran, falls in love with Kalyani, a dark-skinned and uneducated village woman, who demonstrates that character is more important than appearance or education.

The landlord father is on the verge of accepting Kalyani when other members of the household attempt to sabotage the relationship and cast Kaylani out of the house and community. Eventually the couple is reunited. The film earned critical acclaim and was a commercial success. The key song of this early 1960s film, *Kanna karumai nira (The Black-Colored Kannan—Krishna)*, has the protagonist Kalyani plaintively singing to a statue of Krishna ("The Dark One") in the garden of their home: "You are Black, but there are no eyes that will miss you. Nobody refuses you. But when they look at me nobody can tolerate me. They refuse to see what's in my heart."

The song and the film obviously had a great impact, as witnessed by comments such as these in response to the YouTube posting of the song: *"whenever I feel sad and ugly of being dark, I listen to this song"* and *"dedicated to all the black-skinned angels who were rejected for matrimony by guys because of skin color."*

In contrast to the massive, even obsessive, emphasis on the cosmetics and commercialization of skin-care products emphasizing fairness and even bleaching in late-20th century and early-21st century India, the evolution and stardom of the Tamil movie superstar Rajinikanth (Figure 8) reveals an alternative path for colorism in the Subcontinent. His name itself indicates this, literally: "the color of the night." Chosen by the famous director K. Balachander, Rajinikanth emerged in the 1970s and 1980s as a new Tamil and Indian hero in contrast with other actors who were (and are) "milk-white" (Nathan, 2018).

From the film *Apoorva Ragangal to Kala*, Rajinikanth's skin color and his black dress have been seen in a positive light, giving him power, vigor, and a widespread appreciation within and outside the movie world. There was also a song from another film promoting dark skin titled *"Karupputhaan ennaku pudicha coloru,"* meaning that "black alone is my favorite color," a song composed by music director Deva and performed by Anuradha Sriram in the movie *Vettri kodi Kattu* (2000). The song emphasizes the color black, both in dress and skin color, with 20 comely maidens performing in the backwaters of Kerala by a famous waterfall known for its medicinal

Figure 8. Rajinikanth (Wikimedia Commons)

properties.

A key line from the song is *Namma ooru Superstar Rajinikanth oom Karuppu thaan: Our hometown superstar Rajnikanth is also deeply black!* When people asked Rajinikanth why he did not go to North India to act in films, he stated, "I'm not sure they would accept a dark guy like me. . . " (Sreekanth, 2008, p. 47). As Sreekanth, the author of Rajinikanth's biography, remarked, the people of the North want a clean-shaven, fair, lean, pink-lipped, non-mustached man to play the hero. Later, Rajinikanth actually did act in Hindi language movies and was very popular in Bihar and Maharashtra.

One of the most evocative scenes in Indian cinema history regarding colorism can be found in Rajinikanth's *Sivaji the Boss* (Shankar, 2007). This humorous scene shows the hero Sivaji (Rajinikanth) attempting to lighten his skin through a series of bleaching and whitening processes in which the dark-skinned hero who falls in love with a "fair" maiden goes to any extent to look fair, trying a wide range of "fairness" products. Of course, these processes are clearly ridiculous, shown for what they are in this scene, with some of the methods even appearing dangerous (*Sivaji the Boss Comedy Scenes: Rajini vows to get fair*, 2013).

But what of daily life in India today when it comes to color and marriage? The images of superstars in South India may not come close to the impact of images of color from North India and Bollywood and the impact these have on Indian society today.

Color, Cosmetics, Beauty, and Marriage in India Today

"Indians are most racist when it comes to skin colors. . . Why is colorism so tolerated in India?" asks the Indian Administrative Services (IAS) officer Chander Kanta Gariyali in a 2017 essay. The salience of her discussion as an IAS officer, a position imbued with power and authority in India, is powerful. As she points out, the ubiquitous matrimonial ads found in Indian newspapers families are inevitably seeking a "Fair and good-looking bride."

This of course references the almost universal practice in South Asia of arranged marriage versus "love marriages," which are likely less than 10% of marriages. One example of a matrimonial matchmaking website is Shaadi.com, and there are literally hundreds of such sites, in addition to the Sunday Want Ads of major newspapers. KM Matrimonial, for example, asks for a photo as well as caste status ("for the perfect wedding"). Photoshopping is rampant in India at all levels, so other clues and even private detectives might be hired in the case of particularly wealthy families. Caste, color, and marriageability are inextricably linked, the obsession being a daily preoccupation for many in India.

"Fair skin" is big business in South Asia, with a booming cosmetics industry that even leads to bleaching. The desire is for "fairer" skin for young women and, to a lesser extent, for men is called *de rigueur*. The bridal institution of dowry even includes valuation of "fair skin color." Dowry is extremely important in determining marriages in India, despite being outlawed. If one is lighter-skinned, the dowry will be lower. The attractiveness of marriage candidates is thus severely judged and directly monetized according to South Asia's peculiar version of colorism.

One of us (Rajasekaran) remembers how his older brother in his mid-twenties in the 1950s in Madurai, South India had to frequently go out with his parents looking for a suitable partner: "My mother was keener on the fair skin and my father on the economic status. My mother was seen as fair-skinned and did not want someone lighter in the house, not to mention what the future children might look like. Ironically, my father was addressed as *karuppu-vaiki,* the dark lawyer. And I am very dark, so she had to live with it!"

To achieve a "fair complexion," elderly women even today advise younger ones to use the traditional and auspicious practice of applying turmeric paste for fairness (and hair depilation, too, we might add). Saffron is also used, sprinkled into milk or in rice to achieve a lighter skin tone. One often hears comments such as, "She got lucky: despite her [dark] complexion, he married her" (Mishra & Hall, 2017). Mishra has put it succinctly: "It's been the dark man's burden in this majority non-white nation to desire a Westernized concept of beauty, and post-colonial activism has not been able to change this." (Ibid.)

This is partly about ideas of purity and pollution in Indian society, too. Caste or *jati*, too, directly implies a skin gradation spectrum, the highest castes being seen as fairer and the lowest and more Southern castes as darker. The supposedly former Outcastes, Untouchables, or Harijans, now largely calling themselves Dalits, tend to be darker in complexion. Vinay Harpalani has spoken of this in an incisive essay focused on legal issues reflecting color titled, "To Be White, Black, or Brown? South Asian Americans and the Race-Color Distinction" (2015), echoed also by Taunya Lovell Banks on colorism among South Asians and skin tone discrimination (2016). African students in India have experienced racism, too, with horrifying stories of attacks and casual prejudice (BBC, 2016; Prabhu, 2017; see also Harpalani, Ibid.)

The everyday implications of this are found in the ubiquitous advertising of cosmetics with names like "Fair and Lovely" of the major "fairness cream giants" supposedly change skin color and are among the best-selling self-care products. Almost every small town has several beauty parlors, many of them belonging to women's self-help groups. During our field visits we have seen dozens of women sitting with whitening face packs on their faces, waiting to get a shade fairer. As Gariyali (2017) says,

> You know, when we come to USA, African Americans say they want to look like us Indians. They want sultry skin like ours. At the same time white women in America sit doing sun bathing for hours to look tanned like Indians, just as Indian women want to look white. . .
>
> I think we should remember beauty is only skin deep and the black is beautiful, the same as white and pale and brown. . . "Let's scrub out that tan" is a common refrain in beauty parlors in India, where girls grow up with constant reminders that only fair skin is beautiful.

Fair and Lovely, the first whitening product, introduced in the 1970s, aimed at a large and growing middle class, began for what was expected to grow from a $10 billion (2015) to a $31.2 billion (2024) business worldwide, a major share of this being in South Asia (Vox, 2019). Women's "fairness creams" are much sought after by middle- and upper-class women. Cheaper "snow" creams already existed, but the massive marketing of Fair and Lovely dominated the market. The World Health Organization estimated in 2011 that skin lightening or bleaching cosmetics represented over 60% of skin care products (Ibid.). Fairness creams have even been extended to male cosmetics with products like Fair and Handsome. Colorism in cosmetics is also attributed to an

Afghan entrepreneur in Rajasthan who named his cream product after King Zahir of Afghanistan since it reminded him of the snow in that country (Pathak, 2015); after the Indian economy opened up in the 1990s, products like Emami Naturally (with pearl extracts), Fair Herbal Fairness Cream, and Fairever (with saffron and milk) came on the market. To compete, Fair and Lovely switched to stressing women's empowerment and workplace image (Ibid.).

Bollywood superstars such as Shah Rukh Khan, John Abraham, and Miss India Winner and actress Priyanka Chopra frequently advertise these products (Figures 9, 10, 11), though they may later have regrets about their role in these promotions (Jacob, 2017). Some examples include one in which the transition by cosmetic cream from ordinary dark-skinned and dark-haired Indian female to a White, blonde, European-looking temptress, complete with a multi-headed depiction of the transition to "fair" in apparently nine steps (This Indian Skin Lightening Cream Commercial Is Racist!, 2019). South Asia's most-famous male actor Sharukh Khan (Muslim, we might add) in the early 21st century has shown us, too, how to bleach one's skin to get the girl(s), advising his darker friend on the magic of Emami Skin Bleaching Cream (Shahrukh Khan in Emami Skin Bleaching Cream Ad, 2010). As Priyanka Chopra noted,

In India, they advertise skin-lightening creams: "Your skin's gonna get lighter in a week." I used it [when I was very young]. Then when I was an actor, around my early twenties, I did a commercial for a skin-lightening cream. I was playing that girl with insecurities. And when I saw it, I was like, "Oh shit. What did I do?" I started talking about being proud of the way I looked. I actually like my skin tone (Jacob, 2017).

Figure 9. Fair and Lovely Advertisement (Wikimedia Commons)

Figure 10. Shah Rukh Khan and Family (Wikimedia Commons)

Are Fair and Handsome (Figure 12) or Fair and Lovely really the way to happiness and winning one's sweetheart? That many people think so has also led to poisonous products that include steroids, hydroquinone, and even mercury that can cause severe dermatological problems. These products are available throughout India and increasingly online. The obsession for fair skin has led to what has been called "toxic bleaching syndrome" (Hall, 1995), not only in India but elsewhere in the world. That prejudices about skin color are found throughout the world is also echoed by the transcultural nature of the bleaching syndrome, notably in Africa, Southeast Asia, Mexico, and Latin America, the last two where to be dark is associated with *Los Indios*, the native indigenous peoples of Latin America. This bleaching, sometimes literally using household bleach, leads to severe after-effects and even death. Online sales increase the possibility that these products will be privately purchased and used.

Color and cosmetics have even led to "bleaching as toxic syndrome," something which has extended to North America and Latinx communities in the 2010s and today. This bleaching syndrome is not limited to India, with skin bleaching also common in other parts of Asia, Africa, and Latin America (Pather, 2013; Lebsack, 2019). Harvard neuroscientist Allen Counter found hundreds of Mexican-American women in Arizona, California, and Texas suffering from mercury poisoning from skin-whitening creams (Vedantam, 2010), something likely for India as well.

Social media campaigns have emerged that attack these positions, including #unfairandlovely and #darkisbeautiful with their celebration of darker skin as they

Figure 11. Bollywood Actresses (Wikimedia Commons)

attempt to create new narratives of Blackness in India (Pandey, 2016; Peters, 2019). The actresses Nandita Das, Nandita Sen, and others, as well as the TV journalist Bharaka Dutt have been especially strong voices in support of "Black Is Beautiful" (NDTV, 2013). Fair fetish: myth or reality?, 2013; We The People: an 'un'-fair obsession?, 2018) often enduring frequent harassment from many sides in India. Programs with tag lines such as "Fairness Fixation: A Kind of Racism?" are common after 2012 (Ibid.). Their activism was spurred on by the introduction of a new intimate wash cosmetic called Clean and Dry in 2012 which was meant to lighten the vagina (Tilak, 2012), with ads comparing Indian vaginas and coffee (Ibid.; Prolongeau, 2015), followed by a product named "Tampax Deep and White," the purpose of which can only be guessed at by consumers (Mishra, 2015, p. 725).

Advertising companies have continued their inexorable push toward fairness by recruiting even fairer and fairer actresses, actors, and models for their cosmetic products. Miss India Beauty Contests and other similar contests continue to focus on fairer-skinned women whom most Indians are unlikely to encounter in daily life. These prejudices are reinforced by such visible stages of cultural representation as these beauty pageants (see Noronha, 2019; Peters, 2019). Diversity is challenged by these images and their representation of Eurocentric beauty as the ideal in the South Asian context (Figure 13).

"How to choose from such a diverse bunch?!" as Samira Sawlani said (2019), followed by Kamran Shahid, who asked, "Why can't a Miss India be a dusky or a dark brown or darker chocolate brown? So much for the love of fair skin. I sincerely believe

Figure 12. Advanced Whitening for Men—Fair and Handsome
(Wikimedia Commons)

we are the most racist country in the world...!" (Shahid, 2019).

One of the most powerful symbols of resistance around color in the media in India in the 21st century has been centered around ASCI (Advertising Standards Council of India), a self-regulatory organization created by advertisers in 1985 to review products for truth in advertising. ASCI is ostensibly "committed to the cause of self-regulation in advertising ensuring the protection of the interest of consumers." How advertisers treat race, caste, color, creed, and nationality was a main goal of the study, with a draft introduced in 2014 looking for feedback on advertising, specifically about skin color (Pathak, 2015; Shah, 2014).

Not much came of this effort, with advertising continuing into the 2020s to imply that dark skin is inferior and certainly undesirable. Dark-skinned protagonists are seen as unable to advance in life, especially marriage, because of their skin color. "Their fate, so to speak, changes only with a change in their skin color" (Ibid.). Despite this push for color equity through the ASCI Standards, old beliefs and prejudices die hard, literally in the case of skin bleaching. The push by the cosmetics industry for these products led to a major effort by the Indian advertising industry to resist other beauty standards and to continue misleading advertising (Pathak, 2015). These beliefs are still deeply held in Indian society.

Becoming Powerful and Being Black: Discrimination and Pushing Back on Color in India Today

Colorism in India is reflected in recent events among those maintaining the imperial

Figure 13. Femina Miss India Contestants Visit NGO Children
(Wikimedia Commons)

legacy in England who originally ruled India. The "royals" as they were called in England until recently greeted the arrival of a new baby in 2019 who is of mixed blood and will likely have a darker complexion. Archie Harrison Mountbatten-Windsor's mother is the American actress Meghan Markle, the descendant of plantation slaves in the United States (Barry & Karasz, 2019). This is of course not the first time for the royals to encounter color in their family since King George III's wife had African blood (Ibid.).

One solution to the problem of colorism is thus obviously "love marriages," which are often intercaste, interfaith, and interracial. We can see this throughout the world, where the number of cross-cultural marriages has exploded in growth. Yet race in England today continues to be a fraught issue, with both a society that is 87% white (Britain) but one in which the fastest-growing ethnic category is mixed-race children. What has since happened to Prince Harry and Princess Meghan is only too well-known, with details of the story sure to be prominently featured in the media for years to come. As Tanya Compas, a youth worker, told the BBC, "Colorism is definitely a huge thing, and I think that links into it, because if the child does come out darker skinned, then you know that's going to make the news — and not for a good reason" (Barry & Karasz, 2019).

One irony of this in light of colorism in India as well is the presence of a large Anglo-Indian community. A successful, mixed-race community in India that has been briefly discussed above and that is historically linked to the colonial era, Anglo-Indians are an example of a hybrid community that calls for more research on the nuances of colorism in the subcontinent.

Moreover, celebrities and now the younger generation are pushing back as we noted earlier. The poet Aranya Johar published her "Brown Girl's Guide to Beauty" on YouTube (Cichowski, 2017), a spoken-word poem that says "Forget snow-white/say hello to chocolate brown/I'll write my own fairy-tale," which went viral. The Bollywood actor Nawazuddin Siddiqui followed with a Twitter commentary condemning the Indian cinema industry's racist culture (2017). As he said, "Thank U 4 making me realise dat I cannot b paired along wid d fair & handsome bcz I m dark & not good looking, but I never focus on that." He was also responding to a searing account by the actress Tannishtha Chatterjee in 2016 about how she had been bullied on live TV for her skin tone (Ghatak, 2016). Push-back has included humor and outrage such as can be found in spoofs of skin whitening creams (Mirza, 2010) and exposing the racist messaging of these cosmetics (The France 24 Observers, 2017).

Skin-whitening of course is more complex than color alone, with hair texture, class, language, dress, and more reflecting the intersectional nature of colorism. This is unfortunately not about cosmetics alone. Lighter-skinned Latinx people in the United States have been found to earn $5,000 more on average than darker-skinned Latinx people (Vedantam, 2010).

There are many external factors which make a society feel that all dark skin is bad. It is not necessarily even coming from within India. The hyper mode about White skin in the media, companies, pageant holders, boutiques and so on are all hyped to make money. Market forces cannot be underestimated. One by one everyone is just jumping onto the "fairness" bandwagon to see how much they can get out of this. There is a sense that is created that to have white skin has an aspirational value, a colonial hang-over, that "they look better," and that it is simply a fashion tool (Fair fetish: myth or reality? 2013).

Colorism in India: Implications for Practice, Research, & Policy

We conclude this chapter by asking how color in India also has regional and intergenerational dimensions with implications for practice, research, and policy. The South in particular has demonstrated that the historical roots of colorism also reflect the roots of resistance and change. Southern India has traditionally asserted itself against Brahminical dominance more than other parts of India, emphasizing what we have called "Beauty of Another Color." Nonetheless, the dominance of Brahmins, Sahibs, and Caste have meant the continuing march of Aryanization, Sanskritization, and their associated "Fairness," if not Whiteness. The nuances are somewhat different, with, for instance in Tamil, the idea that Whiteness is transposed into "Fairness," the Tamil word for a White person being *Vellaikaran* ("fair" person).

Yet Black is Beautiful is also found in South India in the *Dravidar Kazhagam DK* movement of the 20th century as well as the movement supporting Blackness in Indian Cinema, the elevation of darker skin being resistance against the received wisdom of fairness. This is complicated at the individual level by the powerful sway of the cosmetics industry and the pressing needs of the array of service industries supporting arranged marriage. These industries impress upon families the need for "fair" skin color for their daughters and sons. Younger generations are now pushing back, with the understanding that being Black can be a counter to long-standing social, religious, and caste norms that counter received ideas of privilege and power often associated with "fairness" and increasingly lighter images of South Asians.

Will these conscious moves for a different colorism have an impact on the expected growth of the skin whitening and skin bleaching industry? Will new images of beauty emerge in South Asia? What new narratives of color and colorism might we see going forward?

Process Questions and Considerations

1. What can we learn from transcultural examples of colorism?
2. Why do peoples around the world continue to be driven socially and personally by concepts of color?
3. When and how might the obsession with skin color be transformed?
4. Where can change occur in public and private spheres?
5. How can activists concerned with colorism act in transparent and public spaces to change the narratives of color?

References

Ambai (C. S. Lakshmi). (1992). *A purple sea of short stories: My mother, her crime.* Translated by Lakshmi Holmstrom. New Delhi: Affiliated East West Press Pvt. Ltd.

Banks, T. L. (2016). Colorism among South Asians: Title VII and skin tone discrimination. Volume 14, Issue 4 (2015), *Global Perspectives on Colorism (Symposium Edition).* DOI:https://openscholarship.wustl.edu/law_globalstudies/vol14/iss4/11/

Barry, E., & Karasz, P. (2019). Meghan, Duchess of Sussex, gives birth to a boy. https://www.nytimes.com/2019/05/06/world/europe/meghan-markle-baby-boy.html?action=click&module=Latest&pgtype=Homepage,May 6.

Basham, A. L. (1975). *A cultural history of India.* Oxford: Oxford University Press. BBC News. (2016). What is it like being black in India?, April 15. DOI:https://www.youtube.com/

watch?v=djuAvmn37ug&list=RDTDNIlhq6Mz4&index=10

Cichowski, H. (2017). This 18-year-old wrote a "Brown girls' guide to beauty,' Encouraging Us to 'Love All Shapes and Shades,' https://articles.aplus.com/a/aranya-johar-a-brown-girls-guide-to-beauty-poem-video

Clothey, F. W. (2007). *Religion in India: A Historical Introduction.* London: Routledge.

Darkskin Models Talk About Their Struggles in the Industry | Black Like Me YouTube (2018).BET her. March 13. DOI:https://www.youtube.com/watch?v=emoCRb4wAU0

Deva. (2000). *Vettri kodi Kattu* (Tying a Flag of Victory), sung by Anuradha, Sriram Music, https://www.youtube.com watch?v=AJLx_As6ETE

Diehl, A. (1977). *E. V. Ramaswami Naicker-Periar: A study of the influence of a personality in contemporary South India.* Sweden: Scandinavian University Books.

Dirks, N. B. (2001). *Castes of mind: Colonialism and the making of modern india.* Princeton, NJ: Princeton University Press.

DuBois, A. (2006). *Hindu manners, customs, & ceremonies.* Delhi: Winsom Books India, First published in 1816.

Dumont, L. (1981). *Homo hierarchicus: The caste system and its implications.* Chicago: University of Chicago Press.

Fair fetish: myth or reality? (2013). Fair fetish: myth or reality? Actress Nandita Das talks about how she's campaigning for 'Dark is beautiful' and the pressures on her to lighten her skin, NDTV, https://www.youtube.com/watch?v=TeaGg_ab_28

The France 24 Observers. (2017). The racist messaging of India's skin lightening creams, https://www.youtube.com/watch?v=DeR72SxcZRE

Gariyali, C. K. (2017). Why is colorism so tolerated in India? July 17 Blog. DOI:https://www.quora.com/Why-is-colorism-so-tolerated-in-India

Ghatak, L. (2016). It's 2016, and "Parched" actress Tannishtha Chatterjee gets hit by "dark skin" slur on TV show, channel calls it unfortunate, https://economictimes.indiatimes.com/magazines/panache/its-2016-and-parched-actress-tannishtha-chatterjee-gets-hit-by-dark-skin-slur-on-tv-show-channel-calls-it-unfortunate/articleshow/54562692.cms

Goyal, D. (2017). Nawazuddin Siddiqui hints at racism, tweets about not being cast with fair actors, https://www.ndtv.com/india-news/nawazuddin-siddiqui-hints-at-racism-tweets-about-not-being-cast-with-fair-actors-1726193

Hall, R. E. (1995). The color complex: The bleaching syndrome, *Race, Gender and Class, 2*(2), Winter, pp. 99-109.

Harpalani, V. (2015). To be white, black, or brown? South Asian Americans and the race-color distinction. *Global Perspectives on Colorism (Symposium Edition), 14*(4). DOI:https://openscholarship.wustl.edu/law_globalstudies/vol14/iss4/9/

Hinduwebsite.com. (2000). *Manusmriti: The laws of Manu introduction,* https://www.hinduwebsite.com/sacredscripts/hinduism/dharma/manusmriti.asp

Jacob, M. (2017). Priyanka Chopra on when she starred in a skin-lightening cream commercial https://www.vogue.in/content/priyanka-chopra-on-when-she-starred-in-a-skin-lightening-cream-commercial

Karthick, S. (2012). Color change in politics: Karunanidhi to wear black. *Times of India,* Oct 4. DOI:https://timesofindia.indiatimes.com/city/chennai/Color-change-in-politics-Karunanidhi-to-wear-black/articleshow/16678246.cms

Karupputhaan ennaku pudicha coloru. (2000). Song by Music Director Deva, performed by Anuradha Sriram in the movie Vettri kodi Kattu (2000).

Lebsack, L. (2019). Skin bleaching is poisoning women—but business is booming,https://www.refinery29.com/en-us/2019/05/233409/skin-bleaching-lightening-products-safety-controversy

Lorenzen, D. N. (2005). *Hinduism in the Pre Colonial Period. In Defining Hinduism: A Reader,* J. E. Llewellyn (Ed.), p. 75.

Mines, D. P. (2005). *Fierce gods: Inequality, ritual, and the politics of dignity in a south Indian village.* Bloomington: University of Indiana Press.

Mirza, F. (2010). Fair and Lovely Skin Whitening Cream Commercial Spoof -https://www.youtube.com/watch?v=8cv9w75yz4M

Mishra, N. (2015). India and colorism: The finer nuances. *Global Perspectives on Colorism (Symposium Edition),14*(4) DOI:https://openscholarship.wustl.edu/law_globalstudies/vol14/iss4/14/

Mishra, N., & Hall, R. (2017). Bleached girls: India and its love for light skin. *The Conversation*, July 21. DOI:https://theconversation.com/bleached-girls-india-and-its-love-for-light-skin-80655

Naanum_Oru_Penn (I am a woman, too) (1963). Tamil Movie. DOI:https://en.wikipedia.org/wiki/Naanum_Oru_Penn#Tamil_Film_History_and_Its_Achievements

Nathan, Archana. (2018). The colour black has a starring role in Rajinikanth's films, from 'Apoorva Raagangal' to 'Kaala', March 7. DOI:https://scroll.in/reel/870652/the-colour-black-has-a-starring-role-in-rajinikanths-films-from-apoorva-raagangal-to-kaala

Noronha, C. (2019). Miss India Photo Stirs Debate About White-Washed Beauty Standards, https://www.huffingtonpost.ca/entry/miss-india-colourism-beauty-standards_ca_5cf69d7be4b0a1997b7206c2

Pandey, G. (2016). BBC, #unfairandlovely: A new social campaign celebrates dark skin. https://www.bbc.com/news/world-asia-india-35783348

Paramasivan, T. (2001). *Panpaattu Asaivukal: Essays.* (In Tamil). Madurai: Kalachuvadu Publications.

Parameswaran, R. E., & Cardoza, K. (2009). Immortal comics, epidermal politics. *Journal of Children and Media, 3*(1), 19-34. DOI:10.1080/17482790802576956

Pathak, J. P. (2015). Portrayal of colour discrimination vis-à-vis Indian television advertisements, *IOSR Journal of Humanities and Social Science* (IOSR-JHSS), 20(5), Ver. VI (May. 2015), 45-64, https://www.researchgate.net/publication/304300840_Portrayal_of_colour_discrimination_vis-a-vis_Indian_television_advertisements.

Pather, J. (2013). Fifty shades of black. https://tamilculture.com/fifty-shades-of-black

Peters, A. (2019). Skin bleaching concerns as Miss India Pageant promotes fair skin ideals. https://www.dazeddigital.com/beauty/head/article/44710/1/skin-bleaching-concerns-as-miss-india-pageant-promotes-fair-skin-ideals

Prabhu, M. (2017). African victims of racism in India share their stories. https://www.aljazeera.com/indepth/features/2017/04/african-victims-racism-india-share-stories-170423093250637.html

Prolongeau, H. (2015). India's skin-whitening creams highlight a complex over darker complexions, https://www.theguardian.com/world/2015/jul/24/dark-skin-india-prejudice-whitening

Rajinikanth. (2013). *Sivaji the Boss* - Excerpt on Becoming Fair, https://www.youtube.com/watch?v=OI2oKN2--Uo

Richman, P. (1991). *Many Ramayanas: The diversity of a narrative tradition in South Asia.* Berkeley: University of California Press.

Saivam.org (ND). *Thiruvilaiyadal Puranam - Introduction.* https://shaivam.org/scripture/English-Translation/1488/thiruvilaiyadal-puranam-introduction

Sarangapani, R. (1984). *A critical study of Paripaatal.* Madurai: Publications Division of Madurai Kamaraj University.

Sawlani, S. (2019). Question: who will be crowned Miss India this year? https://twitter.com/samirasawlani/status/1133086119292231681?lang=en

Shah, G. (2014). ASCI seeks feedback on draft guidelines on ads for fairness products. *LiveMint*, 11 Jun. DOI:https://www.livemint.com/Consumer/fEBPDuGv9Im6lyUqPukxKM/ASCI-seeks-feedback-on-draft-guidelines-on-ads-for-fairness.html Shahid, Kamran. (2019). Why can't a Miss

India be a dusky or a dark brown or darker chocolate brown?, https://twitter.com/CitizenKamran/status/1133512143045742592

Shahrukh Khan in Emami Skin Bleaching Cream Ad. (2010). https://www.youtube.com/watch?v=0kqd9zaI698

Shulman, D. (2016). *Tamil—A biography*. Cambridge: Harvard Belknap Press.

Sivaji the Boss. (2013). Sivaji the Boss Comedy Scenes—Rajini vows to get fair, https://www.youtube.com/watch?v=OI2oKN2--Uo, from *Sivaji the Boss* (2007), directed by Shankar, Music by A.R. Rahman.

Sreekanth, G. (2008). *The name is Rajini Kanth*. Noida, India: Om Books International.

Somu, K. (1958). *Sampoorna Ramayanam*, M.A. Venu, Producer.

This Indian Skin Lightening Cream Commercial Is Racist! (2019). https://www.youtube.com/watch?v=J92MBTXO_mA

Tilak, S. (2012). Whitening cream: Fair deal for India's women? https://www.aljazeera.com/indepth/features/2012/07/20127108213972410.html

Vedantam, S. (2010). Shades of prejudice, *New York Times,* Jan. 18. DOI: https://www.nytimes.com/2010/01/19/opinion/19vedantam.html

We The People: An 'un'-fair obsession? (2018). Dark skin Models Talk About Their Struggles In The Industry | Black Like Me YouTube BET her. March 13. DOI:https://www.youtube.com/watch?v=emoCRb4wAU0

Why Is India So Obsessed With Fair Skin?—YouTube. (2018). DOI:https://www.youtube.com/watch?v=9BQc2guo-Lg

CHAPTER 12.

Hair Splitting: Experiences of Prejudicial Treatment of Black Women Based on Hair Texture

Afiya Mangum Mbilishaka
University of the District of Columbia

Introduction

Black hair textures have been weaponized, within a system of White supremacy racism, as a tool of discrimination and bias in most American institutions, such as school, work, romantic relationships, and within families (Lewis, 1999; Mbilishaka, 2018a; Mbilishaka, 2018b; Mbilishaka, 2018c; Mbilishaka & Apugo, 2020; Opie & Phillips, 2015). Not only do these incidences of hair bias arrive on our phones through social media, but are highly litigated in courtrooms, where Black people are usually engaged in a losing battle because it is thought that Black hair can change based on the expectations of perceived authority figures (Greene, 2008). Hair texture is immutable, it cannot change permanently, it is built into our DNA, but Black hair textures are still regulated on the personal and professional level (Greene, 2017). Hair texture bias, also known as texturism, can be defined as prejudicial thinking and discriminatory behaviors directed toward individuals with tightly coiled hair (Mbilishaka & Apugo, 2020; McGill Johnson, Godsil, McFarlane, Tropp, & Goff, 2016). These thought patterns and institutionalized values have garnered individualized traumas and publicized debates on employment, academia, and military services (Mbilishaka, Apugo, & Mangum, 2019). Clinicians and research scientists have a vested interest in resolving these hair related traumas and behavioral loops enforced by institutionalized anti-Black racism (Mbilishaka, 2018a). Black women and girls are often emotionally threatened to express a Black aesthetic in hairstyle and texture because of the implicit and explicit hair texture biases manifested as texturism (Mbilishaka & Apugo, 2020).

This chapter heightens the investigation of the psychosocial significance of hair texture within the lives of Black women. Black women are habitually driven to a crossroad, establishing aesthetic self-worth while embodying social structures of race and gender (Capodilupo, 2015; Ellis-Hervey, Doss, Davis, Nicks, & Araiza, 2016). To stimulate dialogue on the nuances of hair texture within Black communities, this chapter aims to: (1) deepen the bio-psychological and cultural-historical scope of African phenotypic expression; (2) dignify narrative processing of autobiographical memories of hair as a methodology; (3) broadcast the implicit hair texture biases that disenfranchise Black women; and (4) enshrine haircare spaces as locations for healing from hair texture biases and trauma. There is a clear need for researchers to be grounded in the culture and history of processing the meaning of African phenotype.

Praising and Pathologizing African Phenotypic Expression of Hair

With Africa as the origin of human genetic diversity, the human genome ranges from expressions of highly textured to straight hair (Jablonski & Chaplin, 2014). Through the anthropological and socio-political shifts across millennia, the meaning of hair currently reflects internalized projections that were influenced by systems of White supremacy that spread through the globe (Johnson & Bankhead, 2014). Human hair on the head emerged to regulate body temperature, but specifically to decrease heat within the human skull; coiled hair from elliptical shafts was necessary for survival in equatorial regions and sub-Saharan Africa (Jablonski & Chaplin, 2014). Hair follicles with circular shafts emerge as straight hair, while oval shaped shafts result in curled hair (Davis-Sivasothy, 2011). Although most human beings are born with 100,000 hair follicles on the scalp, the texture of hair manifests in extreme ranges to cope with ancestral environments of heat and cold (Davis-Sivasothy, 2011; Jablonski & Chaplin, 2014). There are a myriad of historical, anecdotal, and anthropological narratives about the utility of hair.

The historical narrative of hair spans from the establishment of ethnic groups to modern negotiations of hair styles and statements through social media (Neil & Mbilishaka, 2019). What is common within the narrative, is that hair has been a tool of demarcation, establishing a line or split, to establish in-group and out-group. Anthropological research heightens the conversation on hair texture and length as critical to the meaning making process of group membership. Dating back to the ancient Kemetic tradition, also known as ancient Egypt, hair was a device to establish royalty. Only members of the royal family were permitted to wear ornate hairstyles, wigs, or even shave their hair into patterns (Tassie, 2008). We see that hair can communicate dimensions of identity.

In traditional societies across Africa, like the Himba, Yoruba, and Tuareg, the appearance of hair was indicative of ethnic group membership, age, spiritual practices, economic position, and health status (Byrd & Tharps, 2014). Each ethnic group established cultural meaning related to the texture, style, and length of their hair. For example, the Himba women of Namibia coat the hair shaft with ocher and butter fat to fossilize the hair in its natural coiled texture (Beckwith & Fisher, 1999). Straightening the hair would be considered sacrilegious; hair is viewed as an extension of God's creation and the bond with the earth (Beckwith & Fisher, 1999). The Yoruba of Nigeria often utilize the hair as a spiritual offering to the Orishas or pantheon of gods, first starting with shaving of new born babies' hair for gratitude for a safe journey from the spiritual world to the physical plane (Sherrow, 2006). Throughout the lifetime of a traditional Yoruba woman, her cultural group expects that she maintains ornate braided styles in her highly textured hair, not only as an expression of beauty, but because the hair and the head are entangled in her spiritual destiny (Olugbemi, 2004). Hair grooming is a symbolic deposition with the community, as well as the spiritual world, expressing her completion of rites of passage, marriage rituals, birthing, grieving, and other life transitions (Byrd & Tharps, 2014). Further, the Tuareg women of today's nation states of Mali and Niger, are identified by their long wavy and shiny hair (Beckwith & Fisher, 1999). Women in this ethnic group engage in rituals of shining the hair with specialized herbal oils and buffing the hair with fine black grains of sand, as the shinier the hair, the more attractive (Beckwith & Fisher, 1999). This group still focuses grooming on length retention, braiding the hair to protect the hair shaft and eliminate excessive hair pulling to prevent breakage (Beckwith & Fisher, 1999). In this way, haircare served medicinal purposes of infusing the scalp with herbal remedies for the body and reflecting the health of the individual through the appearance of the hair (see Mbilishaka, 2018a). Unfortunately, these systems were damaged during the processes of slavery.

Enslavement of Africans across the globe by Europeans, starting in the 17th century, disrupted the veins of the language system of hair for African women (Morrow, 1990). To consummate the dehumanization process of enslavement, European captors shaved the hair of their enslaved Africans before entrance onto slave ships, discharging the power of African hair (Byrd & Tharps, 2014). Upon their arrival to the Americas for chattel slavery, enslaved Africans were often not permitted to groom their hair and their hair was labeled as "wool" or "fur" to psychologically condemn highly textured hair (Byrd & Tharps, 2014). Relegated to inhumane living conditions, enslaved African women were mandated to behave as animals, they slept on the floor in barn-like structures, ate food scraps, and utilized sheep carding tools to comb their hair (Byrd & Tharps,

2014). No longer was hair integrated into health care and community spiritual bonding, but now African hair textures were deemed as unsightly and illegal; the Tignon Laws forbid African women to display their hair in public and were forced to cover their hair with fabric (Byrd & Tharps, 2014). Within this American plantation structure, enslaved African women serving in the house, were required to straighten the hair or wear wigs (Morrow, 1990). Enslaved women relegated to the manual labor of field work did not have the same appearance expectations because of the labor differential (Morrow, 1990). In addition, the White male sexual assault that intergenerationally traumatized Black women and the passive sexual consent of Black women led to high populations of mixed-race children among enslaved populations. Often these mixed-race children of the slave monsters/masters with loosely curled hair held a position of privilege in plantation life (DeGruy, 2005). Enslaved Africans internalized this splitting process, thereby associating privilege with hair texture and self-worth (DeGruy, 2005).

The distinctions between hair textures were reinforced by the post-enslavement cultural practices. Black women now generate income and with new income spent measurable funds on highly advertised hair products that promised to straighten the hair, despite the physical consequences (Rooks, 1996). In the late 19th century, Black women used axle grease and lathered butters to penetrate the hair and scorched the hair with metal rods or irons to straighten it (Morrow, 1990). Even further, a combination of potatoes and lye were used to envelop hair follicles to chemically alter the coiled texture of the hair and remove the hydrogen bonds from the hair, sometimes burning the hair right off the scalp (Davis-Sivasothy, 2011). Integration of Black women into the workforce encouraged this population to conform further with Eurocentric aesthetics of straight hair textures (Byrd & Tharps, 2014). Black churches and organizations implemented the hair cousin of the "brown paper bag test" known as the "comb test," suggesting that inclusion in an organization required a woman to easily pass a fine-tooth comb through her hair (Byrd & Tharps, 2014). This method of derision enforced a model of "good hair" and "bad hair" within Black communities that perpetuated an anti-Black aesthetic and implied a phenotypic hierarchy. From this perspective "good hair" was long and straight hair, while "bad hair" was short and tightly coiled (Ellis-Hervey et al., 2016). Black women are motivated to attain "good hair" to secure societal privilege in employment, romantic relationships, the family dynamic, and styling convenience (Bellinger, 2007; Mbilishaka, in press). Any yet, the concept of "good hair" is a cultural myth because hair cannot hold valence in itself but is subject to interpretation from systems of White supremacy and anti-Black racism (Mbilishaka, 2018).

Populations of Black people have remained warriors in confronting White supremacy and racism through choice in hair style. In the 1960s and 1970s, Black men and women embraced the hairstyle of "the natural" or "the Afro," and wore their hair in its unaltered state to reflect their shift in cultural consciousness from devaluing African culture and aesthetics to illuminating the power and beauty of African people (Byrd & Tharps, 2014). In particular, the Black Panther Party for Self Defense encouraged the transition from chemically straightened hair to natural hair as a symbol of racial pride in Blackness (Byrd & Tharps, 2014). During this Civil Rights era, Black women were faced with confronting the Europeanization of aesthetics, standards that inherently oppose tightly coiled hair. Black women internalized the mantra of "Black is beautiful" and adorned their crowns with the braids of their ancestors as an explicit visual cue of resistance and re-Africanization (Byrd & Tharps, 2014). However, populations of all Black women never agreed with this choice to reconnect to African aesthetic values and thereby continue to chemically alter their appearance. Today, 70% of Black women chemically straighten their hair (Davis-Sivasothy, 2011). Social scientists have found evidence that hair straightening is a cultural norm for Black women, as it is actually reinforced by how Black men rank Black women in attractiveness (Capodilupo, 2015) and as a means for Black girls to prevent school bullying (O'Brien-Richardson, 2019).

In the 2000s, the Natural Hair Movement (re)emerged within urban settings and digital spaces for Black women, that embolden choices of chemically unaltered natural hair textures (Ellis-Hervey et al., 2016). Black women have employed systems to evaluate the texture of hair, not for the purpose of comparison or status, but to better understand how to care for hair that ranges in texture (Ellis-Hervey et al., 2016). These "curl patterns" take on number and letter systems to communicate the shape of the hair follicle and shaft. This classification of hair helps Black women determine how much water and oil-based products should be applied to achieve a desired look (Walton & Carter, 2013). This classification system emphasizes hair health and protective styling to reduce excessive hair combing and flattening of hair that defies gravitational sciences (Walton & Carter, 2013). Research scientists have been able to translate the lived experiences of Black haircare into research methodology to study potential bias in hair texture.

Emerging Methodology of Studying Hair Texture Bias

There are limited techniques to elicit race-based stories in a society that deems racism as a pariah. Social scientists and mental health professionals should recognize the ubiquitous role of internalized racism in Black identity development and aesthetics. Over the past twenty years, research scientists have developed methodological frameworks to capture the nuanced meaning in the variation of hair texture. Quantitative techniques, that are sensitive to today's racial climate, have been developed to assess hair texture bias. McGill Johnson and colleagues (2016) modified an existing assessment protocol, the race-based Implicit Association Task (Greenwald et al., 1998; IAT), to spotlight implicit bias against highly textured hair. Since bias is both conscious and unconscious, it is critical to devise techniques to gather significant points of data while eliminating social desirability concerns. In the "Good Hair Study," an image of a Black female model was presented to over 4,000 participants (20% Black men, 25% Black women, 25% White men, 30% White women) online with variations in hair texture, with half of the images displaying highly coiled hair in natural styles (braids, locs, and Afros) and the other half with "smooth" hair textures ranging in hair length (McGill Johnson et al., 2016). These images were paired with "pleasant and unpleasant words" in the English language to ascertain valence of associated images. The result of the Hair IAT suggested that, "the majority of participants, including black women, hold implicit bias against black women's natural hair (McGill Johnson et al., 2016, p. 33)." This metric provides scientific evidence of colloquial concepts of implicit bias related to hair texture.

Even further, McGill Johnson and colleagues (2016) collected data on Black women's hair texture bias through a self-report survey to gather data on explicit bias. The same participants were asked to rate the attractiveness, professionalism, and sexiness of various hair textures on the same Black model. The data suggested that White women are the most explicit in articulating their dislike for Black women's coiled hair textures (McGill Johnson et al., 2016). Here, White women may be asserting dominance over what is considered the ideal beauty using themselves as a standard. The data also indicated that Black women harbor fears and anxiety of publicly displaying their natural hair textures due to social repercussions. McGill Johnson and colleagues (2016) generated research data that evidenced Black women spending more time and money altering their hair texture in comparison to White women, due to societal pressures and anxiety.

Johnson and Bankhead (2014) also developed a survey to assess the hair bias experiences of Black women that wear their unstraightened hair. The 529 Black women with natural hair that responded to their social media-based 52-question survey, shared that they feel a general sense of approval of their hair in everyday life, but a third reported that they experienced discrimination from wearing their natural hair (Johnson & Bankhead, 2014). Some of this hair criticism came from family members, friends, and strangers. Of the participants that responded to this question of bias, 85% reported that they identify hair-based discrimination as "common" for Black women (Johnson & Bankhead, 2014).

Lewis (1999) created a hair combing interaction paradigm to describe and explain the role of hair in shaping emotional bonds for Black women through observational studies. According to Lewis (1999, p. 507), "the hair combing task offers context in which to study structural aspects of the evolving attachment relationship, one that may be especially suited to evaluation and assessment of subtle socioemotional domains of cultural and racial socialization by African American mothers." Lewis (1999) recognized that most of the literature on attachment style and bonding did not include a central variable for identity development for Black women—the variable of hair (Lewis, 1999). Through naturalistic observational techniques, Lewis (1999) identified both the verbal and non-verbal exchanges between mother and child during hair combing interaction that shaped racial and gender identity development through accepting or rejecting hair texture. Lewis (1999) witnessed Black mothers engage in gentle touch and provide words of affirmation to daughters with loosely textured hair, while other Black mothers utilized harsh styling techniques and negative commentary about the thickness of their daughter's hair. This criticism about hair texture may correlate with feelings of shame (Lewis, 1999). In turn, these interactions represented intergenerational cultural transmission about the role of hair texture within Black families (Lewis, 1999). Lewis (1999, p.507) highlights these family dynamics and shared, "attitudes, beliefs, and superstitions about 'good' or 'bad' hair may be the grandmother's legacy, behaviorally transmitted to young girls by their mothers' actions around hair combing." Lewis (1999) presents both research scientists and clinicians with a paradigm for understanding how Black women are socialized initially by other Black women about the role of hair texture. These hair combing interactions can be actively recalled during adulthood and influence self-concept about hair texture (Wilson, Mbilishaka, & Lewis, 2018).

Although surveys and observational studies have been developed in the assessment of hair texture bias by McGill et al. (2016) and Johnson and Bankhead (2014), this does not fully utilize the specific voices of Black women to explain their meaning making process of texturism. To facilitate a conversation for and by Black women related to hair, narrative methodologies are useful in processing race (Winston, Rice, Bradshaw, Lloyd, Harris, Burford, et al., 2004). Race self-complexity is a narrative framework of personality that integrates racial identity theory with narrative identity techniques (Winston et al., 2004). Black women engage in autobiographical reasoning and narrative processing of their hair experiences as an extension of their racial identities (Wilson et al., in press). To stimulate deeper analysis of hair texture bias, the *Guided Hair Autobiography (GHA)* (Mbilishaka, 2014) is a new research instrument designed for this purpose. The GHA is modified from the McAdams (1997) *Guided Autobiography* that elicits a structured life storytelling. The GHA only includes three episodes, but these episodes have a focus on self-defining moments in negotiating the meaning of hair by describing the: (1) the earliest memory of hair; (2) low point experiences of hair; and (3) a turning point related to hair. This research instrument was piloted in 2017 and 2018 to a sample of 300 participants recruited through Washington, DC Black-serving barbershops and beauty salons, as well as through social media postings on hair. The narratives ranged in content, but hair bias emerged as a recurring theme in the narrative data. As emphasized by Johnson and Bankhead (2014, p. 86),

> . . . practitioners working with women and girls of African descent, who intend to have a culturally responsive relationship based on respect and value, must understand that part of getting to know their client/student may mean exploring the meaning of hair to the individuals they serve.

This research instrument may be ideal in the solicitation of meaning making and narrative processing of hair and race. This next section includes the hair stories of a sample of Black women discussing their own experiences of texturism.

Hair Stories

Below are several short hair testimonies that collectively offer a compelling case of how texturism is internalized. There are several implications of these collected hair narratives in processing divisions within Black communities based on skin color, hair texture, and facial features. First, these hair experiences should be shared because they may be defining to the narrative of self. Second, these hair narratives can be used to help Black people learn lessons and gain insight from their race experiences rather than ruminate on negative aspects of race experiences. What follows includes the exact words from a sample of Black women negotiating hair texture biases within their lived experiences prompted by the GHA.

Lisa (18):

> I never really considered its texture until fifth grade and a boy kind of looked through it and pretended to be "lost" and stuck inside and I really did not understand

the joke until someone explained that my hair was nappy. I understood my hair was thick and nappy. I just didn't understand why someone would joke about it.

Lorraine (24):

One of my friends came up to me and said, "Okay we get it, you're black" and another said "Yes, your hair is looking a little nappy today." I remember being so embarrassed. It took so much effort to achieve that look and to be insulted in such a way where I was made to feel embarrassed about my natural curls prevented me from truly feeling comfortable in my own skin for a long time. I think that even today that statement affects me where I do not like to leave my apartment looking unkempt in any way.

Robin (47):

Many of my female classmates and friends had a similar hair story as mine. And my male classmates and friends had watched as the women and girls in their family went through the hair straightening process. Therefore, all of us had accepted the notion that straight hair was better. Anyone who knows a thing or two about the hair straightening process knows that it does not last very long dependent upon weather, water exposure, and body chemistry. My mother had pressed my hair for school but by the time recess was over it began to return to is natural state. As we were lining up to return into the school building I reached the line before one of my male classmates who was upset that I got there before he did. In his anger he pushed me and called me a "nappy-headed little girl." I felt embarrassed, began to cry silently and wanted to die right then. This event served as another reinforcer for the idea that my hair was bad and that I had to make sure no matter what, that I keep it straight even if it meant destroying my hair and scalp.

Samantha (27):

I remember going to a club with a friend, and a drunk guy approaching me and saying "My damn! You are black as hell and your hair is nappy as fuck." He did this in front of a bunch of people. Some laughed—my friend defended me—however the damage was done. I went and installed Senegalese back in my hair. I still wanted to remain natural, but I wanted to keep my natural hair hidden until it got to an "acceptable" length. By constantly trying to hide it and not take care of it or give it time to breathe, I was tearing out my edges and slowing the growth process.

Tia (70):

I remember in middle school someone commenting on my "kitchen" (the short hairs at the back of your neck) being "nappy." I became self-conscious about that and worked hard to make those hairs look less kinky.

Andrea (25):

I felt lowest about my hair in my freshman year of college. I had put a texturizer (a product that loosens curls in the hair) in it just before I started school and by the end of the year my hair was shedding a lot and had broken off very badly in the middle of my head. I had to stop doing the texturizer and cut out the chemical portions of my hair. I was extremely distraught at the feel, the length and the state of my hair. This experience confirmed that I would never put chemicals in my hair again.

Cynthia (22):

I was starting a new school and I went to a hairstylist who put my hair in a straw set. My hair was so tightly curled that it looked like I only had two inches of hair and I hated it. I thought the other girls wouldn't want to talk to me. I also had to take my yearbook picture with this hair and I avoided buying that yearbook because of my hair. This was when I started straightening my hair instead of getting it curled. At that time in my life I felt like I had to straighten my hair to fit in.

Ava (26):

I permed my hair in middle school, then wanted to go back to my natural hair in high school. When I cut my hair off I felt so ugly because my hair was short and some of my friends didn't want to talk to me anymore at school because my hair wasn't long anymore.

Amina (22):

I remember having my hair very short when I was in high school. I think it broke off due to a perm, so I had to have it cut short. I remember a couple of times when I was with a friend and others that my friend was with another boy from a distance. She was with me. That really hurt my feelings and to this day I shy away from even considering short hair styles. Again, my hair's length in my mind contributes to my self-confidence and my attractiveness.

Marisol (37):

I had long hair and decided to get a buzz cut. I remember some people being upset. But others telling me I was beautiful even without much hair. Shallow boyfriend dumped me. But boy next door said he still thought I was beautiful. Showed me the kind of man I wanted in my life.

Shelbie (57):

My first friends were a couple of older girls that had long, thick hair. I remember them teasing me about my short hair. It seemed to be a measure of attractiveness and therefore worthiness.

Rose (43):

My mother had my hair cut into a boyish flat-top when she found that I had split ends during the early 90s. I was severely teased at school by my peers and mistaken by for a boy. I developed anxiety in relation to going to school until I finally refused to leave the house for school until my mother agreed to relax my hair again.

Delicia (34):

I went to Spelman. I took a class on the African Diaspora and decided to research and write a paper on the politics of black hair. After seeing ads for years telling black women that they owed it to themselves not have ugly nappy hair, and men tell women that their hair was their crown and glory. I felt like I didn't have to listen to the lies. I decided to take out my weave and cut off all my hair, which was processed.

Darlene (50):

I remember getting my hair pressed at about four years old. I hated sitting there, I hated the smell, and I hated the fact that I might get burnt. My mom would do my hair. I am currently in my 50s and do very little to my hair. I don't think you should spend so much time altering your hair's natural state.

Qualitative researchers encourage social scientists to categorize stories (Braun & Clarke, 2006), but one of the goals for this chapter is to maintain the authenticity of each account. These are stories to be savored and broadcast for and by Black women.

Healing and Haircare Practice

Given the complexity of these hair stories of texture bias, mental health professionals need to frame the thematic content and emotional tone of the stories into a format that is healing of these aesthetic traumas. These hair stories, which reflect the internalization of past lived experiences, may impact self-concept and social relationships. They deserve the same attention as other forms of trauma. PsychoHairapy (Mbilishaka, 2018a) is a community engagement model that uses hair as an entry point into emotional healing.

This intervention fosters a relationship between haircare professionals and mental health professionals to collaborate on intervention and prevention strategies in the salon and barbershop setting. PsychoHairapy is inclusive of training haircare professionals in mental health first aid, offering group processing, sharing psychoeducational materials, and managing the referral process. These hair stories shared by Black women can help to further tailor this intervention as Black women cope with the discrimination that comes from having tightly coiled hair in a society that rejecting of the African aesthetic.

Specifically, narrative therapy is an ideal intervention model to address stressful hair experiences. The salon space may be ideal for Black women to process the meaning of their hair with other Black women (Mbilishaka, 2018a). Through directive questioning using the GHA, mental health professionals and haircare professionals can elicit and normalize the process of experiencing hair texture bias in a world that is not affirming of Blackness. Shame deserves significant attention in the process. Often this emotion is silenced, but through a group response, it reverses the power of this emotion and offers race-based healing (Mbilishaka, 2018b).

We must acknowledge the power of physical touch and the power of getting one's hair styled. Previous researchers have studied the importance of hairstylists being involved in mental health interventions (Ashley & Brown, 2015). Physically touching the scalp and the hair served to be healing for Black girls that were involved in the foster care system (Ashley & Brown, 2015). These findings should be extended to the adult population. Scholars need to investigate how Black women are physically cared for by hair-care providers, as well as mental healthcare professionals. A multi-pronged research agenda is needed to create a holistic approach to coping with hair texture bias.

Research

The hair stories of texturism affirm the concept of hair stress in the research literature. Hair stress (Winfield-Thomas & Whaley, 2019, p. 162) is conceptualized as the "harmful physical and psychological effects of hairstyling methods used to transform the hair from its natural state to achieve and maintain an unnatural texture and appearance." These stories not only highlight struggles with self-esteem and self-worth, but also challenge the individual to cope with the psychological consequences of being a target of discrimination. Once someone has experienced the discriminatory behavior, they were often motivated to change their own appearance. Unfortunately, popular methods of hair straightening include burning of the hair and scalp thermally or chemically, which has lifelong effects on health outcomes (Winfield-Thomas

& Whaley, 2019). To extend the stories, researchers should gather the antecedent, behavior, and consequences of hair bias within the lives of Black women. Carefully crafting culturally sensitive tools, research scientists should continue to unpack and honor the challenges, and resiliency, that Black women face related to hair texture bias. This research can then translate into policies that are protective of Black hair textures.

Policy

Over the last year, there has been tremendous policy change in addressing hair bias. In February 2019, New York City passed the CROWN Act, an anti-discrimination bill to protect Black people that wear their hair in natural hairstyles. It was swiftly followed by the California State Senate passing the bill. Here CROWN stands for "Creating and Respectful and Open World for Natural Hair." As stated on the Crown Act Website (retrieved March 2020), "The CROWN Act ensures protection against discrimination based on hairstyles by extending statutory protection to hair texture and protective styles in the Fair Employment and Housing Act (FEHA) and state Education Codes." Hair texture is explicitly named. Driven by the Civil Rights Act of 1964 that protects Black people against racial discrimination, this legislature aims to extend racial discrimination to be inclusive of hair texture and hairstyle. Several states have been in alignment to introduce bills that protect Black people during the hiring practice, staying employed, and in-school success. In December 2019, this bill was introduced at the federal level to the Senate and House of Representatives. Lived experiences of bias are now changing policy.

Conclusion

Hair texture bias has been systematically woven into the lives of Black people. This chapter offers an opportunity to extend the research, practice, and policies that can improve lives through the medium of hair. To develop cultural competence in the field of psychology or other social sciences, we all must be informed about the trauma and richness of hair as a strategy of identity development and tool of discrimination.

Process Questions and Considerations:
1. Why is the history of Black hair textures often hidden from broader historical narratives?
2. Why is it important for Black women to articulate experiences of hair bias?
3. How do you conceptualize your growth areas in being able to process texturism in your life?
4. How do you think policy changes related anti-discrimination laws will impact the mental

health of people who have been the targets of hair bias?

5. How might intersectionality serve as a protective factor in coping with hair bias?

References

Alston, G., & Ellis-Hervey, N. (2014). Exploring public pedagogy and the non-formal adult educator in 21st century contexts using qualitative video data analysis techniques. *Learning Media and Technology, 40*, 502-513. DOI:10.1080/17439884. 2014.968168

Ashley, W., & Brown, J. (2015). Attachment tHAIRapy: A culturally relevant treatment paradigm for African American foster youth. *Journal of Black Studies, 46*(6), 587-604. https://doi.org/10.1177/0021934715590406.

Beckwith, C., & Fisher, A. (1999). *African Ceremonies*. Michigan: Harry Abrams.

Bellinger, W. (2007). Why African American women try to obtain "good hair." *Social Viewpoints, 23*, 63-71.

Bianchi, C. (2014). Slurs and appropriation: An echoic account. *Journal of Pragmatics, 66*, 35-44.

Braun, V., & Clarke, V. (2006). Using thematic analysis in psychology. *Qualitative Research in Psychology, 3*, 77-101. DOI:10.1191/1478088706qp063oa

Byrd, A., & Tharps, L. (2014). *Hair story: Untangling the roots of black hair in America*. New York, NY: St. Martin's Press.

Caldwell, K. L. (2004). "Look at her hair": The body politics of black womanhod in Brazil. *Tranforming Anthropology, 11*(2), 18-29.

Capodilupo, C. M. (2015). One size does not fit all: Using variables other than the thin ideal to understand black women's body image. *Cultural Diversity and Ethnic Minority Psychology, 21*, 268-278.

Chapman-Hilliard, C., & Beasley, S. (2018). "It's like power to move": Black students' psychosocial experiences in Black Studies courses at a predominantly white institution. *Journal of Multicultural Counseling and Development, 46*, 129-151.

DeGruy, J. (2005). *Post traumatic slave syndrome: America's legacy of enduring injury and healing*. Portland, OR: Joy DeGruy Publications Inc.

Ellis-Hervey, N., Doss, A., Davis, D., Nicks, R., & Araiza, P. (2016). African American personal presentation: Psychology of hair and self-perception. *Journal of Black Studies, 47*, 869-882.

Gill, T. (2010). *Beauty shop politics: African American women's activism in the beauty industry*. Illinois: University of Illinois Press.

Goode-Cross, D. T., & Grim, K. A. (2016). "An unspoken level of comfort": Black therapists' experiences working with black clients. *Journal of Black Psychology, 42*(1), 29-53.

Greene, D. W. (2008). "Title VII: What's hair (and other race-based characteristics) got to do with it?" *University of Colorado Law Review, 79*(4), 1355.

Greene, D. W. (2017). Splitting hairs: The Eleventh Circuit's take on workplace bans against black women's natural hair in EEOC v Catastrophe Management Solutions. *University of Miami Law Review, 71*, 987-1036.

Harper, K., & Choma, B. (2018). Internalized White Ideal, Skin Tone Surveillance, and Hair Surveillance Predict Skin and Hair Dissatisfaction and Skin Bleaching among African American and Indian Women. *Sex Roles, 79*, 1-10. https://doi.org/10.1007/s1119

Harrison, M. S., & Thomas, K. M. (2009). The hidden prejudice in selection: A research investigation on skin color bias. *Journal of Applied Social Psychology, 39*(1), 134-168. https://doi.org/10.1111/j.1559-1816.2008.00433.x

Hills, P., & Lewis, M. (2006). Reducing the own-race bias in face recognition by shifting attention. *The Quarterly Journal of Experimental Psychology, 59*(6), 996-1002.

Jablonski, N. G. & Chaplin, G. (2014). The evolution of skin pigmentation and hair texture in people of

African Ancestry. *Dematologic Clinic, 32,* 113-121. http://dx.doi.org/10.1016/j.det.2013.11.003

Johnson, T. A., & Bankhead, T. (2014). Hair it is: Examining the experiences of black women with natural hair. *Open Journal of Social Sciences, 2,* 86-100.

Jones, J. M. (2003) TRIOS: A psychological theory of African legacy in American culture. *Journal of Social Issues, 59,* 217-241.

Lewis, M. L. (1999). Hair combing interactions: A new paradigm for research with African American mothers. *American Journal of Orthopsychiatry, 69,* 504-514.

Magubane, Z. (2007). Why 'nappy' is offensive. *The Boston Globe.* Retrieved from https://www.commondreams.org/views/2007/04/12/why-nappy-offensive

Mangum, T., Mbilishaka, A., & Apugo, D. (2019). Protective styles: Documenting and disrupting hair bias towards black girls in schools. *Psych Discourse.*

Mangum, A. M., & Woods, A. (2011). "Psychohairapy": Integrating psychology, public health, and beauty shop talk. Paper read at the 43rd Annual Association of Black Psychologists Convention, Crystal City, VA, 2011.

Mbilishaka, A. M. (2014). *The guided hair autobiography.* [Data collection instrument].   W a s h i n g t o n, DC: PsychoHairapy Research Lab, Department of Psychology, Howard University.

Mbilishaka, A. M. (2018a). PsychoHairapy: Using hair as an entry point into black women's spiritual and mental health. Meridians: Feminism, Race & Transnationalism, 16(2), 382-392.

Mbilishaka, A. M. (2018b). Black lives (and stories) matter: Race narrative therapy in lack hair care spaces. *Community Psychology in Global Perspective,* 4(2), 22-33.

Mbilishaka, A., & Apugo, D. (2020). Brushed aside: African American women's narratives of hair bias in school. *Race Ethnicity and Education.* DOI:10.1080/13613324.2020.1718075

McGill Johnson, A., Godsil, R. D., MacFarlane, J., Tropp, L. R., & Atiba Goff, P. (2017). The "good hair" study: Explicit and implicit attitudes toward black women's hair. *The Perception Institute.*

Meissner, C. A., & Brigham, J.C. (2001). Thirty years of investigating the own-race bias in memory for faces: A meta-analytic review. *Psychology, Public Policy and Law, 7*(1), 3-35. DOI:10.1037//1076-8971.7.13

Morrow, W. (1990). *400 years without a comb.* San Diego, CA: Black Publishers of San Diego.

Neal, A. M., & Wilson, M. L. (1989). The role of skin color and features in the black community: Implications for black women and therapy. *Clinical Psychology Review, 9,* 323-333.

O'Brien-Richardson, P. (2019). Hair harassment in urban schools and how it shapes the physical activity of black adolescent girls. *The Urban Review, 51,* 523-534.

Opie, T. R., & Phillips, K. W. (2015). Hair penalties: The negative influence of Afrocentric hair on ratings of black women's dominance and professionalism. *Frontiers in Psychology, 6,* 1311. DOI:10.3389/fpsyg.2015.01311

Robinson, C. L. (2011). Hair as race: Why "good hair" may be bad for black females. *The H o w a r d Journal of Communications, 22*(4), 358-376. DOI:10.1080/10646175.2011.617212

Rooks, N. (1996) *Hair raising: Beauty, culture and African American women.* Rutgers University Press, New Brunswick.

Rosette, A. S., & Dumas, T. L. (2007). The Hair Dilemma: Conform to mainstream expectations or emphasize racial identity. *Duke Journal of Gender Law & Policy,* 14(407), 407-421.

Rubin, L. R., Fitts, M. L., & Becker, A. E. (2003). "Whatever feels good in my soul": Body ethics and aesthetics among African American and Latina women. *Culture, Medicine and Psychiatry, 27,* 49-75.

Sherrow, V. (2006). *Encyclopedia of hair: A cultural history.* Westport, CT: Greenwood Press.

Smith, T., Mbilishaka, M., & Kennedy, K. (2017). Press and curl: An examination of *Ebony* magazine covers to understand the cultural-historical trends of black women's hair. *Media Psychology Review, 11*(1).

Wilson, I., Mbilishaka, A., & Lewis, M. (2018). "White folks ain't got hair like us": African American mother-daughter hair stories and racial socialization. *Women, Gender, and Families of Color, 6*(2),

226-248.

Winfield-Thomas, E., & Whaley, A. (2019). *Hair stress: Physical and mental health correlates of African American women's hair care practices.* In B. Slatton & C. Brailey (Eds.), *Women and Inequality in the 21st Century*, pp. 159-176. New York, NY: Routledge.

Winston, C. E., Rice, D. W., Bradshaw, B. J., Lloyd, D., Harris, L. T., Burford, T. I., Clodimir, G., . . . & Burrell, J. (2004). Science success, narrative theories of personality, and race self-complexity: Is race represented in the identity construction of African American adolescents? *New Directions for Child and Adolescent Development, 106*, 55-77.

CHAPTER 13.

Protective Factors or Comparative-based Excuses? The Relationship Between Racial Identity and Body Image in Black women

Kristen Gayle, Howard University

Introduction

Western society is preoccupied with women's body size and shape; thus, society continues to impose pressure on women to conform to standards of beauty that are ever-changing. However, one beauty ideal, thinness, has remained somewhat of a constant for generations. Since the 1900s, mainstream media has inundated society with images of increasingly thinner women (Brisbon, 2009; Hunter, 2002; Martin, 2010). The glorification of thinness and weight loss has been so profound in Western society, that the term thin-ideal emerged from what some researchers defined as an epidemic (Low et al., 2003). Rodin, Silberstein, and Striegel-Moore (1984) reported that there is a "normative discontent" of women in the United States where constant preoccupation with their weight and dieting is considered normal. Phenomena such as the normative discontent perpetuates the belief that all women experience the drive for thinness leaving those who do not to be viewed as anomalies as compared to the norm. Although not all women desire to be thin, the thin ideal remains a universal standard in the United States (Capodilupo & Kim, 2014).

Society's idealization of thinness has undergone recent adaptations which now include muscles in addition to thinness (Bozsik, Whisenhunt, Hudson, Bennett, & Lundgren, 2018) also known as #fitspiration (Prichard, Kavanagh, Mulgrew, Lim, & Tiggemann, 2020). Researchers now identify muscular ideals as the pursuit of thinness in disguise (Uhlmann, Donovan, Zimmer-Gembeck, Bell, & Ramme, 2018). Although Western society has been infatuated with thin women for generations, the Black community continues to prefer more voluptuous/curvy/"thick" women (Overstreet, Quinn, & Agocha, 2010). These stark differences have yet to be adequately explored in culturally appropriate studies. Instead, comparative studies contrast Black and White women and deem racial identity as the moderator that reduces body dissatisfaction and the frequency of eating disorders in Black women. However, this is not an accurate depiction. Thomas (2004) reported,

> Comparative research, in many respects, has been detrimental to a complete and accurate understanding of Black women because it often simplistically frames questions and discusses outcomes in terms of "apparent" differences between Blacks and Whites, Black men and women, or Black and non-Black women (p. 289).

Such comparative studies are simply deducing the presentation of body dissatisfaction in White women to a mere standard for all women. These studies attribute between-group differences to the buffering effects of racial identity, cultural conditioning, and acceptance of diverse body types within Black communities (Rogers Wood & Petrie, 2010) thus minimizing the Black women's experience. McClure (2012, p. 18) states that research that does not adequately explore the within-group differences as a means to understand Black women's body image creates the conditions for a between-group categorization (race) and a between-group difference (race-associated body image) to be misapplied as an explanation of a within-group phenomenon (body image among African Americans) (p. 18).Furthermore, McClure (2012) states that Black women who do not want to be thick are thought to have experienced loss or attenuation of authentic racial identity. This resort to acculturation explanations fails to recognize that cultural categories such as race serve to identify within-group similarity but cannot reliably account for the within-group difference. The way women come to understand and view their bodies cannot be surmised based on dichotomies between race differences. Therefore it is important to remember that research that suggests some Black women are impervious to body dissatisfaction is based on using White women's experience as the norm which cannot be used to explain the Black women's experience. Black women have been underrepresented in body image literature, leaving a gap in the knowledge regarding how Black women appraise their bodies and determine what is beautiful as well as what impact objectification/self-objectification has on their psychological well-being.

Identifying race as the sole explanation for between-group differences leads the public and many practicing clinicians to believe that Black women are immune to body dissatisfaction. Gordon, Brattole, Wingate, and Joiner (2006) found that when 91 clinicians were presented with one of three identical scenarios of fictional White, Latina, and Black women who were experiencing disordered eating symptoms, 44% concluded that the White woman's symptoms were problematic, 41% identified the

Latina woman's symptoms as problematic, and only 17% reported the Black woman's symptoms as problematic. Objectification is defined as "the process by which people are dehumanized, made ghostlike, given the status of Other" Cliff (1900, p. 272) . Black women have been dehumanized for centuries in the United States, beginning with slavery. In the modern day, Black women continue to be dehumanized and objectified due to their body parts, particularly their buttocks, being commodified and their essence being hypersexualized. Fredrickson and Roberts (1997) stated that women and girls are conditioned to internalize an observer's perspective as a primary view and opinion of their physical selves. In other words, from a young age, girls appraise their bodies as though they are objects based on how they perceive others to view them rather than on other qualities. The hyperawareness of how others view them can lead to feelings of shame and preoccupation with body surveillance resulting in a reduced cognizance of their internal states of being (Fredrickson & Roberts, 1997). Although it is less explored, men also experience objectification; however, the objectification of women's bodies is unique to the appraisal of men's bodies due to the power dynamic that men typically hold over women in society (Civile & Obhi, 2015). Hesse-Biber (1991) argues that the more social, political, and economic power women obtain, the more pressure they receive to become physically smaller in an attempt for men to maintain their power.

The voices of Black women in the United States have been stifled since 1619 (Hill Collins, 2000) and change is imperative. Black women have arguably been the most oppressed population in the United States (Thomas, 2004). They have continued to be omitted and forgotten in psychological discourse. This issue is not only due to the lack of Black female subjects in research, but also the dearth of Black women researchers whose work is published. Centuries of enslavement and torture only transitioned into modern-day subjugation and objectification.

Body Image

Body image is the way an individual perceives themselves physically and the thoughts and emotions that are derived from that perception. Body image is multifaceted and thus includes body size and shape as well as overall appearance (McClure, 2012). Both body image and body dissatisfaction develop at a very young age. Clark and Clark (1950) found that children as young as three years old acknowledge racial differences based on skin color (Black and White) and a majority endorsed preferences for White skin. Girls as young as five have been found to have concerns about being thin and already have ideas about dieting (Abramovitz & Birch, 2000). Kelly et al. (2012) found that, among their participants, which consisted of 58 girls (66% Black and 35% White) ages 6-11, 99% selected a smaller ideal body size. In another study which included 58 Black parent-child dyads where the children were in first grade, only 12.1% of the children reported body satisfaction, while 85% of 38 average weight children reported body size dissatisfaction (Davis, Sbrocco, & Williams, 2009). Research has also found that between 30% and 50% of adolescent girls are concerned about their weight and many report dieting. In addition, they found that girls as young as 11 years old engage in self-objectification (Murnen & Don, 2012). Young girls are influenced by the unrealistic body image ideals that they are exposed to in the media, the clothes made available to them, and the physical features of the dolls they play with. Black girls, in particular, tend not to internalize mainstream beauty ideals and rather focus more on the appearance of other Black women (Schooler, Ward, Merriwether, & Caruthers, 2004). However, Black women who follow blogs with a Black focus on social media experienced higher symptoms of depression and anxiety (Stanton, Jerald, Ward, & Avery, 2017).

Body Image and Heterosexual Black Women

Burgeoning body image research has included samples of women of color, as mentioned; this is often for the purpose of comparing the population to White women, even when White women are not present in the study's sample (Capodilupo & Kim, 2014). Fewer studies looked solely at women of color and even fewer have attempted to identify the unique aspects that create their perceptions of beauty and influence their body image. Of the studies that have focused on defining the factors that contribute to Black girls' and women's body image and beauty ideals most have identified similar themes: more concern is placed on body type, hair, and skin color (Awad et al., 2015). Awad et al. (2015) found that the women in their study tended to address additional themes such as a drive to be thick/curvy versus thin, which they identified as being for White women, the presence and lack of validation from others, and microaggressions/ oppression. These characteristics proved to be more salient for the population than concerns that are emphasized in traditional body image literature, which often perpetuates the universality of European White women's experiences.

Black body image is embedded in the history of Black persons in the United States beginning with the enslavement of Africans (Awad et al., 2015). Enslavement meant that one's body was not their own and instead the property of another. African bodies were not seen as wholes but rather divisible parts that could be used by the slave master as he saw fit (Hill Collins, 2000). Black women's genitalia became a commodity that could be sold and purchased on an open market (Hill Collins, 2000) further objectifying the Black body. Today, Black women's bodies continue to be objectified in a similar manner due to the commodification of their butts (Hill Collins, 2000). In the media, there is a push for Black women to be sexy and "images of black women and sexuality represent modern-day resurrections of historically constructed derogatory images" (Herd, 2015, p. 578). From music videos to social media, Black women can be found to be hypersexualized in ways that often include an emphasis on large buttocks (Murnen & Don, 2012). Despite being hypersexualized and commodified, Afrocentric features are often considered less attractive and unfeminine, whereas European features are viewed as the ideal (Awad et al., 2015). The undesirability of Afrocentric aesthetics is a message that is transmitted at a young age and is further perpetuated by interpersonal relationships and their communities (Awad et al., 2015). Waldron (2019) stated,

> The bodies of Black women have long been sites of trauma that carry the weight of the past and present stereotypes that dehumanize them. They continue to embody the traumatizing effects of multiple forms of structural violence, historically and in the present day (p. 21).

Black women are considered to be more satisfied with their bodies than White women because their dissatisfaction presents differently. They are less preoccupied with thinness (Capodilupo, 2015), desire more curvaceous body frames (Overstreet, Quinn, & Agocha, 2010), and are more concerned with the ideals such as body shape, skin color, and hair texture (Capodilupo & Kim, 2014). In addition, body image among Black women and girls is intricately woven with intersectionality, which is comprised of a system of "isms." Body image and beauty ideals cannot be thoroughly explored without considering the intersectionality of the systems and ideologies (racism, sexism, colorism, ageism, classism, heterosexism, ableism), that are unabating in their lives (Awad et al., 2015; Thomas, 2004). Black women often experience the intersectionality of at least two oppressed identities, race and gender, which impacts their lived experiences by altering their schema.

Body Dissatisfaction

Disproportionate body image concern is thought to be related to eating disorders, body dissatisfaction, and internalization of thin-ideal (Singh, Parsekar, & Bhumika, 2016), as well as depression and interpersonal struggles such as insecure adult attachment and fear of romantic intimacy (Maillé, Bergeron, & Lambert, 2015). As mentioned, comparative studies report that Black women are experience lower levels of body dissatisfaction compared to White women. This research suggests that Black women are more unlikely to diet and have eating disorder symptoms. Black women's higher levels of body satisfaction have often been attributed to protective factors due to their race and culture (Hesse-Biber, Livingstone, Ramirez, Barko, & Johnson, 2010) despite being inappropriately used as a means of describing within-group differences. These protective factors are said to produce greater acceptance of larger body sizes, less fear of gaining weight (Gordon, Castro, Sitnikov, & Holm-Denoma, 2010), being less impacted by mainstream beauty ideals and racial identity. Abood and Chandler (1997) reported that their Black female participants weighed around 10 pounds more than their White female participants. However, many Black girls and women can attest to experiencing copious amounts of dissatisfaction when they catch a glimpse of themselves in the mirror. Similar to White women, Black women often tend to desire smaller body types (Baugh, Mullis, Mullis, Hicks, & Peterson, 2010). Gustat, Carton, Shahien, and Andersen (2017) found that only 42.2% of their participants reported satisfaction with their bodies and 44.1% selected the correct body size when asked to identify their own body size. Numerous studies have also reported that Black women experience bulimia at the same rate as White women (Smolak, Striegel-Moore, & Levine, 2013).

Although certain body image researchers report a shift away from comparative studies, the December 2019 edition of the *Body Image Journal* there was only one article that focused solely on people of color. Considering these aforementioned factors regarding the major flaws of comparative studies, it remains unclear why body image discourse continues to neglect the concerns of Black women. The answer to this is simple—body image and beauty ideals are essentially defined through a European lens and women who do not subscribe to that paradigm are perceived as less important. Therefore, their displeasure goes unnoticed, leaving Black women who are experiencing body dissatisfaction to go undertreated and virtually unrecognized. Rather than accounting for the unique differences among Black women, some researchers report that some Black women have assimilated and acculturated with European American culture and have a higher probability of internalizing ideals that promote thin bodies. These women are thought to experience difficulty balancing assimilation with mainstream White American culture and identifying with their race, gender, or other identities leaving them to feel as though they do not belong in either group (Hesse-Biber et al., 2010).

The acculturation assumption has led studies to use the desire to assimilate as an explanation for why some Black women continue to do the following: a) desire smaller body sizes than their perceived and actual body size (Ard, Greene, Malpede, & Jefferson, 2007; Baugh et al., 2010; Boyington, Johnson, & Carter-Edwards, 2007), b) partake in skin bleaching, c) are willing to go into financial debt to achieve beauty ideals, d) undergo surgical procedures to fit both culturally relevant and mainstream beauty standards, and e) overindulge in haircare (Awad et al., 2015). The preconceived beliefs that minority women are not affected by disordered eating has the potential to impede proper awareness, diagnosis, and treatment of dangerous medical and psychological conditions in ethnic minority groups (Gordon, Perez, & Joiner, 2002). Additionally, Black women have concerns about their body image that have been understudied and unexplored. For example, in her study, Poran (2006) found that young Black women are indeed feeling (1) pressures to be thin, (2) pressures from the preferences of men of diverse ethnicities, (3) competition with other Black women in the realms of beauty, and (4) a strong sense of being misrepresented by media images of thin Black women.

Skin

For Black women, the evaluation of beauty is not solely based on body type. Skin color is an integral aspect of Black women's body image (Awad et al., 2015). Colorism is a system that is connected to racism, where individuals with lighter skin tones are viewed as more attractive and intelligent than those with darker skin tones. In other words, colorism is prejudice or discrimination against people who are darker-skinned. It is more likely to occur among people of the same ethnic or racial group. The cause for colorism can be linked back to colonialism when skin color was used to determine status in the United States during enslavement. Skin color was used to assign duties and separate the Africans and prevent unity among them (Hunter, 2002). Darker-skinned Africans were often considered to be less valuable. Today, people with lighter skin tend to be offered more opportunities and better treatment than those with darker skin complexions. Hunter (2002) found that Black women with lighter skin tones are more likely to achieve higher education and income and are more likely to get married. Unfortunately, colorism also impacts one's perception of self-worth and attractiveness (Fears, 1998). Moreover, relative to media, Black models that have more European features tend to be more popular than models with more Afrocentric aesthetics (Fears, 1998). Past research underscores this, as the legendary Mamie and Kenneth Clark doll study has revealed that even young children can develop the thought that Black skin equates to being bad. Additional research has confirmed that the darker a person's skin and the more stereotypically Black their features appear to be, the more likely they are to be associated with criminal behavior (Eberhardt, Goff, Purdie, & Davies, 2004).

Due to the ways in which society has treated those with darker skin, many Black individuals maintain the belief that lighter skin is more attractive. Awad et al. (2015) found that many of their participants believed that lighter skin tones continue to be preferred over darker skin tones. This preference implies that White is the preferred skin color due to White privilege (Hunter, 2002) and can lead to skin-bleaching practices. Skin bleaching is a phenomenon across the globe due to colorism (Harper & Choma, 2019) where creams and soaps are used to lighten and in some cases whiten one's skin (Benn et al., 2016). The global prevalence of skin bleaching is estimated to be 27.7% (Sagoe et al., 2019) and can be as high as 67% in certain regions of the world (Benn et al., 2016). This phenomenon has come to be known as Bleaching Syndrome (Hall, 1995). "Bleaching Syndrome is characterized by the efforts of a stigmatized out-group to assume the identity of a dominant in-group via anatomical paradigm" (Hall, 2018, p. 2055). Not only are there psychological implications due to skin bleaching, but there are also health concerns that can arise such as mercury and steroid exposure (Benn et al., 2016).

The term the "Lily Complex," describes the process of African American women attempting to change their natural physical features to fit white beauty standards (Jones & Shorter-Gooden, 2003). The "Lily Complex" is defined as "altering, disguising and covering up physical self to assimilate to be accepted as attractive" (Jones & Shorter-Gooden, 2003, p. 177). The idea to conform and cope with identity begins with making women hate themselves. The self-hate and notion that "Black is not beautiful" (Jones & Shorter-Gooden, 2003, p. 177) leads to additional stress. Jones and Shorter-Gooden (2003) stress the importance of not using the Lily Complex as a generalization for all women who try new styles such as blonde hair, colored contacts, and so on. "Not every woman who decides to straighten her hair or change the color of her eyes by wearing contacts believes that beauty is synonymous with whiteness" (Jones & Shorter-Gooden, 2003). One could argue however, that those who do not believe that beauty is synonymous with whiteness have unconscious biases that they are unable to access.

Hair

Hair texture is another aspect of colorism, where straight, long hair is preferred (Watson, Lewis, & Moody, 2019). In Africa before slavery, the hair of Black men and women once had cultural and spiritual implications (Thompson, 2009). However, in the United States during slavery, Africans with more Afrocentric features, were banished to the fields, whereas their more European-looking counterparts were made to serve the slave master and his family in their home (Patton, 2006), and their ability to tend to their hair was diminished and in most cases fully halted (Thompson, 2009). The duties and location in which the duties were performed by the enslaved persons determined the way they wore their hair. In the field, hair was often unkempt and, for women, it was often covered by scarves, whereas in the slave master's house, looking neat was often strictly enforced (Patton, 2006; Thompson, 2009). In the 18th century, those enslaved who worked in the house wore wigs or in some cases manipulated their hair to resemble a wig due to wigs being stylish for White upper-class men. It was not long before Black hair was regularly styled to mimic that of White hair and Blacks began being appraised by their hair and skin tone. Those with darker skin and kinkier hair were considered substandard (Thompson, 2009).

One of the first hair products developed for and by Black people was Madam C. J. Walker's invention of hair softener and the hot comb in 1905 (Thompson, 2009). Straightening Black hair soon became an expectation of Whites and was predicated on one's ability to obtain employment, education, and wealth (Patton, 2006). Brisbon (2009) states that terms such as, "Hot comb, relaxer, texturizer, perm; tender-headed, hard-headed; good hair, bad hair. . . have come to use in defining haircare, and by extension, in defining this important part of their identity" (Brisbon, 2009, p. 89). Therefore, maintaining their hair has led many Black women to spend excessive amounts of time and money on haircare (Awad et al., 2015). Haircare remains a significant factor in the lives of Black women particularly due to its ability to mediate between one's Blackness and American identity (Brisbon, 2009).

Thin Ideal

For the purposes of this book chapter, the thin ideal is defined as the belief that women who have a slender, feminine physique with limited body fat are considered more attractive. The impact of the thin ideal has been thoroughly researched, revealing the damaging psychological effects (Uhlmann et al., 2018), body dissatisfaction being one. Research has historically classified body dissatisfaction as a White women problem. The majority of the body image discourse focuses on White girls and women and has yielded ample literature about how they experience their bodies. These data have often been used as a baseline to describe all other women.

American media has perpetuated the idea that women have specific standards they must uphold to be accepted by, and viewed as aesthetically appealing to, the general public, particularly to men. Although often unrealistic and unattainable, there is continuous pressure to compare and conform to both cultural and mainstream ideals. The Western standard of beauty is typically white, slender women with long blonde hair. Interestingly, striving for the thin body shape becomes an issue when women attempt to lose large amounts of weight to fit an image (Couch et al., 2016). Research shows that models can be as much as 20% underweight, which puts them 5% below the requirement for anorexia nervosa (Murnen & Don, 2012). Although women desire to fit this ideal body type, females tend to have lower rates of exercise participation and adherence than males (Hyuk, Hee, & Youngsook, 2012). With the passage of time, American society has begun to shift away from the desire to achieve thinness and instead is focusing on being fit and healthy. However, many researchers have deemed the "Fitspiration" (fit inspiration) craze as a way to disguise the thin ideal due to it being as unattainable as ultra-thinness (Uhlmann et al., 2018).

In an attempt to use comparative reasons to explain some Black women's desire to be thin, Harris and Kuba (1997) reported that some Black women strongly identified with the dominant culture, thus increasing their desire to assimilate and acculturate. These women reportedly feel the need to reject their own body type in an attempt to achieve the thin ideal that is so heavily reinforced in the larger social context.

Thick Ideal

For the purposes of this book chapter, the "thick ideal" is the drive for thickness (thick hips, buttocks, and thighs) and the "fit-thick ideal" refers to the drive for thickness and fitness (slender or toned waist). Neither of these ideals has been thoroughly explored in body image discourse and can potentially be the missing link when attempting to understand Black women's body image and beauty ideals. Being thick has been a phenomenon for Black women for centuries; however, little is known about how the pursuit of the thick ideal or fit-thick ideal impacts their psychological well-being.

During the 16th-18th centuries, White people classified Black women as being "monstrous", "unwomanly," and "masculine" (Gentles-Peart, 2016, pp. 8 & 10). The size of Black women in proportion to White women provided excuses for slave masters to make it acceptable to use Black women for labor (Gentles-Peart, 2016). Despite their feigned disdain for the Black female body, White men continued to rape and victimize Black women. Saartjie Baartman (Hottentot Venus), an enslaved African woman was an example of this. She was showcased in a cage, commensurate with that of a circus animal attraction, due to her shapely and voluptuous body. She was severely abused (beaten and raped) repeatedly, and upon her death, later dissected, her body parts were turned into an exhibit (showcasing her vagina) and remained on exhibition until 2002. While she was alive, Sara was essentially tortured and White men outwardly deemed her to be unattractive. Of note, following her death, the Victorian bustle dress was made in her image although she never received the credit (Mastamet-Mason, 2014). Sara has been considered the "Original Video Vixen" (Perkins, 2014, p. 31).

Perkins (2014) states that today's video vixens are similar to Sara, in that they are placed on display and viewed as sexualized commodities due to being glorified for their thickness. Perkins argues that "Black women willingly perpetuate this image that ultimately benefits White men and promotes White supremacy" (Perkins, 2014, p. 32). Additional literature states that idealizing Black women with big buttocks are linked to capitalism, "White supremacy and heteropatriarchy" (Brown, 2013, p. 206). Commoditization of the Black female butt allows clothing companies that attempt to enhance one's butt and plastic surgeons who build a butt to capitalize off Black beauty ideals (Slatton, 2015). Brown (2013) further explains that having a stereotypical Black girl butt provides an elusive benefit of protection due to being perceived as more appealing sexually and thus more likely to marry. Moreover, "thick" or "healthy" (Jones & Shorter-Gooden, 2003, p. 184) bodies have historically been lusted after by Black men overtly, and again, by White men covertly. Likely in concert with Black men's preference, Black women often desire more curvaceous body frames as opposed to more thin body types (Overstreet et al., 2010). Oftentimes, a curvaceous body type in Black culture can also be referred to as overweight, because Black women have different body standards than White women who prefer to be thinner. Unlike White girls, Black adolescent girls tend not to base their self-worth on weight and culturally receive more positive messages about their bodies (Sabik, Cole, & Ward, 2010). However, the pressure to achieve a particular physical prototype remains, thus causing many to strive for a thin waist and big buttocks, in other words, a curvaceous body type (Overstreet et al., 2010). Capodilupo and Kim (2014) found that the women in their study often thought that thickness was perceived as positive by the people in their lives.

In hip hop culture, big butts are glamorized not only in songs but also in dance, social media, fitness, and clothing. Regarding dancing, twerking is a popular dance that unlike dances such as whining, which emphasizes the rotation of a woman's hips and waist, twerking focuses on the woman's buttocks. Many songs are dedicated to twerking tunes that are played on rotation in dance clubs across the United States. On social media, women are praised for having "snatched waists" meaning having very slender waists while maintaining a round buttock (fit-thick). To achieve a slender waist, many women resort to waist trainers, which are "latex undergarments that wrap tightly around the belly and cinch in the waist for an hourglass figure" (Smith, 2018). Waist trainers are thought to have adverse effects on the wearer's lungs, digestive system, and nerves (Adams, 2014).

Social media "Snapbacks" after pregnancy are also popular in hip hop culture. This phenomenon is where a woman "snaps back" to the shape she was prior to her pregnancy only days to weeks after giving birth. This shape is typically that of a slender waist. Snatched and Snapback culture are both influenced by fitness culture (#fitspiration) where women are encouraged to spend excessive amounts of time in the gym and take weight loss supplements detoxes, diuretics, and laxatives, which are often endorsed by celebrities and social media influencers (for example, Flat Tummy Tea, SkinnyFit, Hum, and Teami) to obtain an ideal fit-thick image. Studies on the impact of fitspiration images on Instagram suggest that it is associated with poorer self-compassion, increased negative mood, and body dissatisfaction (Prichard et al., 2020; Slater, Varsani, & Diedrichs, 2017). With regard to clothing, websites such as Fashionova emphasize jeans and outfits that enhance and accentuate one's buttocks. This and similar clothing sites are also endorsed by celebrities and social media influencers.

Cosmetic Surgeries

Black women are being increasingly influenced to undergo elective cosmetic surgery, as Black celebrities flaunt their augmentations, thus diminishing the stigma (Jeffries, 2010). According to the American Society of Plastic Surgeons, in 2018, 6% of the surgeries done on Black women were rhinoplasties. Approximately 20,300 buttock-augmentation surgeries where fat grafting was used took place in 2017. Additionally, 1.6 million African American women underwent cosmetic plastic surgery. This number was a 17% increase from 2016. Between 2017 and 2018 the number of Black people electing for plastic surgery increased by 1%. The prevalence of buttock implants decreased by 28% between 2017 and 2018 buttock augmentation with fat grafting increased by 19%. While buttock implants decreased 28% between 2017 and 2018 buttock augmentation with fat grafting increased 19% and butt lifts remained virtually the same (American Society of Plastic Surgeons, 2018). As for women who cannot afford to go to a certified plastic surgeon, some opt to get a black market, unlicensed service to achieve their desired look which can result in death (Martin, 2015). Further, White women tend to elect for more cosmetic surgeries than Black women, and some of these women are surgically obtaining Afrocentric features (e.g., thick, curvaceous bodies and full lips). Capodilupo and Kim (2014) found that in their study, some participants commented on feeling invisible to Black men, particularly when they praise White women for aesthetics that many Black women naturally have. Patton (2006) states,

> . . . physical and facial features equated with African Americans produce their own beautiful counter-narrative. For example, fuller lips, tan skin, body curves, and curly hair are fashionable. Women who do not naturally have these beauty attributes pay to have what African Americans tend to have naturally by visiting their dermatologist, tanning salons, buying padded undergarments, or going to their hairstylist (p. 38).

Media

Black women tend to be misrepresented in the media, thereby contributing to negative stereotypes about the population, as a whole (Capodilupo & Kim, 2014). These distortions of character are longstanding and can be traced back to slavery and minstrel shows. Blackface originated in minstrel shows, an American theatrical form that gained popularity thanks to Thomas Dartmouth Rice in 1831 (Cockrell, 1996). Intending to look like a Black man, Rice covered his face with burnt cork to blacken his skin and performed a dance in disheveled attire while singing a popular slave song "Jump Jim Crow." And thus, the minstrelsy character, Jim Crow, was born (Johnson, 2012). Jim Crow was just the first of many of the White man's characterizations of plantation slaves and free Black people. These characters revealed how the White Americans of that time perceived Blacks as lazy, worthless, unintelligent, and unattractive.

In the minstrel shows, Black women were also represented by negative images. However, these images continue to be portrayed in modern-day media (e.g., TV, films, video games, and so on). Black women are often portrayed as particular stereotypes. Similar to previous bodies of work (Waldron, 2019, p. 22) states that there are five "Black Female Archetypes" which are negative stereotypes that represent Black womanhood. These archetypes include the Mammy, Matriarch, Welfare Mother, Jezebel, Sapphire, and Black Superwoman.

The Mammy is often portrayed as unattractive, asexual, submissive caregivers who were often overweight with dark skin (Hill Collins, 2000; Waldron, 2019; Watson et al., 2019). Because of her single mother identity, which forces her to work outside of the home to support her family, the Black Matriarch is considered a bad mother. She is the more aggressive, dominant version of the Mammy, causing her to be perceived as less feminine (Waldron, 2019). Women who show Mammy and Matriarch characteristics tend to experience depression due to their focus on the needs of others while neglecting their own (Waldron, 2019). Another caregiver archetype is the Welfare Mother, which portrays Black women as animal-like "breeders" (Waldron, 2019) who are also bad mothers due to their unemployment (Sparks, 1999) and dependence on the government to care for their children.

The Jezebel archetype is a hypersexualized woman with a large sex drive (Hill Collins, 2000). She tends to be promiscuous and is often portrayed as attractive, slender, and has lighter skin (Watson et al., 2019). The Jezebel archetype provides an excuse for Black women to be sexually objectified. This archetype is often portrayed in Hip Hop culture (Hill Collins, 2000). The Sapphire archetype is often loud and obnoxious (Hill Collins, 2000) and tends to be portrayed as the angry Black woman (Waldron, 2019) in films. She is viewed as "hostile, aggressive, bitter, and irate" (Waldron, 2019, p. 24).

The final characteristic is the Black Superwoman archetype (Waldron, 2019) also known as the Strong Black Woman (Watson et al., 2019). She is portrayed as "nurturing, strong, invulnerable, and resilient superwomen" (Waldron, 2019, p. 24). This behavior creates the expectation that Black women must hide or deny their issues because they do not want to be seen as weak (Waldron, 2019).

Herd (2015, p. 579) reported that additional modern-day images of Black women today are "more sexually explicit and demeaning portrayals of black women as ''Freaks, Gold Diggers, Divas, Dikes, and Baby Mamas'' in rap music today." Greenwood and Dal Cin (2012) found that young women's appraisals of their favorite media figures provide insight into how they view themselves and develop self-esteem. Comparing oneself to others often leads to body dissatisfaction (Oney, Cole, & Sellers, 2011). The media also perpetuates the idea that for a Black woman to be considered beautiful she must have a small waist and a large bust and buttock. Many Black men and women also define beauty as having long, straight (Capodilupo, 2015) or loosely curled hair and lighter skin tones (Oney et al., 2011).

A desire to resemble these ideals may damage a woman's self-esteem if she cannot obtain the look she wants. When women attempt to conform their bodies to what society deems beautiful, they often question their own self-identity. Capodilupo and Kim (2014), found that the media's depiction of what women should and should not look like has also impacted the views of Black men, thus causing Black women who do not meet the standard to feel invisible to their male counterparts. Women in the study described low perceived social worth that inevitably negatively impacts their body image and self-esteem.

Racial Identity and Ethnic Identity

Comparative research between Black and White samples often use racial or ethnic identity as a means for understanding between-group differences. Having to identify more strongly with their race, Black women will have higher levels of self-esteem, mastery, and lower levels of symptoms associated with depression; however, the opposite is true for those with a negative racial identity (Hughes, Kiecolt, Keith, & Demo, 2015). The negative views of Black people in the United States have led the group to use "social creativity" to redefine the group, which creates a more positive social identity, thus leading to higher individual self-esteem for those who positively view the group (Hughes et al., 2015). Those who do not view their racial group positively due to the group being devalued and stigmatized are more likely to want to join the dominant group, which will inevitably reject them (Hughes et al., 2015). Henrickson, Crowther, and Harrington (2010, p. 87) explained that ethnic identity includes components such as "a sense of affirmation and belonging" where individuals can develop ethnic pride as well as affirmative feelings about their ethnic group and "ethnic identity achievement or search" where the individual learns more about their ethnicity.

Racial/Ethnic Identity as a Protective Factor

Black body image discourse has repeatedly enforced that having a stronger ethnic identity reduces the internalization of mainstream beauty ideals such as thinness (Rogers Wood & Petrie, 2010). Therefore, research suggests that those with a weaker ethnic identity are less protected from social constructs such as the "thin ideal" (Watson, Ancis, White, & Nazari, 2013). However, Hesse-Biber, Livingstone, Ramirez, Barko, and Johnson (2010, p. 709) stated that racial identity cannot be used as the sole means of explaining the variance among Black women's body appraisals. ". . . race as a contingency of self-worth can have important implications for the extent to which they become vulnerable to White Western norms." Rogers and Petrie (2010) found that Black women with lower "African self-consciousness," which was defined as an awareness of the importance placed on African heritage and African American culture, rated themselves as less attractive after viewing images of White female models. The authors concluded that Black women with a stronger racial identity status are more likely to reject White American standards of beauty (Rogers & Petrie, 2010).

Racial Identity, Body Dissatisfaction, and Disordered Eating

Black women with weak racial identity are thought to be more susceptible to being negatively impacted by White Western beauty ideals and thus have a higher probability of experiencing body dissatisfaction and disordered eating (Hesse-Biber, Livingstone, Ramirez, Barko, & Johnson, 2010). Similarly, research suggests that Black women who closely identify with White American culture are at a higher risk of developing eating disorders (Henrickson, Crowther, & Harrington, 2010). These researchers tend to believe that the promotion of having a healthy body weight by their Black culture acts as a buffer or protection. The problem with this theory is that Black women experience particular eating disorder symptoms such as binge eating and bulimia symptoms at higher rates than White women (Taylor, Caldwell, Baser, Faison, & Jackson, 2007). Black teenagers are 50% more likely than White teenagers to experience bulimia or binging and purging symptoms (National Eating Disorders Association, 2018a). Unfortunately, however, people of color are less likely to get professional help to manage eating disorder symptoms (National Eating Disorders Association, 2018b). Notably, women who struggle with one or both of these disorders are typically a normal or higher-than-normal body weight (Mayo Clinic, 2018; National Eating Disorders Association, 2018a).

As it relates physical health, Black women are known to have the highest rates of obesity (Goode et al., 2018). The prevalence of obesity among Black teens was 19.5% and 20.7% in Black teen girls (Ogden, Carroll, Fryar, & Flegal, 2015). The CDC National Center for Health and Statistics (2015) supports this notion, as they found in a four year study, that the prevalence of obesity was highest among Black adults at 48.1% (Ogden et al., 2015). These statistics may raise the question of whether Black culture promotes a healthy body weight or if it is a disguise for underlying disordered eating in the communities. This consideration is particularly important because binge eating and overeating behaviors are often responses to trauma (Coker Ross, 2019), which Black women perpetually experience. This and other implications must be further explored to adequately assess and treat Black women with disordered eating symptoms.

Conclusion

Implications for Practice

Clinicians should strive to be more sensitive and aware of the unique risks racial and ethnic minorities may have that indicate a higher likelihood for them developing an eating disorder (Gordon et al., 2010). Understanding the cultural influences on the development and persistence of eating disorders is not only essential to treating non-White clients with eating disorders but can also help assess clients with co-occurring disorders such as depression and anxiety. Depression and anxiety have been found to have a positive correlation with binge eating disorders across races and ethnicities (Coker Ross, 2019). Being aware of this association could be beneficial for mental health providers and physicians alike. And due to the low numbers of eating disorders being identified, it can be assumed that medical professionals are less aware of the traits associated with binge eating in Black women. Additionally, clinicians and medical professors are not sufficiently trained and are not provided with culturally sensitive tools to adequately assess for eating disorders and body dissatisfaction in Black women.

Implications for Research

Body image is measured using instruments that are evaluating body image with a Eurocentric lens (disordered eating and the desire to be a lower body weight and/or an unhealthy weight). Middle-class White women were used to norm the majority of the body image related instruments used today (Awad et al., 2015). Therefore, using such measures for Black women would yield inaccurate results. Kelly et al. (2012), state that there remains a need for body image/dissatisfaction and eating disorder instruments that take culture into consideration.

It is essential for research to shift its focus away from comparative studies to a discourse where Black women's lived experiences are central. Body image literature is nearly devoid of instruments that consider cultural context when assessing and treating body dissatisfaction and disordered eating symptoms for Black women. Kelly et al. (2012) state that the majority of measures for eating disorders are developed and validated with mostly White samples. Using these instruments to assess eating disorders in Black women can lead symptoms and risk factors to be exaggerated or minimized (Kelly et al., 2012). Furthermore, the eating behaviors within the Black population could be less stereotyped if instruments were able to more accurately access symptoms and risk factors among the population (Kelly et al., 2012). Refining these instruments and measures would also improve the effectiveness of eating disorder screening programs across the country for diverse populations (Kelly et al., 2012). It would provide more accurate statistics and show the need for an increase in eating disorder-related research in this population.

Implications for Policy

The regulation and diversifying of media as a whole, as well as social media, could potentially reduce body dissatisfaction in Black girls and women. Social media users are flooded with advertisements and endorsements of beauty enhancement and weight loss products, which likely increases the surveillance and appraisals of one's self. Walker, Krumhuber, Dayan, and Furnham (2019) found that the participants reported increased displeasure with their bodies when they used social media for longer periods of time. To limit these problematic outcomes, social media sites could be held accountable for potentially harmful posts/advertisements that promote idealized bodies anesthetics.

Media must be diversified to include a variance of skin tones and body shapes and sizes. Additionally, actors and actresses with darker skin and/or fuller bodies should no longer be typecast to play undesirable characters to reduce the discrimination and stigma around darker skin and obesity.Vartanian (2010) found that their participants reported experiencing disgust in association with obese persons. On the other hand, darker-skinned women are often considered less desirable than their lighter-skinned counterparts (Stephens & Thomas, 2012). Such negative views are influenced by society's perceptions about overweight and darker-skinned individuals.

Process Questions and Considerations

1. How can we as a society reduce the prevalence of obesity in the Black community without encouraging thinness?
2. How can Black women be evaluated based on their personality and intellect opposed to being objectified for their bodies?
3. In what ways can Black Power and Black is Beautiful ideals be restored without receiving opposition from non-Black members of the community?
4. Are Black women more dissatisfied with their bodies than what is currently thought?
5. What are the factors that contribute to body dissatisfaction in Black women?

References

Abood, D. A., & Chandler, S. B. (1997). Race and the role of weight, weight change, and body dissatisfaction in eating disorders. *American Journal of Health Behavior, 21*(1), 21-25.

Abramovitz, B. A., & Birch, L. L. (2000). Five-year-old girls' ideas about dieting are predicted by their mothers' dieting. *Journal of the American Dietetic Association, 100*(10), 1157-1163. DOI:10.1016/S0002-8223(00)00339-4

Adams, R. (2014). Spanx and other shapewear are literally squeezing your organs. *Style & Beauty.* Retrieved from https://www.huffpost.com/entry/spanx-shapewear_n_4616907?utm_hp_ref=style&ir=Style

American Society of Plastic Surgeons. (2018). 2018 plastic surgery statistics report. Retrieved from https://www.plasticsurgery.org/documents/News/Statistics/2018/plastic-surgery-statistics-full-report-2018.pdf

Ard, J. D., Greene, L. E., Malpede, C. Z., & Jefferson, W. K. (2007). Association between body image disparity and culturally specific factors that affect weight in Black and White women. *Ethn Dis, 17*(2 Suppl 2), S2-34-39. Retrieved from https://www.ncbi.nlm.nih.gov/pubmed/17684812

Awad, G. H., Norwood, C., Taylor, D. S., Martinez, M., McClain, S., Jones, B., . . . Chapman-Hilliard, C. (2015). Beauty and body image concerns among African American college women. *J Black Psychol, 41*(6), 540-564. DOI:10.1177/0095798414550864

Baugh, E., Mullis, R., Mullis, A., Hicks, M., & Peterson, G. (2010). Ethnic identity and body image among black and white college females. *J Am Coll Health, 59*(2), 105-109. DOI:10.1080/07448481.2010.483713

Benn, E.K.T., Alexis, A., Mohamed, N., Wang, Y.-H., Khan, I. A., & Liu, B. (2016). Skin bleaching and dermatologic health of African and Afro-Caribbean populations in the US: New directions for methodologically rigorous, multidisciplinary, and culturally sensitive research. *Dermatology and therapy, 6*(4), 453-459. DOI:10.1007/s13555-016-0154-1

Boyington, J., Johnson, A., & Carter-Edwards, L. (2007). Dissatisfaction with body size among low-income, postpartum black women. *Journal of Obstetric, Gynecologic & Neonatal Nursing, 36*(2), 144-151. DOI:https://doi.org/10.1111/j.1552-6909.2007.00127.x

Bozsik, F., Whisenhunt, B. L., Hudson, D. L., Bennett, B., & Lundgren, J. D. (2018). Thin is in? Think again: The rising importance of muscularity in the thin ideal female body. *Sex Roles, 79*(9/10), 609-615. DOI:10.1007/s11199-017-0886-0

Brisbon, A. E. (2009). Good hair, bad hair: African-American hair relations in the early twentieth century. *Undergraduate Humanities Forum 2008-09: Change.*

Brown, R. (2013). *Hear our truths: The creative potential of black girlhood:* University of Illinois Press.

Capodilupo, C. M. (2015). One size does not fit all: using variables other than the thin ideal to understand black women's body image. *Cultur Divers Ethnic Minor Psychol, 21*(2), 268-278. DOI:10.1037/a0037649

Capodilupo, C. M., & Kim, S. (2014). Gender and race matter: the importance of considering intersections in Black women's body image. *J Couns Psychol, 61*(1), 37-49. DOI:10.1037/a0034597

Civile, C., & Obhi, S. S. (2015). Power, objectification, and recognition of sexualized women and men. *Psychology of Women Quarterly, 40*(2), 199-212. DOI:10.1177/0361684315604820

Clark, K. B., & Clark, M. P. (1950). Emotional factors in racial identification and preference in Negro children. *The Journal of Negro Education, 19*(3), 341-350. DOI:10.2307/2966491

Cliff, M. (1900). Object into subject: Some thoughts on the work of Black women artists. In G. E. Anzaldúa (Ed.), *Making Face, Making Soul/Haciendo Caras: Creative and Critical Perspectives by Women of Color* (pp. 271-290). San Francisco, CA: Aunt Lute Foundation Books.

Cockrell, D. (1996). Jim Crow, demon of disorder. *American Music*, 14, 161+. Retrieved from https://link.gale.com/apps/doc/A18563146/BIC?u=howard1&sid=BIC&xid=ded1247c

Coker Ross, C. (2019). African-American women and eating disorders: Depression, and the strong black woman archetype. *Eating Disorders Review.com, 30*(5). Retrieved from https://eatingdisordersreview.com/african-american-women-and-eating-disorders-depression-and-the-strong-black-woman-archetype/

Couch, D., Thomas, S. L., Lewis, S., Blood, R. W., Holland, K., & Komesaroff, P. (2016). Obese people's perceptions of the thin ideal. *Soc Sci Med, 148,* 60-70. DOI:10.1016/j.socscimed.2015.11.034

Davis, D. S., Sbrocco, T., & Williams, J. (2009). Understanding body image in African American and Caucasian first-graders: a partnership with the YMCA. *Progress in Community Health Partnerships: Research, Education, and Action, 3*(4), 277-286. DOI:10.1353/cpr.0.0092

Eberhardt, J. L., Goff, P. A., Purdie, V. J., & Davies, P. G. (2004). Seeing black: Race, crime, and visual processing. *Journal of Personality and Social Psychology, 87*(6), 876-893. DOI:10.1037/0022-3514.87.6.876

Fears, L. M. (1998). Colorism of black women in news editorial photos. *Western Journal of Black Studies, 22*(1), 30-36.

Fredrickson, B. L., & Roberts, T.-A. (1997). Objectification theory: Toward understanding women's lived experiences and mental health risks. *Psychology of Women Quarterly, 21*(2), 173-206. DOI:10.1111/j.1471-6402.1997.tb00108.x

Gentles-Peart, K. (2016). *Romance with voluptuousness Caribbean women and thick bodies in the United States.* University of Nebraska Press.

Goode, R. W., Kalarchian, M. A., Craighead, L., Conroy, M. B., Wallace, J., Jr., Eack, S. M., & Burke, L. E. (2018). The feasibility of a binge eating intervention in Black women with obesity. *Eat Behav, 29,* 83-90. DOI:10.1016/j.eatbeh.2018.03.005

Gordon, K. H., Brattole, M. M., Wingate, L. R., & Joiner, T. E., Jr. (2006). The impact of client race on clinician detection of eating disorders. *Behav Ther, 37*(4), 319-325. DOI:10.1016/j.beth.2005.12.002

Gordon, K. H., Castro, Y., Sitnikov, L., & Holm-Denoma, J. M. (2010). Cultural body shape ideals and eating disorder symptoms among white, Latina, and black college women. *Cultur Divers Ethnic Minor Psychol, 16*(2), 135-143. DOI:10.1037/a0018671

Gordon, K. H., Perez, M., & Joiner, T. E., Jr. (2002). The impact of racial stereotypes on eating disorder recognition. *Int J Eat Disord, 32*(2), 219-224. DOI:10.1002/eat.10070

Greenwood, D. N., & Dal Cin, S. (2012). Ethnicity and body consciousness: Black and white American women's negotiation of media ideals and others' approval. *Psychology of Popular Media Culture, 1*(4), 220-235. DOI:10.1037/a0029411

Gustat, J., Carton, T. W., Shahien, A. A., & Andersen, L. (2017). Body image satisfaction among blacks. *Health Education & Behavior, 44*(1), 131-140. DOI:10.1177/1090198116644181

Hall, R. E. (1995). The Color Complex: The Bleaching Syndrome. *Race, Gender & Class, 2*(2), 99-109. Retrieved from www.jstor.org/stable/41675381

Hall, R. E. (2018). The Bleaching Syndrome Per Colorism Pathology: LGBTQ Perpetuation of Discrimination. *American Behavioral Scientist, 62*(14), 2055-2071. DOI:10.1177/0002764218810759

Harper, K., & Choma, B. L. (2019). Internalised White Ideal, Skin Tone Surveillance, and Hair Surveillance Predict Skin and Hair Dissatisfaction and Skin Bleaching among African American and Indian Women. *Sex Roles, 80*(11), 735-744. DOI:10.1007/s11199-018-0966-9

Harris, D. J., & Kuba, S. A. (1997). Ethnocultural identity and eating disorders in women of color [American Psychological Association DOI:10.1037/0735-7028.28.4.341]. Retrieved

Henrickson, H. C., Crowther, J. H., & Harrington, E. F. (2010). Ethnic identity and maladaptive eating: expectancies about eating and thinness in African American women. *Cultur Divers Ethnic Minor Psychol, 16*(1), 87-93. DOI:10.1037/a0013455

Herd, D. (2015). Conflicting Paradigms on Gender and Sexuality in Rap Music: A Systematic Review. *Sexuality & Culture, 19*(3), 577-589. DOI:10.1007/s12119-014-9259-9

Hesse-Biber, S. (1991). Women, weight and eating disorders. A socio-cultural and political-economic analysis. *Women's Studies Interntational Forum, 14*(3), 173-191.

Hesse-Biber, S., Livingstone, S., Ramirez, D., Barko, E. B., & Johnson, A. L. (2010). Racial Identity and Body Image Among Black Female College Students Attending Predominately White Colleges. *Sex*

Roles, 63(9/10), 697-711. DOI:10.1007/s11199-010-9862-7

Hill Collins, P. (2000). *Black Feminist Thought: Knowledge, Consciousness, and the Politics of Empowerment* (2 ed.). New York, NY: Routledge.

Hughes, M., Kiecolt, K. J., Keith, V. M., & Demo, D. H. (2015). Racial Identity and Well-Being among African Americans. *Social Psychology Quarterly, 78*(1), 25-48. DOI:10.1177/0190272514554043

Hunter, M. L. (2002). "If You're Light You're Alright": Light Skin Color as Social Capital for Women of Color. *Gender & Society, 16*(2), 175-193. DOI:10.1177/08912430222104895

Hyuk, P. S., Hee, J. J., & Youngsook, K. (2012). The Relationship between Gender Role Identity and Intrinsic Motivation of Female University Students Based on Exercise Participation. *International Journal Of Applied Sports Sciences, 24*(2).

Jeffries, A. (2010). Is plastic surgery the new black for black women? Retrieved from https://www.essence.com/celebrity/is-plastic-surgery-the-new-black-for-bla/

Johnson, S. (2012). *Burnt Cork: Traditions and Legacies of Blackface Minstrelsy:* University of Massachusetts Press.

Jones, C., & Shorter-Gooden, K. (2003). *Shifting : the double lives of Black women in America.* New York: HarperCollins.

Kelly, N. R., Mitchell, K. S., Gow, R. W., Trace, S. E., Lydecker, J. A., Bair, C. E., & Mazzeo, S. (2012). An evaluation of the reliability and construct validity of eating disorder measures in white and black women. *Psychological Assessment, 24*(3), 608-617. DOI:10.1037/a0026457

Low, K. G., Charanasomboon, S., Brown, C., Hiltunen, G., Long, K., Reinhalter, K., & Jones, H. (2003). Internalization of the thin ideal, weight and body image concerns. *Social Behavior and Personality: An International Journal, 31*(1), 81-90. DOI:10.2224/sbp.2003.31.1.81

Maillé, D. L., Bergeron, S., & Lambert, B. (2015). Body Image in Women with Primary and Secondary Provoked Vestibulodynia: A Controlled Study. *The Journal of Sexual Medicine, 12*(2), 505-515. DOI:10.1111/jsm.12765

Martin, J. (2010). The Development of Ideal Body Image Perceptions in the United States. *Nutrition Today, 45*, 98-110. DOI:10.1097/NT.0b013e3181dec6a2

Martin, N. (2015). Pursuit of curves ends tragically for woman at Deep Ellum salon. Retrieved from http://www.dallasnews.com/news/crime/headlines/20150319-pursuit-of-curves-ends-tragically-for-woman-at-deepellum-salon.ece

Mastamet-Mason, A. (2014). The Saartjie Baartman's Body Shape versus the Victorian Dress: The Untold African Treasures. *Open Journal of Social Sciences, 2*(8).

Mayo Clinic. (2018). Bulimia Nervosa. Retrieved from https://www.mayoclinic.org/diseases-conditions/bulimia/symptoms-causes/syc-20353615

McClure, S. M. (2012). Body Image among African Americans. In T. Cash (Ed.), *Encyclopedia of Body Image and Human Appearance* (pp. 89-94). Oxford: Academic Press.

Murnen, S., & Don, B. (2012). Body Image and Gender Roles. In (Vol. 1, pp. pp. 128-134).

National Eating Disorders Association. (2018a). Binge Eating Disorder. Retrieved from https://www.nationaleatingdisorders.org/learn/by-eating-disorder/bed

National Eating Disorders Association. (2018b). People of Color and Eating Disorders. Retrieved from https://www.nationaleatingdisorders.org/people-color-and-eating-disorders

Ogden, C. L., Carroll, M. D., Fryar, C. D., & Flegal, K. M. (2015). Prevalence of Obesity Among Adults and Youth: United States, 2011-2014. NCHS *Data Brief*(219), 1-8.

Oney, C., Cole, E., & Sellers, R. (2011). Racial Identity and Gender as Moderators of the Relationship Between Body Image and Self-esteem for African Americans. *Sex Roles, 65*(7-8), 619-631. DOI:10.1007/s11199-011-9962-z

Overstreet, N., Quinn, D., & Agocha, V. (2010). Beyond Thinness: The Influence of a Curvaceous Body

Ideal on Body Dissatisfaction in Black and White Women. *Sex Roles, 63*(1-2), 91-103. DOI:10.1007/s11199-010-9792-4

Patton, T. O. (2006). Hey Girl, Am I More than My Hair?: African American Women and Their Struggles with Beauty, Body Image, and Hair. *NWSA Journal, 18*(2), 24-51. Retrieved from www.jstor.org/stable/4317206

Perkins, R. M. (2014). The Influence of Colorism and Hair Texture Bias on the Professional and Social Lives of Black Women Student Affairs Professionals. *Louisiana State University Digital Commons.*

Poran, M. A. (2006). The Politics of Protection: Body Image, Social Pressures, and the Misrepresentation of Young Black Women. *Sex Roles, 55*(11), 739-755. DOI:10.1007/s11199-006-9129-5

Prichard, I., Kavanagh, E., Mulgrew, K. E., Lim, M. S. C., & Tiggemann, M. (2020). The effect of Instagram #fitspiration images on young women's mood, body image, and exercise behaviour. *Body Image, 33*, 1-6. DOI:https://doi.org/10.1016/j.bodyim.2020.02.002

Rodin, J., Silberstein, L., & Striegel-Moore, R. (1984). Women and weight: A normative discontent. *Nebraska Symposium on Motivation, 32*, 267-307.

Rogers Wood, N. A., & Petrie, T. A. (2010). Body dissatisfaction, ethnic identity, and disordered eating among African American women. *J Couns Psychol, 57*(2), 141-153. DOI:10.1037/a0018922

Sabik, N. J., Cole, E. R., & Ward, L. M. (2010). Are All Minority Women Equally Buffered from Negative Body Image? Intra-Ethnic Moderators of the Buffering Hypothesis. *Psychology of Women Quarterly, 34*(2), 139-151. DOI:10.1111/j.1471-6402.2010.01557.x

Sagoe, D., Pallesen, S., Dlova, N. C., Lartey, M., Ezzedine, K., & Dadzie, O. (2019). The global prevalence and correlates of skin bleaching: a meta-analysis and meta-regression analysis. *Int J Dermatol, 58*(1), 24-44. DOI:10.1111/ijd.14052

Schooler, D., Ward, L. M., Merriwether, A., & Caruthers, A. (2004). Who's that Girl: Television's Role in the Body Image Development of Young White and Black Women. *Psychology of Women Quarterly, 28*(1), 38-47. DOI:10.1111/j.1471-6402.2004.00121.x

Singh, M., Parsekar, S., & Bhumika, T. (2016). Body Image, Eating Disorders and Role of Media among Indian Adolescents. *J. Indian Assoc. Child Adolesc. Mental. Health, 12*, 9-35.

Slater, A., Varsani, N., & Diedrichs, P. C. (2017). #fitspo or #loveyourself? The impact of fitspiration and self-compassion Instagram images on women's body image, self-compassion, and mood. *Body Image, 22*, 87-96. DOI:https://doi.org/10.1016/j.bodyim.2017.06.004

Slatton, B. (2015). *Mythologizing Black Women: Unveiling White Men's Racist Deep Frame on Race and Gender:* Routledge.

Smolak, L., Striegel-Moore, R. H., & Levine, M. P. (2013). *The Developmental Psychopathology of Eating Disorders: Implications for Research, Prevention, and Treatment:* Taylor & Francis.

Sparks, E. (1999). Against All Odds: Resistance and Resilience in African American Welfare Mothers.

Stanton, A. G., Jerald, M. C., Ward, L. M., & Avery, L. R. (2017). Social Media Contributions to Strong Black Woman Ideal Endorsement and Black Women's Mental Health. *Psychology of Women Quarterly, 41*(4), 465-478. DOI:10.1177/0361684317732330

Stephens, D., & Thomas, T. L. (2012). The Influence of Skin Color on Heterosexual Black College Women's Dating Beliefs. *Journal of feminist family therapy, 24*(4), 291-315. DOI:10.1080/08952833.2012.710815

Taylor, J. Y., Caldwell, C. H., Baser, R. E., Faison, N., & Jackson, J. S. (2007). Prevalence of eating disorders among Blacks in the National Survey of American Life. *Int J Eat Disord, 40 Suppl*, S10-14. DOI:10.1002/eat.20451

Thomas, V. G. (2004). The Psychology of Black Women: Studying Women's Lives in Context. *Journal of Black Psychology, 30*(3), 286-306. DOI:10.1177/0095798404266044

Thompson, C. (2009). Black Women, Beauty, and Hair as a Matter of Being. *Women's Studies, 38*(8), 831-856. DOI:10.1080/00497870903238463

Uhlmann, L. R., Donovan, C. L., Zimmer-Gembeck, M. J., Bell, H. S., & Ramme, R. A. (2018). The fit beauty ideal: A healthy alternative to thinness or a wolf in sheep's clothing? *Body Image, 25*, 23-30. DOI:https://doi.org/10.1016/j.bodyim.2018.01.005

Vartanian, L. R. (2010). Disgust and perceived control in attitudes toward obese people. International *Journal of Obesity, 34*(8), 1302-1307. DOI:10.1038/ijo.2010.45

Waldron, I. (2019). Archetypes of Black Womanhood: Implications for Mental Health, Coping, and Help-Seeking. In *Culture, Diversity and Mental Health - Enhancing Clinical Practice* (pp. 21-38).

Walker, C., Krumhuber, E., Dayan, S., & Furnham, A. (2019). Effects of social media use on desire for cosmetic surgery among young women. *Current Psychology.*

Watson, L. B., Ancis, J. R., White, D. N., & Nazari, N. (2013). Racial identity buffers African American women from body image problems and disordered eating. *Psychology of Women Quarterly, 37*(3), 337-350. DOI:10.1177/0361684312474799

Watson, L. B., Lewis, J. A., & Moody, A. T. (2019). A sociocultural examination of body image among Black women. *Body Image, 31*, 280-287. DOI:10.1016/j.bodyim.2019.03.008

CHAPTER 14.

Black Women's Hair Complexities: Cultural and Psychological Implications of Hairstyle Choices

Terra L. Bowen-Reid, Brittany M. Williams, and Shannon N. Smith,
Morgan State University;
Kevin Washington, Grambling State University

In chapter 12, Afiya Mangum Mbilishaka focused on the prejudicial treatment of Black women based on their hair texture. This chapter will continue that investigation by addressing the role of Black women's hair as a social construct related to racial identity. Throughout history and in contemporary times, Black/African American women have faced considerable harsh societal pressures and negative racial stereotypes toward their appearance. The beauty standards of Black women have been traditionally evaluated from a Eurocentric normative cultural frame of reference that is predicated on colorism (Goff, Thomas, & Jackson, 2008; Olney, Cole & Sellers, 2011; Robinson, 2011). Alice Walker (1983) first penned the term colorism in her book, *In Search of Our Mothers' Gardens: Womanist Prose.* Walker defines colorism as the "prejudicial or preferential treatment of people of same-race people based solely on their color." The diversity of skin complexions in the United States and around the world, the predominant within-group and between-group preference, has been lighter skin tone over darker. Although skin tone is the most frequently used criterion, colorism extends beyond the conceptual definition advanced by Walker. Colorism also embodies other phenotypic characteristics, such as hair texture and facial features that manifest in similar kinds of prejudicial treatment (Zhang, 2017).

For Black people, skin color and hair operate as major determinants of social outcomes (Branigan, Wilderman, Freese, et al., 2017). Prior research shows that African Americans with lighter skin complexion and European features (e.g., wavy or straight hair, keen facial features) are associated with higher states of self-worth, intelligence, financial success, attractiveness, and social privileges (e.g., Bankhead & Johnson, 2014; Coard, Breland, & Raskin, 2001; Harvey, LaBeach, Pridgen, Gocial, 2005; Hill, 2002;

Neal & Wilson, 1989; Okazawa-Rey, Robinson, & Ward, 1987; Thompson & Keith, 2001). Contrastingly, Blacks with more Afrocentric features (e.g., darker skin, kinky hair, broader facial features) have carried a greater burden of disadvantages (Bellinger, 2007; Branigan et al., 2017; Guthrie, 1998; Neal & Wilson, 1989; Patton, 2006).

The hegemonic dynamics of women of African descent aesthetics have a longstanding pejorative history within mainstream and scientific communities (Bellinger, 2007; Guthrie, 1998; Patton, 2006). Past studies suggest that Black women are not oblivious to the dominant culture's perceptions of their appearance (Awad et al., 2015; James, Phelps, & Bross, 2001; McGill-Johnson et al., 2017). Black hair in particular has played a pivotal role in shaping the identity of African American women (Coard, Breland, & Raskin, 2001; Hill, 2002; Johnson & Bankhead, 2014; Snider & Rosenberg, 2006; Thompson & Keith, 2001). The complexity of Black women's hair is steeped in historical and sociocultural experiences. It is the one physical feature that is most transformative of colorism. Given the social preference for Eurocentric standards of beauty, Black women commonly feel societal pressure to change or alter their natural hair. Natural hair is defined by the hair texture at birth, which is unaltered by chemical hair straighteners (for example, perms, relaxers, texturizers) or other artificial augmentation (for example, hair extensions, weaves, wigs, or hair dyes). For African American women today, choosing to wear their hair natural is more than a personal attribute or personality style. It provides a mechanism for understanding the way African American women define their identity and navigate their experiences in the world (Jacobs-Huey, 2006). The current article further addresses the research gap in the literature by presenting an empirical study that focuses on the psychological complexities of Black women's hair style choices.

Historical Context of Black Women's Hair

Hair is an important physical attribute for all people regardless of gender or race. For black women in particular, hair texture and hairstyle choices are beset with a myriad of political, psychological, physical, and social implications. The obsession with Black hair is not new. The salient role of hair in Black women is deeply rooted and manifested in their experienced historical-cultural reality (Johnson & Bankhead, 2014; Patton, 2006; Versey, 2014). In ancient African civilization, hair denoted various markers of a person's status, identity, religion, and cultural traditions. For example, in Ancient Egypt, hairstyles were symbolic of power, as reflected in their social and political status (Jahangir, 2015). Historical records further document that a discourse about skin color and hair predates Grecian civilizations. Images of people of various complexions are found in the Medu Neter or hieroglyphics (Diop, 1989; Guthrie, 1998). Herodotus, who is credited with being the Father of History among the Greeks, is recorded as commenting on the Black skin and wooly hair of Egypt (Kemet) inhabitants (Bernal, 1996; Diop, 1989). Although there is no indication that the Greeks placed a value on such phenotypical differences, there is evidence of references to physical characteristics. It was common practice for the Greco-Romans to describe persons of darker hue as *melanchroes*, which mean "dark/Black-skinned" and their hair texture as *oulotriches*, which translates to wooly (Bernal, 1996; Merenptah, 2018).

During the rise of European empiricism, we begin to see a more prominent emergence of valuation on certain physical features. The colonization era led to concerted objectification and vilification of enslaved African women's appearance. The practice of skin color and hair texture biases became an integrative part of the European slave trade, as social strata for race identification, worth, intelligence, and attractiveness (Guthrie, 1998). Upon arrival in the Americas, constant assaults were made about enslaved Africans' physical characteristics. Before the slavery era, many foreigners studied in the temples of Kemet and learned the lifestyles of Africans. Europeans clearly understood the complex magnitude and significance of Black hair. The hair of enslaved Africans was strategically targeted as a mechanism to strip Africans of their identity, dignity, self-worth, and cultural traditions. Systematic efforts were implemented to dehumanize and oppress the African spirit (Johnson & Bankhead, 2014). The plantation master routinely expressed disdain toward the hair of enslaved African women and their descendants by engaging in denigrating practices (Ellis-Hervey et al., 2016). Enslaved Africans were ridiculed to feel ashamed of their hair. Nappy hair is the derogatory term first used by plantation owners to describe the tightly coiled and kinky hair texture of enslaved Africans. Given plantation owners' abhorrence of "nappy hair," head shaving was used as a form of punishment. Head coverings, known as "head rags", "head scarves," or "head handkerchiefs" were also imposed by the slave master to hide the "unsightly" nature of enslaved African women and girls' hair. Later head wraps evolved into a paradox of meaning steering away from their original purpose of servitude to a fashionable style of anti-White resistance (Griebel, 1995).

Hair texture was one of the distinguishing features used to categorized enslaved African women. Miscegenation between enslaved African women and their White slave masters often produced hair textures resembling European features. Enslaved

Africans possessing features similar to the White slave master were deemed a higher commodity compared to those with indigenous African features (for example, darker skin, kinky hair, broader nose, thick lips, and so on). The preference in hair textures from tightly coiled or kinky to looser coils, wavy, or straight became symbolic of "good hair." Modern depictions of good hair is classified by the 2-3a hair type, which is partially straight to wavy hair, and easy to comb. Enslaved African women with good hair received favorable treatment for styling their hair in ways similar to White women. Good hair was viewed as more attractive, civilized, and well-adjusted (Guthrie, 1998; Jacobs-Huey, 2006; Manning, 2010; Neal & Wilson, 1989). Conversely, indigenous African features with tightly coiled or kinky natural hair textures were classified as "bad hair," less attractive, unruly, and barbaric (Guthrie, 1998; Manning, 2010; Neal & Wilson, 1989). The favoring of Eurocentric features created not only a physical divisiveness between enslaved Africans, but a form of mental oppression for generations to come.

Although the abolishment of slavery ended over 150 years ago, the negative connotations against Black hair from mainstream America and intragroup members still exist (Johnson & Bankhead, 2014; Rosette & Dumas, 2007; Snider & Rosenberg, 2006). The psychological indoctrination of what constitutes "good" and "bad" hair has remained a continuous narrative. Many social societies established in the 1900s used hair texture to determine membership. Straight or wavy hair became a prerequisite for admission into certain schools, social groups, and professions. For example, the comb test was used for membership intake into elite social organizations (Johnson & Bankhead, 2014). Prospective candidates were granted membership based upon their hair texture passing smoothly through the comb (Neal & Wilson 1989; Okazawa-Rey, Robinson, &Ward, 1987). Since those times, Black women with tightly coiled or kinky hair have often resorted to using straightening methods (for example, chemical relaxers/perms, hair press, Dominican blowout), wigs, weaves, and extensions to achieve the European standard of "good hair."

Historically, hair alterations were mainly done to fit in with the dominant mainstream culture. In the late 1800s, Sarah Breedlove, also known as Madame C.J. Walker, and Anna Turbo Malone, were responsible for revolutionizing the Black hair industry (Johnson & Bankhead, 2014; Obokohwho & Budznski, 2012). Both ladies helped catapult the Black hair movement with their haircare products and hair straightening methods. Each focused on hair products and techniques designed to emulate Western standards of beauty. The Black hair industry continued to burgeon into developing other hair products, which included permanent hair straighteners or chemical relaxers. Garrett Augustus Morgan, Sr. is credited for inventing the first hair straightening prototype in 1909 (Obokowho & Budzynski, 2012). Morgan serendipitously discovered that alkaline chemicals used to repair sewing machines could also straighten out kinky hair. Over the years, Morgan's initial hair relaxer formula has been tweaked. In 1971, the first lye was commercially produced by Pro-Line (Obokowho & Budzynski, 2012). Chemical hair relaxers, also known as perms or texturizers, are used to straightening the tightly coiled or kinky curl pattern. Consequently, hazardous ingredients have been identified in relaxers. Studies have shown that the application of relaxers can lead to the breakdown of the hair structure, and can cause permanent scalp damage, chemical burns, hair brittleness, breakage, or alopecia (see Shetty, Shetty & Nair, 2013).

Black haircare products and maintenance have evolved into a lucrative and profitable industry. Mintel's (2015) research shows that "nearly two in five (38%) Black consumers report that they are constantly looking for ways to improve their appearance." To achieve that ideal look, Black women are investing a tremendous amount of money into their aesthetics. According to a recent Nielson (2018) report, Black women spend on average nearly nine times more money than their non-Black counterparts on hair and beauty products. Annually, Black women spend over $2.7 billion on beauty with at least $473 million in haircare, $127 million in grooming aids, and $465 million in skincare preparations (Mintel, 2015). In recent years, sales of chemical hair relaxers have significantly dropped to reflect the growing shift in Black women's preference for natural hair.

Similar to those in the Civil Rights era of the 1960s, today's Black women are embracing their natural hair texture more and more. The motivation, however, for this generation is different than that of earlier generations. During the time of the Black Power Movement, natural hair was seen as a political statement of resistance to Europeans' standard of beauty (Rosette & Dumas, 2007). Today, hairstyle choice is a personal preference. Popular social media outlets, blogs, commentaries and qualitative data provide ample anecdotal evidence of the mixed perceptions toward Black hair (Hill, 2002; Lester, 2000; Patton, 2006; Rosette & Dumas, 2007; Williams, 2015). Recent evidence shows that there is still bias against the types of hairstyles worn by Blacks. McGill-Johnson and colleagues (2017) found that relaxed hairstyles are perceived as more attractive and professional among both White and Black women. Consequently, African American women that choose to wear their hair relaxed may experience greater adverse health outcomes (Eberle et al., 2019; Hall et al., 2013; Llanos et al., 2017; Rosette & Dumas, 2007; Versey, 2014). Studies have shown that Black hair products contain more toxic chemicals than those marketed to other ethnic groups. One study in more 23,000 African American women found an association between hair relaxer use and uterine leiomyomata (Wise, Palmer, Reich et al., 2012). More recent research found that hair dye and chemical straighteners may place Black women at greater risk for breast cancer (Eberle et al., 2019).

African American Women's Hair and Self-Concept

In further understanding the implications of Black women's hair, it is important to consider the paradigm that is used to define the cultural reality of African Americans. In many regards, hair represents a social construct that is connected to the racial identity development of Black women (Byrd & Tharps, 2001; Johnson & Bankhead, 2014; Manning, 2010). Perceptions of Black women's hair can generate an inferiority complex, self-consciousness, and social anxiety in those targeted (McGill-Johnson et al., 2017). African American women have continuously struggled with the power to define their unique identity outside of mainstream standards of beauty (Patton, 2006), while negotiating their identity in a country that "idealizes the physical characteristics of White women" (Greene, 1994, p. 18). Jacobs-Huey (2006) asserts that hair provides a mechanism for understanding the way African American women experience the world. For African American women, hair is not only a matter of style or preference; it symbolizes an important aspect of their identity and social acceptance (Patton, 2006: Rosette & Dumas, 2007). In many regards, hair represents a social construct that is fundamentally connected to who they are.

Racial identity has long been studied among African Americans. Racial identity development is very complex and multifaceted. African American identity research scholars argue that African Americans are forced to develop multiple "selves" (see Cross, Parham, & Helms, 1998; Du Bois, 1903; Kambon, 2012; Sellers et al., 1998, 2003). Over a century ago, W.E.B. Du Bois (1903) articulated this schism in his conceptualization of a "double consciousness." Du Bois refers to the dual identities of African Americans as two warring souls that are partially imposed by living between an indigenous African heritage and the other adaptive self in America. Double consciousness also delineates the quandary Black women experience in determining their choice to wear natural or unnatural/altered hairstyles. At the core of this decision are the cultural norms used to define their identity—personality, social status, economic opportunities, and advancements.

Ironically, the aesthetics of Black women have been most paradoxical in that they have been despised and admired by Europeans. Josephine Baker's performance of the Black female body on the Paris stage in the 1920s and 1930s is one example of the admiration and objectification of the Black female body and sexuality (Ruiz, 2012; Syska, 2006). George Cuvier, professor of comparative anatomy at the Natural Museum in Paris in the early 1800s studied Saartjie Baartman, known as the "Venus Hottentot." Baartman was sexually objectified for her enlarged buttocks. She had been on display in London prior to Curvier's research. She was seen as exotic, as well as viewed in disgust in Europe (Werbanows, 2012). Her buttocks inspired the modification of the bustle dress in Europe. Not only were these men attracted to the bodies of these women, but they acknowledged the hair of both Baker (straightened hair) and Baartman (peppercorn/kinky). This has been a contributing factor in the identity formation of African American women within the United States and throughout the African Diaspora.

Implications of Hairstyle Choices on Black Women's Psychological Well-Being

The authentic voice of Black women has been limited with respect to the Black/African perception of beauty. The perceptions of Black beauty, especially as it relates to black hair, have been critical. The "good" and "bad" labels placed on the various textures and styles of Black women's hair carry different political and psychological connotations than those of other ethnicities (Patton, 2006). For White women, bad hair may simply mean a lack of style, physical damage, or unkemptness, whereas with Black women, bad hair carries a plethora of meanings that imply an inherent deficit. If you talk to any Black woman, she has a "hair story" that undergirds the saga she commonly faces—whether it is the snarky comments, glaring stares, or the hassle to manage, style, or maintain her hair.

Although ample anecdotal evidence exists, previous research has not adequately addressed the psychological impact associated with African American women who have to "choose between hairstyles that conform to the norms and expectations of their White colleagues or hairstyles that are central to their African American, African, Caribbean, or other racial or ethnic identities" (Rosette & Dumas, 2007, p. 410). Over the years, indigenous African hair texture (tightly coiled/kinky) has been least preferred. The devaluation of natural hair and other features of Blackness can lead to demoralizing feelings of inferiority and social stratification. Black women who wear their hair in its natural texture are commonly viewed in certain settings as "lower class", "not good enough," or a "badge of shame" (Bellinger, 2007; Byrd & Tate, 2007; Tharps, 2001). For example, in 2007 radio personality Don Imus, sparked outraged in the public sector with his inflammatory racial remarks that referenced the Rutgers University Black women's basketball team players as "nappy-headed hos" (Faber, 2007). Unfortunately, not much has changed since then with the virulent attacks against Black hair. In 2019, a Black male Texas high school senior was barred from school until he cut his dreadlocks. Another high school student was forced to shear his dreadlocks during a wrestling match or risk being disqualified. Such incidents reinforce the eccentric attacks toward Black hair types.

Racist sentiments and institutional discrimination based on Blacks' hairstyles have long existed in the United States. Adorning natural hairstyles have continuously led to discriminatory practices. For years, these complaints were deemed unwarranted or frivolous. To date, three states, California, New York, Colorado, and others to follow, have advanced bills to ban hair discrimination. The CROWN Act, which stands for "Creating a Respectful and Open World for Natural Hair," is part of a national effort to protect against hair style choices and textures of Black people. This is particularly important given the negative appraisals and source of stress generated from internal conflict associated with other's perceptions of their hairstyle choices (Rosette & Dumas, 2007).

Having to deal with demoralizing and microaggressive comments about one's hair can eventually take a toll on Black women's self-esteem. Self-esteem is influenced through social comparisons formulated between the personal self and others. It is also impacted by others' opinions toward themselves, which include appraisals, compliments, and rewards (Thompson & Keith, 2001). According to Thompson and Keith (2001), the self-evaluation theory emphasizes the importance of consonant environmental context for personal comparisons. Consonant environmental context is defined as the appraisal of significant others to affirm one's self-identity. In other words, Blacks will systematically compare themselves with other Blacks in their community. For example, during the Civil Rights era kinky hairstyles and darker skin complexions were viewed as acceptable among African American people (Hill, 2002). Mainstream sectors however, advance images to emulate European standards of beauty. Consequently, African American women are faced with the challenge of redefining Black beauty and self-identity from a vantage point that transcend historical biases.

Present Study

Redefining Black women's aesthetics from an indigenous cultural reality perspective has affirmative psychological and physical implications (Capodilupo, 2014). Internalizing stereotypical messages about Black hair may be particularly damaging for marginalized groups that can perniciously impact significant aspects of their identities and psychological well-being (Davies, Spencer, & Steele, 2005). Given the predominant Eurocentric standard of beauty, more research is warranted that explores the internalization of mainstream messages on Black women's hairstyle choices and psychological well-being. Yap, Settles, and Pratt-Hyatt's (2011) research is one of few studies that have specifically investigated happiness among African Americans. The researchers found that African Americans who identify more strongly with their racial identity are generally happier. Scientific evidence supports many positive benefits to happiness and health. Consequently, past research has not explored the relationship between happiness and the psychological strain emanating from the stereotypical perceptions of Black hair (Capodilupo, 2014).

Although extensive research has been conducted on perceptions of beauty among women, limited empirical evidence exists that focuses on the valuation experienced by Black women's hairstyle choices. Research in this area is particularly salient for college-aged African American women, who are at a developmental stage in establishing their professional identity. By studying this demographic, important insight may be gained in understanding how post-adolescent African American women negotiate their identity in environments that either promote or demoralize their hairstyle choices. More specifically, this study seeks to augment the paucity of scientific research that focuses on the psychological factors undergirding hairstyle choices among Black women attending a historically Black college or university (HBCU). Students at HBCUs come from diverse backgrounds, and in many instances represent a microcosm of their communities. HBCUs also offer an affirmative environment for young people to explore and develop their racial identity.

We explored the following research questions: What are the dominant hairstyle choices of Black women worn at an HBCU? To what extent are Black women's hairstyle choices (relaxed, natural/no chemical straightener) related to their perceptions of racial identity and psychological well-being (as measured by hair esteem, social anxiety, and happiness?

Empirical Evidence

One hundred sixty-six undergraduate female students (mean age 20.02) that self-identified as African American (92%) were recruited from an HBCU in the mid-Atlantic region of the United States. Participants took part in a cross-sectional design study that assessed evaluative psychosocial determinants of their hairstyle choices.

At one point, the majority of the sample (88%) had permed or chemically straightened their natural hair. Only 12% of the respondents indicated that they had never used a hair relaxer/chemical straightener on their hair. The current findings reflect the growing trend of Black women that have transitioned to wearing their hair natural. Sixty percent of the current respondents reported natural hair texture, as defined by no chemical straightener/relaxed permed hair. About 39% of the respondents indicated that they felt pressured to wear their hair a certain way, and that "having straight/wavy hair makes you more attractive." Overall, most of the African American women in the study (73%) indicated that they were happy with their hair.

Perception of Hair and Hairstyle Choices as a Function of Racial Identity and Psychological Well-Being

Pearson's correlations were employed to explore the relationships between perceptions of hair, racial identity, and psychological well-being (self-esteem and social anxiety). Table 1 displays the means, standard deviations, Cronbach's alphas and correlation coefficients for the dependent variables (hair perceptions, racial identity, and psychological well-being). Participants endorsing higher mainstream perceptions of hair reported significantly lower levels of racial identity and ethnic belonging, $r=-.318$, $p<.01$ and $r=-.230$, $p<.01$, respectively; lower levels of happiness, $r=-.192$, $p<.05$; and greater social anxiety/fears of negative evaluation, $r=.419$, $p<.01$). Stronger racial identity was positively associated with happiness and less social anxiety/fears of negative evaluations.

A 2x3 MANOVA was conducted to determine the interaction effect of skin color and hairstyle choice on the racial identity and psychological well-being dependent variables. Table 2 provides the descriptive statistics of the means and standard deviations of the dependent variables by skin tone and hairstyle choice groups.

Table 3 displays the MANOVA and univariate analysis of variance (ANOVA) comparing the mean group differences. There was no significant main effect for skin tone, nor interaction effects of skin color and hairstyle choice on the dependent variables. Significant main effects were found between the two hair texture groups

Table 1.
Intercorrelation Coefficients and Descriptive Statistics for Perceived Hair Attractiveness, Racial Identity and Psychological Well-Being

Variables	M (SD)	Range	Cronbach's Alpha	2	3	4	5
1. Mainstream Perception of Hair	16.46 (6.54)	6-30	.734	-.318**	-.230**	-.192*	.419**
2. MEIM: Overall Ethnic Identity	15.09 (4.89)	5-60	.746		.878**	.377**	-.405**
3. MEIM: Belonging	13.26 (5.18)	4-56	.679			.282**	-.342**
4. Happiness	24.20 (4.61)	4-28	.821				-.470**
5. Social Anxiety	33.30 (11.66)	12-60	.932				

Table 2.

Mean Scores and Standard Deviations for Measures of Perceived Attractiveness, Racial Identity, and Psychological Well-Being as a Function of Skin Tone and Hairstyle Choice

	Hair		Racial Identity				Psychological Well-Being			
	Mainstream Hair Perceptions		Overall MEIM		Ethnic Identity Belonging		Happiness		Fear of Negative Evaluation	
	M	SD	M	SD	M	SD	M	SD	M	SD
Skin Tone										
Very/Somewhat Light	25.82	5.62	36.44	7.66	12.53	2.60	19.41	5.11	36.23	10.73
Medium Brown	23.85	6.45	39.62	8.29	13.72	4.70	21.57	4.92	31.47	11.38
Very/Somewhat Dark	24.22	7.45	37.36	11.99	13.17	7.51	19.50	5.52	33.43	12.85
Hairstyle Choice										
Natural	23.22	6.73	39.62	9.84	14.07	6.29	20.50	5.42	31.88	11.62
Chemical Relaxer	25.72	6.37	35.98	8.15	12.02	2.79	20.37	4.78	36.03	11.40

(natural, chemically straightened/relaxed) on the dependent measures, Wilk's Λ=2.926, F (5, 125), $p<.05$. ANOVA on the dependent variables were conducted as follow-up tests to the MANOVA. Respondents with natural hair reported significantly higher overall racial identity scores, $F(1, 129)=6.856$, $p<.01$, and feelings of belongingness to their ethnic group, $F(1, 129)=5.637$, $p<.01$, compared to the women with chemically straighten/relaxed hair. Contrastingly, respondents with chemically straighten/relaxed hair endorsed more mainstream perceptions of hair, $F(1,29)=8.070$, $p<.01$; and indicated greater fears of negative evaluation, F (1, 129)=6.693, $p<.01$, than the women with

Table 3.

Multivariate and Univariate Analyses of Variance for Skin Tone x Hairstyle Choice Effects on Measures of Perceived Hair Attractiveness, Racial Identity, and Psychological Well-Being

		ANOVA				
		Hair	Racial Identity		Psychological Well-Being	
	MANOVA	Mainstream Hair Perceptions	Overall MEIM	Ethnic Belonging	Happiness	Fear of Negative Evaluation
Variable	$F (5, 125)$	$F (1, 129)$	$F(1, 129)$	$F(1, 129)$	$F(1, 129)$	$F(1, 129)$
Skin Tone (S)	.837	1.594	1.677	.478	2.365	2.189
Hairstyle Choice (H)	2.926*	8.070**	6.856**	5.637*	.095	6.693**
S x H	.481	.470	.245	.049	.189	.943

Note. F ratios are Wilks'Lambda approximation of Fs. MANOVA = multivariate analysis of variance; ANOVA = univariate analysis of variance

$*p<.05. **p<.01$

natural hair.

Discussion

This article expands upon the paucity of research that evaluates the hairstyle choices of young Black women. The current study findings shed critical insight on the cultural and psychological implications of hairstyle choices. Throughout history, the dominant hairstyle preference has embodied Eurocentric features of straight or wavy/curly hair texture. This generation of young Black women is shifting away from mainstream standards of beauty that have typically viewed natural hair as unattractive and unprofessional. Although many Black women still feel pressure to wear their hair a certain way, the majority of the respondents in this study reported hair texture in its natural state (unaltered by chemical relaxers). Young Black women wearing their hair in its natural state represent a growing trend around the world. There were however, discriminative in-group differences between African American women that wear their hair natural compared to those that relaxed or chemically straightened their hair. Implications of the findings are discussed from a theoretical perspective that debunks the hegemonic views held by mainstream society (Johnson & Bankhead, 2014; Patton, 2006; Rosette & Dumas, 2007).

Implications of Hairstyle Choices

Limited research has focused on the self-valuation Black women have of their hair.

Past research on African American women's aesthetics has predominantly focused on the implications of skin color (Coard, Breland, & Raskin, 2001; Harvey, LaBeach, Pridgen, Gocial, 2005; Hill, 2002; Neal & Wilson, 1989; Okazawa-Rey, Robinson, & Ward, 1987; Sellers, 2003; Thompson & Keith, 2001). The current study looks at the intersection of skin tone and hair. Subsequently, skin tone did not emerge as a significant social determinant. There were no significant main or interactive effects found for skin tone on the racial identity and psychological well-being variables. Many young African American women are embracing their skin color, as evident in cultural pride slogans: #BlackisBeautiful, #BlackGirlsRock, or #MelaninPoppin. In this investigation, hair emerged as a viable construct for understanding the psychosocial dynamics of Black women. Particularly, the current findings suggest that Black women's hairstyle choices may play a more salient role than skin tone. While intragroup skin color bias may seemingly be diminishing and an underlying push for colorblindness, colorism remains the "pink elephant" in the room. The onslaught of innocent young Blacks killed by police officers and public citizens suggests that skin color matters. Blacks are continuously treated differently based on the color of their skin.

Consistent with past research, the findings of this investigation support that Black women are cognizant of mainstream perceptions of their hair (Awad et al., 2014). Ellis-Hervey and colleagues (2016) found that "African American women who wear their hair in a natural state may be less inclined to worry about how others perceive and compare them with European standards of beauty" (p. 879). Mainstream perceptions of hair were negatively associated with racial identity and psychological well-being. African American women that embraced mainstream hair standards showed less allegiance to their racial group. Prior research has shown that Black women that wear their hair naturally generally report feeling better about themselves (Johnson & Bankhead, 2014). Similar findings emerged whereby the Black women in the current study that indicated wearing their hair in its natural state were more likely to have stronger racial identity, less social anxiety (fears of others negatively evaluating them), and greater levels of happiness. Contrastingly, those Black women who adopted Eurocentric hairstyles (chemically relaxed) reported significantly lower levels of happiness, greater fears of being negatively evaluated by others, and more often attributed their attractiveness to hair. Given some Black women's internal need to measure up to social norms valued within mainstream society, the findings suggest it may come at a psychological risk of distress. Future studies should incorporate causal research designs to further explore this implication. Such investigations would help determine the direct effects of hairstyle choices on psychological and social outcomes.

Although chemically relaxed hair texture or Eurocentric styles are still valued in today's society, Black women with natural hair in this study displayed a stronger disposition toward happiness than those with chemically relaxed hairstyles. This finding is particularly important given the broader psychological ramifications. Traditionally, African American women adopting natural hairstyles have been portrayed in a pejorative light. Prior theoretical advancements purport that natural hair style choices symbolized cultural pride and political statements to demonstrate a resistant strategy against the Eurocentric normative standard of beauty (Patton, 2006). Many African American women that shift from chemically relaxed hair describe the feeling as "empowering" and "liberating" (Williams, 2015). The findings may also infer that having natural hair is beneficial to Black women's well-being. Accordingly, Black women that embrace their natural hair are experiencing positive mental health outcomes, as an artifact of not living under the duress of conforming to an unrealistic image.

Black women that feel pressured to assimilate to mainstream hegemonic standards could potentially carry insidious health risks (Eberle et al., 2019; Hall et al., 2013; Llanos et al., 2017; McGill-Johnson et al., 2017; Rosette & Dumas, 2007; Versey, 2014). As shown, African American women in this study with chemically relaxed hair indicated greater psychological anomaly and ambivalence about self. These individuals generally feared judgments from others and were more likely to relate their attractiveness to mainstream hairstyles. Almost half of the respondents (39%) in this study felt pressured to wear their hair a certain way. Although African American women that chemically relax their hair will adamantly proclaim that their hairstyle choice is not due to the conformity of Eurocentric aesthetics, the thought of wearing their hair in its natural state tends to invoke unsettling psychological emotions.

A study by Hall and colleagues (2013) further supports the physical risk associated with African American women's hairstyle choices. Of the 123 African American women surveyed in their study, 38% of them avoided exercising because of their hair. Lack of physical activity has been associated with various cardiovascular diseases, obesity, and other health problems. Consequently, some African American women are willing to sacrifice their health in order to maintain the Eurocentric appearance of straight hair. More research is clearly warranted that explores physical and psychological health risks associated with African American women's hairstyle choices.

Study Limitations and Future Implications

Although the current study provides meaningful insight, several limitations must be taken into consideration. First, the current study targeted female students from one historically black college and university (HBCU). It is plausible that the current findings are an artifact of a cultural response set indicative of that environment. Accordingly, these findings may not be generalizable to a broader range of African American women outside of this setting with qualitatively different experiences. For example, past studies have shown that African American students attending HBCUs tend to have a stronger racial identity compared to those African American students at a traditional white institution (Baldwin, Duncan & Bell, 1987). HBCUs foster an environment that cultivates racial pride and cultural identity, which in turn may cause African American women to feel less judgmental about their natural hairstyle choices. Second, the current study did not assess whether those with natural hair (no chemical relaxer) augmented their hair by flat-ironing, pressing, weaves, braids, wigs, or other mainstream looks. Consequently, given the study's cross-sectional design, more research is warranted to determine causal inferences and other factors that influence African American women hairstyle choice. Such choices address the dynamics associated with media, peer, and parental/familial socialization.

Another limitation that should be addressed in future studies is the psychometric properties of the cultural variables. Both the hair and racial identity measures demonstrated moderate to poor internal consistency. The power to operationalize African American aesthetics from a culturally relevant theoretical framework is paramount. African-centered theories provide a viable perspective in representing the cultural reality of African Americans (Kambon & Bowen, Reid, 2009, 2010). African-centered theories challenge hegemonic or egregious assumptions purported of African American women aesthetics. This counter-hegemonic perspective creates a broader range in defining beauty norms among African American women.

Notwithstanding the limitations, the current findings shed light on a controversial topic that forces African Americans to both defend and negotiate their personal identity and well-being. For centuries, the policing of black hair has long been a part of the American culture. Many jobs and academic institutions have incorporated in their corporate grooming policies that target the hairstyles (for example, dreadlocks, Afros, and braids) mainly worn by Blacks. In many instances, Blacks are forced to alter their natural hair to fit into mainstream domains. The way in which African American men and women wear their hair has important implications for how they achieve social and financial success. For example, on March 31, 2014, the United States Army (U.S. Army, 2014) released Army Regulation 670-1: Uniform and Insignia Wear and Appearance of Army Uniforms and Insignia, a guide to help standardized and professionalize soldiers' appearance. The regulations state in section 3-2 of their standards and grooming policies:

(a) Twists. Twists are defined as twisting two distinct strands of hair around one another to create a twisted ropelike appearance. Although some twists may be temporary, and can be easily untwisted, they are unauthorized (except for French twists). This includes twists formed against the scalp or worn in a free-hanging style.

(b) Dreadlocks. Dreadlocks are defined as any matted, twisted, or locked coils or ropes of hair (or extensions). Any style of dreadlock (against the scalp or free-hanging) is not authorized. Braids or cornrows that are unkempt or matted are considered dreadlocks and are not authorized.

The policies as stipulated clearly discriminate against the hairstyles of Black and Brown women. The natural hair of Black women is seen as unprofessional. This negative appraisal can be an extreme source of stress that Black women encounter, thus making their natural hair a barrier for professional advancement and social mobility. Subsequently, in 2017 the U.S. Army lifted the hair ban on dreadlocks and other hairstyles that seemingly targeted African American women (Mele, 2017).

In summary, the current findings support the importance of Black women embracing their natural hair. Black women should not feel demoralized or discriminated against due to their hairstyle choices. Additionally, this line of research should be explored among Black males. Black males are more harshly stereotyped based on their physical features. Although hair straightening is not very prevalent among Black men, many are faced with the hair dilemma of looking too "ethnic" by adopting Afros, braids, or dreadlocks. Prior research has found that Blacks with stereotypical black features (for example, facial hair) are more prone to be associated with crime and violence (Blair, Judd, & Chapleau, 2004; Edwards & Bowen-Reid, 2015). Future research with this population would prove instructive around the dynamics of shame/self-blame, perceived stigma self-esteem, and self-efficacy.

Process Questions and Considerations

1. How has your hairstyle choices contributed to your sense of self and racial identity?
2. How do you currently wear your hair? Do you feel your hairstyle choices play a role your

ability to achieve professional success?

3. Are you more conscious of your hairstyle choice based on your environment?

4. Do you feel comfortable with your appearance based on your hairstyle choice? Does that comfort level change when you are in certain settings, such as in a predominantly white audience?

5. How do the findings of this study impact the valuation you place on your hair or the perceptions of other black hairstyle choices.

References

Awad, G. H., Norwood, C., Taylor, D. S., Martinez, M., McClain, S., Jones, B., Holman, A., Chapman-Hilliard, C. (2014). Beauty and body image concerns among African American college women. *The Journal of Black Psychology, 41*, 540-564.

Baldwin, J. A., Duncan, J. A., & Bell, Y. R. (1987). Assessment of African self-consciousness among black students from two college environments. *Journal of Black Psychology, 13*, 27-41.

Bellinger, W. (2007). Why African American women try to obtain "good hair." *Sociological Viewpoints,* 63-72.

Bernal, M. (1996). Bernal's Blacks and the Afrocentrists. In *Black Athena Revisited*, Mary R. Lefkowitz and Guy MacLean Rogers (Eds.). Chapel Hill: University of North Carolina Press.

Blair, I. V., Judd, C. M., & Chapleau, K. M. (2004). The influence of Afrocentric facial features in criminal sentencing. *Psychological Science, 15*, 674-679. https://doi.org/10.1111/j.0956-7976.2004.00739.x

Capodilupo, C. (2014). One size fits all: Using variables other than the thin ideal to understand black women's body image. *Cultural Diversity and Ethnic Minority Psychology.*

Coard, S., Breland, A. M., & Raskin, P. (2001). Perceptions of and preferences for skin color, black racial identity, and self-esteem among African Americans. *Journal of Applied Social Psychology, 31*, 2256-2274.

Cross, W. E., Parham, T. A., & Helms, J. E. (1998). *Nigrescence revisited: Theory and research.* In R. L. Jones (Ed.), *African American identity development: Theory, research, and intervention.* Hampton, VA: Cobb & Henry.

Davies, P. G., Spencer, S. J., Steele, C. M. (2005). Clearing the air: Identity safety moderates the effects of stereotype threat in women's leadership aspirations. *Journal of Personality and Social Psychology, 88*, 276-287.

Diop, C. A. (1989). The African origin of civilization: Myth or reality? Chicago: Chicago Review Press.

Edwards, E., & Bowen-Reid, T. (2015). Mistaken identity: Intragroup stereotypes of African American males. Unpublished manuscript.

Ellis-Hervey, N., Doss, A., Davis, D., Nicks, R., & Araiza, P. (2016). African American personal presentation: Psychology of hair and self-perception. *Journal of Black Studies, 47.* https://doi.org/10.1177/0021934716653350

Faber, J. (April 12, 2007). "CBS Fires Don Imus Over Racial Slur." CBS News.

Greene, B. (1994). *African American women.* In L. Comas-Diaz & B. Greene (Eds.), *Women of Color: Integrating Ethnic and Gender Identities in Psychotherapy*, pp. 10-29. New York: The Guilford Press.

Grieber, H. B. (1995). The West African origin of the African American headwrap. In J. B. Eicher (Ed.), *Dress and Ethnicity: Change Across Space and Time*, pp. 207-226. https://doi.org/10.2752/9781847881342

Goff, P. A., Thomas, M. A., & Jackson, M. C. (2008). "Ain't I a woman?": Towards an intersectional approach to person perception and group-based harms. *Sex Roles, 59*(5-6), 392-403.

Guthrie, R. (1998). *Even the rat was white: A historical view of psychology.* Harper & Row Publishers.

Hall, R. R., Francis, S., Whitt-Glover, M., Loftin-Bell, K., Sweet, K., & McMichael, A. J. (2013). Hair care practices as a barrier to physical activity. *JAMA Dermatology, 49*, 310-314.

Harvey, R. D., LaBeach, N., Pridgen, E., & Gocial, T. M. (2005). The intragroup stigmatization of skin tone among black Americans. *Journal of Black Psychology, 31*, 237-253.

Hill, E. M. (2002). Skin color and the perception of attractiveness among African Americans: Does gender make a difference? *Social Psychology Quarterly, 65*, 77-91.

Hunter, M. L. (2002). "If you're light, you're alright": Light skin color as social capital for women of color. *Gender & Society, 16*, 175-193.

Johnson, T., & Bankhead, T. (2014). Self-esteem, hair-esteem and black women with natural hair. *International Journal of Education and Social Science, 1*(4), 92-102.

Jacobs-Huey, L. (2006). *From the kitchen to the parlor: Language and African American women's hair Care.* Oxford, England: Oxford Press.

Jahangir, R. (2015). *How does black hair reflect black history?* Retrieved May 4, 2019 from https://www.bbc.com/news/uk-england-merseyside-31438273

James, K. A., Phelps, L., & Bross, A. L. (2001). Body dissatisfaction, drive for thinness, and self-esteem in African American college females. *Psychology in the Schools, 38*(6), 491-496.

Kambon, K. K. (2012). African/black psychology in the American context: an African-centered approach (2nd Ed.). Tallahassee, FL: Nubian Nation Publication.

Kambon, K. K., & Bowen-Reid, T. L. (2010). Theories of African American personality: classification,basic constructs and empirical predictions/assessments. *Journal of Pan African Studies, 8*, 83-108.

Kambon, K. K., & Bowen-Reid, T. L. (2009). Africentric theories of African American personality: basic constructs and assessments. In Neville, H.A., Tynes, B. M., & Utsey, S. O., *Handbook of African American Psychology* (pp. 61-73). Thousand Oaks, CA: SAGE.

Lester, N. A. (2000). Nappy edges and goldy locks: African American daughters and the politics of hair. *The Lion and the Unicorn, 24*, 201-224.

Manning, J. (2010). The sociology of hair: Hair symbolism among college students. *Social Sciences Journal, 10*, 35-48.

Massey, D., & Owens, J. (2014). Mediators of stereotype threat among black college students. *Ethnic and Racial Issues,* 557-575.

McGill Johnson, A., Godsil, R. D., MacFarlane, J., Tropp, L. R., & Atiba Goff, P. (2017). The good hair study: Explicit and implicit attitudes toward black women's hair. Perception Institute. Retrieved from www.goodhairstudy.com.

Mele, C. (2017) Army lifts ban on dreadlocks and Black servicewomen rejoice. Retrieved from https://www.nytimes.com/2017/02/10/us/army-ban-on-dreadlocks-black-servicewomen.html

Mintel Group, Ltd. (2015). Mintel Reports-Mintel Group Ltd. Academic.mintel.com [online] Available at: https://academic.mintel.com [Accessed 17 May 2020].

Neal, A., & Wilson, M. (1989). The role of skin color and features in the black community: Implications for black women in therapy. *Clinical Psychology Review, 9*, 323-332.

Obokowho, P., & Budzynski, B. W. (2012). *Hair relaxers: Science, design, & application.* Carol Stream, IL: Allured Books.

Okazawa-Rey, M., Robinson, T., & Ward, J. V. (1987). Black women and the politics of skin color an hair. *Women and Therapy, 6*, 89-102.

Patton, T. (2006). Hey girl am I more than my hair?: African American women and their struggles with beauty, body image and hair. *NWSA Journal, 18*, 24-51.

Robinson, C. L. (2011). Hair as race: Why "good hair" may be bad for black females. *The Howard Journal of Communications 22*, 358-376.

Rosette, A. S., & Dumas, T. L. (2007). The hair dilemma: Conform to mainstream expectations or emphasize racial identity. *Duke Journal of Gender Law & Policy, 14*, 407-421.

Sellers, R. E. (2003). The kink factor: A womanist discourse analysis of African-American mother/daughter perspectives on negotiating black hair/body politics. In R. L. Jackson II & E. B. Richardson (Eds.), pp. 223-243. New York, NY: Routledge.

Sellers, R. M., Caldwell, C. H., Schmeelk-Cone, K. H., & Zimmerman, M. A. (2003). The role of racial identity and racial discrimination in the mental health of African American young adults. *Journal of Health and Social Behavior, 44*, 302-317.

Sellers, R. M., Smith, M. A., Shelton, J. N., Rowley, S.A.J., & Chavous, T. M. (1998). Multidimensional model of racial identity: A reconceptualization of African American racial identity. *Personality and Social Psychology Review, 2*, 18-39.

Shetty, V. H., Shetty, N. J., & Nair, D. G. (2013). Chemical hair relaxers have adverse effects a myth or reality. *International Journal of Trichology, 5*, 26-28. https://doi.org/10:4103/0974-7753.114710

Snider, S. R., & Rosenberg, J. (2006). The relationship of skin tone and hair to perceived beauty among African American University Students. *The University of Alabama McNair Journal*, 201-212.

Thompson, S. M., & Keith, M. V. (2001). The blacker the berry: Gender, skin tone, self-esteem, and self-efficacy. *Gender and Society, 25*, 336-357.

U.S. Army (2014). https://api.army.mil/e2/c/downloads/337951.pdf

Versey, H. S. (2014). Centering perspectives on black women, hair politics, and physical activity. *American Journal of Public Health, 104,* 810-815.

Walker, A. (1983). In search of our mothers' gardens: Womanist prose. New York: Harcourt, Inc.

Williams, J. J. (2015, March). Natural style. *Baltimore Sun*. Retrieved from http://www.baltimoresun.com/entertainment/bthesite/

Wise, L. A., Palmer, J. R., Reich, D., Cozier, Y. C., & Rosenberg, L. (2012). Hair relaxer use and risk of uterine leiomyoma in African American women. *American Journal of Epidemiology, 175*, 432-440.

Yap, S. C., Settles, I. H., & Pratt-Hyatt, J. S. (2011). Mediators of the relationship between racial identity and life satisfaction in a community sample of African American women and men. *Cultural Diversity and Ethnic Minority Psychology, 17*, 89. https://doi.org/10.1037/a0022535

Zhang, W. (2017). Colorism. *The Wiley-Blackwell Encyclopedia of Social Theory.* https://doi.org/10.1002/9781118430873

CHAPTER 15.

The Role of Skin Tone Dissatisfaction, Body Shape Dissatisfaction, and Disordered Eating on Self-Esteem Among Black Undergraduate and Graduate Women

Charnel Hollier, Private Practice
Marisa Franco, American Association for the Advancement of Science
Martinque K. Jones, University of North Texas
Kamilah Marie Woodson; Howard University

Introduction

Disordered eating behaviors (DEBs) include dieting, binge eating, fasting, laxative use, and self-induced vomiting (National Eating Disorders Association [NEDA], 2015). Black women are not immune to eating disturbance and, in fact, engage in DEBs at rates similar to women of other racial and ethnic groups (Cheng, Perko, Fuller-Marashi, Gau, & Stice, 2019; Gordon, Castro, Sitnikov, & Holm-Denoma, 2010; Talleyrand, 2012; Talleyrand, Gordon, Daquin, & Johnson, 2017; Taylor, Caldwell, Baser, Faison, & Jackson, 2010). In the case of Black college women, one study found that approximately a quarter of women admitted to eating disorder symptoms (Mulholland & Mintz, 2001), whereas another found that three-quarters of the sample reported one or more maladaptive eating behaviors (Flowers, Levesque, & Fischer, 2012). DEBs are associated with a number of harmful physical and psychological outcomes, such as poor diet quality, obesity, depressive symptoms and suicidality, as well as eating disorders (Duarte & DeLee, 2015; Mustapic, Marcinko, & Vargek; 2016; NEDA, 2015). Accordingly, Black college women engaging in DEBs may be at significant health risk.

Despite the prevalence and consequences of DEBs among Black college women, studies examining the contributing factors to DEBs among this specific demographic are limited. Studies of racially diverse girls and women suggest that perceptions of one's body (e.g., body dissatisfaction and body shame) and overall self-esteem are critical factors to consider in understanding DEBs. However, the foundational premise of these investigations is that because of the "thin ideal" women are concerned about gaining weight or losing weight (Brechan & Kvalem, 2015; Mustapic et al., 2016), and thus scholars overlook the fact that many young Black women experience body image concerns related to their body shape, skin tone, and even hair texture (Awad, Norwood, Taylor, Martinez, McClain, Jones, & Chapman-Hilliard, 2014; Thompson & Keith, 2001; Woodson, 2002). In fact, studies show that Black college women experience dissatisfaction with their skin tone and physique, and experience low self-esteem as a result (Awad et al., 2014; Thompson & Keith, 2001). For this reason, the current study investigates both body shape and skin tone dissatisfaction as predictors of disordered eating, as well as the extent to which disordered eating mediates the association between aspects of body dissatisfaction and self-esteem among Black undergraduate and graduate women.

The Importance of Examining DEBs Among Black Women

We center our investigation on Black university (undergraduate and graduate) women because these women have unique experiences that may make them more likely to engage in DEBs. First, college is often a time where food independence (choice over food intake and preparation as well as easy access to new food options) is gained for the first time (Striegel-Moore & Franko, 2002). Additionally, college women are susceptible to heightened salience of body image, which occurs due to an increased amount of social comparison (Striegel-Moore & Franko, 2002). Last, Black women may engage in DEBs as a way to cope with academic, racial, and gendered stress (Beukes, Walker, & Esterhuyse, 2010; Kreig, 2013; Longmire-Avital & McQueen, 2019).

Examining body dissatisfaction and disordered eating among Black women is important given that a majority of research on this topic area is based on the experiences of White Americans, and thus has limited generalizability. For example, previous research has operationalized body dissatisfaction as weight concerns, which is more relevant for White than for Black women (Stice, 2002). Black women's body ideals are more likely to focus on reproportioning weight to be more curvaceous (Jefferson & Stake, 2009; Poran, 2006; Singh, 1994). Media is a main contributor to the desire to be curvaceous. For instance, Watson and colleagues (2015) found that Black college women's media consumption was related to body dissatisfaction via internalization, meaning that women who internalize media portrayals of women's bodies are more likely to experience dissatisfaction as a result. Given that Black women are less focused on a thin ideal (Cheng et al., 2019), Black women are less likely to engage in anorexia-related behaviors and more likely to engage in binge-eating behaviors (Cheng et al., 2019; O'Neill, 2003). A nationally representative study noted that anorexia was the rarest, and bulimia was the most common and persistent eating disorder among Black women (Taylor et al., 2007).

Furthermore, researchers have also identified that skin color dissatisfaction is an aspect of body dissatisfaction unique to Black women (Awad et al., 2014; Capodilupo, 2015; Capodilupo & Kim, 2014; Falconer & Neville, 2000; Jefferson & Stake, 2009; Poran, 2006). A study by Mucharah and Frazier (2013) found that the more satisfied a woman is with her skin tone, the more she is satisfied with her body image. Moreover, skin color may be an important factor to address among Black women due to the issues related to colorism. Colorism, or skin color stratification, is the prejudicial treatment of same-race people based on their skin color (Hunter, 2007). Some studies have identified colorism as an aspect of the Black experience that can influence Black women's feelings of attractiveness, and subsequently decrease   their overall body image satisfaction (Awad et al., 2014; Banks, Harvey, Thelemaque, & Onyinyechi,   2016; Falconer & Neville, 2000). In support of this, Falconer and Neville (2000) found that skin color satisfaction significantly predicted body image among Black college women. Moreover, Harvey and colleagues (2016) found that women's negative perceptions of their skin tone and colorists' attitudes were associated with lower self-esteem. Thus, in decentering a weight-related conceptualization of body image and including a focus on skin tone, the current study serves as a culturally-grounded investigation of how body dissatisfaction relates to disordered eating.

Body Dissatisfaction, DEBs, and Self-esteem

The concerns with body image among Black women are rooted in the history of enslavement that manifests in the subsequent subscription to the Eurocentric physical aesthetic. Body image dissatisfaction predicts the development of DEBs (Gorden, Castro, Sitnikov, & Holm-Denoma, 2010; Stice, 2002; Zeigler-Hill & Noser, 2015). Eating disturbances may serve as a coping response to body dissatisfaction or as a perceived method to obtain a more desirable body (Stice, 2002). DEBs may also then contribute to low self-esteem, as research has shown that body dissatisfaction (including feelings toward both skin color and body) relates to low self-esteem (Brechan & Kvalem, 2015; Thompson & Keith, 2001; Woodson, 2002; Zeigler-Hill & Noser, 2015); however, the mechanism through which this relationship occurs is unknown. Considering established relationships between body dissatisfaction and disordered eating (see Stice, 2002), and relationships between disordered eating and low self-esteem (Lampard, Byrne, & McLean, 2011; Shea & Pritchard, 2007; Zeigler-Hill & Noser, 2015), it is possible that one way that body dissatisfaction might contribute to low self-esteem is through disordered eating. Dissatisfaction about one's body contributes to disordered eating, as a way to cope with negative body image or else to control body shape, and disordered eating may subsequently engender feelings of shame, which compromise self-esteem (Lampard et al., 2011; Shea & Pritchard, 2007). Accordingly, we investigate whether the relationship between body dissatisfaction (that is, body shape and skin color dissatisfaction) and self-esteem is explained by DEBs.

In conceptualizing the links between body dissatisfaction, disordered eating, and self-esteem, we rely on self-discrepancy theory (SDT). SDT indicates that negative consequences arise when individuals perceive a discrepancy between their actual self and their ideal self (Higgins, 1987; Vartanian, 2012). The actual self reflects the individual's perceptions of their own attributes or characteristics. The ideal self represents attributes that the individual would like to possess. The discrepancy between actual and ideal self happens when an individual believes that their appearance or physical attributes do not meet some personally relevant ideal standard (Cash & Green, 1986). This discrepancy then contributes to emotional distress. In order to reduce the distress related to this discrepancy, individuals are likely to engage in externalizing behaviors such as disordered eating, which may lower their self-esteem and contribute to more psychological distress. SDT is particularly useful for diverse populations because it allows for variation in what each individual might consider "ideal." Thus, we conceptualized body shape dissatisfaction as discrepancies between actual and ideal body, and also predict that body dissatisfaction will predict disordered eating which will then predict decreased self-esteem.

The Current Study

The aim of the current investigation is to expand our understanding of the association between aspects of body dissatisfaction and self-esteem, particularly among Black college women. In consideration of SDT, we hypothesize that each type of body dissatisfaction (body shape and skin tone) will negatively predict self-esteem, and that disordered eating will mediate these relationships. A total of 190 self-identified U.S. Black undergraduate and graduate college women (M_{age}=26.5 years; SD=5.4, $range$ =18-54) participated in the study. All participants racially identified as Black but varied in ethnic background: American (98.9%) and multiethnic (1.1%). A majority of the participants were graduate students (66.8%) and, among the undergraduates, 14.7% were seniors, 12.1% were juniors, 3.7% were sophomores, and 1.1% were freshmen;

1.6% reported their student status as "other." In terms of sexual orientation, the majority of the sample identified as heterosexual (91.9%), with a small number of participants identifying as bisexual (6.3%) or lesbian (2.1%); the remaining participants (.5%) did not report their sexual orientation.

The purpose of the study was to better understand the predictors and consequences of disordered eating among Black college women. Disordered eating is important to address considering that it carries the risk of weight gain, obesity, depression, and suicide (Duarte & DeLee, 2015; Mustapic et al., 2016; NEDA, 2015). It is particularly important to address among Black college women as rates of DEBs are substantial among this population (Danso, 2013; Shaw et al., 2004; Taylor et al., 2007), and their gendered-racial university experience predisposes them to unique DEB trajectories (Beukes et al., 2010; Kreig, 2013; Longmire-Avital, & McQueen, 2019).

Results of the current study indicate that there was relatively high body and skin tone satisfaction; this finding aligns with a recent study which also found some Black women to be generally content with their bodies (Cotter et al., 2015). Participants in the current study endorsed low levels of eating disturbance, a finding also mirrored in previous studies that have found sub-clinical thresholds for eating disorders among some Black women (Danso, 2013; Mulholland & Mintz, 2001; Rucker & Cash, 1992). Though rates of eating disorders tend to be lower for some Black women, when risk factors do occur they tend to affect Black women to the same degree as White women (Shaw et al., 2004). It may also be the case that the rates of eating disturbance are low because we measured this construct using the EAT-26. The EAT-26 was normed on a White sample and focuses on ideals of thinness and behaviors associated with weight; therefore, this scale may overlook critical aspects of Black women's perceptions of body (for example, body shape and skin tone) and eating (for example, binging).

We used a culturally-grounded approach, and thus attended to aspects of body and skin tone dissatisfaction in Black college women. Body shape dissatisfaction was conceptualized using self-discrepancy theory and operationalized as discrepancies between ideal and actual body shape, rather than an endorsement of a thin ideal. Past research has shown that some Black women are diverse in terms of their body aspirations and can identify with both curvaceous and/or thin body shape ideals (Awad et al., 2014; Bledman, 2011). Our results demonstrated that no matter the body ideal (thin or curvy), discrepancies in actual and ideal body shape (that is, body dissatisfaction) predicted disordered eating. Post-hoc tests indicated that this discrepancy predicted specific forms of disordered eating, namely bulimia. We did not test the direction of difference between actual and ideal body (for example, desire to gain or to lose weight to achieve ideal), but given the focus on having a curvaceous figure in the Black community (Jefferson & Stake, 2009; Poran, 2006; Singh, 1994), it is possible that our participants saw a larger body as their body ideal. If Black women's ideals are for larger bodies, then binge eating may be more salient and predictive because it is a medium through which a larger body can be obtained.

This study also found that Black women's negative feelings about their skin tone contributed to their DEBs. Few studies have directly examined the relationship between skin satisfaction and eating behaviors. The studies that do exist conceptualize skin appearance as it relates to skin dryness, skin roughness, freckles, and dark circles under the eyes (Gupta & Gupta, 2001), and not skin tone and color. This conceptualization stems from the fact that individuals with eating disorders, specifically anorexia nervosa and bulimia nervosa, tend to experience dermatological changes. These studies are limited because they do not consider skin appearance as related to the lightness and darkness of one's complexion.

The current study was the first of its kind to find links between skin tone dissatisfaction and disordered eating among Black college women. Post-hoc tests indicated that skin tone dissatisfaction predicted bulimia. In line with SDT (Higgins, 1987; Vartanian 2012), generally negative feelings toward aspects of the body (including body shape and skin tone) provoked unhealthy efforts to control body size. Considering that skin tone is less changeable than body size, Black women may cope with distress related to skin tone dissatisfaction through discorded eating (bulimia in particular). It is important to note that in the present study, the effects of skin tone dissatisfaction on DEBs were similar in magnitude to the effect of body shape dissatisfaction on this outcome. Thus, the current study highlights the combined role of body shape dissatisfaction and skin tone dissatisfaction on disordered eating for Black women.

When we explored whether skin and body shape dissatisfaction predicted specific forms of disordered eating, we found that both body shape and skin dissatisfaction predicted binging but not dieting behaviors. Whereas previous research has highlighted elevated risk for binge eating among Black populations, compared to other racial groups (Cheng et al., 2019; O'Neill, 2003; Shaw et al., 2004; Taylor et al., 2007), the current research might explain why. Dissatisfaction with body shape and skin tone contributes to Black women engaging in behaviors characteristic of bulimia, such as binging on food, preoccupation with food and vomiting more so than other disordered eating behaviors, such as dieting. This research verifies the salience of binge eating, rather than dieting, to Black women's disordered eating behaviors.

Previous research has found less strong relationships between body shape dissatisfaction and self-esteem in Black women, compared to White women (Van den Berg, Mond, Eisenberg, Ackard, & Neumark-Sztainer, 2010), and results of the current study suggest that these weaker relationships may have occurred because of the exclusion of skin tone satisfaction in conceptualizations of body satisfaction. Whereas both body dissatisfaction and skin tone dissatisfaction were correlated with self-esteem at the bivariate level, in mediational models, only skin tone satisfaction was correlated with self-esteem when disordered eating was controlled. These findings highlight the importance of considering skin tone satisfaction when understanding Black women's self-esteem, and also the unique body-related psychological experiences of Black women.

The current study found that disordered eating explained relationships between body dissatisfaction—including body shape dissatisfaction and skin tone—and self-esteem, albeit the magnitude of these effects were small. Thus, this study identifies disordered eating as the mechanism through which body dissatisfaction influences feelings of self-worth for Black women. Specifically, findings indicated that discrepancies between actual and ideal body types or negative feelings regarding skin tone contribute to DEBs, which then engenders compromised self-esteem. Individuals feeling that their body is discrepant with an ideal body, or else that their skin tone is undesirable, may engage in unhealthy eating and preoccupation with food as a way to obtain a self-perceived more desirable body. Unhealthy behaviors and preoccupation with food may provoke negative evaluating feelings toward self (for example, "I'm out of control in my eating"; "I'm not dieting enough"), which may then diminish self-esteem. Post-hoc analyses indicated that bulimia-related behaviors specifically, indirectly predicted relationships between both types of body dissatisfaction and self-esteem. This suggests that binging plays a pivotal role in explaining why body dissatisfaction compromises self-esteem (Taylor et al., 2007).

This study also comes with a number of limitations. First, there may have been a selection bias given that individuals self-selected into this study; this form of bias may limit the representativeness of results, such that participants actively struggling with eating disorders may have been reluctant to take part in the study. Also, the findings of this study may be more generalizable to graduate student women in their mid-twenties, given the demographics of the sample. Research indicates that age significantly affects eating disorder experiences, with college freshman being particularly vulnerable to body dissatisfaction (NEDA, 2015), and older adults focusing more on body functioning than aesthetics (Jefferson & Stake, 2009). The sample was mostly homogenous based on age, limiting our ability to test substantive age interactions. Another limitation is the fact that the study utilized self-report measures, which occasionally present accuracy concerns, particularly for sensitive topics such as weight and eating disorder behaviors. Finally, it is significant that the EAT-26 was developed in predominantly White female samples, perhaps limiting the usefulness of this measure to Black women. Given that Black college women tend to evince particular types of disordered eating (that is, binge eating) and are less likely to endorse a thin ideal (Capodilupo, 2015; Shaw et al., 2004; Taylor et al., 2007), it may be important to develop measures of eating disorders specifically for Black women.

Implications for Practice, Research, and Policy

A number of avenues for future directions arise from the current study's findings. Whereas the aim of this study was to focus on body shape discrepancies and skin tone as markers of Black women's overall body dissatisfaction, future research studies could include additional factors (for example, style of dress, hair, facial features) as potential domains of body dissatisfaction. Furthermore, and consistent with studies conducted by Awad and colleagues (2014), future research could include qualitative methods to determine how Black women cope with body dissatisfaction in healthy ways. Given our conceptualization of skin tone as an aspect of body dissatisfaction for Black women, an ideal goal would be to create a comprehensive body satisfaction measure specific to Black women, which captures both cultural and personal experiences and includes skin tone (Bledman, 2011). Last, future research could be used to disentangle whether an idealization of lighter skin among darker-skinned Black women, or of darker skin among lighter-skinned women differentially affects disordered eating behaviors and self-esteem.

The current study's findings inform avenues of intervention. Rather than assuming that Black women are immune from DEBs, therapists should incorporate Black women's unique cultural experiences, such as colorism, in their conceptualizations of predictors of disordered eating among this population. Considering that DEBs explain relationships between body dissatisfaction and self-esteem, counselors might address how evaluative feelings about bodies manifest as eating behaviors and preoccupations in order to promote more positive self-esteem for Black women. Promoting more positive feelings toward body size or else skin tone may each provide for less DEBs.

Considering that DEBs explained relationships between body shape dissatisfaction and self-esteem for Black women, it is imperative that interventions to increase Black women's self-esteem not only address body shape perceptions, but also the effects these perceptions have on eating behaviors. Interventions that address body dissatisfaction alone without addressing its impact on disordered eating may be unsuccessful.

Practitioners treating Black female clients with eating disorders should attend to any transference issues that occur related to body image or skin tone. For example, a practitioner might share: "I'm aware that we're talking a lot about your feelings surrounding your skin tone and that my skin tone may affect what you feel comfortable sharing. I'm wondering if that's come up for you at all." After attending to this, practitioners might help clients understand what negative thoughts or feelings about their body or their skin tone trigger their eating disordered behaviors or self-esteem issues. Mindfulness can help clients avoid acting out on triggers and cognitive-behavioral therapy can help reframe these negative thoughts.

Regarding policy, the DSM currently does not consider dissatisfaction with skin tone as a potential feature of disordered eating. Should results of this study be replicated, skin tone dissatisfaction should be added to the culture-related diagnostic issues section of disordered eating behaviors, particularly for binge-eating disorders. This would help mental health practitioners be more aware of the potential contributions of skin tone dissatisfaction to disordered eating among Black female clients.

Conclusions

In sum, the current study is the first to quantitatively examine the relationship between body dissatisfaction (including both body shape and skin tone), DEBs, and self-esteem among Black undergraduate and graduate women. Specifically, this study is the first to find significant relationships between skin tone dissatisfaction and DEBs. This study serves as a starting point for new research and interventions that go beyond weight, consider the unique views of body ideals among Black female populations, and ultimately contribute to lessening the grave impact of disordered eating among this group.

Process Questions and Considerations:
1. What aspects of your body image affect your sense of self-worth?
2. What experiences have you had that have affected your body image or skin tone perceptions?
3. What do you think would help you improve your body image or skin tone perceptions?

4. What triggers make you feel negatively or positively about your skin tone or body shape?

5. What are some ways you cope when you feel negatively about your body shape or skin tone?

References

Awad, G., Norwood, C., Taylor, D. S., Martinez, M., McClain, S., Jones, B., & Chapman-Hilliard, C. (2014). Beauty and body image concerns among African American college women. *Journal of Black Psychology, 41*, 540-564. DOI:10.1177/0095798414550864

Banks, K. H., Harvey, R. D., Thelemaque, T., & Onyinyechi, V. A. (2016). *Intersection of colorism and racial identity and the impact on mental health.* In F. M. Last Editor (Ed.), *The Meaning-Making, Internalized Racism, and African American Identity* (pp. 261-276). Albany, NY: State University of New York.

Beukes, M., Walker, S., & Esterhuyse, K. (2010). The role of coping responses in the relationship between perceived stress and disordered eating in a cross-cultural sample of female university students. *Stress and Health, 26,* 280-291. DOI:10.1002/smi.1296

Bledman R.A. (2011). *The ideal body shape of African American college women* (Master's thesis). Retrieved from https://mospace.umsystem.edu/xmlui/handle/10355/14193

Brechan, I. & Kvalem, I. L. (2015). Relationship between body dissatisfaction and disordered eating: Mediating role of self-esteem and depression. *Eating Behaviors: An International Journal, 17,* 49-58. DOI:10.1016/j.eatbeh.2014.12.008

Capodilupo, C. C. (2015). One size does not fit all: Using variables other than the thin ideal to understand Black women's body image. *Cultural Diversity & Ethnic Minority Psychology, 21,* 268-278. DOI:10.1037/a0037649

Capodilupo, C. M., & Kim, S. (2014). Gender and race matter: The importance of considering intersections in black women's body image. *Journal of Counseling Psychology, 61,* 37-49. DOI:10.1037/a0034597

Cash, T. F., & Green, G. K. (1986). Body weight and body image among college women: Perception, cognition, and affect. *Journal of Personality Assessment, 50,* 290-301. DOI:10.1207/s15327752jpa5002_15

Cotter, E. W., Kelly, N. R., Mitchell, K. S., & Mazzeo, S. E. (2015). An investigation of body appreciation, ethnic identity, and eating disorder symptoms in black women. *Journal of Black Psychology, 41,* 3-25. DOI:10.1177/0095798413502671

Cheng, Z. H., Perko, V. L., Fuller-Marashi, L., Gau, J. M., & Stice, E. (2019). Ethnic differences in eating disorder prevalence, risk factors, and predictive effects of risk factors among young women. *Eating Behaviors, 32,* 23-30. DOI:10.1016/j.eatbeh.2018.11.004

Danso, A. (2013). *Body image and disordered eating patterns in African American college women* (doctoral dissertation). Retrieved from http://digitalcommons.liberty.edu/cgi/viewcontent.cgi?article=1360&context=honors

Duarte, T., & DeLee, F. (2015). Disordered eating. In R. L. Smith, R. L. Smith (Eds.), *Treatment Strategies for Substance and Process Addictions* (pp. 207-235). Alexandria, VA, US: American Counseling Association.

Falconer, J. W., & Neville, H. A. (2000). African American college women's body image: An examination of body mass, African self-consciousness, and skin color satisfaction. *Psychology of Women Quarterly, 24,* 236-243. DOI:10.1111/j.1471-6402.2000.tb00205.x

Flowers, K. C., Levesque, M. J., & Fischer, S. (2012). The relationship between maladaptive eating behaviors and racial identity among African American women in college. *Journal of Black Psychology, 38,* 290-312. DOI:10.1177/0095798411416459

Garner, D. M., & Garfinkel, P. E. (1979). The Eating Attitudes Test: An index of the symptoms of anorexia nervosa. *Psychological Medicine, 9*, 273-279.

Garner, D. M., Olmsted, M. P., Bohr, Y., & Garfinkel, P. E. (1982). The Eating Attitudes Test: psychometric features and clinical correlates. *Psychological Medicine, 12*, 871-878.

Gleaves, D. H., Pearson C. A., Ambwani S., Morey L. C. (2014). Measuring eating disorder attitudes and behaviors: A reliability generalization study. *Journal of Eating Disorders, 2*, 1-12. DOI:10.1186/2050-2974-2-6

Gordon, K. H., Castro, Y., Sitnikov, L., & Holm-Denoma, J. M. (2010). Cultural body shape ideals and eating disorder symptoms among white, Latina, and black college women. *Cultural Diversity and Ethnic Minority Psychology, 16*, 135-143. DOI:10.1037/a0018671

Gupta, M., & Gupta, A. (2001). Dissatisfaction with skin appearance among patients with eating disorders and non-clinical controls. *British Journal of Dermatology, 145*, 110-113. DOI:10.1046/j.1365-2133.2001.04292.x

Harvey, R. D., Tennial, R. E., & Hudson Banks, K. (2017). The development and validation of a colorism scale. *Journal of Black Psychology, 43*, 740-764. DOI:10.1177/0095798417690054

Higgins, E. T. (1987). Self-discrepancy: A theory relating self and affect. *Psychological Review, 94*, 319-340.

Hunter, M. (2007). The persistent problem of colorism: Skin tone, status, and inequality. *Sociology Compass, 1*, 237-254.

IBM Corp. (Released 2016). IBM SPSS Statistics for Macintosh, Version 24.0. Armonk, NY: IBM Corp.

Jefferson, D. L., & Stake, J. E. (2009). Appearance self-attitudes of African American and European American women: Media comparisons and internalization of beauty ideals. *Psychology of Women Quarterly, 33*, 396-409. DOI:10.1111/j.1471-6402.2009.01517.x

Kreig, B. D. (2013). High expectations for higher education? Perceptions of college and experiences of stress prior to and through the college career. *College Student Journal, 47*, 635-643. DOI: 10.1080/13583883.2016.1188326

Lampard, A. M., Byrne, S. M., & McLean, N. (2011). Does self-esteem mediate the relationship between interpersonal problems and symptoms of disordered eating? *European Eating Disorders Review, 19*, 454-458. DOI:10.1002/erv.1120

Longmire-Avital, B., & McQueen, C. (2019). Exploring a relationship between race-related stress and emotional eating for collegiate black American women. *Women & Health, 59*, 240-251. DOI:10.1080/03630242.2018.1478361

Maxwell, M., Brevard, J., Abrams, J., & Belgrave, F. (2015). What's color got to do with it? Skin color, skin color satisfaction, racial identity, and internalized racism among African American college students. *Journal of Black Psychology, 41*, 438461. DOI:10.1177/0095798414542299

Mulholland, A. M., & Mintz, L. B. (2001). Prevalence of eating disorders among African American women. *Journal of Counseling Psychology, 48*, 111-116. DOI:10.1037/0022-0167.48.1.111

Mustapic, J., Marcinko, D., & Vargek, P. (2016). Body shame and disordered eating in adolescents. *Current Psychology, 36*, 447-452. DOI:10.1007/s12144-016-9433-3

National Eating Disorders Association [NEDA]. (2015). *Eating disorders statistics.* Retrieved from http://www.anad.org/get-information/about-eating-disorders/eating-disorders-statistics/

O'Neill, S. K. (2003). African American women and eating disturbances: A meta-analysis. *Journal of Black Psychology, 29*, 3-16. DOI:10.1177/0095798402239226

Patt, M. R., Lane, A. E., Finney, C. P., Yanek, L., & Becker, D. M. (2002). Body image assessment: Comparison of figure rating scales among urban black women. *Ethnicity and Disease, 12*, 54-62.

Poran, M. (2006). The politics of protection: Body image, social pressures, and the misrepresentation of young black women. *Sex Roles, 55*, 739-755. DOI:10.1007/s11199-006-9129-5

Rosenberg, M. (1965). Society and the adolescent self-image. Princeton, NJ: Princeton University Press.

Rowley, S. J., Sellers, R. M., Chavous, T. M., & Smith, M. A. (1998). The relationship between racial identity and self-esteem in African American college and high school students. *Journal of Personality and Social Psychology, 74*, 715-724. DOI:10.1037/0022-3514.74.3.715

Rucker, C. E., & Cash, T. F. (1992). Body image, body-size perceptions, and eating behaviors among African American and white college women. *International Journal of Eating Disorders, 12*, 291-299. DOI:10.1002/1098-108X(199211)12:3<291::AID-EAT2260120309>3.0.CO;2-A

Shaw, H., Ramirez, L., Trost, A., Randall, P., & Stice, E. (2004). Body image and eating disturbances across ethnic groups: More similarities than differences. *Psychology of Addictive Behaviors, 18*, 12-18. DOI:10.1037/0893-164X.18.1.12

Shea, M. E., & Pritchard, M. (2007). Is self-esteem the primary predictor of disordered eating? *Personality and Individual Differences, 42*, 1527-1537. DOI:10.1016/j.paid.2006.10.026

Shuttlesworth, M. E., & Zotter, D. (2011). Disordered eating in African American and Caucasian women: The role of ethnic identity. *Journal of Black Studies, 42*(6), 906-922. DOI:https://doi.org/10.1177/0021934710396368

Singh, D. (1994). Body fat distribution and perception of desirable female body shape by young Black men and women. *International Journal of Eating Disorders, 16*, 289-294. DOI:10.1002/1098-108X(199411)16:3<289::AID-EAT2260160310>3.0.CO;2-9

Stice, E. (2002). Risk and maintenance factors for eating pathology: A meta-analytic review. *Psychological Bulletin, 128*, 825-848. doi.:10.1037/0033-2909.128.5.825

Striegel-Moore, R. H., & Franko, D. L. (2002). Body image issues among girls and women. In T. F. Cash & T. Pruzinsky (Eds.), *Body image: A handbook of theory, research, and clinical practice* (pp. 183-191). New York, NY: Guildford Press.

Tabachnick, B. G., & Fidell, L. S. (2007). *Using multivariate statistics* (5th ed.). Boston, MA: Allyn & Bacon/Pearson Education.

Talleyrand, R. M. (2012). Disordered eating in women of color: Some counseling considerations. *Journal of Counseling & Development, 90*, 271-280. DOI:10.1002/j.1556-6676.2012.00035.x

Talleyrand, R. M., Gordon, A. D., Daquin, J. V., & Johnson, A. J. (2017). Expanding our understanding of eating practices, body image, and appearance in African American women: A qualitative study. *Journal of Black Psychology, 43*, 464-492. DOI:10.1177/0095798416649086

Taylor, J. Y., Caldwell, C. H., Baser, R. E., Faison, N., & Jackson, J. S. (2007). Prevalence of eating disorders among blacks in the National Survey of American Life. *International Journal of Eating Disorders, 40*, S10-S14. DOI:10.1002/eat.20451

Thompson, M. S., & Keith, V. M. (2001).The blacker the berry. *Gender & Society, 15*, 336-357. DOI:10.1177/089124301015003002

Utsey, S. O., Ponterotto, J. G., Reynolds, A. L., & Cancelli, A. A. (2000). Racial discrimination, coping, life satisfaction, and self-esteem among African Americans. *Journal of Counseling & Development, 78*, 72-80.DOI:10.1002/j.1556-6676.2000.tb02562.x

Van den Berg, P. A., Mond, J., Eisenberg, M., Ackard, D., & Neumark-Sztainer, D. (2010). The link between body dissatisfaction and self-esteem in adolescents: Similarities across gender, age, weight status, race/ethnicity, and socioeconomic status. *The Journal of Adolescent Health, 47*, 290-296. DOI:10.1016/j.jadohealth.2010.02.004

Vartanian, L. R. (2012). *Self-discrepancy theory and body image.* The University of New South Wales, Sydney NSW, Australia. Retrieved from http://www2.psy.unsw.edu.au/Users/lvartanian/Publications/Vartanian%20%282012%29%20SDT%20chapter.pdf

Watson, K. L., Livingston, J. N., Cliette, G., & Eaton, S. (2015). Internalization of the thin ideal, media images and body image dissatisfaction in African American college women: Implications for black female sexuality. *Journal of Black Sexuality and Relationships, 1*(4), 23-43. DOI:10.1353/bsr.2015.0014

Woodson, K. M. (2002). *The impact of hair texture and skin color among black men and women during mate selection on the expression of risky sexual behaviors* (Doctoral dissertation). Alliant International University, Los Angeles.

Zeigler-Hill V, Noser A. (2015). Will I ever think I'm thin enough? A moderated mediation study of women's contingent self-esteem, body image discrepancies and disordered eating. *Psychology of Women Quarterly. 39*, 109-118. DOI:10.1177/0361684313515841

CHAPTER 16.

Breaking the Silence of Colorism: Psychotherapy as a Form of Reflexivity & Liberation

O'Shan D. Gadsden and Darlene G. Colson
Norfolk State University

Introduction

The topic of race has been a common one, throughout African American literature and remains a salient factor in the daily lives of Black Americans in both the United States and abroad (Wingfield & Wingfield, 2014; Ford & Harawa, 2010). Many African Americans often are negatively impacted by having to psychologically hold and make sense of the multiple sociocultural and relational implications of their race (Hooker & Tillery, 2016). Colorism, is thought by many scholars, to be one of the effects of such a convoluted attempt to navigate and psychologically hold the complexities of "African American" selfhood (Norwood & Foreman, 2014; Hochschild, 2007).

Colorism, has been defined by some scholars as, differential discrimination based on skin tone or color (Landor & Barr, 2018; Maxwell et al., 2014; Russell et al., 1992; Neal & Wilson, 1989). Within the African American community, generally, darker skin has been perceived as less desirable; with darker-skinned individuals experiencing greater discrimination from others within and outside of their racial/ethnic communities (Kahn & Davies, 2010; Hall, 1992; Hughes & Hertel, 1990; Freeman et al., 1966. Historically (during the period of slavery), as a consequence of interracial rape and sexual "relationships," many African children were born the products of Black and white parents (Davis, 1941). Consequently, skin tones among African Americans range from very light to very dark brown. The offspring of white slave owners were often treated better than those with two African parents. The terms house nigger and field nigger denoted the jobs and quality of life differences between lighter and darker hued Africans. Predictably, this led to anger within the race that became color-based.

This is not to say that colorism did not exist prior to this time but the proliferation of studies began after it was given a name by Alice Walker (Russell-Cole, Wilson, &

Hall, 2013; Norwood, 2015) and found its way into multiple genres of literature. Social organizations after the Civil War also served as concrete evidence of colorism (Keith & Herring, 1991). Organizations such as the Bon Ton Society of Washington DC and the Blue Vein Society of Nashville allowed membership only to lighter-skinned Blacks (Russell-Cole, Wilson, & Hall, 2013). More recently, Jack and Jill which was founded in 1938, excluded darker-skinned Blacks from membership. Additionally, many African American churches also discriminated on the basis of skin tone (Drake and Cayton, 2015).

Given the move from overt to perhaps covert colorism, its current prevalence is less obvious (Rusell-Cole, Wilson, & Ronald, 2013). However, colorism can be inferred from some practices and trends (Snell, 2017; Hunter, 2011, 2007). In popular black films, such as, *All About the Benjamins*, fair-skinned women are often cast in lead roles more often than darker-skinned females (Maddox & Gray, 2002). A preference for light skin can also be seen in heterosexual relationships (Hamilton et al., 2009). Most often, the female is the lighter-skinned partner, resulting from Black men's preference for lighter-skinned partners (Hill, 2002). It seems then that colorism results in a two-tiered system within the African American community, with lighter-skinned individuals occupying the top tier. This can be seen in terms of economics, with lighter-skinned African Americans earning more money (Hill, 2002; Wade et al., 2005) and having greater occupational status (Monk, 2003). Divisiveness is a predictable result of colorism. Darker-skinned African Americans often resent the preferential treatment afforded to lighter-skinned African Americans. (Esmail & Sullivan, 2006).

A conversation regarding the complexity of colorism within the African American community cannot be complete without an examination of how colorism has presented itself and functioned similarly and/or differently as a consequence of gender. According to Hunter (2007), African-American women have been more negatively impacted by colorism compared to African-American men through a phenomenon he has coined as, "gendered colorism" (Wilder & Cain, 2010). Similarly, Keith et al. (2010) remarked that "issues of racial identity, skin color, and attractiveness are central concerns for women" (p. 54). There is some seminal research that has postulated that African-American women have contended with issues of skin tone color in highly significant ways (Piper, 1973). Historically, the literature has noted that darker-skinned African-American women have been socially impacted for their skin tone; while also having experienced differential wages and economic access, lower levels of success in educational pursuits, and higher levels of racial slurs and abusive treatment by others (Edwards, 1973).

Ogungleye (1998) also observed that darker skin toned African-American women often feel responsible for strengthening the family; particularly related to self-esteem.

When accounting for gender differences in experiences of colorism between African-American women and men, some research has found that African-American men were not as negatively impacted as African American women. However, darker-skinned African-American men were found to internalize feelings of hostilities toward lighter-skinned individuals and there were differential employment opportunities found between darker-skinned African-American men and lighter-skinned African-American men, with the latter being privileged (Harrison & Thomas, 2009; Goldstein et al., 2007; Hill, 2000; Hughes and Hertel, 1990).

Current research has found a strong correlation between color discrimination (that is colorism) and violence toward African-American males at the hands of police (Jones, 2014). The Washington Post reported that from January 2015 to July 10 2016, 50% of those murdered at hands of police officers were African-Americans; despite African-Americans being only 13% of the total U.S. population (U.S. Census Bureau, 2014). However, when one looks more closely at this high rate of killing of African-Americans, there seems to be an unmistakable pattern of police prejudice against darker-skinned toned African-American victims (Chavers, 2015; Correll et al., 2007). Crutchfield et al. (2017) also found that when exploring the relationship between gender, skin tone, and police violence, 57% of African-American males and 63% of African-American women were darker-skinned. Additionally, the highest percentages of dark skin tones were among African-American men from the ages of 18-28. This particular study seems to point out that although there is a slight higher percentage (6%) of darker skin toned African-American women being negatively impacted by police violence that darker-skinned African-American men are also highly impacted. Suffice to say, regardless of the gender differences, both African-American males and females historically and currently are psychologically and relationally impacted by colorism; both from within their communities and without.

But what does these issues of colorism and the trends of colorism between Black Americans have to do with the treating psychotherapist? Is there a need to make clinical and dynamic sense out of the phenomenon of colorism, for Black/African American patients who are directly and indirectly impacted by colorism, in multiple dimensions of their lives? Aren't we (that is the treating psychotherapist) also in danger of being complicit, as a consequence of our own racialized socialization and its impact on how we view and "emotionally take in" Black/African-Americans along the lines of skin tone? We would argue that before any of these questions can be answered, we must first acknowledge how the mental health field has and continues to create and practice forms of psychotherapy that are often marginalizing and out of step with the needs of Black/African-American patients who seek healing (Gadsden & Howard, 2016). Even when receiving mental health services, Black/African-Americans have often been treated as identity categories outside the margins of psychological-emotional engagement (Gadsden & Howard, 2016). The internalization of this treatment has led to many Black/African-Americans feeling invisible, muzzled, misunderstood, and even colonized by mental health providers and treatment recommendations (Delphin-Rittmon et al., 2015).

It is evident that the mental health field has been in step with and continues to collude with the problematizing of African-American psychology and cultural subjectivities (Delphin-Rittmon et al., 2015). This continues to be enacted by psychological-clinical models and interventions being normed and presented as a set of universally true theories and clinical practices that are efficacious in both explaining and responding to the "human" condition; often in direct disregard of cultural differences, particularly to issues dealing with race and colorism. One might ask, how can the writers make such a declaration. It is our contention, like many other critical theorists and practitioners; that the field of psychology, counseling, social work, and psychiatry have placed their "universal" conceptualizations/formulations/theoretical models, and clinical interventions as the standard by which Black/African-Americans are to be understood, compared, and acted upon (Comas-Diaz, 2000). As such, many of these Western/European/white models are no more than a culturally narcissistic mirroring of themselves and consciousness; implicitly and explicitly enforced. In light of this, one can see the imperativeness of a framework of psychotherapy, that is fundamentally and qualitatively dissimilar to Western/European psychology, counseling, social work, and psychiatry (Owen et al., 2016) in both its epistemology and ontology. A model or framework of psychotherapy in the words of Nobles (2010) that is free of "conceptual incarceration" (that is distorted [cultural] conceptions of reality that have negative psycho-cultural-spiritual consequences); particularly when conceptualizing and treating issues that are directly a consequence of the psycho-cultural-spiritual impacts of colorism.

As such, we would like to use this paper as a challenge to psychotherapists, to continue to more deeply explore and understand the connections between both their own, and their Black/African American patients' understanding and subjective experiences of colorism; as well as how that understanding and those experiences of colorism may have and continue to impact their sense of selves, the therapy dynamic, and ultimate therapy interventions/treatment chosen. To that end, we will introduce the Black Centered Decolonizing Clinical Framework that can be used by clinicians of varying theoretical orientations to assist them to frame their assumptions and motivations when working with African American patients in general; and in particular when issues of skin tone discrimination and/or internalized colorism are the primary presenting issues. We will also discuss the components needed and the clinical efficacy of integrating reflexivity into the psychotherapeutic process when helping Black/ African American patients explore and heal (that is become liberated) from the impacts of skin tone discrimination and colorism in their lives. Lastly, we present some clinical implications and ways to think about the assessment process when treating patients who present with issues of related to skin tone discrimination and internalized colorism.

The Black Centered Decolonizing Clinical Framework

The Black Centered Decolonizing Clinical Framework was created by Dr. O'Shan Gadsden and transposed from the work of Linda Tuhiwai Smith (2012) and her seminal book, Decolonizing Methodologies: Research & Indigenous Peoples. In this book Smith provides a nuanced condemnation and critique of western frameworks of research and knowledge from the positionality of an indigenous and "colonized" Maori woman. In it she calls for the "decolonization" of methodologies; which for her is defined as having, "a more critical understanding of the underlying assumptions, motivations and values that inform research practices." As such, her new form of "decolonized research" includes a systematic process that allows "researchers" to re-learn what is needed when working with indigenous peoples, what is appropriate or inappropriate as it concerns both the epistemologies used to frame research inquiry as well as the dynamics of engagement. In this way, Smith redefines the enterprise of research as one that is culturally loaded and political in nature; and as such, must fundamentally be a body of work that is, the "voice of" indigenous folks.

One can see the correlation of her work and the idea of decolonizing the nature of clinical frameworks, methodologies and interventions. More precisely, the emergence of a framework that provides a more critical understanding of the underlying assumptions, motivations and values that inform clinical paradigms and interventions with Black/ African-American patients in general; and specifically, around issues of skin tone discrimination and colorism. As such, Gadsden (2019) has proposed a Black Centered Decolonizing Clinical Framework as a way to begin to formulate such an endeavor.

Fundamental Assumptions:

The Black Centered Decolonizing Clinical Framework (BCDCF) makes a number of assumptions about the nature of western psychology's epistemologies, motivations, and values and situates it in direct juxtaposition to what Black/African-American patients need in context to their cultural subjectivities and positionalities. As such, there are four major assumptions of the BCDCF. First, normative clinical paradigms are inextricably linked to European imperialism and colonialism and often perpetuate patriarchal-sexist-racist-ableist-deterministic values and assumptions, that fundamentally disadvantages and re-victimizes Black peoples-patients. Second, normative clinical paradigms and interventions often misses a fuller nuanced understanding of the cultural-subjectivity of Black peoples-patients. Third, normative clinical paradigms and interventions do not inform and/or support Black peoples-patients right toward cultural-self-determination. Finally, clinical paradigms and interventions must not be a perpetuation or enterprise of privileged identities authorizing their own views of Black peoples-patients, describing/observing them from/through their own limited cultural epistemologies. As such, clinical paradigms and interventions for Black/African-American patients should be created from the lived experiences of Black/African American patients and created by African American (and other Black and Brown) clinicians who are committed to their own racial identity development and that continue to be integrated in community contexts/work that inform their clinical suppositions and interventions.

The Black Centered Decolonizing Clinical Framework Operationalized

Although these assumptions are paramount in understanding the positionality of the BCDCF, they do not provide a conceptual juxtaposition in which we can build by themselves. As such, here are the tenets of the BCDCF operationalized:

1. The BCDCF is both political and spiritual in nature, offering a vehicle for Black peoples-patients to, "retrieve what they were and remake themselves."

2. Decolonizing clinical treatment for Black peoples-patients must include a reflexive analysis that explores the multi-complex impacts that imperialism and colonialism has on how Black peoples-patients have been understood and treated.

3. Decolonizing clinical treatment for Black peoples-patients must include an explicit understanding of the history and impacts of racism/discrimination through the eyes of and via the voices of Black peoples and Black/racialized clinicians.

4. Decolonizing clinical treatment for Black peoples-patients must be by nature,

resistance in action; a form of healing that creates counter-narratives for Black peoples-patients.

5. Decolonizing clinical treatment for Black peoples-patients should be a space to deeply deconstruct and analyze both the motivation and types of treatment interventions; particularly those focused on Black peoples-patients. Black centered Decolonizing clinical treatments are about its results being a vehicle to assisting Black peoples-patients to become culturally integrative, healthy, and confident. Black centered decolonizing clinical treatments should be both epistemologically and ontologically social justice oriented by nature.

Psychotherapy as a Form of Reflexivity Against the Impacts of Colorism

As one can see, utilizing a Black centered decolonizing clinical paradigm provides a framework to deepen our psychotherapy process, making it a real process of reflexivity for Black/African American patients and sets up the psychotherapeutic space to be one in which the patients' narratives about both the etiology and continuance of their difficulties with colorism can be deconstructed more fully. Before we can more fully discuss the ways in which a black centered decolonizing clinical paradigm can be integrated into a process of reflexivity focused on combating issues related to skin tone discrimination and internalized colorism, it seems important for us to first define how we are operationalizing the term reflexivity in our chapter. The Dictionary of Human Geography (2009, 627) defines reflexivity as the consideration of a variety of personal biography, social situation, and political values. From this vantage point, it is the ability and willingness to recognize the influence of our personal subjectivities and the influence of our social and cultural contexts on how we navigate our lives as well as how we relate to our environment and others (Kessl, 2009; Fook & Ashland, 2006). This act of reflexivity then, is about journeying into the 'not-knowing', entertaining the possibility that there could be very different ways of perceiving, framing and experiencing issues or phenomena. It's about a radical openness to fresh possibilities, new horizons, hitherto unimaginable ideas. It's a recognition that all assumptions and preconceptions about reality could be limiting or flawed. In this vein, reflexivity is an invitation first to oneself (then patient) to embark on an ongoing journey and adventure of deeply understanding the multiple functions of one's thoughts and behaviors as well the complexity of motivations toward oneself and the other.

This type of personal and clinical reflexivity allows the psychotherapist to deeply consider all types of cultural determinants and how they get internalized into the identity structure of both themselves and their patients via systems and developmental socialization processes; often not in the realm of consciousness. Reflexivity is an ongoing process of deconstruction and examination of how socialization processes (gender, race, orientation, class) and society's reinforcement of said rigid social constructions of identity have helped to construct and perpetuate inauthentic and split off cultural selves.

One could readily see how fusing a Black centered decolonizing clinical paradigm into a process of reflexivity for both the clinician and Black/African American patient could be beneficial when exploring issues related to skin tone discrimination and internalized colorism. For the purpose of this chapter let us highlight a few ways in which this fusing can be beneficial to both the patient and clinician, when delving into issues related to skin tone discrimination and internalized colorism:

1. The clinician has the opportunity to more deeply examine their own racial-pigmentation and how this impacts their social location and capacity to understand (cognitively and affectively) the material in which their patients brings to regarding them their subjective experiences with skin tone discrimination and colorism;

2. The clinician has the opportunity to create a theoretical framework and interventions that explicitly allow for the patient to work through the relational and internal dissonance that skin tone discrimination and internalized colorism has created in their lives;

3. Black/African American patients have the opportunity to deconstruct the ecological-cultural variables that inform their sense of self while the clinician provides a holding environment that allows Black/African American patients to *"remake"* themselves in ways that are more congruent to their cultural subjectivities and needs;

4. Black/African American patients who are working through issues related to skin tone discrimination and internalized colorism have the opportunity to deeply explore the multiple ways in which racism/discrimination both historically and currently may have informed their developmental experiences that have impacted the ways in which they navigate their skin tone; as well as how those experiences and the ways in which they have attempted to cope with skin tone discrimination and internalized colorism has impacted their overall sense of worth;

5. Clinicians have the opportunity to provide a continual space for patients to articulate their own experiences with skin tone discrimination and colorism and

the various ways they attempted to make meaning of those experiences;

6. This type of space of reflexivity also provides an opportunity for the clinician to validate the patient's meanings and experiences and communicate cultural-empathy; while also challenging the patient to more deeply make connections between their own consciousness and the collective consciousness of this society that they've internalized, related to skin tone;

7. Black/African American patients who are struggling with issues related to colorism, through the process of reflexivity have the opportunity to create counter-narratives from the ones they've internalized concerning the psycho-social-political-relational meaning of their skin tone; and their subsequent worth;

8. The clinician has an opportunity for her/his own process of reflexivity by deeply exploring what types of interventions would be best suitable in assisting the patient at hand to work through issues related to skin tone discrimination and internalized colorism. This process includes an examination of the chosen theoretical orientations' epistemologies and whether or not said orientation can be transposed in ways that compliment and speak to the subjectivity of his/her Black/African American patient regarding their understanding and experience with skin tone discrimination and of colorism. Additionally, this must then be presented to the Black/African American patient in a spirit of collectivism and collaboration; and to also determine if it "fits" the patient's subjectivity, impressions of healing, and stated goals; all in a spirit of openness;

9. This process of reflexivity provides the clinician an opportunity to more deeply explore their motivation for their work. Critical exploration should be had regarding whether or not their work with the patient regarding skin tone discrimination and internalized colorism, should just lie in the dimension of the psychological, or whether or not they should take the stance that the psychological is political; thus shifting the nature of their work, to one in which sees their work exploring skin tone discrimination and the effects of internalized colorism as an act of social justice; thereby linking psycho-cultural-spiritual healing to social justice;

10. The patient, through this type of reflexivity, is given the opportunity to develop new narratives about the self that is in resistance to their former distorted racialized views of self that have resulted from skin tone discrimination and internalized colorism;

11. This form of reflexivity also provides the space for the Black/African

American patient to explore and work through how the societal projected fantasies and projections, manifesting as skin tone discrimination and colorism, has impacted their multiple identities; as well as the ways in which internalized colorism conditions and primes the patient to psychically and relationally interpret themselves as unworthy and others as dangerous/invalidating;

12. This form of reflexivity provides a space for both the patient and clinician to ask of themselves: who am I; and how does skin tone discrimination and colorism impact my ideas of myself? How and with what do I regularly identify with and as; and how does my feelings regarding my skin tone impact said identifications? What self-concepts/self-schemas control my life; and how might my internalization of skin tone discrimination inform those self-concepts/self-schemas? How did my cultural-relational patterns originate and emerge?; and how has internalized colorism impacted my cultural relational patterns?;

13. This process of reflexivity provides an opportunity for the clinician to deeply expose their own racism and/or internalized notions of colorism; while honestly and bravely considering their part in the maintenance and perpetuation of skin tone discrimination. This process then provides the clinician an ongoing space to notice her/his own psychological-cultural-relational internalizations of race and skin tone, while deconstructing how his/her own worldview, values, socialization, ideology, and biases related to race and skin tone are being perpetuated onto how they conceptualize and treat their Black/African-American patients, no matter how benevolent their said conceptualization, treatment plan, or intentions may be;

14. This type of reflexivity allows the clinician the opportunity to utilize their cultural observing ego and inviting the patient to do the same. In this vein, they ask together:

15. What are we observing, with regard to the patient's navigation of race and psycho-relational difficulties related to their skin tone?

16. How are we emotionally-culturally-politically-spiritually observing this phenomenon of race and skin tone of the patient and how is it impacting the ways in which we are or not taking each other in?

17. Is my observation of the patient, as the therapist, reifying my own psycho-cultural subjectivities related to race and skin tone, perpetuated as objective and clinical expertise?

18. Am I creating a space for the patient to observe themselves from an

intersectional perspective; assisting them to be curious about what they might have taken for granted about their racial socialization-identity as natural or innate in nature?

19. How I am assisting the patient to observe how their sense and definition of power and agency have been impacted by race, skin tone discrimination, and colorism?

Psychotherapy as a Form of Liberation From the Impacts of Colorism

This indeed is what we mean by a liberatory process. This is a process, framework, and foundation to clinical work that is both contextual and multi-dimensional. It provides the patient with an opportunity to move beyond self-blame to more deeply understanding the systemic, cultural, familial, and spiritual nature of their difficulties regarding selfhood that manifest as internalized colorism in their lives. Utilizing the Black centered decolonizing clinical framework in a reflexive manner sets the stage for Black/African American patients to become liberated. The liberation comes as a direct consequence of their ongoing deconstruction of the multiple variables of causation related to their issues of selfhood manifesting as internalized colorism. The liberation is really in the process of their exploring the possibility that much of their distorted ideas about the self is not innate (intrapsychic in nature) but responses to social structures, mono-cultural epistemologies regarding identity and worth; which have hindered them from walking in their full humanity, creativity, and power. This type of psychotherapeutic engagement, as an exercise of liberation, has the capacity of freeing both the clinician and patient in deeply mutually constructive ways.

Implications for Practice

Thus far we have provided a theoretical argument for the need of a reflexive Black Centered Decolonizing Clinical Framework as a means to assist clinicians and patients more deeply explore issues related to skin tone discrimination and internalized colorism. We shall end this chapter with some helpful clinical tips that can be utilized in the clinical moment and/or integrated into the clinical process. We believe that any clinical work focused on skin tone discrimination and internalized colorism must by nature be an explicit process of self-revelation. This should be explicitly discussed in the first session or immediately when these issues become materialized and bought forth by the patient. The patient should receive some psychoeducation about the psycho-cultural-spiritual efficacy of discovering new parts of themselves and being open to the process, albeit painful that such opening will produce in their lives.

During the assessment/gathering of data process, there are a number of things the clinician would do well to assess and ask. Here are some things to consider and observe as you are involved in assessment:

1. How does the patient react emotionally to questions regarding race and skin tone?

What is the patient's overall thoughts and feelings about racism, their racial identity, and it salience in their lives?

2. How do they present physically? What parts of their appearance have they seemed to focus on or adorned more?

3. What is the tone and nature of their feelings about other persons that share their racial/ethnic background?

4. What is the tone and nature of their feelings about persons who have a different skin tone from themselves?

5. What is the tone and nature of their feelings about persona who have a similar skin tone as themselves?

6. Does the patient fit the criteria for any mood disorder? And is there a correlation between their affective symptomology and experiences with skin tone discrimination or internalized colorism?

7. If, so to what extent? And what areas of functioning do you think it has historically and currently impacted?

How does the patient react to your physical appearance and skin tone?

Additionally, here are some questions that might be helpful during the assessment/ data gathering/rapport building process:

1. When was the first time you became aware of your skin tone? Was it a positive or negative experience?

2. How did your parents, siblings, and other salient family members discuss skin tone? Did you feel held by such conversations or shamed?

3. How do you think others that are racially different from you think about your skin tone? Have their thoughts impacted you? If so, in what ways?

4. How do you think the history of your racial/ethnic group influences your own thoughts and feelings about your skin tone and worth?

5. Have you ever fantasized about having another skin tone or complexion? If so, what type of feelings did that image bring up for you?

6. Have you ever been depressed or anxious about your skin tone complexion?

7. Have you ever been suicidal as a result of negative feelings about your skin tone complexion or perceived mistreatment regarding your skin ton complexion?

8. Do you have many friends who share your skin tone complexion? What are the quality of those relationships?

9. What are your general feelings about your skin tone complexion?

10. What were your mother's and/or father's skin tone complexion? Did (do) you find them attractive/beautiful/handsome?

11. If you have siblings, what were their skin tone complexions? Was it different or similar to yours? If different, were you or they treated differently because of it?

12. How do you think whiteness impacts your current views of your skin tone and self-worth?

13. Do you think my phenotypical traits impact our dynamic and work? How do you think I experience you as a lighter-skinned/darker-skinned patient?

Conclusion

It is apparent that Black/African-American patients are in need of a psychotherapeutic dynamic and experience that includes a black centered clinical reflexivity in general; and specifically, when working through issues of selfhood, skin tone discrimination, and internalized colorism. It is our belief that this process must include an explicit discussion of the ways in which the ecological contexts (both historically and currently) in which the patient navigates has set them up for lives fraught with psychic and relational survival and dissonance. Here both the psychotherapist and patient have an opportunity to extend their healing beyond the therapy room and collaboratively deconstruct the many ways in which the collective consciousness of their society, families, and communities have projected into them distorted ways of seeing themselves and the other. Through the ongoing process of reflexivity, vulnerability and a re-telling of the patient's cultural-subjective narratives, the patient is provided a space to understand themselves more deeply and understand their community more deeply; with the hopes of positively shifting the collective consciousness of their communities regarding their worth.

This process of black centered decolonizing reflexivity is both aspirational, theoretical, but can be implemented in pragmatic and empathic ways. It is our hope that this piece serves not as a prescriptive piece but one in which assists psychotherapists begin to think more deeply about the theoretical underpinnings that inform their work with Black/African-American patients; and how those epistemologies could be both triggering and perpetuating whiteness and be complicit in perpetuating skin tone discrimination or the patient's internalized colorism. We ask that you think deeply about the black centered decolonizing clinical framework's suppositions and how it, along with the process of reflexivity might better inform your practice with Black/African American patients in general but in assisting those patients who are wrestling with the psychic and relational strain of skin tone discrimination and internalized colorism. There is hope and it starts in and with you, your cultural epistemologies, and willingness to shift in consciousness. Ase!

Process Questions and Considerations

1. When thinking about the relationship between racial identity and self-image, how would you as a psychotherapist assess the impact of your client's developmental history on their racial identity and sense of self?

2. How would you assist a client to tease out the affective differences between skin discrimination that occurred within their own racial group and skin discrimination that resulted from other racial populations?

3. When thinking about your own experience with skin discrimination and possible internalized colorism, how would you utilize the process of reflexivity to work through your own material?

4. Can social justice, reflexivity, and psychotherapy co-exist? How so? Why not?

5. When thinking about a black centered clinical framework, how can the paradigm of intersectionality be integrated?

References

Chavers, L. (2015). Cops ignore me because I have light skin. That just affirms their racism. Retrieved from http:www.theguardian.com/commentisfree/2015/aug/13/cops-racial-profiling-light-skinned-blackwoman.

Comas-Diaz, L. (2000). An ethnopolitical approach to working with people of color. *American Psychologist, 55*, 1319-1325.

Correll, J., Park, B., Judd., C. M., Wittenbrink, B., Sadler, M.S., & Keesee, T. (2007). Across the thin blue line: Police officers and racial bias in the decision to shoot. *Journal of Personality and Social Psychology, 92*(6), 1006-1023. DOI:10.1037/0022-3514.92.6.1006.

Crutchfield, J., Fisher, A., & Webb, S. L. (2017). *The Western journal of black studies, 41*(3/4), 81- 91.

Davis, K. (1941). Intermarriage in caste societies. *American Anthropologist, 43*(3), 376-395. doi.org/10.1525/aa.1941.43.3.02a00030.

Delphin-Rittmon, M. E., Flanagan, E. H., Andres-Hyman, R., Ortiz, J., Amer, M. M., & Davidson, L. (2015). Racial-ethnic differences in access, diagnosis, and outcomes in public-sector inpatient mental health treatment. *Psychological Sciences, 12*, 158-166. DOI:10.1037/a0038858.

Drake, St. C., & Cayton, H. R. (2015). *Black metropolis: A study of Negro life in a northern city.* University of Chicago Press: Chicago, IL.

Edwards, O. L. (1973). Skin color as a variable in racial attitudes of Black urbanites. *Journal of Black Studies, 3*, 473-483.

Esmail, A., & Sullivan, J. M. (2006). African American college males and females: A look at color mating preferences. *Race, Gender, & Class, 13*(1/2), pp. 201-220.

Freeman, H. E., Armour, D., Rose, J. M., Pettigrew, G. E. (1966). Color gradation and attitudes among middle income Negros. *American Sociological Review, 3*, 365-374.

Ford, C. L., & Harawa, N. T. (2010). A new conceptualization of ethnicity for social epidemiologic and health equity research. *Social Science & Medicine, 71*, 251-258. http://dx.doi.org/10.1016/j.socscimed.2010.04.008.

Gadsden, O., & Howard, L. (2016). *Beyond Trayvon Martin: A clinical deconstruction of the negative internalized archetype of African American masculinity.* In Ross, W. (Ed.) *Counseling African American males: effective therapeutic interventions and approaches.* NC: Information Age Publishing.

Goldsmith, A. H., Hamilton, D., & Darity, W. (2007). From dark to light skin: Skin color and wages among African Americans. *The Journal of Human Resources, 4*, 701.

Gordon, L. R. (2007). *Problematic people and epistemic decolonization: Toward The postcolonial in African political thought.* In N. Persam (Ed.), *Postcolonialism and Political Theory*, New York: Lexington Books.

Gregory, D., Johnston, R., Pratt, G., & Watts, M. (2009). *The dictionary of human Geography* 5th ed.. Wiley-Blackwell.

Hall, R. (1992). Bias among African Americans regarding skin color: Implications for social work practice. *Research on Social Work Practice, 2*, 479-486.

Hamilton, D., Goldsmith, A.H., & Darity, W. (2009). Shedding "light" on marriage: The influence of skin shade on marriage for black females. *Journal of Economic Behavior & Organization, 72*(1), 30-50. https://doi.org/10.1016/j.jebo.2009.05.024.

Hanisch, Carol (January 2006). "The Personal Is Political: The Women's Liberation Movement classic with a new explanatory introduction

Harrison, M.S., & Thomas, K.M. (2009). The hidden prejudice in selection: A research investigation on skin color bias. *Journal of Applied Social Psychology, 39*(1), 134-168.

Hill, M. E. (2002). Skin color and the perception of attractiveness among African Americans: Does gender make a difference? *Social Psychology Quarterly, 65*(1), 77-91. https://doi.org/10.2307/3090169.

Hochschild, J.L., & Weaver, V. (2007). The skin color paradox and the American racial order. *Social Forces, 86*, 643-670. DOI:10.1093/sf/86.2.643.

Hooker, J., & Tillery, A.B. (2016). The Double Bind: The politics of racial and class inequalities in the Americas, Washington, DC: American Political Science Association.

Hughes, M., & Bradley, R. H. (1990). The significance of color remains: A study of life chances, mate selection, and ethnic consciousness among Black Americans. *Social Forces, 68*, 1105-1120.

Hughes, M., & Hertel, B. R. (1990). The significance of color remains: A study of life chances, mate selection, and ethnic consciousness among Black Americans. *Social Forces, 68*(4), pp.1105-1120.

Hunter, M.L. (2007). The persistent problem of colorism: Skin tone, status, and Inequality. *Sociology Compass, 1*(1), 237-254. https://doi.org/10.1111/j.1751-9020.2007.00006.x.

Hunter, M.L. (2011). Buying racial capital: Skin-bleaching and cosmetic surgery in a globalized world. *Journal of Pan African Studies, 4*(4), 142-164.

Jones, S. (2014). Michael Brown and the effects of colorism. Retrieved from http://www.solomonjones.com/michael-brown-effects-colorism.

Kahn, K.B. & Davies, P.G. (2010). Differentially dangerous? Phenotype racial Stereotypically increases implicit bias among ingroup and outgroup members. Group Processes & Intergroup Relations, 10-12. DOI:10.1177/1368430210374609.

Keith, V.M., & Herring, C. (1991). Skin tone and stratification in the Black community. *American Journal of Sociology, 97*, 760-778. https://doi.org/10.1086/229819.

Keith, V. M., Lincoln, K.D., Taylor, R. J., Jackson, J. S. (2010). Discriminatory Experiences and depressive symptoms among African American women: Do skin tone and mastery matter? *Sex Roles, 62*(1-2), 48-59.

Lanor, A. & Barr, A. (2018). Politics of respectability, colorism, and the terms of social exchange in family research. *Journal of Family Theory & Review, 10*, 330-347. DOI:10.1111/jftr.12264.

Maddox, K.B., & Gray, S.A. (2002). Cognitive representations of Black Americans: reexploring the role of skin tone. *Personality and Social Psychology Bulletin, 28*(2), 250-259. https://doi.org/10.1177/0146167202282010.

Maxwell, M., Brevard, J., Abrams, J., & Belgrave, F. (2014). What's color got to do with it? Skin color, skin color satisfaction, racial identity, and internalized racism among African American college students. *Journal of Black Psychology, 41*, 438-461. https://doi.org/10.1177/0095798414542299.

Neal, A. M., Wilson. M. (1989). The role of skin color and features in the Black community: Implications for Black women and therapy. *Clinical Psychology Review, 9*, 323-333.

Norwood, K.J., & Foreman, V. (2015). The ubiquitousness of colorism: Then and now. In K.J. Norwood (Ed.), *Color matters: Skin tone bias and the myth of a Post-racial America* (pp. 9-28). New York, NY: Routledge.

Ogunleye, T. (1998). Dr. Martin Robison Delany, 19th century Africana Womanist: Reflection on his avant-garde politics concerning gender, colorism, and nation building. *Journal of Black Studies, 28*(5), pp. 628-649.

Owen, J., Tao, K., Drinane, J., Hook, J., Davis, D., & Foo Kune, N. (2016). Client perceptions of therapists' multicultural orientation: Cultural (missed) opportunities and cultural humility. *Professional Psychology: Research and Practice, 47*, 30-37.

Russell-Cole, K., Wilson, M., & Ronald, E.H. (2013). *The color complex: The politics of skin color in a new millennium*, New York, NY: Anchor Books.

Russell, K., Wilson, M., Hall, R. (1992). *The color complex: The politics of skin color among African Americans.* Anchor Books.

Smith, L.T. (2012). *Decolonizing methodologies: Research and indigenous peoples.* London, UK: Zed Books.

Snell, J. (2017). Colorism/Neo-colorism. *Education, 138*(2), 205-209.

Wade, T. J., & Bielitz, S. (2005). The differential effect of skin color on attractiveness, personality evaluations, and perceived life success of African Americans. *Journal of Black Psychology, 3*(3),215-236. https://doi.org/10.1177/0095798405278341.

Wilder, J., & Cain, C. (2010). Teaching and learning color consciousness in Black families: Exploring family processes and women's experiences with colorism. *Journal of Family Issues, 32*(5), 577-604. https://doi.org/10.1177/0192513x10390858.

Wingfield, A. H., & Wingfield, J. H. (2014). When visibility hurts and helps: How intersections of race and gender shape Black professional men's experiences with tokenization. *Cultural Diversity and Ethnic Minority Psychology, 20,* 483-490. http://dx.doi.org/10.1037/a0035761.

CHAPTER 17.

Colorism and Skin Bleaching: Implications for Advancing Multiple Critical Literacies for Equity and Social Justice

Petra A. Robinson, Louisiana State University
Paula A. Barbel, The College at Brockport State University of New York

Introduction

Even when broadly defined to include a focus on facial physical features or other phenotypic characteristics beyond skin complexion, colorism is a disturbing and oppressive dilemma for people of color. Colorism is a privileging process (Hunter, 2002) which relies on a mechanism of stratification that affords preference through prestige and favor to people with lighter skin over people with darker skin (Robinson, 2011; 2013). It extends to also other physical attributes and features such as hair texture, eye color, and other facial features (Cain, 2006) in which preference/privilege is shown and extended to people with features that are more closely connected to racialized beauty standards, specifically those described as part of a Eurocentric model of beauty (Robinson, 2011) and the Caucasian color code (Charles, 2003a). While this is not a new phenomenon, studying colorism and the skin bleaching practice situated within a critical theory and critical literacy framework has not been done in the academic literature.

Some scholars have studied and described colorism using terms such as skin color bias, shadism, color complex, skin tone bias, and pigmentocracy (Adams, Kurtz-Costes, & Hoffman, 2016; Harrison & Thomas, 2009; Russell, Wilson, & Hall, 1992; Telles, 2015). While we embrace a broad and more inclusive definition of colorism, for purposes of this paper we utilize the Blair, Judd, Sadler, and Jenkins' (2002) definition which explicates that colorism is the result of a positive evaluation that favors lighter skin over darker skin. This definition is appropriate in this context because our central focus in the chapter is on the skin bleaching phenomenon, which we frame in light of the global colorism problem.

Purpose of the Chapter

The purpose of this chapter is to investigate skin bleaching, as a complex societal problem rooted in colorism and to frame it in terms of critical literacy. This will help further our understanding of the phenomenon and contribute to filling the gap related to various critical literacies related to the problem of colorism described herein as a kind of disease with skin bleaching as a metaphorical symptom.

Background

Predicated on tenets of White supremacy (Hunter, 2007) and connected to an ideology of Black inferiority, like Dixon and Telles (2017), we argue that colorism (at least in the Western Hemisphere), as a form of discrimination, has roots in racism and European colonialism, but importantly, like Robinson (2011) explains, it stretches beyond the traditional discourse of the Black/White race dichotomy since it includes discrimination from and among people of the same race.

Colorism is a significant, pervasive, and disturbing problem that has implications for people of color across the world. In commenting on the ubiquitous and harmful nature of colorism juxtaposed to that of racism, Wilder (2008) suggests that similar to "the daily experiences of racism, everyday colorism is a system of language, internal scripts and external practices that govern the everyday interactions and experiences of young black women as it relates to skin tone" (p. 12). Indeed, colorism affects people of color across race and gender in multiple ways and this suggests that colorism is significant as a topic for scholarly inquiry with multiple implications for research, theory, and practice.

As Webb and Robinson (2017) illustrate, studying and addressing colorism is important as evidenced by numerous interdisciplinary studies that highlight color-based inequality in various aspects of life, particularly among people of color. Colorism, as Hunter (2002) describes, is a major sociological issue which often results in disparities in areas such as income (Goldsmith, Hamilton, & Darity, 2007), employment (Johnson, Bienenstock, & Stoloff, 1995; Harris & Thomas, 2009), courtship and marriage (Hunter, 2002; 2004) education (Murguia & Telles, 1996), school disciple—especially for girls (Hannon, DeFina, & Burch, 2013).

Further, research suggests that conforming to a white beauty standard would lead to a more rewarding life (Bond & Cash, 1992; Gatewood, 1988) because colorism has significant impact on one's positionality (Robinson, 2011), status (Dixon & Telles, 2017); on one's life chances (Herring, 2002; Hunter, 1998; Telles & Murguia, 1990);

and life choices (Matthews & Johnson, 2015). As colorist messages permeate through advertising and the cosmetic industry (Collins, 2018) and through social media such as Twitter (Webb & Robinson, 2017), formal and informal stakeholders participate in and capitalize on the dynamic network of the multi-billion-dollar global skin-lightening industry (Glenn, 2008) which we describe as central to the skin bleaching practice.

The process of skin lightening through skin bleaching is a global phenomenon for which the motivations are explained in various ways in the increasingly global literature. Hall (1995) suggests that it occurs because of cultural domination and from pressure to assimilate in the dominant group (Hall, 1994; 1995) while Charles (2003b; 2003c) suggests it is because of miseducation about Blackness in general and about beauty more specifically. Other scholars suggest that skin bleaching may have emerged as a result of a lingering colonial influence (Charles, 2003a), described by Robinson (2011) as an imperialist and colonial legacy. Additionally, Robinson and Alfred (2013) found in their study, among male and female skin bleachers in Jamaica, that some people report to bleach for fashion suggesting that bleaching is the "in-thing" and for staying current with beauty trends in urban communities (such as Kingston or for self-image, acceptability, and popularity (Robinson, 2011). In this chapter, we, like other scholars, argue that skin bleaching is directly connected to colorism and, as such, we use a critical lens to examine the nuances and implications of the phenomena.

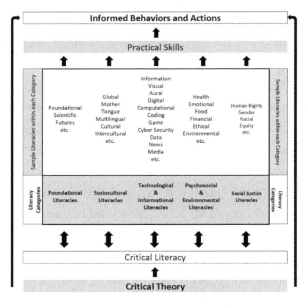

Table 1: Critical Literacies Advancement Model. (Robinson, 2020)

Theoretical Framework

We situate our examination of colorism and the skin bleaching phenomenon on the core principle of Critical Theory. Further, we frame the implications of colorism and skin bleaching in terms of critical literacy by way of the Critical Literacies Advancement Model (CLAM) (Robinson, 2020). Critical literacy is based on critical theory which focuses on the fact that there are unequal power structures and relationships prevalent in society and that these are systematically legitimized, even through education. Critical Theory focuses on issues of marginalization, power, and privilege and its main goal is to seek positive change through reflective analysis, critique, and challenge of society's power structures. Critical literacy, as a practical application of critical theory, is one mechanism that can be used to challenge the status quo.

Freire (1970), for example, describes the necessity for critical literacy and how it can be developed in an educational context. In this case, students become more socially aware through critiquing multiple forms of injustice as they learn how to explore and construct knowledge and as educators move away from the traditional "banking" concept of education.

This is useful as a framework since critical literacy is "derived, in part from Critical Social Theory, particularly its concern with the alleviation of human suffering and for the formation of a more just world through the critique of existing social and political problems and the posing of alternatives" (Cervetti, Pardales, & Damico, 2001, p. 5). Therefore, as highlighted in the CLAM (Robinson, 2020) we use critical literacy as a means to understand, critique, and challenge colorism, the skin bleaching phenomenon, and to discuss these in critiques in light of other critical non-traditional literacies.

We build on this idea of the critical literacy model as an analytical tool and/ organizing device to further our critique and challenge of colorism and the skin bleaching phenomenon, but also as one that broadens our focus to encompass other non-traditional critical literacies toward the goal of positive social change. In the next section of the chapter, we provide more details about the skin bleaching practice in terms of the science behind the practice as well as some of the side effects of engaging in the practice.

The Science of Skin Bleaching

Skin bleaching is the use of chemical products to lighten skin pigmentation. Melanin (derived from the Greek word *melanos*, which means "dark") is the primary pigment responsible for skin, eye, and hair color (Solano, 2014). Melanin is produced by melanocytes (cells in the basal layer of the epidermis) through a complex chemical process known as melanogenesis, with the enzyme tyrosinase playing a key role in the production of melanin. The melanin is then transferred to keratinocytes (present in the epidermis of the skin) resulting in visible skin pigmentation.

Skin bleaching products inhibit the synthesis of tyrosinase, leading to destruction of melanocytes and decreased production of melanin resulting in lightening of the skin (Mohammed, Mohammed, & Bascombe, 2017). Skin bleaching products are available in several formulations such as topical creams, soaps and ointments, as pills or capsules, or as injections for intravenous administration (Darj, Infanti, Ahlberg, & Okumu, 2015). Hydroquinone, steroids, retinoids, alpha-hydroxy acids, glutathione, kojic acid, vitamin C, mercury derivatives, and several other herbal extracts are all used for skin bleaching. However, the most commonly used products are hydroquinone, corticosteroids, mercury derivatives, and kojic acid (Couteau & Coiffard, 2016; Sonthalia, Daulatabad, & Sarkar, 2016). Cosmetic products containing hydroquinone have been banned in Europe, however, they are readily available over-the-counter (OTC) in the United States and other countries around the world (Couteau & Coiffard, 2016). Topical prescription combination creams containing hydroquinone can be effective in treating hyperpigmentation skin conditions such as melasma.

Other methods of skin lightening include the use of alpha hydroxyl acids such as "glycolic acid (derived from sugarcane), lactic acid (from fermented milk or honey), malic acid (from apples, quinces and mountain ashes), citric acid (from citrus fruits), tartaric acid (from grapes) and mandelic acid (from bitter almonds)" (Couteau & Coiffard, 2016, p. 5). Very superficial cosmetic peels destroy the outermost layer of the skin while a superficial peel destroys part of the epidermis. A medium peel destroys the epidermis and part of the dermis and a deep peel destroys the epidermis and the deeper layer of the dermis (Couteau & Coiffard, 2016).

Melanin protects exposed skin from the damaging effects ultra violet (UV) radiation from sunlight (Solano, 2014). Given that the rate of skin turnover is approximately 28 days, skin bleaching products need to be repeatedly applied or used in order to achieve and maintain the lighter skin tone. Similarly, exposure to sunlight increases the production of melanin, this again requires repeated use of skin bleaching products to maintain lighter skin pigmentation. Additionally, in order to achieve an even skin tone, skin bleaching products would need to be applied over large areas of the body (Olowu & Ogunlade, 2013). Many of the skin bleaching creams available worldwide contain levels of mercury that exceeds the limits recommended by the World Health

Organization (WHO) (Michalek, et al., 2019). Use of mercury-containing creams can result in mercury being absorbed systemically by either inhalation or absorption through the skin leading to elevated systemic mercury levels (Agrawal & Sharma, 2017; Mohammed, Mohammed, & Bascombe, 2017). These products are readily available for purchase OTC in many countries as they are considered cosmetic products or dietary supplements or have the status of "Generally recognized as safe" (Sonthalia, Daulatabad, & Sarkar, 2015).

Side Effects of Using Skin-Bleaching Products

Skin bleaching products are associated with several known harmful side effects. They are dangerous and harmful to the skin and to a person's overall health (Mahe, Ly, & Peret, 2005; Faye, Keita, Diakite, Konare, & Ndiaye, 2005). Notably, these chemicals have proven to be so dangerous that they have led to disfigurement and even death (Miyanji de Souza, 2008). Topical steroids (major component) used over large areas can lead to hypercorticism, skin atrophy, arterial hypertension, osteoporosis, and diabetes (Couteau & Coiffard, 2016). Hydroquinone used topically can result in exogenous oochronosis (a bluish-black discoloration of the skin), dermatitis (reddened itchy skin), leukoderma (depigmentation of the skin), post-inflammatory pigmentation, bone marrow toxicity, and kidney and liver diseases. Creams containing mercury can lead to mercury poisoning and can present with symptoms such as anorexia, excessive sweating intense itching, rashes, skin discoloration, peripheral neuropathy, renal tubular necrosis resulting in acute injury to the kidneys, nephrotic syndrome (edema or swelling of the face and extremities, protein in the urine, increased cholesterol levels and decreased serum albumin levels) and neurological and behavioral problems. Mercury also crosses the placenta and can lead to birth defects and damage to the fetal brain (Agrawal & Sharma, 2017; Mohammed, Mohammed, & Bascombe, 2017; Aramide, Olatunji, & Ayandele, 2019). Use of retinoic acid can result in redness and desquamation of the skin.

According to Robinson (2011), "other side effects of bleaching creams include skin cancer, thinning of the skin, irreversible stretch marks, easy bruising and tearing of the skin, rashes, enlarged blood vessels, susceptibility to infection, delayed wound healing, hyper pigmentation, acne, and hormonal disturbances. Additionally, commenting on the prevalence and use of bleaching creams and other bleaching chemicals, dermatologist, Andrew (2002) reported that Dr. Neil Persadsingh explained,

Some of these creams work by killing the melanin, the substance that lends skin pigmentation and protects the skin from the cancer-causing ultraviolet rays of the sun. All people have melanin in their skin; the more melanin present, the darker the skin. In addition, he says, the preparations contain large amounts of hydroquinone- a white crystalline de-pigmenting agent that is fatal in large concentrations. Victims suffer from nausea, shortness of breath, convulsions and delirium. Damage to the skin- wrinkles, severe acne marks- may be irreversible after prolonged use. ...When we are faced with this type of damage, there is nothing that we can do except to advise the patient to live with their condition. The prolonged and continued use of these creams will lead to a face looking like a grater (para. 6).

Despite the potential adverse effects, the practice of skin bleaching continues to be prevalent in many countries around the world. Several factors contribute to this phenomenon including lack of knowledge regarding the ingredients in the skin bleaching products and potential adverse effects.

In the next section of the chapter, we explain Critical Literacy as a central theme of our organizing framework in terms of critiquing colorism and the skin bleaching practice and phenomenon. This is followed by discussions and implications section which includes ideas for future research.

Critical Literacy

In this instance, we use a critical literacy stance to analyze the skin bleaching phenomenon as part of the global colorism problem. Critical literacy is an analytical tool that is grounded in the sociocultural perspective (Robinson, 2019) which encourages examination, questioning, and dispute about power relations (Bradford & Harris, 2003). Not restricted to reading material, critical literacy represents all forms of communication which can influence peoples' perspective and lead to positive social change (Freire, 1970). Essentially, critical literacy is a means by which people learn to "read both the word and the world in relation to power, identity, difference and access to knowledge, skills, tools, and resources. It is also about writing and rewriting the world: it is about design and redesign" (Janks, 2013, p. 227). Therefore, we suggest that critical literacy is an integral skill for combating colorism and more specifically the skin bleaching phenomenon.

The impact of colorism is well documented and its prevalence is supported by colorist messages in advertising, editorial content, and widely by popular, mass, and social media. We suggest, therefore, that a critical approach to problematizing these messages is required for addressing the problem of colorism. This also means being able to decode and developing skills to unearth the hidden curriculum and other hidden agendas that can, especially in a seemingly innocent way and even through educational settings, communicate overt and covert messages that perpetuate colorism.

The hidden curriculum refers to the unspoken and unofficial norms, behaviors, and values that students learn in formal education settings in addition to the official curriculum. Considerations in this context include a broader examination of the informal ways we learn unofficial norms, behaviors and values in society-- the hidden societal curriculum. This societal curriculum refers to "massive, ongoing, informal curriculum of family, peer groups, neighborhoods, mass media and other social forces that 'educate' us throughout our lives." (Cortes, 1979). Through critical literacy, individuals can learn strategies on how to discriminate, problematize and carefully evaluate various messages and therefore promote or advance other critical non-traditional literacies such as media and health literacy. The CLAM (Robinson, 2020) can therefore be used to help further illustrate the ways in which critical theory can support critical literacy and how critical literacy can help advance the development of various categories of literacies. This is all with the aim of having practical skills that can result in informed behaviors and actions that promote positive social change.

Health Literacy

Colorism (the disease) and skin bleaching (the symptom) more specifically, have implications for a host of non-traditional literacies. Most obvious in this instance and pertinent for this discussion is health literacy. It is evident that being cognizant of the dangers of skin bleaching and responding appropriately, despite the many social and cultural pressures to bleach, requires a specific level of health literacy.

Health literacy can be defined as "the degree to which an individual has the capacity to obtain, communicate, process, and understand basic health information and services to make appropriate health decisions" (Centers for Disease Control [CDC], 2019). This includes skills such as being able to read and understand labels, proper use of medications and access to health- related information such as potential side effects like those seen with the use of skin bleaching products (Berkman, et al., 2011). There are many factors that contribute to health literacy including socio-economic status, social support, media, language, family, age, gender, historic discrimination and culture (lgüm, Turaç, & Orak, 2015). Minorities, the elderly, having lower levels of education and persons from low socio-economic groups have the highest rates of low or limited health literacy (Berkman, et al., 2011; Center for Health Care Strategies, 2013).

Health literacy has significant effects on health-related outcomes. Low health literacy has been associated with an increased rate of hospitalization and use of the emergency department, decreased rates of vaccination and cancer screening, poor health choices, riskier behaviors, improper use of medications and increased rate of death and chronic disease (lgüm, Turaç, & Orak, 2015; World Health Organization [WHO], 2013). Higher health literacy can result in increased perceived quality of life, better overall health and decreased hospitalization. It is therefore imperative to develop interventions and strategies that will increase health literacy in persons who use skin bleaching products in an effort to increase self-efficacy and reduce disparities.

Overall, we suggest that in order to help advance health literacy, it would be essential to develop skills in critical literacy, as posited in the Robinson (2020) Critical Literacies Advancement Model which suggests that Critical Literacy is important for advancing other critical literacies such as psycho-social and environmental literacies to include health literacy.

Discussion and Implications

In this chapter, we used the Robinson (2020) Critical Literacies Advancement Model which outlines the connection between Critical Theory and Critical Literacy by explaining the ultimate goal of Critical Theory to promote positive social change. By doing this and by framing this chapter with the Critical Literacies Advancement Model (Robinson, 2020), we show how critical literacy can serve as the mechanism through which non-traditional critical literacy skills can be developed and promoted toward the goal of informed behaviors and actions especially, in this case, decision-making related to eradicating colorism and combating the skin bleaching practice.

Developing critical literacy skills is an important step in seeking to address complicated societal problems (such as colorism and skin bleaching) and the implications of this skill development can be far reaching particularly as we seek to live and thrive in a globalized, technologically-dependent world. This chapter highlights the significance of critical literacy and it has implications for practice, policy, and research.

Implications for Practice

Stakeholders interested in advancing critical literacy skills may consider creating learning opportunities in both formal and informal learning environments. This means addressing these problematic areas directly in the formal curriculum whether through integration of important topics such as colorism into already existing curricula through practical activities, reflections, small group facilitation, assignments, modular topics, scholarly writings, and so on. This may also be done by developing specific courses aimed at engaging students in a critical analysis of colorism while focusing on the cultural, theoretical, and practical aspects related to various disciplines. These initiatives and learning opportunities can also be provided and in other environments such as in the informal learning network.

Regardless of the learning environment, it means creating instruction in non-typical ways. In terms of practice, instructors may consider using strategies that include learners using their experiences to draw from their own cultural knowledge in ways that can initiate discussion and critique of systems that promote colorism and in turn, skin bleaching. Additionally, such as those used in family-literacy programs where various members of the family are included in learning, or in helping to address gaps in the home and in other social environments. Framed by models such as CLAM (Robinson, 2020), and used in conjunction with a curriculum that is based on a critical-thinking, critical literacy, and social justice agenda, this can have far-reaching effects in terms of reducing negative multi-generational ideas about skin color and unhealthy practices such as skin bleaching. This also has significant implications for policy makers who are concerned with the welfare and well-being for people of color.

Implications for Policy

As policy makers consider designing and implementing policies that affect the experiences of people of color, especially those who face discrimination and marginalization based on the color of their skin, they should consider putting things in place such as public health campaigns that address issues such as skin bleaching and colorism. Using the CLAM framework to help guide policy design and implementation, key stakeholders can negotiate their role in terms of design, administration and execution. Colorism and other social concerns should be at the forefront of policy makers' agendas similar to other key issues that make up protected class concerns for federal law.

Implications for Research

In terms of future research, the Critical Literacies Advancement Model (Robinson, 2020) is a useful tool that can be used as a stand-alone model or in conjunction with other frameworks to further guide researchers interested in using a critical lens in other studies related to public health and other non-traditional literacies. This is significant because of its implications for theory building and for the creation of refined models to help frame our understanding of how to promote critical thinking skills and to encourage thoughtful analysis of policy and systematic structures that marginalize people and promote inequities in society. Research on colorism framed by this model that uses a variety of methodological approaches will provide important information related to developing skills in a wide range of literacies and can help improve health outcomes, enhance critical thinking skills among learners, as well as promote equity and social justice.

Process Questions and Considerations

1. In what ways do you think skin bleaching is connected to the concept of colorism?

2. How can educators promote health literacy to address skin bleaching?

3. What is the role of technology in promoting colorism and how can it be used to counteract it?

4. What strategies can educators build into their pedagogical practice to disrupt systems that promote colorism?

5. How can the Critical Literacies Advancement Model be used across disciplines to address colorism and other forms of prejudice and oppression?

References

Adams, E. A., Kurtz-Costes, B. E., & Hoffman, A. J. (2016). Skin tone bias among African Americans: Antecedents and consequences across the life span. *Developmental Review, 40,* 93-116.

Agrawal, S. S., & Sharma, P. (2017). Current status of mercury level in skin whitening creams. *Current Medicine Research and Practice, 7,* 47-50.

Andrew, M. (2002, September 1). The skin bleaching phenomenon—Commentary. *Jamaica Primetime.* Retrieved from http://www.jamaicans.com/articles/primecomments/0902_bleaching.shtml

Aramide, O., Olatunji, O. S., & Ayandele, O. (2019). *Health information literacy on the risks of using skin bleaching products.* Library Philosophy and Practice. https://www.researchgate.net/publication/335857124_Health_Information_Literacy_on_the_Risks_of_Using_Skin_Bleaching_Products

Berkman, N. D., Davis, T. C., & McCormak, L. (2010). Health literacy: What is it? *Journal of Health Communication, 15,* 9-19.

Blair, I. V., Judd, C. M., Sadler, M. S., & Jenkins, C. (2002). The role of Afrocentric features in person perception: Judging by features and categories. *Journal of Personality and Social Psychology, 83*(1), 5-25.

Bond, S., & Cash, T. F. (1992). Black beauty: Skin color and body images among African-American college women. *Journal of Applied Social Psychology, 22*(11), 874-888.

Bradford, A. C., & Harris, J. L. (2003). Cultural knowledge in African American children. *Language, Speech, and Hearing Services in Schools, 34,* 56-58.

Cain, C. (2006). *Sources, manifestations and solutions: Examining colorism among African American and Afro-Caribbean women.* Master's Thesis. University of Florida. Retrieved from http://etd.fcla.edu/UF/UFE0014221/cain_c.pdf

Centers for Disease Control. (2019). What is health literacy? Retrieved from https://www.cdc.gov/healthliteracy/learn/index.html

Center for Health Care Strategies. (2013). Health literacy and the role of culture. Retrieved from http://www.chcs.org/media/Health_Literacy_Role_of_Culture.pdf

Cervetti, G. N., Pardales, M. J., & Damico, J. S. (2001). A tale of differences: Comparing the traditions, perspectives, and educational goals of critical reading and critical literacy. *Reading Online, 4*(9). Available at: http://www.readingonline.org/articles/art_index.asp?HREF=/articles/cervetti/index.html.

Charles, C.A.D. (2003a). Skin bleaching and the deconstruction of blackness. *IDEAZ, 2*(1), 42-54.

Charles, C.A.D. (2003b). Skin bleaching, self-hate, and black identity in Jamaica. *Journal of Black Studies, 33,* 711-778.

Charles, C.A.D. (2003b). The crowning of the browning: Colour and identity in the dancehall cultural space. Paper presented at the Caribbean Studies Association Conference, Belize City, Belize.

Couteau, C. & Coiffard, L. (2016). Overview of skin whitening agents: Drugs and cosmetic products. *Cosmetics, 3,* 27.

Darj, E., Infanti, J. J., Ahlberg, B. M., & Okumu, J. (2015). "The fairer the better?" Use of potentially toxic skin bleaching products. *African Health Sciences, 15*(4), 1074-1080.

Faye, O., Keita, S., Diakite, F. S., Konare, H. D., & Ndiaye, H. T. (2005). Side effects of de-pigmenting products in Bamako, Mali. *Journal of Dermatology, 44*(1), 35-36.

Freire, P. (1970). *Pedagogy of the oppressed.* New York, NY: Seabury Press.

Gatewood, W. B. (1988). Aristocrat of color: South and north and the black elite, 1880-1920. *Journal of Southern History, 54,* 3-19.

Glenn, E. N. (2008). Yearning for lightness: Transnational circuits in the marketing and consumption of skin lighteners. *Gender & Society, 22*(3), 281-302.

Goldsmith, A. H., Hamilton, D., & Darity, W. (2007). From dark to light: Skin color and wages among African-Americans. *The Journal of Human Resources, 42*(4), 701-738.

Hannon, L., DeFina, R., Burch, S. (2013). The relationship between skin tone and school suspension for African Americans. *Race and Social Problems, 5*(4), 281-295.

Harrison, M. S., & Thomas, K. M. (2009). The hidden prejudice in selection: A research investigation on skin color bias. *Journal of Applied Social Psychology, 39*(1), 134-168.

Herring, C. (2002). Bleaching out the color line? The skin color continuum and the tripartite model of race. *Race & Society, 5,* 17-31.

Hunter, M. (1998). Colorstruck: Skin color stratification in the lives of African American women. *Sociological Inquiry, 68*(4), 517-535.

Hunter, M. (2002). If you're light you're alright: Light skin color as social capital for women of color. *Gender & Society, 16*(2), 175-193.

Hunter, M. (2004). Light, bright, and almost white: The advantages and disadvantages of light skin. In C. Herring, V. Keith, & H. Horton (Eds.), *Skin deep: How race and complexion matter in the "color-blind" era* (pp. 22-44). Chicago: University of Illinois Press.

Ilgün, G., Turaç, S., & Orak, S. (2015). Health literacy. *Procedia-Social and Behavioral Sciences, 174,* 2629-2633.

Janks, H. (2013). Critical literacy in teaching and research. *Education Inquiry, 4*(2), 225-242.

Johnson Jr., J. H., Bienenstock, E. J., & Stoloff, J. A. (1995). An empirical test of the cultural capital hypothesis. *The Review of the Black Political Economy, 23*(4), 7- 27.

Mahe, A., Ly, F. Perret, J. (2005). Systemic complications of the cosmetic use of skin-bleaching products. *Journal of Dermatology, 44*(1), 37-38.

Michalek, I. M., Benn, E.K.T., Caetano dos Santos, F. L., Gordon, S., Wen, C., & Liu, B. (2019). A systematic review of global legal regulations on the permissible level of heavy metals in cosmetics with particular emphasis on skin lightening. *Environmental Research, 170,* 187-193.

Miyanji de Souza, M. (2008). The concept of skin bleaching in Africa and its devastating health implications. *Clinics in Dermatology, 26,* 27-29.

Mohammed, T., Mohammed, E., & Bascombe, S. (2017). The evaluation of total mercury and arsenic in skin bleaching creams commonly used in Trinidad and Tobago and their potential risk to the people of the Caribbean. *Journal of Public Health Research, 6,* 184-189.

Murguia, E., & Telles, E. E. (1996). Phenotype and schooling among Mexican Americans. *Sociology of Education, 69,* 276-289.

Olowu, A., & Ogunlade, O. (2013). Pathophysiology and Psychopathology of Skin Bleaching and Implications of Skin Color in Africa. *In The Melanin Millenium,* R. E. Hall (Ed.). pp. 39-48. Dordrecht: Springer.

Robinson, P. A. (2011). *Skin bleaching in Jamaica: A colonial legacy.* (Doctoral dissertation, Texas A&M University). Retrieved from http://oaktrust.library.tamu.edu/bitstream/handle/1969.1/ETD-TAMU-2011-05-9220/ROBINSON-DISSERTATION.pdf?sequence=2.Accessed

Robinson, P. A., & Alfred, M. V. (2013). Colorism and skin bleaching in Jamaica: Global implications for communities of color and urban classrooms. National Journal of Urban Education and Practice, 6(3), 29-40.

Robinson, P. A. (2020). The Critical Literacies Advancement Model (CLAM): A framework for promoting positive social change. Retrieved from https://digitalcommons.lsu.edu/cgi/viewcontent.cgi?article=1000&context=shrewd_pubs

Robinson, S. A. (2019). Critical literacy and its impact on African American boys' reading identity. Gifted Child Today, 42(3), 150-156.

Statistical Institute of Jamaica. (2017). Census 2011. Retrieved from https://statinja.gov.jm/Census/PopCensus/Popcensus2011Index.aspx

Solano, F. (2014). Melanins: Skin pigments and much more—types, structural models, biological functions and formation routes. *New Journal of Science,* 1-29.

Sonthalia, S., Daulatabad, D., & Sarkar, R. (2016). Glutathione as a skin whitening agent: Facts, myths, evidence and controversies. *Indian Journal of Dermatology, Venereology and Leprology, 82*(3), 262-272.

Telles, E. E. (2014). *Pigmentocracies: Ethnicity, race, and color in Latin America.* Chapel Hill, NC: University of North Carolina Press.

Telles, E. E., & Murguia, E. (1990). Phenotypic discrimination and income differences among Mexican Americans. *Social Science Quarterly, 71,* 682-696.

Webb, S. L., & Robinson, P. A. (2017). Mentions and melanin: Exploring the colorism discourse and Twitter culture. In H. D. Horton, L. L. Martin, C. Herring, V. Keith, and M. Thomas (Eds.), *Color struck: How race and complexion matter in the "color-blind" era* (pp. 19-35). Brill Publishers.

Wilder, J. (2008). *Everyday colorism in the lives of young black women: revisiting the continuing significance of an old phenomenon in a new generation* (Doctoral dissertation, University of Florida). Retrieved from http://etd.fcla.edu/UF/UFE0022480/wilder_j.pdf

World Health Organization. (2013). Health literacy, the solid facts. Retrieved from https://apps.who.int/iris/bitstream/handle/10665/128703/e96854.pdf

CHAPTER 18.

In Between the Shade: Colorism and Its Impact on Black LGBTQ Communities

Jamal H. N. Hailey, Howard University
Joyell Arscott, Johns Hopkins School of Nursing
Kalima Young, Towson University

"…French-vanilla, butter-pecan, chocolate-deluxe.
Even caramel sundaes is gettin' touched.
And scooped in my ice cream truck.
Wu tears it up."
  –Raekwon ft. Ghostface Killah, Method Man, Cappadonna "Ice Cream"

Introduction

The impact of colorism has influenced many facets of cultures globally. It is no more evident than among Black people living in the United States. For years, theorists, researchers, and other intellectuals have hypothesized about the impact of colorism within Black communities. Academicians and scholars such as Patricia Hill Collins (*Black Sexual Politics*), Eric Jerome Dyson (*What True Sounds Like*), Keith Boykin (*For Colored Boys Who Have Considered Suicide When the Rainbow Is Still Not Enough*), and Marc Lamont Hill (*Nobody*), have long documented the impact of colorism among Black people. While not a new concept or phenomenon, the topic of colorism has seen an uptick in popular media, being covered in various news segments (*Colorism*, PBS) and pop culture (basketball, *Housewives of L.A.*, VH1). However, little attention has been paid to the impact of colorism in Black lesbian, gay, bisexual, and transgender communities.

In the larger American culture, phenotype is said to largely influence standards of beauty and concepts of attractiveness (Charles, 2011). White or lighter skin tone, finer hair textures, and European features are generally valued over darker skin, tightly coiled hair textures, and Afrocentric features. So much so, that some Black people take extreme measures to appear White and appeal to the European aesthetic. For example, some Black Americans engage in the controversial cosmetic procedure skin bleaching and other cosmetic alterations to appeal to the Eurocentric standard of beauty (Charles, 2011; Choma, & Prusaczyk, 2018; Hall, 2016, 2018), and while most empirical and surveillance data had focused on Black women it is worth noting that Black men are also prone to skin bleaching to appeal to Eurocentric standards of beauty (Brown-Glaude, 2013). Other, less extreme forms of cosmetic procedures (that is, hair relaxers, hot combs, colored contact lenses) are practiced and used regularly to appeal to the European aesthetic. While seemingly benign, a number of these practices are said to have long-term consequences on overall health and mental wellness (Charles, 2011; Hall, 2018). Yet some Black Americans continue to participate in these dangerous cosmetic procedures, despite the known health risk associated with many of them, underscoring the impact that colorism has on self-concept.

Colorism is said to have a detrimental impact on the psychological well-being of Black people living in America. It is thought to impact concepts around self-esteem and self-worth and is conceptualized as a salient factor influencing interpersonal relationships among Blacks. While colorism is thought to impact individuals across gender, there are some unique ways in which it manifests. For example, Black women with lighter skin tone, finer hair, and more European features are viewed as having prime characteristics as they relate to attractiveness, intelligence, and upward social mobility (Alon, Smith, Liao, & Schneider, 2019; Charles, 2011). However, Black men with darker skin, tightly coiled hair, and more African features are more associated with beauty and attractiveness (Charles, 2011). It is worth noting that darker skin tone, tightly coiled hair, and more African features on Black men do not translate to a higher social status or even gain Black men access to power and privilege. Instead, the darker skin tone on Black men is seen as linked to their sexual prowess, playing into stereotypes of the Mandingo Black man and the continued fetishization of the Black body (Collins, 2008; Flores, Watson, Allen, Ford, Serpe, Choo, & Farrell, 2018; Poulson-Bryant, 2005).

As discussions regarding colorism in the United States expand, it is important to understand the historical context of colorism, and the nuanced ways in which it impacts society, culture, and the individual. In doing so, discussions of colorism must include its roots in racism, and how it feeds into ideals of White supremacy, sexism, heterosexism, and transphobia. Moreover, special attention is needed to understand how colorism manifests and is maintained within the Black LGBTQ+ community. To date, there has been scant research examining the impact of colorism among Black LGBTQ+ communities (Alon et al., 2019). The purpose of this chapter is to explore how colorism may impact Black LBGTQ+ individuals and provide directions for future research.

Colorism in Lesbian and Bisexual Communities

Discussing the politics of race and gender in filmic representations of LGBTQ persons, QTIPOC (queer, trans, intersex person of color) filmmaker Campbell X posits, "gender identities are racialized, racialized identities are gendered, and all of them are sexualized and classed" (2016). Black lesbian and bisexual women are a subgroup within a marginalized group. Very little sociological, psychological, and public health research has specifically focused on their lives and livelihoods. Empirical evidence about the impact of colorism on the lives of Black lesbian and bisexual women is scarce. However, a scan of the literature on Black women and colorism and Black lesbian and bisexual identity provides several paths for potential investigation.

Distortions

Regardless of their sexual orientation, Black lesbian and bisexual women are socialized as Black women. As such, they too must deal with the oppression that comes from existing within a White supremacist capitalist, hetero-patriarchal (bell hooks, 2010) society. Black women are always working to stand up straight in a room that is made crooked by stereotypes and distortions (Harris-Perry, 2013). Many of those stereotypes and distortions intersect with skin tone privilege. Scholars seeking to learn more about colorism in the lesbian and bisexual community may want to investigate Black lesbian and bisexual women's strategies for resisting distortions and managing self-care. Some of these strategies may affect gender expectations, gender performance, and romantic relationships because all of these choices are buttressed by societal and cultural norms that privilege Whiteness. As Black lesbian and bisexual women navigate spaces, their strategies of resistance and self-care may differ from their heterosexual counterparts, providing new avenues for intervention for all Black women.

Capital

Racial formation is the "socio-historical process by which racial categories are created, inhabited, transformed, and destroyed" (Omi and Winant, 2015). This process of historically situated projects organizes and redistribute resources along racial lines. White supremacy is a racist racial project which relies on the privileging of light skin tones over darker skin tones to maintain its hegemony. Colorism is a product of slavery and has been a long-standing factor in the well-being of Black communities in the

U.S. During enslavement, and many mixed-raced Black people were afforded levels of social privilege due to their ancestral and physical proximity to Whiteness. During and after enslavement, lighter-skinned Black people were afforded more access to education and property, contributing to the creation of Black wealth in the U.S (Coard, Breland & Raskin 2001; Ajayi & Syed 2016; Keith 2009). Scholars have found colorism still impacts Black people's abilities to acquire and maintain capital. Black women face a double economic barrier. The persistent devaluing of Black women's work results in lower wages, economic instability, income inequality, and less overall wealth. This limits their ability to strengthen and build their economic sustainability over the long term (Black Women's Roundtable, 2018). An analysis of 32 Black women in same-sex households found that partners share the economic burden more equitably, but the biological mother assumes more responsibility for nurturing the children (Mignon 2008). A study of colorism and dating choices in the African American community found that many African Americans associate light skin tone with feminine characteristics (Hill 2002). Does this same association relate to biological mothering and nurturing? Furthermore, how much does skin-privilege affect Black lesbian and bisexual women's expectations of who mothers and who works? In what ways do colorism affect their job opportunities and stability? Scholars investigating Black lesbian and bisexual economic health should consider the role of colorism in shaping responsibility structures within the family. As scholarship surrounding colorism and its impact on Black bisexual and lesbian women is cultivated, it is worth examining its impact on gender and gender role expectations. Gender Expectations

Colorism influences ones' personal feelings of self-worth and physical attractiveness (Keith, 2009). This suggests colorism is a form of internalized oppression. Pulitzer Prize-winning author Junot Diaz suggests the African Diaspora, "doesn't look the way it looks without systematic rape" (Diaz, 2016). His provocative statement reminds us that regardless of the privileges afforded to light-skinned Blacks, its legacy is rooted in a system of violence and exploitation meant to create and maintain hierarchies of social control. Beauty standards are one such hierarchy. Western standards of beauty are often associated with Eurocentric physical features such as light skin, thinness, light eyes, thin lips, and narrow noses. For these features to be considered "standard," they need an abject other for comparison. Afrocentric features: darker skin, textured hair, darker eyes, larger noses, lips, body shapes, and sizes fulfill the role of the abject.

Western culture tends to believe in a gender binary that links gender expression to biological sex. Femininity is a set of attributes, behaviors, and roles generally associated with women and girls though both sexes exhibit feminine and masculine traits. Heteropatriarchy links the well-being of a nation to the well-being of the heteropatriarchal family (Smith, 2016). In a heteropatriarchal society such as the U.S., the feminine is synonymous with the domestic/private sphere, while masculinity is generally associated with the public and social sphere. Heteropatriarchy assumes women are naturally attracted to men, and only through the union of a heterosexual family can future productive citizens be created. In the U.S., Black women violate all of these gender expectations. Black women have always worked in both the domestic and public sphere. This contributes to the perception that Black women lack femininity. Black women must fight against the stereotype that they create degenerate and unproductive children. Black women in the U.S. must combat negative perceptions of their looks, controlling images that position them as emasculating and domineering (Collins, 1990) and stereotypes that assume they are hypersexual. The internalization of heteropatriarchal messaging has been linked to higher rates of alcohol misuse and psychological distress among self-identified Black lesbian women (Lewis, Mason, Winstead, Gaskins, & Irons, 2016). Some Black lesbian and bisexual women, however, violate gender expectations by eschewing heteropatriarchy and all of its trapping. Researchers should consider investigating the way abjection structures Black lesbian and bisexual women's performance of gender, mothering, and sexual fulfillment.

Social Identity

Social identity is a person's sense of who they are based on their group membership. The group to which one belongs is an important source of pride and self-esteem and gives one a sense of belonging in the social world. In order to increase one's self-image, individuals elevate the status of the group to which they belong. The creation of an "us" versus "them" process of social categorization is referred to as in-group and out-group (Austin, 1979). Within this framework, the in-group discriminates against the out-group to bolster in-group self-image. White Americans have historically situated Black Americans in the out-group status via White supremacy. The U.S. history of racial discrimination and state-sanctioned terrorism relies heavily on maintaining this in-group/out-group boundary. Narrowing further, within Black intra-racial social identity, heterosexual Black Americans situate queer Black Americans as an out-group. In her study of gender presentation in Black lesbian communities, Mignon Moore (2008) states the:

"fear of stigmatization from one's own group members can be paralyzing, particularly when those whose opinions matter most, those to whom one feels closest, and those to whom one turns for support and protection from outsiders become one's harshest critics" (p. 118).

Black lesbian and bisexual women exist at the intersections of multiple social identities, all of which are impacted by colorism. A robust investigation into the impact of skin privilege on Black lesbian and bisexual women's in-group and out-group status has the potential to expand the field of social identity theory; broadening our understanding of which factors impact healthy social identity developments among sexual and gender racial minorities.

Safety and Abuse

In Black lesbian and bisexual communities, physical representations of gender help "structure women's expectations for and within relationships" (Moore, 2006). Gender presentation is not simply gendered play. It is a vital tool for shaping their social identity. If lighter skin is often associated with femininity and darker skin is associated with masculinity, how does colorism impact physical presentations of the self? The 2017 documentary, *Out in the Night*, tells the story four young Black lesbians who are violently and sexually threatened by a man on the street. They defend themselves against him and are charged and convicted in the courts and in the media as a 'Gang of Killer Lesbians.' As the documentary charts the course of these young women's lives, it sheds light on the way media depictions of darker-skinned lesbian and bisexual women often situate them as hyper-masculine. What are the consequences of darker skin bias on Black lesbian and bisexual women's engagements with the carceral system? How does the double marker of same-sex orientation and darker skin affect their strategies of survival within these systems? Does it extend to their sentencing and rehabilitation plans? According to the most recent federal data, Black girls' suspension rates are much higher than girls and boys of any race. Additional research shows darker-skinned girls are suspended and expelled more harshly than those with lighter skin (Black Women's Roundtable, 2018). It would behoove scholars to clarify the impact of perceptions of lesbian and bisexual identity and colorism on outcomes for Black girls in the school to prison pipeline.

One of the leading causes of death for Black women aged 15-35 is domestic/ intimate partner violence. Although Black women comprise only 8% of the population, compared to 30% for White women, Black women are almost three times as likely to be killed as a result of domestic violence. Despite the prevalence of domestic violence in the lives of Black women, they are less likely to seek help and more likely to fight back. In a study of intimate partner violence among 168 African American women in same-sex relationships, 27.9% of respondents reported racism as a primary factor in their abuse because of low self-esteem (Hill, 2016). With this in mind, it is vitally important that scholars further investigate the impact of internalized racism and colorism on Black lesbian and bisexual women's physical safety and livelihood. As our understanding of colorism and its impact on Black lesbian and bisexual women expands, we must consider how colorism impacts safety this vulnerable community.

Colorism in Transgender and Gender Diverse Communities

As noted by Flores et al. (2018), transgender and gender diverse individuals represent one of the most marginalized and vulnerable groups within the United States. In a recent national survey on transgender health, Black transgender and gender diverse communities were disproportionately represented in HIV prevalence rates and were more likely to report experiences of sexual assault (for example, rape, unwanted genital contact, and so on) (James, Herman, Rankin, Keisling, Mottet, & Anafi, 2016). Black transgender women, specifically, are nearly four times as likely to engage underground economies, such as sex work, when compared to White transgender women (Nuttbrock & Hwahng, 2016). Exploring colorism in relation to the experiences of Black transgender and gender diverse communities may offer new insights into the unique ways that this community is impacted by oppression and discrimination. A review of the literature on Black transgender and gender diverse communities provides several paths for potential investigation.

European Standards of Beauty and Body Image

In the groundbreaking documentary, *Paris is Burning* the impacts of European beauty standards on Black trans bodies was ever-present. As many of the Black and Latinx transgender women were interviewed, they spoke of their desires to achieve the American Dream, which was related to their proximity to Whiteness. While the documentary was filmed in the late nineteen-eighties and early nineteen-nineties, many of the messages regarding beauty and its proximity to Whiteness for Black transgender and gender nonconforming (TGNC) exist today. Numerous studies have suggested that skin tone has more of an impact on Black cis-women than on Black cis-men (Hall, 2017; Hill, 2002; Landor & Smith, 2019). It can be argued that the same holds true for Black women of trans experience. The limited research on colorism on

TGNC people of color suggests that European standards of beauty may be internalized, leading to feelings of anxiety related to skin tone (Flores et al., 2018). In recent years, the experiences of transgender and gender diverse communities have taken center stage as TGNC individuals have become more visible in their fight for equality and better representation in media. However, much of this conversation as centered on the experiences of White or lighter-skinned individuals over the looking the experiences of Black and darker-skinned transwomen. When the experiences of darker-skinned Black transgender individuals are prioritized, they are frequently depicted in more sexual and sensationalized ways (Allen, 2017). This is similar to the experiences of cis-gender Black women who are often oversexualized in the media and depicted as sexual objects (Lamb & Koven, 2019).

As transgender men and other transmasculine individuals begin to experience greater congruence (that is, feelings that their body and gender identity match), they may be faced with different challenges. Black men's bodies have long been the subject of many theories related to colorism. While often regarded for their sexual prowess, Black masculine bodies are often seen as inherently violent and dangerous (hooks, 2004). As many systems in the United States work to perpetuate that myth (for example, media), and protect White bodies from the imagined threat of Black masculine bodies through legislation and over-policing of Black men. The intersection of being both an object of sexual prowess and a perceived threat may create a new reality for Black transgender men, particularly those of darker skin. Darker-skinned Black men have historically been the object of sexual fantasies for both White men regardless of sexual orientation (that is, cuckold and Black bull fantasies in adult heterosexual themed films) and White women who are attracted to men (Poulson-Bryant, 2005; Nero, 2005). For example, Flores et al. (2018) noted that some Black transgender males noted their struggle with now being fetishized as savage sexual objections. They also noted an intensified focus from their potential sexual partners on their genitals related to their transition.

Safety and Harassment

As noted in previous sections of this chapter, colorism is said to have adverse outcomes across a number of domains. One way that colorism uniquely impacts Blacks in American is through the criminalization of Black bodies. Darker-skinned Black people are viewed as more dangerous and often receive harsher penalties for non-violent and drug-related crimes. Skin tone is said to greatly influence outcomes for Black people involved in the criminal justice system in the United States (Monk, 2018).

Despite this, little attention has been paid to the ways in which colorism potentially impacts Black TGNC involved in the criminal justice system who are overrepresented in jails and prisons and are more likely to face street harassment from law enforcement (U.S. Department of Justice, 2016).

It has been suggested that Black transgender individuals are more likely to engage under economies due to historic marginalization and discrimination, limiting access to more traditional sources of income and thereby increasing their involvement in the criminally justice system (Graham, 2014; Rosario, 2009). Incarcerated TGNC individuals are at an increased risk of encountering physical violence, sexual assault, and harassment (Grant, Motter, Tanis, Harrison, Herman, and Keisling, 2011). For example, the U.S. Federal Bureau of Justice Statistics reported that of the 3,200 known transgender individuals incarcerated, approximately 40% experienced sexual assault within the past year (Marksamer & Tobin, 2014). Black TGNC youth report experiences of harassment, criminalization, and punishment from law enforcement who target them for not adhering to prescribed gender role behaviors and expectations (Graham, 2014). These data suggest that transgender individuals experience violence at nearly ten times the rate of other prisoners (Marksamer & Tobin, 2014) While not explicitly stated in the academic literature it can be surmised that skin tone greatly impacts the experiences of Black TGNC persons involved in the criminal justice system based on the literature regarding the experiences of dark-skinned Black persons and the criminal justice system (Monk, 2018). However, more research is needed in this area.

The harassment and violence experienced by transgender people from law enforcement are not germane to the prison setting. Non-incarcerated transgender individuals, particularly transgender women of color, are at an increased risk of encountering harassment and violence from law enforcement. Approximately 22% of transgender individuals surveyed reported experiencing some form of harassment by police officers (Grant et al., 2011). In a report by the U.S. Department of Justice (2016), Black transgender women in one city were routinely harassed and intentionally misgendered by local law enforcement. As a result of these types of interactions with police, transgender individuals are less likely to seek help when in times of crisis (Grant et al., 2011). They are also more likely to experience poor psychological outcomes, including suicidality, sexual risk-taking, illicit drug and alcohol abuse, and experience higher rates of gender dysphoria (Graham, 2014).

But what of the experiences of Black gay and bisexual men living in American? As our we theorize as to the impact of colorism on Black LGBTQ+ we must consider the experiences of Black gay and bisexual men living in American. The following section is an effort to describe the impact of colorism on Black gay and bisexual men in American.

Colorism and Black Men: Exploring the intersections of Gender, Sexuality, and Skin Tone

To properly discuss the role of colorism in the lives of Black American gay and bisexual men, there needs to be an in-depth examination of the role of patriarchy, structural violence, systematic oppression on Black men's bodies. In bell hooks' book, "We Real Cool: Black Men and Masculinity," she asserts that "In patriarchal culture, all males learn a role that restricts and confines" (hooks, 2004), p xii). The attributes of masculinity have historically been defined as a male who is strong, independent, a leader, assertive, and emotionally reserved. For men who have appeared to embody such masculine attributes, they are also seen as having sexual prowess and more power and control in both their intimate relationships and in the world. Men who subscribe to this definition of masculinity are often rewarded socially with reaffirming accolades, the automatic assumption of competence, and virility. However, what does such attributes of masculinity mean for Black gay and bisexual men? How does the intersection of their race, gender, and sexuality align with "traditional" models of masculinity? Patriarchal culture defines what is masculine, how it should be expressed, and who can label themselves as such. Patriarchal culture, steeped in White supremacy, shifts the narrative and benchmarks of identity to ensure the preservation of social and racial hierarchies (The Grassroots Policy, n.d.). The intersection of Black gay and bisexual men's gender and race has put their bodies, and sexuality, under the microscope for examination and scrutiny. Moreover, as in any social experiment, Black gay and bisexual men have been mislabeled, misclassified, and restricted to limited characteristics based on their skin color and body.

Skin Tone as a Commodity

For some gay and bisexual men, the hue of another Black man's skin is an indication that he is suited for a stable romantic partnership, or merely a sexual object. In Corrin Pinkney's (2014) study about internalized oppression, several participants articulated that lighter-skinned Blacks were seen as more attractive and were treated better than their darker-skinned counterparts. In the late 1980s, R&B singers such as Al B. Sure, El Debarge, and Prince were examples to many of Black male sex symbols. Eurocentric features, fairer skin-tone, loose curls, or "silky" or "good" hair was the benchmark for Black men's beauty. It may have been the fact that these men sang primarily love songs, but the perception that lighter-skinned Black men were more sensitive, financially stable, self-confident, sometimes to the point of conceitedness, and highly desired as romantic partners was solidified. This perception, of course, could be tied to the days of enslavement and Jim Crow, where fairer-skinned Black people were able to pass as White in society and establish financial stability and even wealth. In Beth Turner's (2013) *"Colorism in Dael Orlandersmith's Yellowman: The Effect of Intraracial Racism on Black Identity and the Concept of Black Community,"* she highlights the fact that during slavery, enslaved mulattos were more likely to be valued and sold at a higher price, and more likely to be released from slavery, be educated, employed, and own property, even other Black persons. Even today, Black men with lighter skin tones are more likely to secure better positions and have higher earning potential (Kreisman & Rangel, 2015).

These historical factors have laid the foundation for colorism in same-gender loving relationships for Black men. The implications of racism and internalized racism cannot be overlooked and must be examined to gain a deeper understanding of the role of colorism in Black men's search for intimacy. If society, particularly in the Black community, has deemed lighter-skinned men with European features as highly attractive, and therefore worthy of love and adoration, what does it mean for partner selection? Darker complexioned Black gay and bisexual men may seek partnerships with lighter-skinned Black men as a proxy for social mobility they might not have if they partnered with another darker complexioned Black man. Could such partnerships between some men be more about power, privilege, and access than true compatibility? In Lawerence Otis Graham's (2009) book "Our Kind of People," he discussed the important role of skin color for the Black elite to ensure popularity, prestige, and social mobility. This point also illustrated in Lance Hannon's (2015) study, where White respondents consistently rated lighter-skinned Blacks as highly intelligent over darker-skinned Blacks. In a society where Black men, especially darker-skinned Black men, have been labeled as predators to be feared, having a lighter complexioned partner can help Black men navigate institutions and social relationships easier. A darker-skinned man may send his fairer-skinned partner to interact with a White manager (particularly a White woman) in a retail operation or to take the lead in business transactions, with the expectation that his partner would be better received during these interactions. This type of social mobility and privilege is not just limited to society-at-large, as there are also benefits within the Black community. Goldsmith et al. (2007) assert that within the Black community, lighter-skinned Blacks benefit from increasing privilege the closer their physical features, mannerisms, skin color, and even names are to that of White people. Therefore, by proxy, by partnering with a lighter-skinned Black man, the darker-skinned man has now gained access to spaces, resources, economics, and transactions that he might otherwise have been excluded from, both within and outside the Black community.

Colorism is also about physical attractiveness as it is about social standing. In Graham's book, he describes how "the rules were loosened" (2009) p 17) to allow dark-skinned men into young adult social halls after the women (mainly lighter-skinned) grew tired of their existing dating options. Even then, these men were only found in the "dark outer circle" where Black folks deemed darker, less affluent, and less attractive were found at social events (Graham, 2009). Of course, not every fairer-skinned Black man has amassed wealth, as they are still subjected to racial discrimination in employment (Marira & Mitra, 2013), housing (Subramanian et al., 2005), and are victims of mass incarceration (Tucker, 2017). However, for the darker-skinned Black man who has been told the depth of his melanin made him unattractive and lower on the selection hierarchy, having a lighter-skinned Black man desire him for more than sexual relations can be a boost to their concept of self. Gaining the attention and securing a relationship with a person that society has deemed attractive and worthy of love can be seen as a step up on the social ladder, a gateway to an easier life with more privilege (Jackson, 2014). However, in these relationships, imposter syndrome can manifest, where the darker-skinned partner may believe that he is not worthy of his fairer-skinned partner's love and affection. This way of thinking is destructive and can create a dangerous dynamic within same-gender relationships. Imposter syndrome in relationships can lead to submission, leading to a relinquishing of control and ignoring red flags within a relationship, because the fear of losing the "prized partner" becomes greater than self-preservation (Alvarado, 2015). Of course, there are plenty of relationships with Black gay and bisexual men that span the hue of Blackness. However, we cannot ignore the impact of systematic oppression, and White supremacy has had on partner selection for Black gay and bisexual men.

Conversely, darker-skinned Black men have been characterized as primal, aggressive, and someone to be feared and have a more difficult time navigating institutions and achieving economic mobility. However, in Pinkney's (2014) study, some participants only preferred partners with darker completions, as the darker hue of melanin symbolized to them strength, protection, and a deeper Black identity (Pinkney, 2014). Perhaps these stereotypes of Black men are what informed the participants' perception of a suitable partner in Pinkney's study? Again, we cannot ignore the impact of the legacy of slavery and Jim Crow on the psyche of the Black community today. It is said that Wesley Snipes turned the tables for darker-skinned brothers to be considered attractive and suitable as romantic partners, stemming the tide to see men like Taye Diggs, Morris Chestnuts grace the big screen as sex symbols.

The 1990s saw a resurgence of Black empowerment and Black ethnocentricity in everyday life and through the arts. In a New York Times article, writer Lena Williams compared this period of ethnocentricity to the 1960s during the civil rights movement (Williams, 1991). Was this resurgence enough to counteract hundreds of years of stereotyping Black men? Pinkney's study gives us an indication that the resurgence of Black ethnocentricity created a new dynamic and criteria for Black men, "How Black are you?" Blackness is political. We saw such debates when Former President Barak Obama was seeking the Democratic Presidential nomination. Even though there was an acknowledgment of his privilege due to his skin tone and biracial identity, there was still the question, was he Black enough to truly say he was the first Black president. Black men seeking to reaffirm their Black identity in the face of ever-present oppression may select a darker-skinned Black man, whose Black lineage will not be questioned, as their romantic partner. A darker-skinned Black man partnered with another darker-skinned Black man is a show of power, strength, and unquestioned Blackness. However, for some in the Black community, Black gay and bisexual men's Blackness gets mixed up with identity politics, bred from a White supremacist patriarchal framework that dictates the value of men based perceived masculinity. This framework of Blackness does not always include the needs of Black gay and bisexual men. However, the Black Lives Matters (BLM) movement turned this outdated framework upside-down, putting not only Black women, but also the Black lesbian, gay, bisexual, and transgender (LGBT) community at the forefront of leadership (Cobb, 2016). BLM not only helped to galvanize a new generation of people within the Black community, but it has also ensured the visibility of their Black LGBT kin. Galvanized by social media (Anderson et al., 2018), the Black community has had a resurgence of not only pride in their Blackness — skin tones, culture, history — but also a renewed commitment to social justice that is more inclusive of the entire Black community. Now, for Black and bisexual men, appearing in public together, as a loving couple, is the ultimate act of resistance. It is an affront to White supremacist patriarchy that has laid the foundation of who can have access to power and how they can use and express it.

Sexualization and Fetishization of Black Men

Black racist tropes of Black men, especially darker-skinned Black men, have been that of aggressive, overpowering men with uncontrollable sexual urges. These stereotypes of Black men have persisted from the days of slavery until the present day and has influenced how society views and interacts with Black men. bell hooks (2004) asserts that these tropes were formed through the lens of the patriarchal White supremacist lens. This lens has reduced Black men to not sensual beings, but a sexual beast with innate sexual urges that they cannot control or modulate (Ferber, 2007). For Black gay and bisexual men, the stereotyping of their sexual selves has seeped into society and influenced how Black men view themselves and each other.

Black gay and bisexual men have reported that they have been sought out by other racial groups for sexual experiences because of "positive stereotypes" of Black men' sexuality and sexual characteristics (for example, large penis size)(Rhodes et al., 2011). Czopp (2008) defines positive stereotypes as:

> . . . compared to negative stereotypes, people are less likely to perceive positive stereotypes as inappropriate and consequently do not correct for their influence in social judgments...[positive] stereotypes can be considered positive and confer some sort of "advantage" to members of these groups over non-members.
> . . they are inherently restrictive [and] are based solely on group membership rather any individuating information, maintain a complementary relation with more negative stereotypes to ensure that members of target groups can always be denigrated (Czopp, 2008), p. 414.

Positive stereotypes of Black men's sexuality (for example, large penis size, hypermasculine, sexually dominant, and rhythmic) is based on sexual objectification. In his study, Teunis (2007) reported that Black gay men who internalize these messages were more likely to assume the penetrative position during sex, unprotected, despite having a different preference in sexual positioning, upon the request of their White gay sexual partners. However, this sexual objectification is not just limited to other racial groups. Black gay and bisexual men also apply these stereotypes to their Black sexual partners. In one study, Black same-gender-loving men described other Black men as "good in bed," "dominant," "thug," "aggressive," and having a large penis (Wilson et al., 2009). It is not surprising that the same terms used by White supremacists to justify the castrations and lynching of Black men are used by Black men to describe their own bodies and sexual selves. Until now, Black men, particularly darker-skinned Black men, have not been given the freedom and space to accurately describe and name their own sexuality. For Black gay and bisexual men, being a part of the lesbian, gay, bisexual, and transgender (LGBT) community has given them a safe space and creative license to explore what it means to be a sexual being. However, despite this space, colorist themes about their sexuality still seep into their vocabulary to describe themselves and interact with each other. The same way that White gay men may seek out Black men with the assumption they pose larger penises and provide sexually satisfying sexual experiences; this may be the same for Black gay and bisexual men.

Conclusion

The chapter explored how colorism among Black LGBTQ+ communities. The suggested research pathways outlined in various sections are an opportunity to understand the shape and structure of Black LBGTQ+ lives. Each one offers avenues across multiple disciplines to broaden our cultural understanding of this subgroup's structural make-up, and unique strategies of survival within a White supremacist, hetero-patriarchal system. As the U.S continues its march toward a broader and more comprehensive racial demography, a better understanding of colorism within this subgroup will only expand our ability to develop social justice frameworks in all fields. Understanding the impact of colorism on Black LGBTQ+ communities offers an opportunity for psychologists and other mental health professionals as well. How does colorism impact sense of self-worth and overall self-concept? How does colorism impact partner selection, and does that impact relationship satisfaction? And what does all of this mean for the development of interventions for Black LGBTQ+ individuals who come into therapy experiencing racialized trauma? As our understanding of colorism expands, it must include the unique experiences of sexual and gender diverse communities.

Implications for Research, Policy, and Practice

The topics covered in this chapter underscore the limitations of what is currently known about colorism and its direct impact on the Black LGBTQ+ community. While inferences can be drawn from the experiences of Black cisgender and heterosexual persons, considerations must be made that include a lens that centers the experiences of Black gender and sexual minorities. As discussed throughout the chapter, Black LGBTQ+ individuals encounter many individual and structural level oppressions, which have long term implications on health and mental wellness, relationships, and experiences of violence and harassment. As such, information is needed on how colorism is experienced by the Black LGBTQ+ so that psychologists and other mental health professionals are better positioned to provide a more robust assessment and develop more tailored mental health interventions. Understanding the impact of colorism on Black LGBTQ+ communities may also offer an opportunity to expand our knowledge about this community beyond HIV/AIDS research, which has been the predominant foci on much of the Black LGBTQ+ research (Hailey, Burton, & Arscott, 2020).

Process Questions and Considerations

1. What clinical implications are the for Black LGBTQ+ person who experience colorism? How does that shape their racial, gender, and sexual identities?

2. How do we prepare mental health professionals to better assess for intra-racial microaggressions experienced within Black LGBTQ+ communities?

3. How can mental health professionals begin to address their own bias related to the skin tone and complexion of Black LGBTQ+ individuals?

4. Are their existing theoretical frameworks that can help us better under how colorism manifest and is maintained in the Black LGBTQ+ community?

5. Can centering the experiences of Black TGNC individuals and colorism, help us better understanding colorism within the larger LGBTQ+ community?

References

Allen, S. (2017). We're failing trans women of color: Say her name. The Daily Beast. https://www.thedailybeast.com/were-failing-trans-women-of-color

Alon, L., Smith, A., Liao, C., & Schneider, J. (2019). Colorism demonstrates dampened effects among Young Black men who have sex with men in Chicago. *Journal of the National Medical Association, 4*(111), 413-417. https://doi.org.10.1016/j.jnma.2019.011

Alvarado, C. (2015). I'm not all that: a look at the imposter phenomenon in intimate relationships. *EWU Masters Thesis Collection., 277.* http://dc.ewu.edu/theses/277

Anderson, M., Toor, S., Rainie, L., & Smith, A. (2018). Activism in the Social Media Age. *Pew Research Center.*

Austin, W. G., & Worchel, S. (Eds.). (1979). *The Social psychology of intergroup relations.* Brooks/Cole Pub. Co.

Blog | bell j Institute. (n.d.). bell hooks Institute. Retrieved March 13, 2020, from http://www.bellhooksinstitute.com/blog

Coard, S. I., Breland, A. M., & Raskin, P. (2001). Perceptions of and preferences for skin color, black racial identity, and self-esteem among African Americans. *Journal of Applied Social Psychology, 31*(11), 2256-2274. https://doi.org/10.1111/j.1559-1816.2001.tb00174.x

Cobb, J. (2016). The Matter of Black Lives: A new kind of movement found its moment. What will its future be? *The New Yorker*, 10.

Czopp, A. M. (2008). When is a compliment not a compliment? Evaluating expressions of positive stereotypes. *Journal of Experimental Social Psychology, 44*(2), 413-420. https://doi.org/10.1016/j. jesp.2006.12.007

Denton, C., Martin, H., & Christy, E. N. (2015). 'Not everyone's gonna like me': Accounting for race and racism in sex and dating web services for gay and bisexual men. *Ethnicities, 16*(1), 3-21. https://doi. org/10.1177/1468796815581428

Ferber, A. L. (2007). The construction of Black masculinity: White supremacy now and then. *Journal of Sport and Social Issues, 31*(1 Denton, C., Martin, H., & Christy, E. N. (2015). 'Not everyone's gonna like me': Accounting for race and racism in sex and dating web services for gay and bisexual men. *Ethnicities, 16*(1), 3-21. https://doi.org/10.1177/1468796815581428

Ferber, A. L. (2007). The construction of Black masculinity: White supremacy now and then. *Journal of Sport and Social Issues, 31*(1), 11-24.

Goldsmith, A. H., Hamilton, D., & Darity, W. (2007). From dark to light: Skin color and wages among African-Americans. *Journal of Human Resources, 42*(4), 701-738.

Graham, L. F. (2014). Navigating community institutions: Black transgender women's experiences in schools, the criminal justice system, and churches. *Sexuality Research & Social Policy: A Journal of the NSRC, 11*(4), 274-287. https://doi.org/10.1007/s13178-014-0144-y

Graham, L. O. (2009). *Our kind of people: Inside America's black upper class.* Harper Collins.

Grant, J.N., Mottet, L.A., & Tanis, J. (2011) *Injustice at every turn: A report of the national transgender discrimination survey.* National Center for Transgender Equality and National Gay and Lesbian Task Force,

Greene, B. (2000). African American lesbian and bisexual women. *Journal of Social Issues, 56*(2), 239-249. https://doi.org/10.1111/0022-4537.00163

Hailey, J., Burton, W., & Arscott, J. (2020). We are family: Chosen and created families as a protective factor against racialized trauma and anti-LGBTQ oppression among African American sexual and gender minority youth. *Journal of GLBT Family Studies,* 1-16. DOI:10.1080/1550428X.2020.1724133

Hall, J.C. (2017). No longer invisible: Understanding the psychosocial impact of skin color stratification in the lives of African American women. *Health & Social Work, 42*(2), 71-78. DOI:10.1093/hsw/hlx001

Hall, R. E. (2018). The Bleaching Syndrome per Colorism Pathology: LGBTQ perpetuation of Discrimination. *American Behavioral Scientist, 62*(14), 2055-2071. https://doi.org/10.1177/0002764218810759

Hannon, L. (2015). White colorism. *Social Currents, 2*(1), 13-21.

Harris-Perry, M. V. (2011). *Sister citizen: Shame, Stereotypes, and Black women in America.* Yale University Press.

Hill-Collins, P. (2009). *Black feminist thought: Knowledge, consciousness, and the politics of empowerment* (2nd ed.). Routledge.

Hill, M. E. (2002). Skin color and the perception of attractiveness among African Americans: Does Gender Make a Difference? *Social Psychology Quarterly, 65*(1), 77. https://doi.org/10.2307/3090169

Hill, N. (2016). *Intimate Partner Abuse Among African American Same Gender-Involved Females: A Collision at the Intersection of Poverty, Trauma, Mental Health Symptoms, and Racialized, Sexist, Heterocentrism* [Dissertation]. Howard University.

hooks, b. (2004). *We real cool: Black men and masculinity.* Psychology Press.

James, S.E. Herman, J.L., Rankin, S., Keisling, M., Mottet, L., & Anafi, M. (2016). *The report of the 2015 U.S. Transgender Survey.* National for Transgender Survey. https://www.transequality.org/sites/default/files/docs/USTS-Full-Report-FINAL.PDF

Jackson, K. C. (2014). *5 Truths About Colorism That I've Learned As a Black Woman In NYC.* Bustle. https://www.bustle.com/articles/37427-5-truths-about-colorism-that-ive-learned-as-a-black-woman-in-nyc

Jones-Dee Weaver, A. (n.d.). *The State of Black Women in the U.S. and Key States 2019* [Roundtable Summary].

Keith, V. (2009). *A Colorstruck World Skin Tone, Achievement, and Self-Esteem Among African American Women* (E. N. Glenn, Ed.). Stanford University Press.

Kreisman, D., & Rangel, M. A. (2015). On the blurring of the color line: Wages and employment for Black males of different skin tones. *Review of Economics and Statistics, 97*(1), 1-13.

Lamb, S., & Koven, J. (2019). Sexualization of girls: Addressing criticism of the APA report, presenting new evidence. *SAGE Open*. https://doi.org/10.1177/2158244019881024

Lewis, R. (2016). 'At the site of intimacy': An interview with Campbell X, January 2015. *Fashion, Style & Popular Culture, 3*(2), 193-207. https://doi.org/10.1386/fspc.3.2.193_

Lewis, R. J., Mason, T.B., Winstead, B.A., Gaskins, M., & Irons, L.B. (2016). Pathways to hazardous drinking among racially and socioeconomically diverse lesbian women: Sexual minority stress, rumination, social isolation, and drinking to cope. *Psychology of Women Quarterly, 40*(4), 563-581. DOI:10.1177/0361684316662603

Lundquist, J. H., & Lin, K.-H. (2015). Is love (Color) blind? The economy of race among gay and straight daters. Social Forces, 93(4), 1423-1449. https://doi.org/10.1093/sf/sov008

Marksamer, J. & Tobin, Harper, J. (2014). *Standing with LGBT prisoners: An advocate's guide to ending abuse and combating imprisonment*. National Center for Transgender Equality.

Marira, T. D., & Mitra, P. (2013). Colorism: Ubiquitous Yet Understudied. *Industrial and/organizational Psychology, 6*(1), 103-107. https://doi.org/DOI:10.1111/iops.12018

Mirella, M.J., Watson, L.B., Allen, L.R., Ford, M., Serpe, C.R., Choo, P.Y., & Farrel, M. (2018). Transgender people of color's experience of sexual objectification: Locating sexual objectification within a matrix of domination. *Journal of Counseling Psychology, 65*(3), 308-323. https://doi.org/10.1037/cou0000279

Monk, E.P. (2018). The color of punishment: African Americans, skin tone, and the criminal justice system. *Ethnic and Racial Studies, 42*(10), 1593-1612.   DOI:10.1080/01419870.2018.1508736

Moore, M. R. (2008). Gendered power relations among women: A study of household decision making in black, lesbian stepfamilies. *American Sociological Review, 73*(2), 335-356. https://doi.org/10.1177/000312240807300208

Moreno, C. (2018, February 9). *Junot Díaz: The African Diaspora "doesn't look the way it looks without systematic rape."* HuffPost. https://www.huffpost.com/entry/junot-diazafrican-diaspora-systematic-rape_n_5a7dbbefe4b08dfc9303693f

Nero, C.I. (2005). Why are the gay ghettos White. In E. P. Johnson & M. C. Henderson (Eds.), *Black Queer Studies* (pp. 228-245). Duke University Press.

Nuttbrock, L.A. & Hwahng, S.J. (2016). Ethnicity, sex work, and incident HIV/STI among transgender women in New York City. AIDS and Behavior, 21, 3328-3335.

Omi, M., & Winant, H. (2015). *Racial formation in the united states* (Third edition). Routledge/Taylor & Francis Group.

Phillips, G., Birkett, M., Hammond, S., & Mustanski, B. (2016). Partner preference among men who have sex with men: Potential contribution to spread of HIV within minority populations. *LGBT Health, 3*(3), 225-232

Pinkney, C. (2014). The effects of internalized oppression on the Black community. *Stylus Knights Write Showcase Special Issue*, 94-100.

Poulson-Bryant, S. (2005). *Hung: A mediation of the measure of Black men in America*. The Doubleday Broadway Publishing Group.

Rhodes, S. D., Hergenrather, K. C., Vissman, A. T., Stowers, J., Davis, a B., Hannah, A., Alonzo, J., & Marsiglia, F. F. (2011). Boys must be men, and men must have sex with women: a qualitative CBPR study to explore sexual risk among African American, Latino, and White gay men and MSM. *American Journal of Men's Health, 5*(2), 140-151. https://doi.org/10.1177/1557988310366298

Rosario, V.A. (2009). African-American transgender youth. *Journal of Gay & Lesbian Mental Health, 13*,

298-308. DOI:10.1080/19359700903164871

Smith, A. (2016). Heteropatriarchy and the Three Pillars of White Supremacy: Rethinking Women of Color Organizing. In INCITE! Women of Color Against Violence (Ed.), *Color of Violence* (pp. 66-73). Duke University Press. https://doi.org/10.1215/9780822373445-007

Subramanian, S. V, Acevedo-Garcia, D., & Osypuk, T. L. (2005). Racial residential segregation and geographic heterogeneity in black/white disparity in poor self-rated health in the US: A multilevel statistical analysis. *Social Science & Medicine, 60*(8),1667-1679. https://doi.org/10.1016/j.socscimed.2004.08.040

Teunis, N. (2007). Sexual objectification and the construction of whiteness in the gay male community. Culture, *Health & Sexuality, 9*(3), 263-275. https://doi.org/10.1080/13691050601035597

The Grassroots Policy. (n.d.). *Race, power, and policy: dismantling structural racism.* 38.

Tucker, R. B. (2017). The color of mass incarceration. *Ethnic Studies Review, 37*(1), 135-149.

Turner, B. (2013). Colorism in dael orlandersmith's yellowman: The effect of intraracial racism on Black identity and the concept of Black community. *Southern Quarterly, 50*(3), 32.

Vass, V., Sitko, K., West, S., & Bentall, R. P. (2017). How Stigma Gets Under the Skin: The role of stigma, self-stigma and self-esteem in subjective recovery from psychosis. *Psychosis, 9*(3), 235-244. https://doi.org/10.1080/17522439.2017.1300184

Williams, L. (1991, November 30). In a 90's Quest for Black Identity, Intense Doubts and Disagreement. *The New York Times*, 1. https://www.nytimes.com/1991/11/30/us/in-a-90-s-quest-for-black-identity-intense-doubts-and-disagreement.html

Wilson, P. A., Valera, P., Ventuneac, A., Balan, I., Rowe, M., & Carballo-Diéguez, A. (2009). Race-based sexual stereotyping and sexual partnering among men who use the internet to identify other men for bareback sex. *Journal of Sex Research, 46*(5), 399-413.

CHAPTER 19.

A Qualitative Exploratory Analysis of Tweets on Twitter about Colorism: The Case of the Proud Family Animated Series

Velma LaPoint and Jo-Anne Manswell Butty, Howard University
Stacey McDonald Lowe, US Department of Education

Introduction

The purpose of this chapter is to present a qualitative exploratory analysis of tweets about colorism on Twitter of The Proud Family, an animated series featuring a Black family. It ran on the Disney Channel from 2001 to 2005 with information that it would be continued in 2020 as the Proud Family: Louder and Prouder (The Associated Press, 2020). The authors selected The Proud Family as a product marketed primarily to Black youth and their families and communities as a Black family on television— for which they could be proud as cited by promoters (Knight Steele, 2016). Although the Proud Family originally aired on the Disney Channel between 2001 - 2005, the authors examined more recent online activity suspecting that recent analysis by Knight Steele (2016) may have prompted renewed public interest in the characters as well as an additional consideration of the topic of colorism and the Proud Family. We found that there was data, in the form of tweets on Twitter, colorism as well as other academic literature. Tweets on Twitter about the Proud Family series are assumed to characterize the views of a sample of Black people generally and others during a selected chronological period.

The chapter will cover several areas. First, the chapter will include a literature review with (a) definitions of key terms (for example, Black, colorism, Twitter); (b) three person-environment theoretical frameworks that are useful in understanding colorism locally, nationally and globally: Bio-ecological Systems Theory (BEST), Phenomenological Variant Ecological Systems Theory (PVEST), and Cultivation Theory; (c) an overview of marketing products and services to youth and their families; and (d) The Proud Family, one product, an animated series that aired on the Disney Channel that garnered tweets about colorism on Twitter. Second, the chapter describes how Twitter was used to collect consumer reports of colorism and how these reports were analyzed and interpreted. Third, findings are presented as data, namely, tweets by consumers on Twitter between December 11, 2019 and March 9, 2020. Fourth, the chapter will focus on advantages and disadvantages in using Twitter reports as a qualitative methodology in research. Fifth, and finally, we will cite implications of findings (a) for future research (b) how the findings relate to the lives as Black youth and parents and families who rear Black youth, and (c) how findings may relate to professional and advocacy organizations that advocate policies and programs for all youth and families generally and some with a focus primarily on Black youth and families. These organizations are generally in the area of health, education, and human services.

Review of the Literature

This section of the chapter focuses on definitions of key terms, a brief overview of theoretical frameworks that may be useful in understanding colorism and its impact on youth and families as well as the marketing products, services, and messages to youth.

Definitions and Conceptualizations: Black, Colorism, and Complexions

The authors use the term, "Black," in this chapter to refer to refer to people who refer to themselves as "Black" although people may refer to themselves and others with other terms such as African Americans, people of color, Africans, people of African descent, minority group, or mixed. It also seems important to use the term "Black" when writing about colorism as a topic because this book focuses on skin color tones. Black, as used in the chapter, also refers to the descriptive hair texture of Black people without chemical or cosmetic straightening or grooming processes on hair strands that are mostly or more natural, curly, kinky, or coiled. The authors will, correspondingly, use the term White people, to refer to people who label themselves or are labeled by others as Caucasian people or people of European decent. Colorism has similar definitions among social scientists and university professors in the fields of communication, education, psychology, sociology, and others. These definitions can be applied to colorism issues locally, nationally, and globally.

Colorism, according to Kendi (2019), is a powerful collection of racist policies that lead to inequities between Light and Dark people, supported by racist ideas and assumptions about Light and Dark people. He further states that colorism, like all forms of racism, rationalizes inequities with racist ideas, where the differences between Light and Dark persons are not due to racist policies, per se, but to alleged differences in so-called right or wrong in the behaviors between Light and Dark persons. DeFreitas (2019) indicates that colorism, a type of intragroup racism, is a form of discrimination that happens both within an ethnic group and among the members of that group. Colorism places persons of a darker skin tone and with more African physical features based on nose width and hair texture in a position of inferiority when compared with individuals with lighter skin and more European features (DeFreitas, 2019). Belgrave and Allison (2018) discuss colorism as discrimination and inequality based on skin color, hair texture, and facial features, and overall preference for Eurocentric physical attributes over African attributes. This results in the cultural assumption that White is superior to Black. It is not unique to Black people in the U.S. but is found throughout the world in most African, Asian, and Latin American countries (Belgrave & Allison, 2019).

Dines, Humez, Yousman, and Yousman (2018) extend their definition of colorism as a form of racism where the root word "race" is a convenient fiction. They indicate that it has a complex historical significance but no biological reality. Racism can refer to holding or showing prejudiced or bigoted attitudes or indulging in discrimination toward a person based on the person's apparent race, ethnicity, or skin color. However, in their work and critical theory, they use the term racism, and by extension colorism, to refer specifically to the White supremacist ideology encoded into and characteristic of major social, cultural, political, and economic institutions (Dines, et al. 2018).

Complexions and Skin Tones

There are other considerations related to definitions of colorism that should be cited to further our understanding of colorism. The term "skin tone" and "complexion" are also used to describe skin color. Colorism, as cited in above definitions, are defined as a form of racialized, political, and legal discrimination as noted by Dines et al., 2018. Behavioral scientists and practitioners have provided studies and applications on the topic of skin color, hair texture, and body weight. Belgrave and Allison (2019) indicate that skin color, hair texture, and body weight are attributes in which Black Americans psychically differ, and with a great deal of diversity. An early child early child learning specialist and Black American suggests that it is developmentally appropriate to explore colors of complexions especially among young children—it precedes color consciousness (Marah, personal communication, March 20, 2017). Very young children need a safe space to explore and celebrate the spectrum of skin tones, hues, and complexions. She indicates that developmentally appropriate early childhood curricula build positive cultural associations in effort to lay a value-based foundation in color consciousness that is a critical component of cultural appreciation (Marah, personal communication, March 20, 2017). Children will then be less likely to perpetuate and/or tolerate color prejudice or discrimination in later years when diversity is normalized and celebrated in the early childhood years at home and in classrooms. She believes all "isms" develop in stages and therefore "isms" (for example, racism, colorism) could be redirected given timely and effective intervention strategies. Skin tone and complexion exploration is one of the more essential and well overdue education interventions This view may be a way to begin socialization of children with neutral understanding about complexion, skin tone, and skin color. Marah's views seem to be the basis for the proactive approaches in books, magazines, products and other resources that seek to celebrate the diversity of Black youth's skin color, hair texture, and cultural lives.

Theoretical Frameworks

A few theoretical frameworks are useful in furthering our understanding of colorism. First, is the Bio-ecological Systems Theory (Bronfenbrenner, 1979, 1995). Children are reared in multiple ecological contexts that influence their development—families, schools, peers, faith-based, media, marketplace, workplace, and other broader socioeconomic, political, and cultural settings. These settings and interactions between these multiple and interrelated settings that influence and shape human behavior (Danzy, LaPoint, Small, & Butty, 2010). Bronfenbrenner theorized that, in addition to being shaped by bioecological factors, children develop in five distinct, but interrelated contexts: (a) microsystem is the context that most directly impacts and child and is comprised of the immediate surroundings such as caregiver settings and households, neighborhoods, and schools; (b) mesosystem is comprised of the structures that connect aspects of the microsystem (for example primary caregiver interaction with formal educators); (c) exosystem is comprised of the larger contexts that impact a child, but are settings where a child has no direct interaction (for example caregiver workplace settings and community resources); (d) macrosystem—which is comprised of cultural norms, values, laws and societal expectations; and (e) chronosystem—which is the time in which a child exists (Danzy, et al., 2010).

Connections and interactions between and among each of the multiple contexts work together to shape children's knowledge, attitudes, beliefs, behaviors, and worldviews. Many ecological settings are replete with structural barriers and inequalities in areas such as education, housing, healthcare where there are major disparities among European American children and various ethnic groups of children of color. Ethnic group children of color must often learn to navigate between mainstream American culture, which often views them from a negative perspective and negates their culture. While these structural barriers may exist, ethnic group children of color have learned optimal coping skills and have become resilient which often emanates from their parents, family members, community members, and other stakeholders who provide supportive networks, resources, and systemic change in an effort to provide for children's optimal development.

We can apply examples of colorism in the BEST. Within the microsystem children can learn information about colorism from parents and family members where they can impart positive or negative evaluations, namely, knowledge, attitudes, and behavior about children's skin color. These evaluations can originate from previous generations or timelines, or across or within the chronosystem. It should be noted that previous generations obtained their information about skin color and colorism from the prevailing macrosystem comprised of cultural norms, values, laws and societal expectations. And parents and previous generations have used various terms to label themselves, their children, and others according by ethnicity or race across various time periods, namely within the chronosystem. These include terms such as Colored, Negro, Black, and African Americans (DeFreitas, 2019).

A framework that is based on the BEST framework is the Phenomenological Variant Ecological Systems Theory (PVEST) by Margaret Beale Spencer (Spencer, 1995; Spencer et al., 1997; Spencer et al., 2012). PVEST, grounded in BEST, was created specifically to apply to Black youth and families as they navigate a system that has both facilitators and barriers to their optimal development (DeFreitas, 2019). PVEST seeks to understand adaptive processes in identity development throughout the lifespan and what events mean to the person in shaping this meaning making—their phenomenology. A major PVEST tenet is that it is important to consider people's evaluations of what events mean and their belief of their impact on them. One major application of PVEST relates to a person's ethnic-racial identity, namely, their beliefs about their ethnic group and sense of belonging to that group (DeFreitas, 2019).

PVEST examines five areas that are all linked bi-directionally: (a) net vulnerability, an evaluation of whether a person has more risks or protective factors that determines protection from vulnerable negative outcomes; (b) net stress engagement focusing on a person's daily experiences with risk factors and their impact that support or challenge encounters with risks; (c) reactive coping strategies focuses on how persons can react negatively or positively to events; (d) emergent identities are persons' methods of coping, which can become stable, within living contexts; and (e) life staging coping outcomes, future self-beliefs and coping strategies that further influence identity and positive or negative outcomes (DeFreitas, 2019). These PVEST areas apply to colorism because it presents a major risk for Black youth and adults in their abilities to cope with current and future events relating to their ethnic identity. The context and how persons make sense of it influences their stress level, how they cope with stress, and how they formulate their understanding of who they are within their smaller and larger living contexts (DeFreitas, 2019).

The third theoretical framework is Cultivation Theory founded by Gerbner in 1976 (DeFreitas, 2019; Gerbner, Gross, Morgan, Signorielli, & Shanahan, 2002; Dines et al., 2018). Cultivation Theory focuses on the effects of television content on viewer knowledge, attitudes, and behavior. We use the term "screens" to refer to newer devices where content is televised such as computers, pads, cell phones, apps, and others. Cultivation Theory postulates that long exposure to screen content makes those who view content believe that the real world is similar to what they have been viewing on screens—even when those worlds are very different (Gerbner et al., 2002; DeFreitas, 2019; Dines et al., 2018). Cultivation theory suggests that the consequences of persons growing up with screens, in particular, are subtle, gradual, but ultimately powerful. Scholars posit that the more screen-time a person watches, the more likely they are to accept screens' content although it is often distorted and misleading narratives and images especially in areas of race, violence, and gender portrayals (Dines, et al., 2018).

Cultivation theory posits that because screen content is mass produced and occupies a central role in American culture, it is more influential than other forms of mass media where it shapes people's attitudes and beliefs about society and other people. The content cultivates values and attitudes already present in the culture and serves to reinforce the status quo, not challenge it. This information is particularly relevant to colorism where youth or adults can be influenced about knowledge, attitudes, and behaviors about colorism emanating from programming, both fiction and non-fiction.

Overview of Marketing to Children and Adolescents

The marketing and messaging of products and services to youth is a multibillion-dollar business in the U.S. and globally (CCFC, 2020; Dines et al., 2018). One major research-based, nonprofit advocacy organizations for children and their families is the

Campaign for Commercial Free Childhood (CCFC, 2020) with over 40,000 members. It is the leading nonprofit organization committed to helping children thrive in an increasingly commercialized, screen-obsessed culture—and the only organization committed to ending marketing to children (CCFC, 2020). It indicates that they are grounded in the overwhelming evidence that child-targeted marketing - and the excessive screen-time encourages and undermines kids' healthy development. Working with an interdisciplinary group of health and child development experts, educators, health, and policymakers CCFC sustains a new vision of childhood shaped by what is best for children's development and not is what is best for corporate profits (CCFC, 2020).

CCFC views pernicious marketing as a social problem. We suggest that marketing to children and adolescence can be viewed as the "commercialization of childhood." Research suggests that areas of commercial culture: (a) sexualizes youth; (b) glorifies violence; (c) promotes unhealthy eating leading to obesity, overweight, and eating disorders; (d) encourages materialistic values and greed (e) undermines appearance and identity development; and (f) invades and targets youth's privacy (CCFC, 2020). Over-consumption also negatively impacts the earth causing harm to the oceans and climate (Klein, 2014). Youth across age, gender, race/ethnicity, social class, ableness, and other characteristics have specific vulnerabilities within consumer culture where they are the targets of this pernicious marketing. And it should be noted that multinational corporations with messages, products, and services created in the U.S. are changed and marketed globally to targeted youth and adult populations (for example, Disney, Mattel) Dines, et al., 2018).

Colorism relates to the problems of pernicious marketing where youth's identity is compromised and undermined in appearance and identity development. White, European models are those that are generally depicted in marketing messages, products, and services. Screen content marketed to youth and their families has been used as a powerful tool to socialize the young to societal preferences toward image and beauty (Baron, 2007; Dines et al., 2018; Knight Steele, 2016). The impact of televised media may be especially damaging during childhood and adolescence, the period in which identity is developing. Contributing to this is the fact is that Black youth watch more screens than some American youth groups (Belgrave & Allison, 2019). Black youth, ages 13-18) reportedly spend more hours daily with media in (that is, television, computers, Internet) during non-school hours than White or Latinx youth: Black youth (11 hrs.), White youth (9 hrs.); Latinx youth (8 hrs.). In general, teens from all three racial/ethnic groups are equally likely to engage in each media related activity on any given day (Common Sense Media, 2015).

The Proud Family

The Proud Family was an animated series that aired between mid-September 2001 to mid-August 2005 on the Disney Channel. It was announced that it will air new episodes in 2020 (The Associated Press, 2020). The Proud Family was touted as the first Black animated series by a Black production company with a Black female as the lead character in a Black family context (Knight Steele, 2016). Although the series offered Black viewers an opportunity see themselves reflected in characters on the television screen, criticisms allege that negative stereotypes related to colorism existed among characters:

1.Penny Proud: Penny is a light skinned, conservative dressing, talented, straight A student who is portrayed as being respectful to her parents (Knight Steele, 2016).

2.Trudy Proud: Trudy is also a light skinned and is portrayed as being a stable, level-headed professional who comes from a family who is highly educated from a high socioeconomic status. Trudy is a veterinarian, mother of three and wife to Oscar (Knight Steele, 2016).

3.Oscar Proud: Oscar is a dark-skinned male who is portrayed as a buffoonish character who is loud, argumentative and a failed businessman (Knight Steele, 2016).

4.Dijonay Jones: Dijonay is Penny's best friend. She is a very dark-skinned character who embodies negative stereotypes about Black Americans. She is portrayed as being sassy, loud, obnoxious and misbehaving. Although not directly cited, the writers indicate that she comes from a lower socioeconomic status when compared to Penny. Dijonay lives in an apartment with some siblings and a cousin named after condiments and spices (for example, Tabasco, Caramel, Cinnamon, Nutmeg, Paprika, Basil, Cayenne, Oran, Bethan) (Knight Steele, 2016).

5.The Gross Sisters. These sisters are depicted as darkest blue-black skin tone with tightly curled or braided hair. They are portrayed as being criminals and bullies who rob and steal from the other high school students. The other students fear these sisters who were clearly social outcasts (Knight Steele, 2016).

Twitter

Twitter, used primarily by 38% of the people between ages 18-29 years, is a free social networking platform that allows registered members to broadcast short posts called Tweets (Rouse, 2015). Although Twitter may have this age range, younger persons or persons of any age, can use Twitter with their own free account. Persons can register for a Twitter account and use it as long as they agree to the terms of use. They can create and broadcast tweets and follow other users' tweets by using various platforms and devices (for example, cell phone text messages, desktop client, posting at Twitter.com website). The default settings for Twitter are public where anyone can follow anyone on public Twitter (Rouse, 2015). Tweets, which may include hyperlinks, were initially limited to 140 characters. Tweets can be delivered to followers in real time and are posted on the Twitter website. They are permanent, public, searchable by anyone whether they are a member or not. Twitter users can post their own Tweets or remain a follower and observer (Rouse, 2015).

While there is a Black Twitter social media platform, the authors did not use Black Twitter in analyzing tweets. It should be noted that Black people have long formed digital communities long before using the Internet as we know it today according to a report, "How Black Twitter and Other Social Media Communities Interact with Mainstream News" (Freelon, Lopez, Clark, & Jackson, 2018). Twitter has become a major online venue for communities of all types and sizes given its emphasis on public accessibility and real-time production content (Freelon et al., 2018).

Data Collection Procedures on Twitter

Brand24.com, a social listening and analytics tool was used to track and analyze hashtag activity that was cited on the Twitter social media platform. The authors conducted an online search using the terms #Colorism and #ProudFamily to determine the number of times these terms were mentioned online between December 11, 2019 and March 9, 2020. Although the Proud Family originally aired on the Disney Channel between 2001 - 2005, the authors opted to examine more recent online activity suspecting that the analysis by Knight Steele (2016) may have prompted resurgence of public interest in the characters as well as an additional consideration of the topic of colorism and the Proud Family.

1. Analysis included tweets that expressed either positive, negative, or neutral sentiment as designated by the Brand24.com analytics tool.

2. During this time period, the volume of mentions using #Colorism was 152 with 346 likes. A mention is when a Twitter user introduces the @ sign immediately followed by another Twitter user's Handle.

3. Of the 152 mentions, 100 were on the Twitter platform, 35 mentions were in the

form of videos, 8 mentions were found on news platforms, 2 mentions were in the blogosphere and 1 mention was made in an online forum and 6 were made generally on the web.

4. The top 15 trending hashtags associated with this search included #colorism, #proudfamily, #lightskinned, #lightskinwomen, #darksinmen, #blackpeoplebelike, #darkskinned, #darkskin, #lightskinboys, #racism, #blackpeople, #darkskinwomen, #lightskinlove, #melanin, #lightskinmen.

5. One tweet specific to the colorism depicted in the children's animated television show Proud Family stated:

COLORISM IN CARTOONS. So, the darker skin sisters had to be "blue black" with braids and called the "GrossSisters," while the light skin girls are part of the "Proud Family" FOH. Oh and the one dark skin friend had to have all the attitude. #Colorism #Hairism #ProudFamily. Readers are referred to the urban dictionary for the meaning of the letters FOH, urban dictionary.com.

A Google search of the search term "Colorism Proud Family" yielded about 96,200 results in .36 seconds. The authors adopted a purposive sampling approach. Selected posts met preselected criteria relevant to the exploratory nature of this investigation. The use of purposive sampling is designed to uncover rich descriptions of online sentiments expressed by online users in online forums (Whitehead & Whitehead, 2016). Selected posts were selected based on the following criteria: (a) poster self identifies as Black and/or African American; (b) poster responds to an online prompt related to colorism as it relates to the animated Disney series, The Proud Family; and (c) poster expressed feelings about their reaction to colorism as it was depicted by the animated series The Proud Family.

1. The results of the search uncovered a forum at lipstickalley.com that was posted on February 28, 2019. One post stated:

It's glaring obvious if you re-watch the episodes and completely turns me off from introducing this show to present day Black children.

How did Disney (I am aware the showrunners were Black) get away with showcasing the worst stereotypes of our community? Black people will accept the bare minimum for representation.

2. This post received 76,596 positive ratings, 7,022 neutral ratings and 6,602 negative ratings.

3. Another post stated:

Oh, and how about the Gross sisters being blue because they were "ashy"? What a mess.

I wish color-ism (sic) doesn't happen when it comes to black television shows. It reinforces stereotypes and hurts the viewers they try to pander to, giving them life-long insecurities and self-esteem. I hope it ends soon.

4. This post received 3,540 positive ratings, 133 neutral ratings and 87 negative ratings.

5. A third post in this forum stated:

That's what I meant by bare minimum. It's not just the Proud family. It's on so many shows you learn to accept whatever you can get. I could make a thread on Black female character development or outright stereotyped but Black girls clung so hard to, desperate for some representation.

6. This post received 76,596 positive ratings, 7 022 neutral ratings and 6,602 negative ratings.

7. A forum posted at reddit.com gave bloggers an opportunity to respond to the prompt "Is Disney's The Proud Family colorist?" This thread had 26 responses.

The initial post stated:

I just saw a promo image for the show recently (where exactly I don't remember, maybe on some buzzfeed-like site), and looking at the picture now and with my knowledge of colorism today. I can't help but remember how certain characters with darker skin acted and/or were treated by the writing of the show in comparison to the lighter-skinned characters. It's not even like they casted real people who happen to look a certain way, it's an animated show, and they had total control over what every single character looked like to a precise degree. Does anyone looking back on the show now feel the same way?

8. Another post stated:

Of course. I love the show to death cuz of the nostalgia but the way they treated Dijonay and the Gross Sisters was clearly an indictment of dark-skin black women, especially in comparison to the biracial Penny Proud.

Dijonay is the fat loud black girl w/a billion siblings who constantly chases after Sticky, who clearly don't want her. The Gross Sisters are the aggressive bullies.

The Google search engine offered the following as searches related to colorism proud family: the proud family; proud family lipstick alley; Michael proud family, boondocks colorism; colorism in animation; penny proud skin color change; colorism in children's shows; and proud family problematic.

In conclusion, the Brand24.com social listening and analytics tool was used to track and analyze hashtag activity and mentions on the Twitter social media platform using the terms #Colorism to determine the number of times these terms were mentioned online between December 13, 2019 and March 12, 2020. Analysis included tweets that expressed either positive, negative, or neutral sentiment as designated by the Brand24.com analytics tool.

Themes of Characterizations of Tweets
For Entertainment Purposes Only

One theme that emerged from this analysis highlighted the sentiment that Black viewers experienced while viewing the Proud Family during its original airing between 2001 and 2005. These viewers tweeted that they were so happy that there was Black representation on television. They overlooked the colorism and stereotypical portrayals of Blacks that were inherent in the storylines and characters developed by the Black production company. Some stated that they would not allow their children to watch the program (after more time) given what they now know about negative depictions of Blacks on the Proud Family.

Beauty Is Only Skin Deep

A second theme that emerged focused on the stereotypes and characteristics that have been attributed to Black people based on skin color: lighter or darker. They seem to address the Eurocentric view of beauty that is propagated in the U.S. and Western culture. This view dictates that physical attributes (for example, hair texture, skin color, or nose width) that are closer to people of European decent is deemed most desirable. This suggests that media content is a powerful tool to enculturate societal norms and this includes images portrayed in animations marketed to children. These depictions rarely challenge societal norms or racial stereotypes (Baron, 2007). An analysis by Knight Steele (2016) suggests that the animators of the Proud Family incorporated stereotypic images of Blacks which when creating their characters. Lighter-skinned characters were portrayed as possessing positive prosocial attributes while darker-skinned characters were depicted as being less refined, clownish and in some cases criminal (Knight Steele, 2016).

It's Complicated

A third theme that emerged from the analysis of #Colorism and #ProudFamily suggests that colorism within the Black community is complicated. Some responders to threads offered opportunities to show pride about their skin color regardless of skin hues. Some people on tweets expressed love for themselves regarding their skin color (typically in terms of light vs. dark). This behavior highlights the impact of stereotypes associated with Eurocentric views of beauty that some may view as a part of their economic and career upward mobility. Some may view Black people with physical features that are closer to the White physical features as being more aesthetically pleasing as well as intelligent. Some Black people may argue that screen images and content reinforce negative stereotypes associated with skin color as only entertainment; others may insist that stereotypic enculturation maintains the status quo. They may view that they seem locked in place without opportunities to transcend their current SES boundaries.

Advantages and Disadvantages of Using Twitter for Data Collection

Using a social network as a data source offers social scientists a wealth of information that chronicles human behavior and online social interaction (Goritz, Kolleck & Jörgens, 2019). There are some limitations associated with use of this data in the conduct of social science research although Twitter, as social platform, can provide a unique, unprecedented amount of data, and rich glimpse into social interaction (Ruiz-Soler, 2017). However, there are some considerations that researchers must consider when conducting analysis.

One limitation is representation bias. Participants in the Twitter-sphere are not representative of the general population and as a result it is difficult to make generalizable inferences (Ahmed, 2015). The authors acknowledge this as a limitation that is most impactful when using inferential statistical techniques for the purpose analyzing quantitative data and making broad generalizations.

A second limitation concerns data retrieval from Twitter. In this case of tweets about the Proud Family, data was retrieved using Brand24.com. By using Brand24.com, the authors had to accept the methodology and assumptions that Brand24.com uses to extract data from Twitter. As a result, it may be impossible to replicate the dataset (Ahmed, 2015; Ruiz-Soler, 2017). The authors decided that the use of Twitter data to explore the issue of colorism is appropriate because the purpose here is to identify themes in narrative data by adopting a qualitative analytic approach. The authors had to accept the policies and procedures of the platform for data collection and analysis.

Implications of Findings for Future Research

The authors acknowledge that one of the limitations associated with the use of

Twitter data for social science research involves issues related to generalizability due to representation bias (Ahmed, 2015). However, by initiating this exploratory qualitative analysis the authors have been able to shed light on recurring issues related to the role of screen content to amass and spread social constructs that maintain colorism as a race-based stereotypes to mainstream social structures.

Future research should include studies that use quantitative research methodologies that could produce data analysis that could be generalized more broadly. Research database searches of the terms "colorism" and "Black children's media" yielded 35 peer-reviewed journal articles. Two of these articles were related to Black children's exposure to colorism through their consumption of screen content. This highlights a gap in the literature related to this topic and dire need for future research in this area.

Implications for Practice by Black Youth, Parents, Families, and Professionals Who Work with Black Youth

This chapter conducted a qualitative exploratory analysis of Twitter tweets that were assumed to characterize views of The Proud Family aired between 2001-2005. The characterizations generally suggested three major themes. First, viewers tweeted that they were so happy that there was Black representation on television. Yet, they overlooked the colorism and stereotypical portrayals of Blacks that were inherent in the storylines and characters developed by the Black production company. Second, viewers cited stereotypes and characteristics that have been attributed to Black people based on lighter or darker skin color. Viewers seemed to address the Eurocentric view of beauty that is propagated in the U.S. and Western culture. Third, viewers offered tweets that showed pride about their skin color regardless of skin hues. Some people on tweets expressed love for themselves regarding their skin color (typically in terms of light vs. dark) and others suggested that screen images and content reinforced negative stereotypes associated with skin color. Some viewed content as only entertainment others insisted that stereotypic enculturation maintains the status quo where Black people seemed locked in place without opportunities to transcend their current SES boundaries.

Conclusions

This chapter presented a qualitative exploratory analysis of tweets about colorism on Twitter of The Proud Family an animated series featuring a Black family with children and extended relatives. It ran on the Disney Channel from 2001 to 2005 with information that it would be continued in 2020 as the Proud Family: Louder and Prouder. We presented information on literature review including definitions and conceptualizations of key terms, person-environment theoretical frameworks, an overview of information on the Proud Family (b) how Twitter was used to collect consumer reports of colorism and how these reports were analyzed and interpreted; (c) findings on tweets by consumers on (d) selected advantages and disadvantages in using Twitter reports as a qualitative methodology in research; (d) implications of finding for future research; and (e) resources that may be useful to Black youth, parents and families who rear Black youth. This includes advocacy and professional organizations that specifically suggest strategies to balance and reduce screen-time use among children, parents, and families as a way to promote youth identity and appearance and that promote optimal development of children and families in general and in specific areas.

There are some promising interventions, examples of entrepreneurism that Black youth, parents, and families are creating for themselves, in collaboration with others, to counter negative stereotypes and advance discussions about skin tones and complexions. This includes books, magazine, films, and other products. One example is Hair Love, a short, animated film that was nominated in 2019 by the Academy of Motion Picture Arts and Sciences (AMPAS) and won a 2020 Oscar Award (Cherry, 2019). The film written and directed by Mathew Cheery and co-producer Karen Rupert Toliver, two African Americans media professionals as well as other film production experts (Cherry, 2019). The story focuses on a father who must do his daughter's hair for the first time and features the voice of the mother who is later depicted in a hospital, wheelchair bound, who reveals her bald head—implying that she has a chronic illness. The creator of Hair Love stated that he was inspired to create the film to counter stereotypes in mainstream media (for example, uninvolved in childrearing, non-paying child custody supporters) and increase the diverse representation of Black hair (Cherry, 2019). Hair Love creators also released as a children's book in 2019 (Cherry, 2019a).

In a second example is the crayon set created by a nine-year-old, Black girl Bellen Woodward in Louden County, VA. The crayon set is a color pallet of crayons that presents a set of skin colors reflective of diverse colors (More Than Peach, 2020). Bellen, her family, and others created the Peach Project to market the crayons to others in retail stores and online (More Than Peach, 2020). The last example is a magazine, Sesi (means "sister" in the Sotho language of South Africa). It is a quarterly, print magazine for Black teen girls. Its website states that it seeks to fill that void in the mainstream media where Black girls are virtually invisible (Sesi Magazine, 2020). Entrepreneurism, especially among Black youth, families, and communities, is applauded and celebrated. However, we note that often these created products must have financial backing which can mean accepting finances from some corporations who may seek content that is more commercial and moves away from images, and other characteristics that reflect Black culture. Yet, Black entrepreneurs and others in Black communities have to remain proactive and diligent in monitoring and promoting positive images of Black youth, families, and communities.

Process Questions and Considerations

1. How does social media impact Colorism?

2. Is it the responsibility of the media to restrict negative messages to youth?

3. Outside of the interventions listed in this chapter, what are some creative ways of mitigating the impact of Colorism in social media on Black adolescents?

4. Should social media be censored?

5. Which social media platforms are most influential on Black youth?

References

Ahmed, W. (2015). Challenges of using Twitter as a data source: An overview of current resources. *Impact of Social Sciences Blog.*

Associated Press (The) (2020, February 27). Disney Plus to revive The Proud Family animated series: The Proud Family is making a comeback. https://abcnews.go.com/Entertainment/wireStory/disney-revive-proud-family-animated-series-69262788

Baron, R. J. (2007). A Part of Your World: Issues of Patriarchy, Nature, and Technology in Walt Disney's The Little Mermaid. *In Conference Papers--National Communication Association* (Vol. 1).

Belgrave, F. Z., & Allision, K. W. (2019). *African American psychology: From Africa to America.* SAGE.

Bronfenbrenner, U. (1979). *The ecology of human development. Experiments by nature and design.* Harvard University Press.

Bronfenbrenner (1995). Bronfenbrenner, U. (1995). The bioecological model from a life course perspective: Reflections of a participant observer. In P. Moen, G. H. Elder, Jr., & K. Lüscher (Eds.), *Examining lives in context: Perspectives on the ecology of human development* (p. 599-618). American Psychological Association. https://doi.org/10.1037/10176-017

Cherry, M. A. (2019). Hair love. Penguin Random House.

Cherry, M. A. (2019). Hair love. Full short film. http://www.matthewacherry.com/hair-love.

Common Sense Media. (2015). The common sense census: Media use by tweens and teens. https://www.commonsensemedia.org/

Danzy, C., LaPoint, V., Manswell Butty, J. L., Small, C. (2010). Sociocultural factors. In C. S. Clauss-Ehlers (Ed.). *Encyclopedia of Cross-Cultural School Psychology,* pp. 904-911. Springer.

DeFreitas, S. (2019). *African American psychology: A positive psychology perspective.* Springer.

Dines, G., Humez, J. M., Yousman, B., & Yousman, L. B. (2018). *Gender, race, and class in media: A critical reader.* SAGE.

Freelon, D., Lopez, L., Clark, M. D., & Jackson, S. J. (2018, August 5). *How Black Twitter and other social media communities interact with mainstream news.* https://doi.org/10.31235/osf.io/nhsd9

Gerbner, G., Gross, L., Morgan, M., Signorielli, N., & Shanahan, J. (2002). *Growing up with television: Cultivation processes.* In *Media effects* (pp. 53-78). Routledge.

Goritz, A., Kolleck, N., & Jörgens, H. (2019). *Analyzing Twitter data: Advantages and challenges in the study of UN climate negotiations.* SAGE.

Kendi, I. X. (2019). *How to be an antiracist.* Random House.

Klein, N. (2014). *This changes everything: Capitalism vs. the climate.* Simon & Schuster.

Marah, M. (2017, March 20). *Teaching African cultural appreciation through early literacy.* Paper presented, Office of the State Superintendent of Education (OSSE), Washington, DC.

Rouse, M. (2015, December 31).*What is Twitter?* https://whatis.techtarget.com/definition/Twitter

Ruiz-Soler, J. (2017). Twitter research for social scientists: A brief introduction to the benefits, limitations and tools for analyzing Twitter data. *Revista Dígitos, 1*(3), 17-32.

Spencer, M. B. (1995). Old issues and new theorizing about African American youth: A phenomenological variant of ecological systems theory (PVEST). In R. L. Taylor (Ed.), *Black youth: Perspectives on their status in the United States* (pp. 37-69). Praeger.

Spencer, M. B., Dupree, D., & Hartmann, T. (1997). A phenomenological variant of ecological systems theory (PVEST): A self-organization perspective in context. *Development and Psychopathology, 9*(4), 817-833. DOI:10.1017/80954579497001454

Spencer, M. B., Dupree, D., Tinsley, B., McGee, E. O., Hall, J., Fegley, S. G., & Elmore, T. G. (2012). *Resistance and resiliency in a color conscious society: Implications for learning and teaching.* In K. R. Harris, S. Graham, T. Urdan, C. B., McCormick, G.M., Sinatra, J. Sweller. In J. Sweller (Eds.). *APA educational handbook, Vol 1: Theories, constructs, and critical issues* (pp. 461-494). Washington, DC: American Psychological Association, DOI:10.1037/13273-016.

Steele, C. K. (2016). Pride and prejudice: Pervasiveness of colorism and the animated series Proud Family. *Howard Journal of Communications, 27*(1), 53-67.

Whitehead, D., & Whitehead, L. (2016). Sampling data and data collection in qualitative research.

CHAPTER 20.

The Color of Sin: Colorism in Christian Worship

Ronald E. Hopson, Howard University

"I am black, but comely, O ye daughters of Jerusalem, as the tents of Kedar, as the curtains of Solomon. Look not upon me, because I am black, because the sun hath looked upon me: my mother's children were angry with me; they made me the keeper of the vineyards; but mine own vineyard have I not kept."
Song of Songs 1:5-6

"And this is the condemnation, that light is come into the world, and men loved darkness rather than light, because their deeds were evil."
John 3:19

A hymn written during the Jim Crow era (1876), and still a favorite of the Christian church (especially the Black church) is entitled "Nothing But The Blood." The refrain is as follows:
"Oh, precious is the flow!
That makes me white as snow
No other fount I know,
Nothing but the blood of Jesus"

Overview

Imagine, a room full of Black congregants enthusiastically singing of becoming "white as snow;" celebrating their own divine negation while experiencing the morose joy of the repentant sinner. Indeed, references to whiteness as a symbol of virtue and purity abound within the Christian faith. The second century theologian Origen envisioned the conversion of the "black soul" to a "white and heavenly state" (Cited in Davies, 1988). From the ancient poetic and prophetic traditions of Hebrew scripture (for example, Psalms, Ecclesiastes, Song of Songs, Isaiah), through some of the letters of Paul and the Gospels, to the late apocalyptic literature of Revelation, white is the symbol of virtue, purity, and godliness, while black is the symbol of sin and evil. White is the color of holiness, black is the color of sin.

As is developed in other essays in this volume, this idealization of whiteness would ramify through generations of Black families. Such sayings as: "if you're white you're right, if you're brown, stick around, if you're black, get back" or "yellow wasted" (invoked when an African-American person of lighter skin tone was considered otherwise unattractive), have been common in Black families for generations. Affiliations and preferences based upon color-coding among African Americans even today remains the impolitic background in many arenas of Black life (that is churches, fraternities and sororities, social/community groups such as "Jack and Jill," dating and marital partner choices, ideals of beauty, and so on).

Skin color continues to be a determining factor in how persons are regarded within families and in the larger society. At the beginning of the 20th century, W.E.B. Dubois stated, "the problem of the Twentieth Century is the problem of the color line." Now, here, at the beginning of the 21st century, it still matters if you're black or white, dark or light. And though Dubois was referring to the problem of color in America, the color line pervades the cultural landscapes in much of the world, most dramatically in those areas which have been impacted by European colonialism (Davies, 1988). Color is an issue from South Africa to the Philippines, and from Alaska to Brazil and all of America. Colorism is also experienced in Black America.

The abnegation of blackness in America began before the trans-Atlantic slave trade and continued after emancipation, into the Jim Crow era (Painter, 2010). After their defeat in the Civil War, white Southerners were faced with how to reconcile their participation in enslavement and their resistance to emancipation. This effort took two forms: revisionist history, and the denigration of blackness. There began an immediate rewriting of the facts of slavery to sanitize the actual brutality of such a system. Depictions of the "happy slave," portraits of the enslaved posed as part of the "owning" family, and stories of the virtuous patient "owners," providing food, shelter, and lifetime health care to the enslave, proliferated during this era. Post-emancipation, the denigration of blackness began in earnest. The formerly enslaved were depicted as the shiftless, lazy, or dangerous black "other." Minstrelsy shows provided stock images of the black person as: ever patient and nurturing, rotund sexless Mammy; irresponsible, untrustworthy, cunning "Zip Coon" Dandy; rapacious, physically (and sexually) overpowering, threatening, and always dark skin, Buck; hapless Sambo; and compliant, stupid "darkie" Jim Crow. All of these depictions were set upon the black body as rationale, excuse and justification for both enslavement and resistance to emancipation.

Confirming de Tocqueville's contemporaneous observation of religion as the first of America's political institutions, Christianity played a major role in the denigration of blackness. Christian preachers wrote the majority of the apologies/rationale for slavery. The public face of Christianity embraced, excused and tolerated the exploitation and domination of dark people. Many debates were held among clergy concerning whether indeed the enslaved had a soul, and therefore was in need of salvation. During enslavement, and after, the African was understood to be in need of civilizing. Such groups as the Freedmen's Bureau arose to provide assistance to the recently emancipated, and to provide both moral and intellectual instruction. Such institutions as Howard University were created to civilize, elevate and educate the formerly enslaved. Indeed, one of the first three departments of Howard University was named "Anatomy and Physiology in Their Relations to Hygiene." The recently freed black bodies needed to learn how to be clean.

Even among a progressive movement of the latter part of the 19th century (the Social Gospel movement), the conviction of black inferiority prevailed. Though the leaders of the Social Gospel movement developed incisive critiques of the economic inequalities of the "robber baron" era, they held to ideas of white racial superiority. Rauschenbusch, a hero of those critical of acquisitive capitalism, wrote ardently of the "virility, talent for freedom" and otherwise positive marks of the Aryan race (cited in Davies, 1988).

During the first half of the 20th century, American Christianity would again play a prominent role in buttressing America's social hierarchy. The newspaper baron William Randolph Hearst had come to hear of a young fiery preacher named Billy Graham. He found Graham's brand of Christianity friendly to the expansion of capitalism and patriarchy. He sent a telegram to all of his newspapers around the country with the words: "puff Graham." Under the aegis of Hearst, Graham began to spread his version of Christianity---personal relationship with Jesus Christ and unquestioning cooperation with (non-communist) governing authorities. Graham took up the mantel of fundamentalist Christianity developed decades earlier at the behest of California oil millionaires and propagated through the network of Young Men's Christian Associations (Ammerman, 1987). Graham promoted a civil religion for the capitalist era which emptied Christianity of its strong critique of wealth and systems of power and domination, and instead defined the Christian faith as personal piety and right beliefs about Jesus. Any concerns about social justice, civil rights or economic justice were eliminated from the 'fundamentals of the faith.' The critiques of exploitative capitalism of the prior generation of Social Gospelers, and the emerging civil rights movement led by a Black Christian preacher, were ignored. Early in his career, Graham even allowed segregated crusades. In the early 1960's Graham advised Dr. Martin Luther King to cease his agitation of the government and display patience and cooperation rather than active resistance to racial discrimination, and Graham never took a prominent role in publicly supporting the civil rights movement. Indeed Graham's deafening silence on this contributed to the ease with which conservatives and southerners were able to hijack Christianity in the latter part of the 20th century, and become the public face of the faith, though embracing and advancing racist, sexist, and homophobic ideologies.

As Graham's anemic personal Christianity took root in America, the political turmoil of the latter 1960's and early 1970's provided fodder for the rise of politically effective backlash rhetoric aimed to blunt and reverse the progress of the Civil Rights movement. White conservatives utilized the intransigent resistance of white America to civil rights gains as an ideological resource to turn back the few advances made during the height of the civil rights movement. They employed what came to be known as the "southern strategy" to mobilize white racial resentment and secure electoral victories based upon racial dog-whistle politics (Carter, 2000; Hopson and Williams, 1999). Though the South had been a Democratic party stronghold for a century (Abraham Lincoln was a Republican), the South became Republican within a decade, and within a generation there was a complete transformation of political alignments. The industrial states of the mid-west, usually friendly to critiques of exploitative capitalism, heartily began to embrace the values offered by corporate interests. This backlash against the civil rights movement began to employ political tropes rooted in the negation of blackness and the black body. Jim Crow was resurrected through such rhetoric as: "law and/order," "family values," "anti-abortion," critiques of big government, "welfare queen," "moral majority." These ideas and terms functioned as rhetorical props for the underlying ideology of anti-blackness. The black body is: lawless and out of order (for example the revolts following the killing of Dr. King); lacking in family values (Daniel P. Moynihan's infamous report describing impoverished black families as a "tangle of pathology"); sexually irresponsible (preferring abortion, unwilling to bear the consequences (children), of their insatiable sexual appetite); lazy (Black mothers living extravagantly on the government); and essentially immoral. This period could rightly be termed a "second redemption" period. The rhetoric of restoring "American" values and rescuing the country from a dark threat among us (in the form of undeserving black bodies draining the resources of the body politic through "big government" (that is social welfare) programs) resembled the rhetoric of restoration which Southerners advanced during the Jim Crow era.

Some conservative white religious leaders joined this second redemption effort

(Crawford, 1981). Growing out of the moral majority movement, New Christian Right groups such as Promise Keepers and the Christian Coalition were developed by secular right wing neo-conservatives to provide a sacred canopy for regressive race-based policies aimed at expanding exploitative capitalism and undermining the progress of Blacks toward full equality in the society (Hopson and Williams, 1999). Public Christianity was defined by white evangelicalism. White evangelicalism resisted the effort of civil rights leaders to ground the civil rights movement in the religion of Jesus as represented in the Gospels. Rather, White evangelicalism redefined Christianity along the lines of individualism, personal piety, moral asceticism, the white middle class male dominated nuclear family as the social ideal (for example James Dobson's Focus on the Family), and acquisitive capitalism (for example Pat Robertson's 700 Club). These groups opposed social welfare programs and criminal justice reforms and provided religious rationale for the rise of the practice of aggressive policing of Black communities and black bodies. Collectively, these "Christian conservatives" represented in the Southern Baptist denomination, large non-denominational mega-churches, and radio and television networks such as TBN, became the public face of Christianity, and the moral cover for the second redemption efforts of anti-blackness and white supremacy. These "conservative Christians" heartily embraced the political tropes of the backlash era and successfully advanced the project of the re-stigmatization of blackness.

The disdain for darkness/blackness is buttressed by and sourced in the larger cultural positioning of blackness in American society. The horror of police violence upon innocent black bodies is the inevitable result of a society which disdains blackness and sees the black body as a threat. Morrison aptly wrote: "The ease, therefore, of moving from the dishonor associated with the slave body to the contempt in which the freed blackbody was held became almost seamless because the intervening years of the Enlightenment saw a marriage of aesthetics and science and a move toward transcendent whiteness" (Morrison 2019, p. 76). The "Buck" of enslavement becomes the "Thug" of contemporary America. This is a contemporary extension of the old trope of the Black threat first deployed as justification for the "redemption" of whiteness at the beginning of the Jim Crow era. Vigilantism morphed into police forces as the earliest attempts to control the threat of recently freed dangerous black bodies "loosed" on southern society by emancipation and the loss of the Civil War. Then, and indeed now, the Black (dangerous) presence served/serves Whiteness as a source of identity-through-negation: White identity is that which is not Black. Black is dirty, evil, and rapaciously sexual, therefore White is clean, virtuous, and chaste.

The denigration of blackness finds its ultimate expression in the cultural tropes about the Black body (Baldwin & Morrison, 1998). The Black body is bad. The Black body is hyper-sexual. The Black male body is threatening, 'thuggish,' and excessively sexually endowed. The Black female body is seductive, vexing, excessively physically endowed and insatiable. The Black person is irresponsible, lazy, and entitled. (It should be noted in this context that these tropes served as effective excuse/cover for the abuse, rape and exploitation of Black (especially female) bodies by white males during and post the period of slavery). Not only is sin black, but the paradigmatic sin, non-normative sexuality, is most dramatically potentiated in the black body. The challenge of the Black church and Black culture is to counter the pervasive stigmatization of blackness, and to counter the hypersexualization of the black body, to redeem the Black body, and to redeem blackness.

Redeeming Blackness

There have been various responses to the cultural anti-blackness in America. Initially, the black church tried to redeem blackness by elevating the status of Black folk, supporting the adoption of aesthetic and social norms of the larger society (one could call it the Booker T. Washington approach). Following the period of enslavement, some Black religious movements took as their charge to "redeem" the black body from its perilous state by a strict asceticism and "saintliness" (that is Sanders: Saints in Exile). Early revivalists movements such as the Azusa street revival and the new Black Pentecostals, as well as some of the neo-Pentecostal ("Holiness") traditions such as the Church of god, are examples of such movements. Some of these churches were within larger white traditions. They became an example of what results from the unholy ménage a trois of western dualism, Christian asceticism, and white supremacist colorism. Black and White, sin and salvation, sex and holiness, are irreconcilable opposites. James Baldwin deftly depicts this separation in the opening pages of his magnum opus "Go Tell It on the Mountain." The Grimes family (aptly named) make their way to church Sunday morning, struggling to rid themselves of the grime of sin and poverty; mother Grimes clothed in white ("the uniform of holy women"), with John, the protagonist, and his little brother Roy watching, and avoiding, the sinners who populated the street corners and doorways after having spent the night partying and having sex. John looked down upon these "sinners" as those knowing not the hope that lies in the efforts of the chaste faithful:

"These men and women they passed on Sunday morning had spent the night in bars, or in cat houses, or on the streets, or on rooftops, or under the stairs. They had been drinking. They had gone from cursing to laughter, to anger to lust" (Baldwin, p. 12).

Baldwin's Grimes family attempts to defy the expectation of blackness as lustful, sinful and dirty by embracing personal piety and ideals of personal asceticism. Similarly, some Black churches (that is Baptist, Pentecostal, Neo-Pentecostal) have embraced doctrines of personal salvation and personal asceticism (particularly sexually) characteristic of the conservative white church (Pentecostals, some Evangelicals and Baptists, especially Southern Baptists). While these black churches support civil rights efforts and describe themselves as "pro-black," they do not understand the work of social justice, equality, and indeed inclusion, as defining of Christianity. Thus, they are resistant to the expansion of rights to some groups considered marginal or deviant by the dominant society. Recall the National Baptist Convention (leadership) was so resistant to Dr. King's initial civil rights efforts the group splintered, creating the National Progressive Baptist denomination. The current efforts at justice and inclusion involve GLBT-QI persons. These churches are populated by such persons (including in the pulpit) and allow the active participation of such persons in their fellowship. Yet they are reticent to publicly and formally extend affirmation, welcome and sanction, practicing what we have called "constructive hypocrisy," (Douglas and Hopson, 2003), a 'don't ask don't tell' policy. Some of these churches also continue to practice discrimination against women, insisting women cannot occupy pastoral leadership. As these churches came late and reluctantly to the civil rights struggle and the women's rights struggle, though making a contribution to the redemption of blackness, these churches may be able to play only a limited and later role in finally overturning all vestiges of patriarchal heterosexist white supremacy and it's anti-black/anti-body ethos.

Another strategy of redemption of blackness can be seen in the Civil rights Black power, and Black nationalist movements. During the 1950's and 1960's, a "mood ebony" emerged: described by C. Eric Lincoln as a "mystique of blackness...through which the alienated negro of America could "rediscover himself as a black man linked to the ancient civilizations of Mother Africa" (Davies, 1988, p. 107) emerged. This new Black man and woman began to push back against the anti-black cultural norm, declaring as a proclamation of defiance and of self-affirmation: "I'm black and I'm proud!" The designation of U.S. born persons of African descent changed from Negro to Black, and now, African American. Each change an effort to affirm black as a color, and Black people, and embrace the "dark continent," the origin of all humanity, as a point of pride and power. Black people redeeming "black," just as persons of homosexual orientation redeemed "queer," and changed the valence of a term initially intended to separate and stigmatize. "Black is beautiful" became the (protest/progress) proclamation. Some of the leadership of these groups were Black clergy and religious leaders who were members of Baptist and Black Methodist denominations or more progressive white denominations (for example James Bevel, Jeremiah Wright, clergy in the United Church of Christ). Rather than accommodating to white standards of propriety, beauty or godliness, these leaders were unapologetically Black and unashamedly Christian. To be Christian meant to be pro-Black people, pro Black culture, pro Black aesthetic (for example unprocessed hair), pro darker skin, pro black. Rather than 'if you're white you're right,' they insisted 'the blacker the berry the sweeter the juice' and 'once you go black you never go back.'

Academic religionists also participated in the redemption of blackness with the emergence of a theological movement among Black scholars. The first generation of Black religious scholars, though educated by white scholars at white institutions, began to read the Bible anew (that is, Gayraud Wilmore, Cain Hope Felder). Utilizing some of the tools of their education, and inventing new tools, they insisted the Hebrew scriptures and the Gospel record pointed toward a different God and a different faith than that of the Black or white conservative or fundamentalist Christians. Rather than a God of personal piety embracing the social status quo and the ideals of capitalism, interested solely in personal propriety and the afterlife; the God of the Bible was inarguably God of the oppressed (James Cone). Reading sacred texts, historical documents and artifacts within the context in which they emerged, they insisted the Christian faith is a revolutionary faith by definition; in conflict with unjust social structures and governmental regimes, aligned with the marginalized, the disenfranchised, the minority, the sinners, the oppressed. God preferred the harlot Rahab and the bereft widow of Zarephath, God liberated the enslaved Israelites from bondage, God celebrated the poor and frowned upon the rich, God de-stigmatized the half-breed (Samaritans), and critiqued the esteemed leaders (Pharisees), and ultimately God rejected the Roman effort to silence justice (the crucifixion) and liberated Jesus' faith from death through the resurrection. Though the Black presence has been deemed profligate, useless, worthless or threatening, God has identified with just such persons. God is indeed pro-black. Perhaps, as Bishop Henry McNeil Turner declared: God is Black!

Black female theologians (for example, Jacquelyn Grant,) furthered the redemption of blackness work. They took issue with Black Liberation theology's relative silence on the status of women. They also critiqued White feminism's ignorance and indifference to the plight of the poor and women of color and developed a rich theological tradition of Womanism. They demonstrated that in patriarchal hetero-normative white society, blackness, femaleness, economic status, and sexual minority status, all must be considered together in any efforts to redress any of them. A civil rights movement is incomplete if only attending to matters of racial oppression, ignoring gender, sexuality, and economic oppression. And, going beyond the Black theology developed by their male colleagues, Womanists challenged the embrace of atonement theology, the centrality of the cross, and the necessity of a bodily death to effect salvation or atonement. Though James Cone began to indicate some comprehension of this danger in his final book *The Cross and the Lynching Tree,* he did not fully illuminate the implications of his insights. Feminist and Womanist theologians (Grant, Nakishima-Brock, & Parker Townes) have understood the danger of theologies of sacrifice. Societies will always and only be willing to sacrifice those whom they value least. If a body must die to achieve salvation for the society, then black bodies are the most at risk of death in white supremacist societies. Kelly Brown-Douglas has convincingly demonstrated this in her compelling book *Stand Your Ground* (Douglas, 2015). Bringing together the tragedy and travesty of the death of Trayvon Martin and other black bodies killed by the guardians of the society, with her previous work illuminating the strong anti-body/anti-black ethic of prevailing white theology, Douglas shows the devastating impact of these intersecting "isms" (racism, sexism, heterosexism, colonialism) on Black bodies.

Robin Lakoff (2001) masterfully demonstrates the simple yet elusive reality—language matters. The meanings we place on words create the world in which we live. The term "Black" has been the dumping ground of negativity for much of the time in Western hegemony. Now our challenge is to exercise discipline in the work of expunging the term "black" from the culture's lexicon of negativity. It is the challenge of "woke" people to change the easy references of black as negative. Rather than black as the color of sin and darkness the place of danger, what if we followed nature? Black is the context in which all other colors achieve their definition. Black is the absorption of all colors, the container within which all colors rest and against which all other colors emerge. Thus, Black is necessary, foundational, definitional and transformative, intensifying or muting all other colors. Black is richness, fecundity, nutrient rich, growth producing and growth enhancing. Indeed, in the financial lexicon of today, to be "in the black" is a good thing!

Black is not the color of sin; black is the color of the sacred. The Christian religion needs a conversion experience. Womanist theologians are leading the way out of the deeply embedded equivalence of blackness and sin. For them, the body is not the instrument of sin; the Black female body is not the site of sin; black is not the color of sin; and the Black male body is not the paradigm of sin. The Black Christian church can stop singing of red blood washing Black bodies, making them white as snow. Black is comely, too; darkness is the place from which light emerges; Blackness is just as sacred as every other color.

Implications for Research, Policy, and Practice

The work of those who are concerned to redeem blackness, particularly within religious contexts is both theological and practical. Theologically, the church must take seriously the work of Womanists theologians who are highlighting the implicit "anti-body" ethic in traditional Christian theologies and the implications of this anti-body ethic for Black bodies. Research may be conducted at the intersection of theology and social attitudes such as implicit bias research and research into the impact of veneration of the cross, on attitudes toward violence. Within ecclesiastical structures, policies requiring seminary training to include some exposure to concepts in social and developmental psychology may also be initiated. Finally, as suggested above, Black contexts must continue to do the difficult work of modeling inclusion and non-discrimination which Black people have called for in White contexts. This must go beyond issues du jour (that is, race, gender, or sexuality) and include attention to how colorism may be inadvertently operating in these contexts.

Process Questions and Considerations

1. Why suggest the color of sin is black?

2. How did former slave holders and people in former slave states, rationalize their participation in the enslavement of People of Color?

3. How might Billy Graham have played a role in buttressing the American social hierarchy and eliminating social justice from the center of Christianity in America?

4. What ideological resource in the broader society supports anti- black sentiment?

5. What are two ways the redemption of blackness was attempted?

References

Ammerman, N. T. (1987). *Bible Believers: Fundamentalists in the Modern World.* Rutgers University Press.

Baldwin, J. (1985). *Go tell it on the mountain: [A novel].* Dell.

Brock, R. N., & Parker, R. A. (2008). *Saving paradise: How Christianity traded love of this world for crucifixion and empire.* Beacon Press.

Brock, R. N., & Parker, R. A. (2015). *Proverbs of ashes: Violence, redemptive suffering, and the search for what saves us.* Beacon Press.

Carter, D. T. (1995). *The politics of rage: George Wallace, the origins of the new conservatism, and the transformation of American politics.* Simon & Schuster.

Cone, J. H. (1997). *God of the oppressed.* Orbis Books.

Cone, J. H. (2011). *The cross and the lynching tree.* Orbis Books.

Crawford, A. (1981). *Thunder on the right: The "new right" and the politics of resentment.* Pantheon Books.

Davies, A. T. (1988). *Infected Christianity: A study of modern racism.* McGill-Queen's Press— MQUP.

Douglas, K. B. (2018). Sexuality and the black church: A womanist perspective. Orbis Books.

Douglas, K. B., & Hopson, R. E. (2000). Understanding the black church: The dynamics of change. *The Journal of Religious Thought, 56*(2), 95-113.

Grant, J. (1989). *White women's Christ and black women's Jesus: Feminist christology and womanist response.* Scholars Press.

Heim, M. S. (2006). *Saved from sacrifice: A theology of the cross.* Wm. B. Eerdmans Publishing.

Hopson, R. E., & Smith, D. R. (1999). Changing fortunes: An analysis of Christian right ascendance within American political discourse. *Journal for the Scientific Study of Religion, 38*(1), 1-13. https://doi.org/10.2307/1387579

Kelly, D. B. (2015). *Stand your ground: Black bodies and the justice of God.* Orbis Books.

Morrison, T. (2020). *The source of self-regard: Selected essays, speeches, and meditations.* Knopf Doubleday Publishing Group.

Painter, N. I. (2011). *The history of white people.* W.W. Norton & Company.

Sanders, C. J. (1999). *Saints in exile: The holiness-pentecostal experience in African American religion and culture.* Oxford University Press.

Townes, E. M. (2006). *Breaking the fine rain of death: African American health issues and a womanist ethic of care.* Wipf and Stock Publishers.

AFTERWORD

Kamilah Marie Woodson

It is noteworthy that one of the most influential studies of colorism was conducted by a daughter of Howard University, Dr. Mamie Phipps Clark, in partial completion of the master's degree program in developmental psychology. This famous "doll study" has been utilized in seminal law cases such as Brown v Board of Education and other cases arguing for equality. In this study, Dr. Clark used four dolls, identical except for color, to test children's racial perceptions. The participants were children between the ages of three and seven who were asked to identify both the race of the dolls and which color doll they prefer. By and large, the children preferred the White doll and assigned positive characteristics to it, which suggested that "prejudice, discrimination, and segregation" created feelings of inferiority among Black children and that it damaged their self-esteem. This pivotal piece on colorism, without ever being labelled as such, laid the foundation for the study of colorism from a developmental perspective. The study was published in 1947, and is still one of the most significant works almost 75 years later.

As a tenured full professor at Howard University (HU. . . You Know) I am not only humbled but honored to carry the torch. I cited this study in my dissertation and never could have imagined having this opportunity to put together a compendium of scholarship to advance the literature in this area. I have been studying and presenting at national and international psychological conferences about colorism for the last 23 years. As a graduate student in the 90s, my first query into the construct occurred when I was attempting to study HIV risk among people of color, while asking the question, "What is it at a core level that makes them want to risk their lives when we know how to prevent its transmission?" My master's thesis and dissertation yielded data that allowed me to posit that, for some, it was colorism/colorist ideologies that impacted their self-esteem and/or self-concept, thereby leading to risky sexual behavior. Thus, it was then that I began to study the colorist phenomenon, recognizing that traditional self-esteem measures were not nuanced enough to capture the self-concepts of many African Americans who have negative perceptions of their phenotypic presentations, but who simultaneously score high on those self-esteem measures. While on this academic journey, I have witnessed the phenomenal job my colleagues have done in studying the concept, legitimizing its impact and consideration, and advancing the literature. I am "tickled pink" to be able pick up the baton and carry it even further, as colorism is a huge antagonist to the health and well-being of all people. Interestingly, while on this voyage, I have had the great fortune to travel around the world and observe colorist ideologies at work. I travelled to South Africa, Brazil, and the Caribbean, all places where there is nomenclature to describe various phenotypes and serious life repercussions because of them. Moreover, I have practiced as a clinical psychologist, providing therapy for the last 22 years, and themes of colorist ideologies surface often, with many of those colorist ideologies existing at the core of the client's expressed psychological difficulties.

As such, my travels, research, and clinical experiences serve as the impetus for soliciting contributions to this volume. My goal with this treatment is to engage critical thought about the psychology of colorism, with a global focus on the impact of the remnants of the triangular trade in humans and the trans-generational effects of the epoch of enslavement and colonization. It is my supposition that through examining the impact of the remnants of the more than 500 years of globally sanctioned human trafficking, the trans-generational effects of forced bondage and its resultant historical/cultural trauma, colorism, can be contextualized and redefined (Rowe & Woodson, 2018). The book allows readers to explore the theoretical and empirical research on colorism from an intersectional identity perspective, with interventions that promote conceptions of holistic mental health, personality, and spirituality development. This exploration occurs through the engagement of the work from the foremost Black psychologists and other prominent scholars. In addition to traditional treatment modalities, readers are exposed to healing techniques that emanate from the essence of "Afrikan people's being." It is my hope that readers will further learn the cultural considerations necessary to properly address the psychological needs of African Americans and people of the African Diaspora, as well as those who have been impacted by European domination, while taking into account the events encountered by, and the history of, traditionally marginalized people. Finally, a critical examination of the limits of Western psychology, grounded in the privileging of European cultural aesthetics while simultaneously denigrating Afrikans' and people of color's aesthetics, is presented. Although this volume is informative and voluminous, there is still more work to be done. Stay tuned…

References

Clark, K. B., & Clark, M. P. (1947). Racial identification and preference in Negro children. In T. M. Newcomb & E. L. Hartley (Eds.), *Reading in Social Psychology*. New York: Holt, Rinehart & Winston.

Rowe, D., & Woodson, K. M. (2018). How to heal African American traumatic history. The conversation. Retrieved from https://theconversation.com/how-to-heal-African-Americans-traumatic-history-98298.

About the Authors

Josephine Almanzar, MA is currently a doctoral candidate from the Florida School of Professional Psychology and is projected to graduate with a Psy.D. in Clinical Psychology in Spring 2020. Josephine earned a Masters' of Arts in Clinical Psychology from the Florida School of Professional Psychology in 2017. Josephine has a passion in exploring the impact of colorism, identity development, and group belonging across the African Diaspora, particularly in Latin America. Josephine has dedicated her dissertation on exploring the impact of cultural homelessness, self-esteem, and skin color satisfaction among Latinxs, with a particular interest in the experiences of Latinxs of African descent. Through a strength-based approach, Josephine's other clinical interests include childhood trauma, depression, suicide prevention, grief, and identity development in young adults.

Dr. Joyell Arscott is a trauma and violence research post-doctoral fellow at Johns Hopkins School of Nursing (T32HD094687). Dr. Arscott graduated from Duke University with a PhD in Nursing and the University of Maryland, Baltimore, with her B.S.N. She is also an AIDS Certified Registered Nurse (ACRN). Her research examines the historical impact of social, structural, and institutional factors that contribute to the health inequities in marginalized populations, particularly African American/Black, sexual and gender, minority adolescents and young adults. Dr. Arscott scholarship aims to understand the impact that cumulative trauma has on the HIV risk, sexual decision-making for Black adolescents and young adults from underserved communities, especially persons with intersecting identities.

Paula A. Barbel, PhD, CPNP-PC is an Associate Professor at State University of New York (SUNY) Brockport in the Department of Nursing. Dr. Paula Barbel earned a Bachelor of Science in Biology from Rochester Institute of Technology and she worked in biotechnology prior to earning a second Bachelor of Science in Nursing, a Master of Science in Nursing and a PhD in Health Practice Research from the University of Rochester. She currently teaches pediatric didactic and clinical courses in the undergraduate and graduate programs. Dr. Barbel's research interests include child maltreatment, childhood trauma, child abuse prevention, foster-care and parenting.

Dr. Terra L. Bowen-Reid is an Associate Professor in the Department of Psychology at Morgan State University. She earned her Bachelor of Science and Master of Science Degrees in Community Psychology from Florida A&M University; and PhD in Personality Psychology from Howard University. Dr. Bowen-Reid is committed to mentoring and the scholarly advancement of her students. Accordingly, Dr. Bowen-Reid has served as the Program Director/Principal Investigator of the Minority Mental Health Research Scholars Program (MMHRSP), an undergraduate research training program funded by the National Institute of Mental Health. She is also a current mentor in the federally funded ASCEND program. Her personal research interests are in the areas of African American mental health; racial health disparities; psychological and cardiovascular risk behaviors; and cancer prevention. She is a recognized expert in the field of African/Black Psychology in teaching and conducting research that provides an African-centered theoretical framework in understanding the human behaviors of people of African-descent. Dr. Bowen-Reid is enshrined in Florida A&M University Gallery of Distinction. She has been recognized as one of top 20 psychology professors in the state of Maryland.

Dr. Dwayne M. Bryant is a graduate of Howard University, where he received his doctorate in School Psychology. He has gained experience in the field of psychology from working with the American Psychological Association, Educational Testing Service, and the National Association of School Psychologists. He has a passion for advocacy and fairness for all people and strives to create a balanced and positive narrative of black mental health. Also, he has published a series of children's books that highlights attentional concerns, executive functioning, spelling and self-esteem.

Jo-Anne Manswell Butty, PhD is the Education Expert at the NOAA Cooperative Science Center in Atmospheric Sciences and Meteorology (NCAS-M) at Howard University. She is responsible for implementing the education strategy for 13 partner institutions through education, training and professional development and helping underrepresented postsecondary students attain working skills and competencies for the NOAA-mission workforce. Dr. Manswell Butty was formerly a Co-Director and Senior Evaluator on the Pre-K Evaluation and Child Care Subsidy Evaluation Programs in Washington, DC. She has been an Adjunct Professor in educational psychology and similar courses at Howard University, George Mason University, and Prince George's Community College. She has published in refereed journals and presented at national and global conferences on topics related to the evaluation of youth, parents, and teacher participation in STEM and other education programs across contextual settings.

Dr. Darlene Gould Colson is a licensed clinical psychologist. Currently, she is an associate professor in the psychology department at Norfolk State University. She earned Bachelor's and Master's degrees from Case Western Reserve University and a PhD from the University of North Carolina at Chapel Hill. She completed her internship at what was then Portsmouth Psychiatric Center. She has taught undergraduate and graduate classes. From December 1998 until June 30, 2004, she served as the coordinator of the Master of Arts Program in Community/Clinical Psychology. From January 2002 to July 2004 she served as the NSU Director for the Virginia Consortium Program in Clinical Psychology. She served as the Psychology Department head from 2004 to 2012. She is a licensed clinical psychologist. Her research interests include cyberpsychology, resilience, non-traditional students, women, and minority issues. Her favorite course to teach is Positive Psychology.

Antonio M. Cooper, PhD, NCSP is an Assistant Professor in the Department of Psychology and M.S. in Applied Psychology/Specialist in School Psychology program at Francis Marion University (Florence SC). Dr. Cooper completed his internship in the District of Columbia Public School System at the first African-American High School in the United States, Dunbar Senior High School. He received his PhD in School Psychology from Howard University in Washington, DC. His practice experience includes the emphasis on cultural implications in effective education training in grades K-12 (in the realms of administration policy, teacher effectiveness and environmental impact). His research is guided by the psychosocial factor(s) impact on education success among minorities in both rural and urban areas. His research interests include academic success (preventative and intervention), minority males, education policy, rural and urban education, cultural competency, mentorship, colorism, program evaluation, and mental health.

Dr. Maya Corneille is a Visiting Associate Professor at Morehouse College and a Curriculum Fellow for the Institute for Social Justice Inquiry and Praxis at the Andrew Young Center for Global Leadership at Morehouse College. She is the co-director of the Collective Health and Education Equity Research (CHEER) Collaborative. Dr. Corneille's work focuses on examining strategies to dismantle structural inequalities and understanding ways to build upon collective strengths of the Black community. Her work has been funded by the National Science Foundation, the National Institutes of Mental Health, and the Center for AIDS Prevention Studies at the University of California, San Francisco. She received a Master's degree in clinical psychology and a PhD in social psychology from Virginia Commonwealth University.

Dr. Danielle D. Dickens, PhD, is an Assistant Professor in the Department of Psychology at Spelman College. Dr. Dickens earned her B.A. in psychology from Spelman College, and her M.S. and PhD from Colorado State University in Applied Social and Health Psychology. Her program of research focuses on Black womanhood and their implications for health behaviors, academic performance, experiences of discrimination, coping strategies (for example, identity shifting), and psychological well-being. Due to her productivity and innovations in teaching, research, and service, she often serves as an expert scholar and invited speaker on issues affecting underserved and underrepresented individuals in education and in the workplace.

Dr. Patricia S. Dixon is an Assistant Professor at the Florida School of Professional Psychology (FSPP) at National Louis University in Tampa, FL. She is a licensed clinical psychologist and maintains a private practice working with children, adolescents and adults in Palmetto, FL. Her research interests focus on social and psychological factors that contribute to positive mental health outcomes among minority populations. She is passionate about issues of diversity and her greatest hope is to utilize her position in the field of psychology to be impactful in the area of promoting diversity awareness and competency within the field as well as the community. In addition to her passion for teaching, clinical practice and research she is passionate about community involvement and engagement. She has a podcast entitled Healing Mentalit-Tea where she discusses all things that promote emotional well-being and a positive mentality. She is a proud member of the SOLVE Maternity Homes Board of Directors, which is a faith- based organization that seeks to provide services to women and teens throughout their pregnancy.

Dr. Janicia Dugas is a school psychologist for the San Jose Unified School District in California. She received her PhD in school psychology from Howard University where she remained fully invested in advocacy of quality education, health, and most importantly human rights. She gained experience from Children's National Hospital in Washington, D.C., with a specialized focus on Neuropsychological Disorders and Autism related Disorders. Her primary research interest is consultation among home, school, and medical institutions to support vulnerable youth.

Dr. Zoeann Finzi-Adams is the Associate Director of Clinical Training and Assistant Professor for the Clinical Psychology program at the Washington D.C. campus of The Chicago School of Professional Psychology. Dr. Finzi-Adams received her PhD in Counseling Psychology from Howard University and is a licensed psychologist in the District of Columbia. She completed her APA accredited internship at the Texas Woman's University Counseling Center and her postdoctoral fellowship at the George Washington University (GW) Counseling and Psychological Services (CAPs). Following her postdoctoral fellowship, Dr. Finzi-Adams was promoted to senior staff clinician and Diversity Services Coordinator at GW CAPs. In this position she was responsible for overseeing diversity services for the Colonial Health Center and providing diversity training for the entire staff, comprised of providers from mental health, medical, health promotion, and business operations. Dr. Finzi-Adams' research and clinical interests both revolve around experiences of discrimination and intersecting identities among ethnic and racial minorities and their impact on other life contexts (for example interpersonal relationships, academics, and mental health). She has specialized focus on issues pertaining to Colorism and unique stressors that impact Women from the African Diaspora. Clinically, she specializes in diversity trainings, group psychotherapy, interpersonal dynamics, women's issues, emerging adulthood, and working within university/college settings.

Dr. Marisa Franco was a former professor of Counseling Psychology at Georgia State University and she currently works as an AAAS Science and Technology Policy Fellow. Her research has focused on racial discrimination, and she has published over 20 peer-reviewed articles and has received grants from the National Institute of Health and Society for the Psychological Study of Social Issues. She is currently writing a book on friendship.

Dr. O'Shan Gadsden is an applied psychologist and a cultural-relational psychoanalytically trained psychotherapist. He currently holds a Tenure-Track appointment as Assistant Professor of Psychology at Norfolk State University where he teaches specialty courses in the undergraduate program and teaches and supervises students (that is dissertation and TA supervisor) in their APA accredited PhD Clinical Psychology Program (Virginia Consortium Program in Clinical Psychology). Dr. Gadsden earned a PhD in Counseling Psychology from Howard University's APA accredited program and completed a pre-doctoral internship at the University of Delaware Center for Counseling and Development and served as Postdoctoral Clinical Fellow at JFK Behavioral Health Center in Philadelphia, PA before assuming his first academic appointment. Prior to that, he earned a Master's degree in Clinical Psychology at Columbia University. His scholarship and professional work serve traditionally marginalized-minoritized populations; with a specific focus on the impact of psycho-socio-cultural-spiritual variables that impact African American adult males' emotional capacity and self-agency. Currently, he has as number of article manuscripts in progress and is collecting national data for a study exploring the relationship between masculinity development and the capacity toward emotional intimacy with African-American adult males in non-marital romantic relationships. Dr. Gadsden also has made media appearances on The Root and was featured in the Huffington Post as one of the 15 Black male therapists you should know. Clinically, he currently treats patients in a clinic setting in Downtown, Norfolk and is a Psychoanalytic Candidate at the Object Relations Institute in NYC. Professionally, Dr. Gadsden provides consultation and evaluation to organizations and individuals.

Kristen Gayle, MA, LCPC is a 3rd year student in the Counseling Psychology PhD program at Howard University. She has a Master's Degree in professional counseling from Seton Hall University and a bachelors in psychology from Pace University. Ms. Gayle is also a Licensed Professional Counselor in the state of Maryland. Her research interest focuses on intersectionality, racial identity, and body image within oppressed communities.

Nana K. O. Gyesie, MA, MSW is a seasoned Administrator of Student Affairs. He was born in Ghana, Wes Africa, spent his formative years in Ghana and moved to New York City. He earned his Bachelor's Degree in Psychology and African American Studies at SUNY New Paltz. He holds two Master's Degrees, one in Social Work from the University of Maryland, Baltimore and the other in Language, Literacy and Culture from University of Maryland at Baltimore County. His research interest intersect in the areas of identity negotiations of foreign-born blacks, language and student success/study abroad programs. He has also taught several courses including Cultural Anthropology,

Cultural Diversity, The Urban Community, and Sociology courses. Nana enjoys good food, a healthy lifestyle and spending time with his family.

Jamal H.N. Hailey, MA is a doctoral-level counseling psychology trainee in the Department of Human Development and Psychoeducational Studies at Howard University. As a behavioral researcher and social justice advocate, Mx. Hailey works to improve the lives of vulnerable and underserved communities. His research examines the intersections of race, gender, and sexuality on the psychological well-being of teens and emerging adults. Mx. Hailey seeks to understand the impact of sociocultural influences, Black racial identity, masculinity, and resilience on attitudes toward violence. Mx. Hailey's career has spanned all aspects of community service, most notably through professional roles as the former Program Director for STAR TRACK Adolescent Health Program at the University of Maryland, School of Medicine, where he created a leadership development model which focused on creating new public health leaders from Black and LGBTQ+ communities. He has been recognized nationally as LGBTQ+ health expert by GLMA: Health Professionals Advancing LGBT Equality, and the Presidential Advisory Council on HIV/AIDS (PACHA). Mx. Hailey received a Master of Arts in Psychology as well as a dual Bachelor of Science in Psychology and Sociology with a minor in LGBT Studies from Towson University. He is also a member of Rooted, a Black LGBTQ healing collective.

Paula Quick Hall earned the doctorate in Political Science from the University of North Carolina at Chapel Hill in 1998, specializing in Public Administration and Public Policy. In 1999 she founded the African American Education & Research Organization (AAERO). Her research and writing has drawn attention to issues of educational equity, racial discrimination in desegregated schools, and opportunities for groups underrepresented in science careers. Hall served as Associate Professor and Chair of the Political Science Department at Bennett College in Greensboro, North Carolina, and has worked more than fifteen years in not-for-profit organizations, including the College Board and the American Association for the Advancement of Science. She also worked as personnel specialist at the Niagara Falls Board of Education, project coordinator at the North Carolina School of Science and Mathematics, political science and public administration faculty at North Carolina Central University, North Carolina A&T State University, and University of North Carolina, Chapel. She worked at Research and Evaluation Associates, Inc. on several projects addressing issues such as disproportionate confinement of minority youth in the juvenile justice system and childcare provider training. Hall's early education included a summer at N.C. Governor's School, graduation from E.E. Smith Senior High in Fayetteville, N.C., a Bachelor of Science degree from Howard University in Washington, DC, and a Master of Public Administration degree from the University of Southern California.

K. Melchor Quick Hall is a faculty member in the Human and Organizational Development doctoral programs in Fielding Graduate University's School of Leadership Studies. During the 2019-2020 academic year, she also has been a Visiting Scholar at Brandeis University's Women's Studies Research Center. Her book, Naming a Transnational Black Feminist Framework: Writing in Darkness, advocates for a Black +feminist tradition in international relations. Recent publications include an article entitled "Technology in Black Feminist World" in Frontiers: A Journal of Women Studies and a chapter entitled "El pan, el poder y la política: The Politics of Bread-Making in Honduras' Garifuna Community" in Ploughing Our Own Fields: Black Political Women Demanding Citizenship, Challenging Power and Seeking Justice (2018). Previous articles have appeared in Journal of Human Development and Capabilities, Meridians: Feminism, Race, Transnationalism, and JENdA: A Journal of Culture and African Women Studies.

Dr. Naomi Hall-Byers is a Professor of Psychology in the Department of Psychological Sciences at Winston-Salem State University (WSSU). She is an applied social psychologist, with an advanced degree in public health. She is the Director of the Race and Cultural Context (RC2) lab and her overarching program of research focuses on psychological, social, cultural, and contextual factors associated with health disparities and inequities among youth and emerging adults (YEAs) of African descent. Her research has been funded by the National Science Foundation, National Institutes of Health, American Psychological Association, University of California (San Francisco), and the University of North Carolina (Chapel-Hill). Dr. Hall-Byers has received numerous awards for teaching and research, and was the 2018 recipient of the WSSU Wilveria B. Atkinson Distinguished Research Award. She is involved professionally and in the community and swerves as an Advisory Committee member for LEAD Girls of NC, Inc., a grassroots organization focused on empowering at-risk pre-teens girls in the Piedmont Triad area of North Carolina.

Dr. Ashley Hill identifies as a Black, African American, Christian brown skin, loc'd, cisgender, able-bodied, heterosexual woman. She earned her Bachelor of Science in psychology from Howard University and her master's degree in psychology from Virginia Commonwealth University. She is presently a pre-doctoral medical/health psychology intern at the University of Florida. She will earn her doctorate in Counseling Psychology from Virginia Commonwealth University upon completion of internship in 2020. Ashley is an aspiring clinical health psychologist and researcher, who aims to work in an academic health center. Her research interests are rooted in the psychology of the Black experience. More specifically, her research emphasizes the psychological well-being of Black women, their intersectional oppression and their navigation of psychosocial stressors. She has worked on several projects that investigated the effects of colorism on obesity, self-esteem, teen dating violence, and eating disorders. Other avenues of research include the internalization of media stereotypes among Black emerging adults, the utilization of cultural coping strategies (that is, Shifting, Strong Black Woman schema) among Black women, and the effects of race-related stress. Recently, her research interests have expanded to include health disparities in Black maternal health. Her dissertation in Black perinatal bereavement examined culturally congruent coping strategies following perinatal loss and noted recommendations for clinical care. Beyond her clinical and researcher career, Ashley enjoys eating different cuisines, reading romance novels and watching science fiction movies with partner.

Courtney Hives-Gunn, PhD is a mental health practitioner at the Feliciana Forensic Facility, which is an inpatient forensic psychiatric hospital within the Louisiana Department of Health and Hospitals. Her research interests focus on the continued unmet need of mental health services to people of color who are involved in the criminal justice system with a special emphasis on community, family, school, and peer/individual risk factors. She lives in Baton Rouge, Louisiana with her husband and son.

Dr. Charnel Hollier is a Licensed Psychologist in the state of Texas. She has a private practice where she provides psychotherapy to adults with a wide array of concerns such as anxiety, depression, anger, substance abuse, body image dissatisfaction, relationship issues and identity concerns. Her research focuses on skin tone dissatisfaction, body shape dissatisfaction, and disordered eating on self-esteem among Black college women. She also has research experience in adolescent dating violence, sexual health, and mental health. Dr. Hollier is a former research assistant at Georgetown University Medical Center in the Department of Psychology. She received her Bachelor of Arts in Psychology from the University of Texas at Austin and her Doctor of Philosophy in Counseling Psychology from Howard University.

Ronald E. Hopson, PhD, holds a joint faculty appointment (Associate Professor) at Howard University in the Department of Psychology and the School of Divinity. Hopson earned his M.A. and PhD in Clinical Psychology from Michigan State University and the B.A. degree from Indiana University. Additionally, Dr. Hopson attended Garrett-Evangelical Theological Seminary of Northwestern University and completed the doctoral residency in Clinical Psychology at the Institute of Psychiatry at Northwestern University in Chicago, Illinois. He served as interim associate dean for academic affairs in the School of Divinity 2009-2013. Dr. Hopson teaches courses in psychoanalytic/psychodynamic psychotherapy, psychopathology, the psychology of religion, pastoral care, and sexuality and the Black church. He is an ordained clergy in the United Church of Christ and a licensed clinical psychologist. He has published on the role of faith in psychotherapy, the understanding and treatment of addictions and the efficacy of self-help programs, the social psychology of Christian fundamentalism, and pastoral issues in the Black church. Dr. Hopson's current research focus is in theology and psychology. He is conducting research on the impact of theologies of sacrifice and atonement on psychological well-being, attitudes toward the body, and attitudes toward violence.

Dr. Marilyn M. Irving is a Professor of Science Education at Howard University, a Doctoral/Research-Intensive university located in Washington, DC. For more than twenty-four years, she has directed a wide range of science initiatives to help improve the academic performance and increase the participation of under-represented minorities in science and mathematics. She has served as principal and co-principal investigator on funded projects for the National Science Foundation, National Institutes of Health, General Electric and U.S. Department of Education. Her research has focused primarily on professional development of secondary science teachers and increasing the number of teachers to teach science. She is currently the executive director for the Research Association of Minority Professors that seeks to address educational and health disparities through their research findings. She is currently the recipient of a Minority Science and Engineering Improvement Program grant funded by the US Department of Education. Dr. Irving serves as a consultant with the University of Illinois Urbana-

Champaign to conduct Research Experiences for Teachers. She continues to shape the next generation of science leaders.

Steven D. Kniffley Jr., PsyD MPA ABPP HSP is the Associate Director for the Center for Behavioral Health and an Assistant Professor in Spalding University's School of Professional Psychology. He received his doctorate and master's degree in clinical psychology from Spalding University where he specialized in child, adolescent, and family therapy. He completed his post-doctoral training at Harvard Medical School. Dr. Kniffley also has a Master's in Public administration from Wright State University. Dr. Kniffley's area of expertise is research and clinical work with Black males. Specifically, his work focuses on understanding and developing culturally appropriate interventions for Black male psychopathology as well as barriers to academic success for this population. As an educational consultant Dr. Kniffley has worked internationally with students and school administrators in South Africa and India. Dr. Kniffley also serves as an organizational diversity consultant and works with law enforcement departments on addressing conflicts between communities of color and police officers. Some of his books include: "Knowledge of Self: Understanding the Mind of the Black male," "Out of KOS (Knowledge of Self): Black male psychopathology and its treatment, " and "Black males and the Criminal Justice System."

Velma LaPoint, PhD is Professor, Department of Human Development and Psychoeducational Studies, School of Education at Howard University where she engages in teaching, research, and service. She is or has been Principal Investigator, Co-PI, or Senior Researcher conducting research, publishing in refereed journals, and presenting at national and global conferences on various topics: youth screen exposure to consumer culture; youth and parental/family educational strategies to promote youth academic achievement, social competence, and career development; and hip hop pedagogy in universities. Dr. LaPoint teaches and has taught undergraduate and graduate courses related to youth, consumer culture, screens and the earth; youth placed at risk and their resilience; integrative, complementary, and expressive therapies to promote mental health and wellness; and diverse youth and families of color in the U.S.: African Americans, American Indians, Asian Americans, European Americans, and Latin Americans.

Dr. Anna Lee is an Associate Professor of Psychology at North Carolina A&T State University. She received her Bachelor of Science degree in Psychology from Southern University Agricultural and Mechanical College and her Doctor of Philosophy from Howard University. Her work examines the impacts of structural inequities on health and education outcomes of African Americans. She is co-director of the Collective Health and Education Equity Research (CHEER) Collaborative. Dr. Lee's work uses mixed-method, quantitative and qualitative approaches, to examine experiences of Women of Color faculty in the academy, African American high school students' experiences in STEM and the impact of obesity on diabetes risk. Her work has been funded by the National Institutes of Health, the National Science Foundation and the Spencer Foundation.

Stacey McDonald Lowe, PhD is a Senior Education Research Analyst at the Department of Education where she leads efforts to increase student financial empowerment as they prepare for post-secondary education. Her primary policy, evaluation and research interests and work include culturally responsive evaluation of teaching practices in schools for marginalized student populations; student achievement motivation and outcomes in higher education using interdisciplinary contexts to understand students' motivation, persistence, and self-efficacy; and improving access to post-secondary education leading to degree completion with a special focus on women and African Americans in STEM. Dr. McDonald Lowe has published in refereed journals on topics related to increasing participation in STEM by students of color and the intersectionality of STEM participation and African American female students.

K. A. McFarland is a dedicated educator in Baton Rouge, LA. As a McNair Scholar, she studied under the tutelage of Dr. Kamilah Woodson while obtaining her Bachelor's of Science in Psychology at Howard University. After graduation, McFarland decided to pursue her true passion in education. Since gaining experience as an early childhood educator in the District of Columbia and a Literacy Ambassador in Southern Louisiana, she now works as an Academic Counselor in IDEA Public Schools. Her short- term plans include obtaining a Master's of Arts in Teaching in 2021 from Trinity Washington University and then pursuing a doctorate in Curriculum and Education. She hopes to write her own Social Emotional Learning Curriculum specifically for Black and Brown children living and learning in underserved and disenfranchised communities.

Dr. Jannis F. Moody has dedicated her life's work to promoting emotional, psychological and spiritual wellness; as well as increasing mental health education and awareness. For more than a decade, her career has focused on teaching; mentoring; conducting research; consulting; directing community based mental health programs; program development; motivational speaking; and providing direct clinical and support services to individuals, families and groups. Dr. Moody obtained her PhD in Clinical Psychology with an emphasis in Multicultural Community Clinical Psychology and is currently an Assistant Professor at Texas Southern University. Her demonstrated passion and commitment to community service has provided Dr. Moody with a comprehensive and culturally sensitive approach to conceptualizing and implementing treatment with diverse populations. Her knowledge and experience have also facilitated the development of innovative approaches to addressing issues uniquely impacting the psychological wellness of minority and underserved populations. Dr. Moody's research interests and clinical work focuses factors impacting the emotional and psychological wellness of oppressed and underserved populations, with current research focusing on Black women's mental health, factors impacting the relational patterns of African American heterosexuals, and oppressive psychological pedagogy.

J. Rajasekaran is CEO of the Chella Meenakshi Centre for Educational Research, Madurai, Tamil Nadu, South India. He was the Coordinator of the University of Wisconsin Madison Year Abroad Program in Madurai from 1981-2008 and advisor to the Wisconsin Benares Program 2010-2015. "Sekar" has served as a consultant and coordinator for a range of scholars from the United States, Japan, and Europe from 1975-Present, including those from UCLA, UNICEF, and the Troppen Museum-Amsterdam, as well as Harvard, Princeton, Wisconsin, UC-Berkeley, Aarhus, and a range of other Universities. He has published a number of ethnographic articles in collaboration with scholars from outside India. His current research projects include the first extensive folklore study of the Vaigai River, work on Gandhian transformative leaders, and support for Dalit children and their education through a STEM Program. Sekar is also a rock 'n roll musician who has recorded and performed widely, including with David Byrne, and has been a documentary film-maker, producer, and music director for films on temples, cobblers, potters, and the Vaigai River.

Petra A. Robinson, PhD, is Associate Professor at Louisiana State University (LSU) in the School of Leadership and Human Resource Development. Her scholarly work and teaching delve into matters of power and privilege with a focus on contributing to the understanding of institutionalized disparities among traditionally marginalized and underserved adult populations in educational and/organizational contexts. Dr. Robinson has widely-published on issues related to colorism, critical literacies, diversity and social justice, global lifelong learning, and professional development in the academy.

Dr. Taasogle Daryl M. Rowe is a licensed psychologist and Professor Emeritus of Psychology - having taught in both the doctoral and masters programs in clinical psychology at the Graduate School of Education and Psychology of Pepperdine University. His area of focus was on socio-cultural influences on human behavior, theories and strategies of clinical intervention, and clinical supervision. Dr. Rowe has published on topics such as African-centered theory, treatment and training, inter-ethnic and marital relations, cultural competence, and religious leadership and diversity; and has presented at professional organizations, nationally and internationally. His scholarly work has appeared in a number of journals, including the *Journal of Ethnic And Cultural Diversity in Social Work, Journal of Pan-African Studies, Drugs & Society, Journal of Child Sexual Abuse,* and the *Journal of Psychoactive Drugs*, and he has written book chapters on a variety of topics related to psychological interventions and clinical training with persons of African ancestry. He served as National President of the Association of Black Psychologists (ABPsi) from July 2013-15, where he was able to improve the organization's infrastructure, expand its social media presence, and establish critical partnerships with sister organizations that share the mission of the ABPsi. He is the former National Chair of The African Psychology Institute, the training arm of the Association, where he coordinated the development of a comprehensive curriculum for African Psychology. He has been working closely with the Community Healing Network, developing a community empowerment program, entitled *Emotional Emancipation: Defying the Lie of Black Inferiority and Embracing the Truth of Black Humanity.* As a psychologist and consultant, Dr. Rowe maintains a small private practice emphasizing the psychological and communal needs of persons of African ancestry, with special focus on marital and family relationships.

Shannon Smith MA , LMHC-A is proud native of North New Jersey . She attended Morgan State University and received her Bachelor of Arts in Psychology in 2012. Continuing her education she received her Master of Arts in Clinical Mental Health Counseling at Fairleigh Dickinson University in Madison, NJ. After obtaining her graduate degree and state license she has worked as a Mental Health Clinician in the State of Indiana targeting at -risk families in trauma and crisis, conceptualizing with a CBT and Solution focused orientation.

Dr. Sarah J. Stewart received her Bachelor's Degree from Michigan State University, her Master's Degree in education from Loyola University Chicago and her Doctoral Degree in Counseling Psychology in 2016 from Howard University. Dr. Stewart is currently working on a certificate in Women in Entrepreneurship from Cornell. Dr. Steward is an Assistant Professor of Psychology at Livingstone College in Salisbury, N.C. Dr. Stewart teaches general psychology courses and studies mental health in HBCU student athletes. One of her goals has been to integrate mental health into the athlete development program. Prior to working at Livingstone College, Dr. Stewart worked as a Staff Psychologists at University of North Carolina - Charlotte. Dr. Stewart has experience working on various health grants and is currently a peer reviewer for the Office of Justice Programs. Dr. Stewart resides in Concord, NC with her husband Perryn and three children, Kellen, Xavier, Channin.

Kevin Washington (Mwata Kairi), PhD is an African-Centered psychologist licensed in Florida and Washington, DC. He has taught/lectured at several colleges nationally and internationally. Roland Martin as well as Essence Magazine, Black Entertainment Television (BET) News, Vocal Point and many other national and international organizations. He is a Past President of the Association of Black Psychologists and is currently an Associate Professor and Head of the Sociology and Psychology at Grambling State University is the National Director of Black Marriage Day. As a Fulbright-Hays scholar Kevin (Mwata) researched the impact of socializing institutions on the healing or restructuring of post-apartheid South Africa (Azania). It was in South Africa where he researched Ubuntu and how it can inform mental health service delivery to people of African ancestry and others. Not only does he work on healing the psycho-spiritual wounds that are present within people as a result of Cultural and Historical Trauma, he continues developing healing paradigms for persons of African ancestry who have been impacted by Persistent Enslavement Systemic Trauma (PEST). This work is critical to his advancing of *Ubuntu* Psychology/Psychotherapy. He is the founder of *Ubuntu* Psychotherapy and Black Coaching. As the founder of *Ubuntu* Psychotherapy (Psychology) he advances a culturally sensitive modality for mental health counseling and Psychotherapy for Black men and boys as well as Black/African families. He advances culturally-relevant trauma informed care and interventions to be utilized by psychotherapists, that is culturally inclusive and particularized concomitantly. Through his research and writing he seeks to assist people to live life with power, purpose and passion.

Brittany Williams is an educator and professional counselor in the Maryland school system. She has a B.S. degree in Psychology and a Masters' of Education degree in Counseling, graduating in the top 1%of her class. She has experience studying Black women haircare, hair styles and products, which revolve around the complexities of cultural versus the psychological struggle. Her passions and interests involve student motivation at an early age, through mentoring and sponsoring extracurricular activities, such as, the all girls' book club that addresses systemic issues within the African American community at large. Brittany resides in metropolitan Washington DC area with her dog Blue.

David Blake Willis is professor of anthropology and education at Fielding Graduate University and professor emeritus of anthropology at Soai Buddhist University, Osaka, Japan. He taught and did research at the University of Oxford and was Visiting Professor at Grinnell College and the University of Washington. His interests in anthropology, sustainability, social justice, and immigration come from 38 years living in traditional cultural systems (Japan and India). His scholarly work is on transformational leadership and education, human development in transnational contexts, the Creolization of cultures, transcultural communities, and Dalit/Gandhian liberation movements in South India. His publications include *World Cultures: The Language Villages (Leading, Learning, and Teaching on the Global Frontier)* with Walter Enloe (2016); *Sustainability Leadership* with Fred Steier and Paul Stillman (2015); *Reimagining Japanese Education: Borders, Transfers, Circulations, and the Comparative* with Jeremy Rappleye (2011); *Transcultural Japan: At the Borders of Race, Gender, and Identity* with Stephen Murphy-Shigematsu (2007); and *Japanese Education in Transition 2001: Radical Perspectives on Cultural and Political Transformation* with Satoshi Yamamura (2002).

Dr. Kalima Young is an Assistant Professor in the Department of Electronic Media and Film where she teaches Principles of Film and Media Production and African American Cinema. She received her PhD in American Studies from the University of

Maryland, College Park. Her scholarship explores the impact of race and gender-based trauma on Black identity, media, and Black cultural production. A videographer and writer, Ms. Young has written, produced and directed two feature films Grace Haven (2006), Lessons Learned (2009) as well as several political campaign videos. A gender-rights activist, Dr. Young served on the leadership team for the FORCE: Upsetting Rape Culture's Monument Quilt Project, a collection of stories of survivors of rape and sexual abuse. Collecting over 6,000 quilt squares from across the nation. She is also a member of Rooted, a Black LGBTQ healing collective. Additionally, Dr. Young is a frequent host on local radio where she provides media and cultural criticism. Her new manuscript, Mediated Misogynoir: The Erasure of Black Women and Girls' Pain the Public Imagination is scheduled to be released by Rowman and Littlefield's Lexington Books in Spring 2020.

Dr. Sinead N. Younge is the Danforth Endowed Professor of Psychology, and Andrew Young Center for Global Leadership, Prison Fellow, at Morehouse College. Dr. Younge is the principal investigator of Project Ujima, a research laboratory that focuses on community based participatory action research methodologies with regard to health equity and access in underserved populations. Dr. Younge also studies critical pedagogy in higher education and has worked across a variety of settings including her work with the Emory Tibetan Science Initiative where she taught introduction to biology to Tibetan Buddhist Monks, and with Common Good Atlanta, where she helps to bring college courses to students who are incarcerated. Dr. Younge received her Bachelor of Arts degree in Psychology with a minor in Africana Studies from San Diego State University, and a Doctoral degree in Ecological-Community Psychology with a cognate in Urban Affairs from Michigan State University.

About the Editor

Kamilah Marie Woodson, PhD is the former Associate Dean/Director of Graduate Studies and a Professor in the Howard University School of Education, Department of Human Development and Psycho-educational Studies, Counseling Psychology Ph.D. Program. Dr. Woodson is also a Professor in the Department of Psychiatry at the Howard University College of Medicine/Howard University Hospital. In addition to her dual appointment at Howard University, Dr. Woodson was an adjunct professor at the Chicago School of Professional Psychology, DC, served on the Editorial Board of the Journal of Negro Education as the Book Review Editor for 7 years, has been the program evaluator on several NSF-Sponsored research projects, and worked as a consultant with the QEM Network, Washington, DC. She was previously the Director of Training for the Counseling Psychology Ph.D. Program (7 Years), Director of the Howard University Office of Nursing Research, Division of Nursing, College of Pharmacy, Nursing & Allied Health Sciences and the Director of the NSF sponsored (AGEP) Alliance for Graduate Education and the Professoriate Program at Howard University. Dr. Woodson is a graduate of the California School of Professional Psychology, Los Angeles, where she received the Ph.D. & MA., degrees in Clinical Psychology and earned her Baccalaureate degree in Psychology from the University of Michigan, Ann Arbor. Dr. Woodson is currently working to earn a Doctorate Degree in Ministry from the Howard University School of Divinity. Dr. Woodson conducted research as a MHSAC Research Fellow at the Morehouse School of Medicine, Atlanta GA and works with the Howard University College of Medicine, Department of Psychiatry as a Research Associate, Professor, and Clinician. Her research is in the area of health disparities, including the factors that impact health-related risk behaviors (HIV/AIDS & Substance Abuse) among people of color, including incarcerated populations, as well as the impact of human trafficking on young women of color. Dr. Woodson began her career conducting research on the impact of global colorism and furthered this agenda through this current publication and through research as result of being a recent Fulbright-Hayes Fellow (Brazil, South America). She has presented her colorism research all over the world, in places like Ghana, Kenya, Egypt, South Africa, the Caribbean, Mexico, France, Amsterdam, Prague, Hong Kong, and Cuba. As a licensed Clinical Psychologist and the previous Associate Managing Director of the Association of Black Psychologists, Dr. Woodson has over 25 years of experience working with individuals, couples and groups. Her clinical interests include, but are not limited to, sexual victimization, sexual orientation concerns, interpersonal relationships, trauma, and depression. She has a small private practice in Maryland/Washington DC, works closely with the LGBTQ Homeless Shelter and Treatment center, Casa Ruby, Washington DC, and is in the process of developing a Training Consortium in the DMV area to service under resourced and traditionally marginalized clients.